Paying the Toll

American Business, Politics, and Society
Series Editors: Richard R. John, Pamela Walker Laird, and
Mark H. Rose

Books in the series American Business, Politics, and Society explore
the relationships over time between governmental institutions and the
creation and performance of markets, firms, and industries large and
small. The central theme of this series is that public policy—
understood broadly to embrace not only lawmaking but also the
structuring presence of governmental institutions—has been
fundamental to the evolution of American business from the colonial
era to the present. The series aims to explore, in particular,
developments that have enduring consequences.

A complete list of books in the series is available from the publisher.

Paying the Toll

Local Power, Regional Politics,
and the Golden Gate Bridge

Louise Nelson Dyble

PENN

University of Pennsylvania Press

Philadelphia

Publicaton of this volume was aided by a generous grant from the Keston Institute for Public Finance and Infrastructure Policy at the University of Southern California.

Published by
University of Pennsylvania Press
Philadelphia, Pennsylvania 19104-4112

Printed in the United States of America on acid-free paper
10 9 8 7 6 5 4 3 2 1

Library of Congress Cataloging-in-Publication Data
Dyble, Louise Nelson.
   Paying the toll : local power, regional politics, and the Golden Gate Bridge / Louise Nelson Dyble.
      p. cm. — (American business, politics, and society)
   Includes bibliographical references and index.
   ISBN 978-0-8122-4147-1 (alk. paper)
   1. Golden Gate Bridge (San Francisco, Calif.) I. Title.
   TG25.S225D93 2009
   388.1'320979461—dc22   2008047366

To those who don't pay bridge tolls:
to the walkers and bikers, and bus, train, and ferry riders.

Contents

Introduction
"Agency Run Amok"

An architectural masterpiece, the Golden Gate Bridge instantly evokes the natural beauty of northern California and the cosmopolitan pleasures of San Francisco. Tourists from around the world marvel at the scale of the graceful structure, the vision of the architects and engineers who designed it, and the bravery of the workers who built it. For generations, its towers have beckoned weekend adventurers to cross the mile-long span; ominously, its low railings have also lured the despondent, suggesting an easy way to end it all. But for the commuters whose cars crowd onto its narrow roadway every workday morning and evening, the bridge represents something else entirely. To them, the agency that was created in 1928 to build the bridge and has collected its tolls ever since is as notorious as the bridge is beautiful. This is the story of the Golden Gate Bridge and Highway District, the government agency that grew into an empire in the shadow of the bridge.

In 1994, a *San Francisco Chronicle* exposé explained some of the reasons for the notoriety of the bridge district, tracing its problems back to 1971 when the agency entered into the business of mass transportation. That year, the bridge district retired the last of its original construction bonds. Paying this debt had been its raison d'être for decades, and bridge district officials often evoked their obligations to bondholders to fend off attempts to dissolve the agency. Many San Francisco Bay Area residents expected that bridge tolls would finally be eliminated and the bridge incorporated into the state highway system, as campaign publicity promoting the bonds suggested in 1930. After all, the bridge district was wildly unpopular, and its officials were under fire for corruption, mismanagement, racism, and general imperviousness. Nevertheless, they managed to build a "transit empire," taking on expensive new ferry and bus operations that ensured the agency's survival. In 1969, the bridge district secured exclusive control over all modes of transportation from San Francisco to the north, raising bridge tolls steeply to cover operating expenses. This "bid for eternal life," as one reporter described it, made the bridge district indispensable to the Bay Area and transformed the agency "from a relatively simple toll-taking operation to a smug transit authority so impregnable that it has spurned all attempts to reform it." Twenty-three years later the bridge district had three major divisions, a $77 million budget, and a staff of 900. According to *Chronicle* editors it was a "hydra-headed oddity" and an "agency run amok."[1]

Chronicle editors also blasted the bridge district board of directors for its lack of accountability and skewed composition, which heavily favored the residents of small northern California counties over the many toll payers of San Francisco and Marin. They pointed out that the nineteen-member board was a "bastion of white men," with only five women and one minority member. Many of the directors were political appointees, occupying their posts for decades or even inheriting them across generations.[2] Local activists called the insular agency "the last vestige of bossism," and "a perfect example of the type of self-perpetuating, inaccessible, obsolete, fiscally abusive bureaucracy we're increasingly subject to as citizens." Reporters cited charges of inefficiency and extravagance, including high salaries; the Golden Gate Bridge general manager earned 20 percent more than the director of the California Department of Transportation, who was in charge of nine toll bridges as well as many other facilities. To make matters worse, both the Federal Bureau of Investigation and the San Francisco district attorney were investigating bridge district officials for "bid-rigging, skimming, contract improprieties, and financial illegalities."[3]

Even as they cataloged a wide variety of transgressions at the bridge district, *Chronicle* reporters suggested that the fame and beauty of the bridge actually obscured the offenses of its officials. They speculated that the bridge itself was a "technical achievement so daring that it has all but overshadowed the institution that runs it."[4] Over the course of bridge district history, journalists, politicians, and activists have instigated dozens of official investigations, grand jury hearings, reform bills, audits, refinancing drives, and even a few resignations. Still, bridge district scandals seem to fade quickly in the public consciousness, regardless of the size of the headlines they inspire or their importance to the Bay Area.[5]

Contemporary bridge district culture provides some clues to the reasons for this obscurity. I made my first inquiry about bridge district records in 1997, and discovered that its officials guard its resources and history from outsiders. When I explained my research interests and asked to view some of the district's early files, the bridge district public relations officer met my request with prohibitive insurance requirements, claiming that the agency could not accept liability for my presence at its offices. The bridge's history had already been written, I was told, and it was available at the toll plaza gift shop.

This unexpected response heightened my interest in the bridge district. The Golden Gate Bridge was the only span in California managed by an independent local agency, and the records of other state-operated toll bridges were easily available in a variety of public libraries and archives. I discovered that the California Public Records Act makes very clear provisions for access to bridge district records and accommodations at its facilities, even naming the agency specifically.[6] Armed with new determination and knowledge of the law, I resubmitted my request. This time, bridge district officials informed me that they simply did not have the manpower or the budget to accommodate research—and that district vaults were "not libraries." The public relations officer described the records that I was requesting, perhaps thinking it would deter me: hundreds of boxes of unknown materials in several locations had not been moved for decades. They would require significant time and expense to sort, and an attorney would have to review all documents before I saw them. This only encouraged me; not only did a large cache of untouched historical records and unknown secrets beckon, but also governmental transparency and accountability were at stake. After appealing directly to the directors individually and fending off demands that I agree to "approval" of anything I wrote, I was finally allowed to inspect bridge district records more than a year after my initial request.[7]

Installed at a desk in an old modular building near the toll plaza, I faced the daunting task of sorting through more than three hundred boxes of documents, reports, correspondence, and a variety of other disorganized and deteriorating materials dating back to the 1920s. Some had been stashed and forgotten in a damp paint tunnel within the bridge itself and were brittle, moldy, and dusted with rust from staples and paper clips. Many of the records were moved to a private storage facility soon after I began research, where they were slightly more accessible and much better preserved. Nevertheless, they often seemed to disappear after my initial inspection if I requested them again. In the end, I was presented with material vastly exceeding the parameters of my original request, perhaps in the hope that its sheer volume would dissuade me. Making sense of it was a formidable job that stretched on for months.

I know now that secrecy and aversion to public scrutiny are central to bridge district culture, products both of the agency's nature as a special district and its distinctive history. Generations of fiercely loyal bridge officials have had a proprietary attitude toward the span, and those in charge when I made my request were no exception. Fortunately, although they rightly suspected that there were many skeletons in bridge district closets, they also shared a sense of pride in its accomplishments and a keen awareness of the bridge's importance as a landmark in the history of architecture and engineering. Because of this, they preserved records that many government bureaucrats would long since have destroyed.[8] Thousands of memos, letters, reports, photos, and artifacts provided a rare and intimate view of the inner workings of a special district, its character, and its development over time. Ultimately, they revealed how and why the bridge district transformed from a relatively simple agency intended to finance and build a bridge into an expansive regional transportation authority.

The bridge district came into existence as a formal organization with clearly defined powers and rules, charged with fulfilling a specific purpose. Immediately, it began to develop its own unique characteristics, its officials expanding its authority, changing its rules, and redefining its purpose. Over time a compelling culture developed that gave value and meaning to the bridge district in the minds of its officials, who promoted and protected the agency's interests as they understood them. Their sense of loyalty and duty led them to identify personally with the bridge district, in addition to recognizing their rational stake in its success; the interests of the agency converged with and even superceded the interests of individuals associated with it. Because of this, the bridge district can be understood as a collective actor in its own right, an organization with its own agency. Its status as a corporate body was more than just a legal metaphor, but also one of the many attributes that contributed to its coherence as an institution.[9] This history traces the life of the bridge district from its conception in the 1920s, continuing through its youth as it developed its own identity and set of interests after the opening of the bridge in 1937, through its maturation with the retirement of the original construction bonds and its perpetuation in 1971. As the bridge district increased its power, jurisdiction, and political engagement, it shaped the landscape and government of the San Francisco Bay Area. This book is about the development of an institution that transcended the intentions of its founders and the interests of the leaders at its helm—it is a biography of the Golden Gate Bridge and Highway District.

To a large degree, the remarkable power that the Golden Gate Bridge and Highway District developed over the course of its history can be attributed to its characteristics as a special district. Special districts (including authorities, commissions, and boards) are autonomous government agencies with independent decision-making power, often considerable financial resources, and little outside accountability. They are neither part of traditional local governments (cities and counties) nor divisions of state or federal government, and their operations are distinct from other governmental agencies.[10] Special districts are public corporations modeled after private firms with the goal of bringing the benefits of businesslike administration and market incentives to the public sector. They are managed by professional administrators, who have all of the independent initiative of corporate executives and are insulated from the vicissitudes of public opinion and electoral politics. In general, their governing boards are appointed rather than elected; while in theory, citizens are the shareholders of these government businesses, their operations are designed to deflect public interest.

Special districts made up the fastest-growing sector of local government in the United States throughout the twentieth century. These agencies took on a variety of public works projects and services early on, and later they were adapted to provide for limited collaboration between cities and suburbs. Starting in the late nineteenth century, drainage, levee, irrigation, and road districts promoted rural development and agriculture, particularly in the West. In cities and suburbs, special districts developed new water and sanitation systems, built parkways and bridges, and took over the operation of major seaports.[11] The Golden Gate Bridge and Highway District operated an unusually famous facility, an iconic, celebrated bridge that raised the profile of the organization that operated it. However, as a government agency, the bridge district was far from unusual. Its history is important because it was a *typical* special district—neither its size, jurisdiction, nor resources were out of the ordinary.

The bridge district was conceived in 1923, and like those of many other special districts, its main backers were local businessmen who hoped to facilitate public enterprise in the service of growth and development. As the most important mile of the Redwood Highway, Golden Gate Bridge promoters expected it to bring automobiles, tourists, and rising property values to rural northern California. However, the proposal was expensive and risky and did not necessarily promise profit to private sector investors. Leading northern California boosters, including Santa Rosa banker Frank P. Doyle and Marin County attorney George H. Harlan, proposed a special district that would harness public resources to finance, build, and operate an ambitious and expensive bridge. A regional special district could take advantage of San Francisco's valuable real estate to secure construction bonds while at the same time ensuring northern California civic leaders and businessmen a voice in its policies and management and, ideally, insulating its administration from political interference and corruption.

While the bridge fulfilled and even exceeded hopes that it would stimulate development and economic growth, bridge district founders were almost immediately disappointed with the agency they had created. The independence that was built into the structure of the bridge district meant its backers surrendered control to the expert professionals they put in charge. As it turned out, these professionals were not immune to corruption or incompetence, and they were very successful in using the resources at their command to secure power and to fend off interference or reform. After the bridge district was incorporated in 1928, it became clear that there were many opportunists among the politicians and local businessmen on its staff and board of directors. A struggle for control commenced, intensifying once the agency was funded and construction was under way. Valuable contracts and patronage were at stake, and various outside business interests and political factions sought to gain control of the agency and the windfalls of construction. A series of scandals generated charges of corruption and led to the resignation of several top bridge district officials.

After the bridge opened and its officials began collecting tolls in 1937, pressure on the agency intensified. Critics, including State Senator John F. McCarthy, instigated investigations and grand jury hearings that revealed inefficiency, extravagant spending, and a general disregard for bridge safety and engineering concerns. Repeated attempts to dissolve or reform the bridge district failed, as its officials united against outside critics and became adept at fighting outside interference. James Adam, the formidable bridge district publicity director and lobbyist, rose to power and took control as general manager in 1953, inaugurating an era of tight solidarity and fierce independence. During Adam's reign as the top bridge district official, which lasted until 1968, the agency endured a series of scandals involving questionable accounting, no-bid contracts, undocumented expenses, racist hiring practices, and negligent maintenance. Nevertheless, Adam built the bridge district into a regional power, taking advantage of the impressive resources at his disposal. He reinforced an emerging organizational culture that emphasized the importance of financial security and political autonomy, and deemphasized safety, bridge maintenance, and other engineering concerns. He also cultivated strategic political alliances and established new procedures to promote bridge district interests, including lobbying and public relations activities. Adam refined a mythic account of bridge district origins based on a story of heroic and righteous struggle that helped justify questionable policies and encouraged bridge district officials to view embattlement and unpopularity as normal and appropriate.

Under Adam, the bridge district developed a reputation in the Bay Area as an intractable, imperious, and corrupt organization, and as a behind-the-scenes power in Sacramento. Bridge district officials increased their engagement in regional policy-making, both by expanding their public activities and by covert political maneuvering. A tightly knit cadre of leading directors and top staff was instrumental in defeating proposals for Bay Area planning that threatened bridge district autonomy. Adam and bridge district engineer Arthur C. Jenkins also succeeded in fending off competition for toll revenue by defeating plans to run rapid transit rails on the bridge. Their actions on behalf of the bridge district flew in the face of public opinion, defied economic and political elites, and even offended the agency's traditional allies. By the end of the 1950s, bridge district leaders had a reputation for mismanagement and corruption, and the agency itself was widely seen as a major impediment to the development of effective and rational regional government and transportation policy.

At the time of its inception in 1923, the Golden Gate Bridge and Highway District was an innovative and ambitious organization with few precedents. It represented the application of new theories of public administration and a strategic breakthrough in public finance.[12] A series of closely watched court cases were necessary to establish its legality and legitimacy in California. However, the bridge district was on the crest of a tsunami of new special districts in metropolitan areas in California and throughout the country.[13] Criticism of bridge district administration contributed to increasing concern among policy analysts and politicians about the implications of special districts. As early as 1930, economist Paul Studenski asserted that governmental fragmentation resulted in uneven standards of public services and "radical inequities in the tax resources of the several political divisions," and warned that special districts, "removed from the people whom [they] serve, may become arbitrary or bureaucratic." Political scientist Victor Jones pointed out in 1942 that the more special districts increased in number, the less likely it was that centralized, comprehensive metropolitan government could ever be established. In 1957 political scientist John C. Bollens published the first comprehensive study of special districts, condemning them for being "uneconomic," calling their rapid proliferation a "piecemeal, unintelligent attack on the problems of government . . . hinder[ing] the orderly development and sound utilization of the resources of an area."[14]

There was a virtual consensus among policy analysts, state politicians, and federal leaders on the need for governmental centralization and effective planning in rapidly growing metropolitan areas at the end of the 1950s. However, in the absence of regional government and planning, the creation of new special districts was an obvious, quick, and easy way to address major problems that existing local governments did not have the capacity or the political will to take on themselves. Special districts proliferated in the decades following World War II, initiated at the local level in the context of an urban and suburban crisis of rapid growth and encouraged by a variety of new federal programs.[15] Jones explained that local government officials saw special districts as "useful devices" to "meet a crisis without disturbing current organizational arrangements . . . [they are] an easy and painless way of eating one's regional cake and having one's local cake too."[16] Accommodating state governments authorized them as stop-gap measures to manage growth and ameliorate its side effects, despite concern about the consequences of political fragmentation. From 1942 to 1952, the total number of special districts in the United States went from 8,299 to 12,340. During the same ten years, the number of special districts in metropolitan areas more than doubled, and many of these were bigger and more powerful than their predecessors, with broader functional and geographic scope and greater fiscal independence than ever.[17] In 1962 there were 18,323 autonomous special districts in the United States, and their numbers continued to rise.[18]

By the 1960s, the inability of government to direct growth and control its impact in rapidly growing cities and sprawling suburbs was widely attributed to special districts. Max A. Pock, professor of law at the University of Michigan, summed up the scholarly consensus in 1962: "[The] 'metropolitan problem' has principally come to serve as a synonym for the proliferation of ineffectual units of local government which . . . are pitifully inadequate to the task of rendering urban services or performing regulatory functions that peremptorily demand area-wide jurisdiction and control."[19] The unintended effects of special districts were not limited to the issue of effective metropolitan area coordination. Although for the most part these agencies operated out of the spotlight, their leadership and policy-making process intentionally shielded from public scrutiny, various scandals brought attention to the consequences of too much special district autonomy.[20] After half a century of special district administration in the United States it was clearly apparent that these agencies did not always serve the interests of their creators or of the public at large, and that efforts to make government more efficient and businesslike sometimes generated new sorts of mismanagement and corruption. These agencies often could not be effectively controlled or regulated once they were created and had a variety of unintended effects. The story of the Golden Gate Bridge and Highway District and its influence on the San Francisco Bay Area provides insight into the consequences of thousands of similar agencies that were created in metropolitan areas throughout the United States.

Once new special districts came into existence, their officials and associates had obvious incentives for protecting their jurisdiction and extending their lifespan. In the San Francisco Bay Area a number of large, regional special districts joined the Golden Gate Bridge and Highway District, including the Bay Area Regional Water Pollution Control Board (1949), the Bay Area Air Pollution Control District (1955), the

Alameda–Contra Costa Transit District (1956), and the Bay Area Rapid Transit District (1957). Not only did these agencies relieve pressure for regional government, but their leaders, like those of the bridge district, opposed any infringement on the jurisdiction or autonomy of their agency. They closed ranks with local politicians, particularly those of suburban cities and counties, to rally against any centralized regional government or planning that would diminish the sovereignty of existing governments.

Ultimately, the survival of the bridge district depended on the outcome of an epic battle over the form of metropolitan area government. Bridge district officials fought to protect their agency from dissolution alongside provincial defenders of "home rule," including city, county, and other special district officials, who rallied to oppose any new regional authority. This coalition squared off against regionalist advocates of centralized planning and government, including Bay Area civic and business leaders, state and federal officials, and high-profile intellectuals and policy analysts. These two factions waged a war in the 1950s and 1960s that took place in the context of major shifts in regional politics, including the rise of environmentalism and the growth-control movement. The bridge district played a small but critical part in the victory of the home rule coalition and the adoption (or acceptance) of decentralization as the permanent structural form of metropolitan area government. Because of this outcome, special districts, including an expanded and permanent Golden Gate Bridge, Highway and Transportation District, took over as the de facto regional government of the San Francisco Bay Area.

The history of the Golden Gate Bridge and Highway District and the San Francisco Bay Area demonstrates how the officials of even the most unpopular special district can mobilize its resources and independent power to fend off reform and protect its interests as an agency. It also reveals how immensely influential a single, relatively modest special district can be. A multitude of limited-purpose governments have shaped policy in distinctive and ever more significant ways as their numbers have increased over the last century. All of them have the potential to engage in the regional decision-making process and influence its outcome, and while their purpose, culture and political orientation varies, they all share a basic institutional interest in survival. In alliance with other local governments they form a massive fortress protecting a decentralized, federalist system of government in American metropolitan areas. They also represent a significant step away from democratic decision-making, political transparency, and government accountability.

Max Weber observed in 1917 that government bureaucracy was "far more persistent and 'escape proof'" than "other historical agencies of the modern rational order of life." He noted with apprehension the "irresistible advance of bureaucratization" and the "practically indestructible" power of public officials. Weber posed the question: "In view of the growing indispensability of [government] bureaucracy and its corresponding increase in power, how can there be any guarantee that any powers will remain which can check and effectively control the tremendous influence of this stratum? How will democracy even in this limited sense be *at all possible?*"[21] The development of the Golden Gate Bridge and Highway District and its influence on the politics and policy of the San Francisco Bay Area highlights the continued importance of these questions, as well as more specific dilemmas: are the pragmatic advantages of special districts worth the risk of corruption and abuse? Have special districts removed public decisions and policy-making too far from the democratic process? Is the decentralization of metropolitan area government inevitable and irreversible? Other special districts, public agencies, and even private organizations share some of the essential characteristics that made the Golden Gate Bridge and Highway District so powerful and enduring. In a sense, this story is about bureaucracy as the basic organizational form of the modern state, and of the major American social, business, and political institutions of the twentieth century.

Chapter 1

A Bridge to Prosperity

Bridging the Golden Gate, the narrow opening of the San Francisco Bay to the Pacific Ocean, was a daring proposal in 1923, and the challenge of financing a bridge was as daunting as its engineering. On January 13, more than two hundred men, most representing northern California government, civic, or business groups, crowded into the assembly room of the Santa Rosa Chamber of Commerce, determined to take on that challenge. They had been called together by the chamber president Frank P. Doyle, the president and majority shareholder of Sonoma's largest bank and a founding member of the Redwood Highway Association.[1] Doyle and his fellow bridge supporters from the rural north wanted to promote regional economic development, population growth, and tourism in the dawning age of the automobile. As a group they were practical and conservative, hoping to build the bridge quickly with minimal political complications or financial risk. The meeting also included a large contingent of San Francisco officials, who had very different expectations and goals for a Golden Gate bridge. San Francisco's delegates, including Mayor James Rolph, Jr., and city engineer Michael M. O'Shaughnessy, held progressive political ideals, including a commitment to public enterprise and an enthusiasm for large public works projects. They believed that a bridge to new suburbs and a vast northern hinterland would help ensure San Francisco's place at the center of the regional economy and its status as a great city.[2]

While no one questioned the desirability of a bridge, many doubted its engineering feasibility and financial advisability. Doyle called the meeting not to address these concerns but rather to get the job under way despite them. Bridging the Golden Gate was too risky to be attractive to the private sector, and even if existing governments had the will, they did not have the wherewithal to undertake it publicly. A bridge required an innovation in government that could inspire the confidence of conservatives, appeal to the ideals of progressives, and at the same time command the resources needed to build the ambitious bridge.

Appropriately, it was a resident of Marin County, situated between San Francisco and the rest of northern California, who suggested a means of bridging this political divide. George H. Harlan of Sausalito had introduced legislation for the state's first municipal water district in 1911 during his single term as a state assemblyman. Now he proposed the creation of another special district to take on the task of building the bridge. California's first and only bridge and highway district garnered support from both progressives and conservatives by depoliticizing the financing and administration of the bridge but keeping it in the public sector. It removed the bridge from the jurisdiction of politicians and, presumably, protected it from corruption.

Creating a bridge district would mean a redistribution of power and resources, and a significant minority of civic leaders, including O'Shaughnessy, eventually came to oppose it. The campaign for this new public agency evoked questions about the relationship between public and private enterprise that were central to American politics. Its creation was part of an ongoing process of state-building and an important stage in the development of public works bureaucracy. On the vanguard of a multitude of similar organizations, the bridge district became a test case for special districts in California. It was the product of determined and resourceful local leaders and businessmen who sought to achieve their goals by expanding the capacity of local government in the early twentieth century.

The Redwood Highway

The northern California conservatives who met in Santa Rosa to discuss a Golden Gate bridge had powerful incentives to overcome their suspicion of public enterprise and their aversion to taxes. Real estate investors and businessmen saw exciting potential in the region north of San Francisco, which was largely rural and sparsely populated. They imagined traffic streaming out of San Francisco, tourists infusing forests and coastlines with money, and suburban development boosting real estate values. The fact that this potential remained untapped provided the principal reason for building a bridge, but at the same time, it hindered its financing. While enormous growth was possible, without it a bridge could never attract enough traffic to pay for itself, much less make a profit. It was a gamble these men were eager to make.

They were not alone on their chosen path to prosperity. "Good Roads" campaigns swept the country in the 1890s, spurred by bicycle manufacturers and funded by railroad companies. They were primarily aimed at improving local farm-to-market routes, particularly those leading to railroad terminals. With the rise of the automobile and a widespread enthusiasm for touring among middle-class as well as wealthy citizens, the orientation and goals of road advocates changed. As in northern California, small-town leaders began creating organizations throughout the country to promote ambitious long-distance routes that would open new territory to the motoring public. Among the earliest of these was the Lincoln Highway Association, formed in 1913 by Carl Graham Fisher, a headlight manufacturer from Indianapolis who envisaged a continuous, paved route linking New York and San Francisco. Other associations sought funding and rallied support for the Dixie Highway, the Yellowstone Highway, the Pacific Coast Highway, the Bankhead National Highway, and dozens of other long-distance, tourist-oriented roadways.[3] By the 1920s federal and state governments were providing subsidies for road building, spurring local boosters to lobby for their share.[4] However, nothing yet suggested that a project as expensive as the Golden Gate Bridge could rely on state or federal funding—it had to be paid for locally.

To northern California businessmen, the costs and risks of building a bridge must have paled in comparison with the danger of being left behind in the nationwide rush for roads. The region suddenly seemed to be cut off from San Francisco by a bay that benefited ferries and ships but hindered automobiles and trucks. In 1920 Doyle and a select group of civic leaders and businessmen formed the North Bay Counties Association, both to compete for state and federal road funding and to advertise to motorists. They soon renamed the organization the Redwood Highway Association, focusing their efforts on a north-south artery for motorists. In 1925, they hired publicist Clyde Edmondson as its full-time general manager. Edmondson described the Golden Gate Bridge as the most important mile of the anticipated Redwood Highway, the northern California route that would integrate the region and stimulate its economy.[5]

The North Bay Counties Association consisted of Marin, Sonoma, Napa, Mendocino, Humboldt, and Del Norte counties in California, and Josephine County in Oregon. Already oriented toward San Francisco economically, these counties supplied San Franciscans with agricultural products and timber. Marin County, just north of the Golden Gate, offered the best evidence of the region's potential for development. Marin encompassed the peninsula extending southward toward San Francisco, ridged with mountains sheltering the bay. The fog and mist that often blanketed the county, particularly in western areas, made its pastures lush and productive. Its dramatic rocky shoreline, pastoral beauty, and proximity to San Francisco made the county a favorite retreat for the city's leisure class. Starting in 1896, visitors could enjoy views of the bay from the prominent Mount Tamalpais on a twisting railroad devoted to sightseeing. Most significantly, Marin already hosted a small population of commuters, many of whom left the city after the earthquake of 1906 and took advantage of ferries to downtown San Francisco. Its promoters described Marin as a "mecca for the homemaker, where suburban life in a beautifully wooded and flowered countryside may be combined with business of the metropolis."[6]

Napa and Sonoma County partisans boasted of bountiful farms and picturesque rural landscapes. With 52,090 residents in 1920, Sonoma was the most populous county north of San Francisco and an important supplier of dairy, poultry, eggs, beef, vegetables, and apples. Sonoma also had some of California's best-known wineries and resorts, including the legendary Bohemian Grove, a favorite retreat for the rich and powerful. Napa County, while smaller both in population and in area than its coastal neighbor, also had significant vineyards and pasture. While some Napa and Sonoma products were shipped to eastern markets, San Francisco residents consumed the vast majority.[7]

Although there was some agriculture north of Sonoma, including vineyards and ranches, the timber industry dominated the economy of Humboldt, Mendocino, and Del Norte counties. In the nineteenth century, mill towns sprang up along the Pacific coast as vast and dense redwood forests were harvested and shipped as lumber to San Francisco. Reconstruction after the 1906 earthquake increased demand for the prized wood, and timber production boomed. By 1920, the combined population of Mendocino and Humboldt topped 60,000 and all of the easily accessible forests had been cleared.[8] Most of this activity bypassed the remote Del Norte County, however, which was traversed by a single, unpaved road and had only 2,759 residents, no rail service, and few prospects for growth.[9] Redwood Highway boosters there hoped to attract motoring visitors with a "zestful outdoor life," ample trout and salmon, grand forests teeming with game, rugged terrain, remote beaches, and even interaction with Native American inhabitants.[10]

As planned, the Redwood Highway would run north from San Francisco, through Marin County and Santa Rosa in the Sonoma Valley, then northwest through Mendocino County along the south fork of the Eel River toward Eureka on Humboldt Bay. From there, it would trace the Pacific coast, cross the treacherous Klamath River on its way to Crescent City in Del Norte, and finally turn inland toward Grant's Pass, Oregon.[11] State engineers had surveyed the entire route from Sausalito in Marin to Crescent City in Del Norte by 1917, but construction stalled. While El Camino Real running south from San Francisco to San Diego was entirely paved by 1920, little progress had been made on the Redwood Highway.[12] It was "replete with chuck-holes, washboard surface—extremely crooked and often impassable in winter," and autos crossed

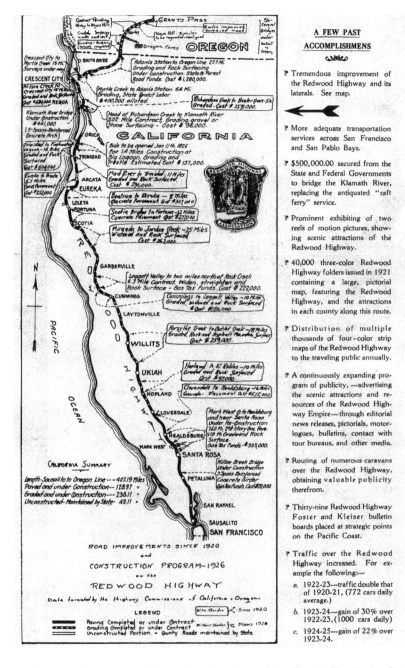

Redwood Highway Association, *Your Harvest from More Tourists Vacationists Settlers in the Redwood Highway Empire* [1925]. Courtesy of The Bancroft Library, University of California, Berkeley.

the Klamath River by raft as weather permitted. Near Crescent City the road disappeared entirely: "motorists had to drive over the sand beach and take their chances on a tricky tide. Many a car was lost in the Crescent City surf by motorists unfamiliar with tide conditions."[13] While these challenges may have appealed to adventuresome motorists, they deterred most tourists. Members of the new Redwood Highway Association were determined to change this. Decades of boosterism in the western United States had enforced the idea that prosperity was a zero-sum game, and that localities had to actively compete for resources, investment, and growth.[14]

To achieve their goals, Redwood Highway advocates forged a metropolitan-level alliance. While they might be successful in winning state and federal subsidies for road-building, Northern California boosters knew they could never bridge the Golden Gate without support from San Francisco. California's major financial institutions were based in the city, and its delegation dominated the state legislature.[15] The bridge required War Department authorization and right-of-ways through two military bases on either side of the Golden Gate; the influence of well-connected San Francisco leaders in Washington would be critical to winning federal permission. Most importantly, though the city was a tiny peninsula in comparison to the expanse of farmland and forest to the north, its immensely valuable property was vital to securing bonds. Northern California boosters had to convince city leaders that the bridge was a necessity. James H. Wilkins, a reporter for the *San Francisco Bulletin* and a Marin County ferry commuter, outlined their argument in 1916: "The vast Bay region will never be complete without a bridge across the Golden Gate." In a lengthy front-page feature, he pointed out the advantages of an "empire" for San Francisco: "These counties are growing faster, on the basis of merit alone, than any other part of northern California. They offer room and opportunity for at least two million people. Nature has, in a way, tied their fortunes, beyond recall, to San Francisco. That city must always be their final market place— their clearing-house. Nothing can be more important to San Francisco."[16] Wilkins, who had a degree in engineering, asserted that a bridge across the Golden Gate would be "the greatest advertisement in the world . . . the most stupendous, awe-inspiring monument of our modern civilization." He also supported public ownership, predicting that the bridge would "pay for itself," but that a private bridge would have little chance of winning War Department permission.[17]

In 1918 Wilkins spoke throughout the region on behalf of a Golden Gate bridge. He drafted legislation and even commissioned engineering plans to present to local leaders. The most enthusiastic endorsement came from Michael F. Cochrane, publisher of the *San Rafael Independent*, who instigated a meeting of Marin County civic leaders in August 1919 that resulted in the first formal organization to promote the bridge. Elected chairman of the Marin Committee on the Golden Gate Bridge, Cochrane predicted that the span would triple the county's property values. Also on the committee was William Kent, the county's largest landowner and a former U.S. congressman. Other northern California boosters promised to rally behind the project once Marin started "the ball rolling." Cochrane, Kent, and the rest of the Marin committee met with San Francisco city engineer O'Shaughnessy a week later to plan the next step, an expert assessment of feasibility. Significantly, O'Shaughnessy was a Marin commuter, residing in Mill Valley. Northern California partisans had a much more vital and immediate interest in the proposed bridge than did San Francisco officials, and they provided the leadership, the resources, and the determination to build the bridge.[18]

Public Enterprise

In San Francisco, the Golden Gate Bridge proposal had to compete with several ambitious construction projects for the attention of city leaders, who were embroiled in a decades-long battle over public enterprise. City officials around the country were undertaking technically advanced and expensive large-scale public works projects by the turn of the century. James Duval Phelan, Jr., elected mayor of San Francisco in 1897, inaugurated a bold program of city-sponsored improvements. Phelan and other like-minded progressive reformers not only restructured municipal government to reduce abuse and fraud, but they also sought to expand its responsibilities and power. They backed city managers, nonpartisan elections, and other measures designed to reduce the influence of political parties and "machines" and put responsibility into the hands of expert administrators. Trained professionals replaced patronage-based appointees and civil service bureaucracies removed administrative functions from traditional "politics." Reformers had new confidence that city government could be effectively and efficiently used to promote the public interest—without undue corruption. In pursuing the goal of responsible, active, and powerful city government, Phelan had the support of Governor Hiram Johnson as well as many other members of the patrician elite who believed in public enterprise. After passing a major charter revision in 1898 that expanded the city's administrative capacities and reduced the power of elected officials, Phelan's primary ambition was to provide public water and electricity to the city by damming the Hetch Hetchy Valley hundreds of miles away in the Sierra. He also initiated the construction of a municipal railway in 1900, the first public rail system in the country.[19]

However, these projects languished after Phelan left office in 1901.

While he continued to pursue the effort to dam Hetch Hetchy, Phelan's opponents blocked federal authorization. Many conservatives viewed the huge scale and cost of the project with alarm, and preservationists such as John Muir sought to protect the beautiful valley itself.[20] The election of James "Sunny Jim" Rolph as mayor in 1911 revived Phelan's projects. Back in control, San Francisco progressives restarted municipal railway construction and lobbied intensively for the Hetch Hetchy Dam, which the federal Raker Act authorized in 1913. Rolph recruited O'Shaughnessy to build the monumental dam and aqueduct, promising the highly regarded engineer a free hand in its design and ample city funding.[21]

All of the activity surrounding public enterprise meant that, by the time northern California boosters began campaigning for the Golden Gate Bridge in San Francisco, they had to contend with a backlash against large public projects. The municipal railway generated persistent controversy over its cost as well as speculation about graft and corruption, and by the 1920s voters consistently rejected bond issues for its extension. The first phase of the Hetch Hetchy project, the construction of O'Shaughnessy Dam, immediately went dramatically over budget. Conservatives mocked "More Money" O'Shaughnessy after repeated supplemental bond issues, and argued that the San Francisco supervisors were out of their league and that large-scale undertakings were better left to experienced businessmen.[22]

By the 1920s public enterprise was the central, defining issue of San Francisco politics. The city's two rival political factions, conservative and progressive, were both nominally Republican.[23] They agreed that new infrastructure was needed to provide San Francisco with water, electricity, and transportation, but differed on whether it should be built publicly or privately. The dispute played out in the pages of San Francisco newspapers. The *San Francisco Examiner* and the *Call-Bulletin* were both owned by William Randolph Hearst and overseen by John Francis Neylan, a devoted advocate of municipal ownership and a leader among San Francisco progressives. In the 1920s, Neylan focused his attention on *Examiner* editorials, regularly arguing the case for expanding the role of local government and even proclaiming support for municipal ownership with a daily front-page byline. No candidate won an *Examiner* endorsement without supporting public enterprise, and Neylan earned the moniker of political "czar."[24] The *San Francisco Chronicle*, owned and operated by members of the conservative de Young family, provided a political counterweight to the *Examiner*. Michael de Young operated the *Chronicle* until his death 1925, when his son-in-law George T. Cameron took over as its manager and publisher. Cameron, known as the "cement king," was a prominent businessman and a leading member of the city's chamber of commerce, and used the *Chronicle* to back its political positions and policy recommendations. His conservative allies held fast to their faith in the private sector, arguing that public officials did not have the business sense or honesty to handle large projects responsibly.[25]

While all Bay Area public works were controversial at the time, the Golden Gate Bridge was especially problematic because its financing depended upon speculation. The bridge could never attract enough traffic to cover the cost of construction without spectacular, unprecedented population growth north of the bay. In addition, it had to compete with other more sensible projects, including a bridge connecting San Francisco and Oakland. Comparison of the two proposed bridges, both of which were endorsed by the San Francisco supervisors in 1918, reveals the relative weakness of the Golden Gate span. The transbay crossing was to connect two major cities that were economically interdependent, with ferries already transporting millions of foot passengers and automobiles between them each year. Thirteen private companies had applied for permits to build a San Francisco-Oakland bridge by 1921, and conservatives wanted to grant one of them a franchise and the right to collect tolls.[26] Progressives, determined to keep any new span public, argued that interest from the private sector indicated its potential profitability,

Joseph B. Strauss with Frank P. Doyle, 1927. San Francisco History Center, San Francisco Public Library.

but that any profits should benefit the people directly. A tug-of-war between the two factions delayed construction, but interest in the span did not wane: in 1927 there were eighteen active applications from private companies eager to build a San Francisco-Oakland crossing.[27]

In contrast, the Golden Gate Bridge generated almost no private sector interest. Not only was it highly speculative financially, but its engineering feasibility was also uncertain. Its location presented formidable challenges: two steep, rocky shorelines were divided by rough waters that rushed through a deep, narrow outlet into the Pacific. United States Coast and Geodetic Survey technicians conducted soundings at the request of state legislators in 1920 and found inadequate bedrock and unstable currents, convincing them that building a bridge in that location was virtually impossible. Although the San Francisco supervisors declared a reasonable cost for the project to be $25 million, early estimates were in the range of $100 million.[28] Bridging the Golden Gate would obviously be difficult and expensive, if it could be done at all. Ongoing battles over other municipal projects in San Francisco meant that problems of organization, administration, and finance for the Golden Gate Bridge had to be solved elsewhere.

While the initial investigation of the bridge site discouraged most engineers, it inspired unquenchable ambition in Chicago-based engineer Joseph B. Strauss. In 1919, O'Shaughnessy asked a number of prominent bridge engineers to submit plans and bids for the project, including Strauss.[29] Although he had no experience with long span bridges, Strauss had built many other types of bridges around the world. O'Shaughnessy was familiar with his work because he had designed a successful ride for the Panama-Pacific International Exposition and a small drawbridge for San Francisco in 1917. This was an exciting opportunity for Strauss; the Golden Gate Bridge was a spectacular project that could propel him to the forefront of his profession.[30]

In his eagerness, Strauss discounted the discouraging results of 1920 soundings and quickly developed plans for a cantilever-suspension hybrid bridge. The awkward design caused O'Shaughnessy considerable apprehension, and later he remarked that it "had a greater resemblance to an inverted rat trap than to a bridge and lowered considerably my estimate of [Strauss's] capacity for designing a large bridge."[31] Strauss argued that beauty came at a price, and indeed, the next lowest estimate of $56 million dwarfed his $17 million price tag. Despite misgivings, O'Shaughnessy and other bridge backers realized that any design was better than none, and that serious, credible plans could not be obtained without paying for them. Plus, Strauss was willing to volunteer his time to promote the span. Strauss began touring northern California to present his plan, and O'Shaughnessy released the initial design along with formal cost estimates in a privately printed booklet in December 1922.[32]

Strauss's original design for a bridge across the Golden Gate, 1921. From M. M. O'Shaughnessy and Joseph B. Strauss, *Bridging the Golden Gate* (San Francisco, 1921).

Although one observer described Strauss as "the world's worst speaker," his efforts and O'Shaughnessy's endorsement convinced northern California boosters that if the bridge could be financed, engineering problems could be solved.[33] Soon after the plans were released, Doyle called the fateful meeting in Santa Rosa. The conservative northern California businessmen and San Francisco progressives who attended the meeting formed the Bridging the Golden Gate Association. Doyle, James G. Stafford of Santa Rosa, San Francisco Supervisor Richard J. Welch, California Assemblyman Frank L. Coombs of Napa, and Captain I. N. Hibbard of San Francisco formed the executive committee. Thomas Allen Box, an attorney from southern Marin, was elected president, and Sonoma's W. J. Hotchkiss, vice president of the California Packing Company, chaired the finance committee.[34]

All of the San Francisco attendees, including Rolph, O'Shaughnessy, and supervisors Welch and Warren Shannon, were enthusiastic about the prospects for a grand public bridge. The northern California businessmen who made up most of the assembly were much more wary. However, Harlan could point to the record of the Marin Municipal Water District (MMWD) as evidence that a special district could operate effectively and in the interest of business and growth. Harlan conceived of the agency, wrote its enabling legislation, and now served as its attorney. The original purpose of the MMWD was similar to that of the proposed bridge district. At the time of its creation in 1912, Marin did not have the water it needed for vigorous growth, and a reliable supply required the construction of several dams. Leaving these projects to private companies would mean high water rates, slowing hoped-for development. Even as San Francisco supervisors sought to solve a similar problem themselves by damming the Hetch Hetchy Valley as a city project, Marin leaders opted to support the creation of a special district rather than to trust the elected officials of existing local governments with more responsibility. They hoped to benefit from cheap public water while maintaining control over its provision; some of Marin's wealthiest and most influential men sat on the MMWD board, including William Kent, O'Shaughnessy, and Robert H. Trumbull, the director of three San Rafael banks. MMWD revenues exceeded expectations immediately, and the Alpine Dam was complete by 1919. A $500,000 bond issue to expand MMWD operations and watershed holdings passed by a margin of five to one in 1920, proving the agency's popularity among voters, as well.[35]

The success of the MMWD gave credibility to Harlan's proposal for creating a special district to finance and build the Golden Gate Bridge. Indeed, the Municipal Water District Act turned out to be one of the most influential pieces of legislation in California history, spawning dozens of water districts and providing the template for a variety of other legislation. Harlan described the California Bridge and Highway District Act as an "almost an exact copy of the Water District act," but he did make several significant modifications to address conservative concerns.[36] While MMWD was relatively democratic, with elected as well as appointed directors all subject to recall, bridge district representation was much further removed from voters and strongly favored smaller counties. County supervisors appointed all bridge directors for four-year terms, and they could not be recalled. Harlan limited San Francisco, whose population was nearly ten times greater than any other county being considered for inclusion, to five representatives. He hoped to reassure northern California conservatives by guaranteeing that the city could not gain a majority on the board of directors.[37]

Harlan also adjusted the process of creating the bridge district to sidestep potential opposition. A new municipal water district required a petition signed by 25 percent of its property owners as well as a majority vote of its citizens. The enrollment of a county in the bridge district required only an application from a private citizen and a petition signed by 10 percent of property owners. Once an application had been submitted to county supervisors, they had sixty days to pass an ordinance to join the proposed district before the question had to go to a public vote. Harlan advised bridge promoters to use the time limit to put pressure on county supervisors. Elections would cost counties thousands of dollars, Harlan explained, and certainly they would not be "in the position of crawling as a supplicant before the throne."[38] Only after ordinances were passed could individual property owners file legal challenges to their inclusion in the district. Once these challenges were settled in local courts, the California secretary of state would issue a certificate of incorporation, and at that moment the new agency would have the authority to levy property taxes and incur nonbonded debt. No public vote on the question of membership or the creation of the agency was ever required.[39]

These provisions reflected Harlan's justifiable concern that the impressive powers he proposed for the bridge district would arouse public anxiety. The agency would be able to acquire "real or personal property of any kind," and could purchase or construct "bridges . . . roads, tunnels, railroads, streetcar lines, interurban lines, telephone and telegraph lines, foot paths, viaducts, toll gates, toll houses, subways, and all other forms of property." It would have the power of perpetual succession and the right of eminent domain. Its officials would establish tolls and charges, levy property taxes, and incur nonbonded debt at their own discretion. Its surplus revenue had to be distributed among bridge district counties annually, making it impossible to acquire reserves. This encouraged district officials to spend whatever income they did have and also made tax levies more likely in lean years.[40] There was no requirement for independent audits. The general manager wielded "full power to employ and discharge all subordinate officers, employees and assistants at pleasure, prescribe their duties and . . . fix their compensation," as well as "charge and control of the construction, maintenance and operation of all works of the district." Only the general manager would report to the directors, who met just three times a month, effectively limiting their involvement in day-to-day operations and administration.[41]

Harlan designed the bridge district to operate as a business, with a strong executive, a professional staff, and a corporate structure. Because he could count on progressives such as Rolph to support almost any public enterprise, Harlan adjusted its organizational form to appease the conservative businessmen who doubted the competence and honesty of elected officials. The spectacle of San Francisco's municipal public works projects, plagued as they were by inefficiency, budget overruns, and the constant need for new bond issues, alarmed the bridge boosters of northern California. They hoped that Harlan's bridge district, insulated from electoral politics, could operate effectively, profitably, and without corruption.

Bridge Boosters Rally

Only a few months after the Bridging the Golden Gate Association was formed, the California Bridge and Highway District Act, authored by

Harlan and introduced by Coombs, passed easily in Sacramento. Association members wasted no time getting their campaign under way, touring northern California in the spring and summer of 1923 to promote the bridge. According to one account, Box and Hotchkiss traveled more than two thousand miles in two weeks. Strauss and O'Shaughnessy presented preliminary plans before ever-larger crowds, and representatives of twenty-seven different counties attended a San Francisco rally in June.[42] "You will have to keep the counties out of this district, rather than urge them to come in," Hotchkiss predicted.[43] By the time the enabling act went into effect in September, association members were poised to circulate petitions and persuade northern California county supervisors to commit to the district.

Unexpectedly, the campaign stopped short when Colonel Herbert Deakyne of the Army Corps of Engineers declared his opposition to the project because it could interfere with navigation. Bridge boosters had not anticipated military resistance; Strauss claimed that the secretary of war and several members of Congress had promised him personally that permission would be granted.[44] Obviously, Strauss had not contacted Deakyne, who commented indignantly that the "scheme to place a bridge across the Golden Gate . . . has not yet reached my office."[45] His objections meant that no county would be willing to join before the bridge had formal War Department approval. That would require detailed engineering plans, which would have to be paid for privately rather than with the bridge district's initial tax levies.

Well-heeled members of the Bridging the Golden Gate Association, particularly Hotchkiss, came through with donations.[46] They commissioned Leon S. Moisseiff, one of the country's leading suspension bridge engineers, to review and elaborate on the original design. He was working in Philadelphia on the Benjamin Franklin Bridge over the Delaware River at the time, and it was a year before his report on the Golden Gate Bridge reached Washington.[47] Although several hundred eager boosters from throughout northern California testified at a hearing on behalf of the project in San Francisco in May 1924, Secretary of War John W. Weeks did not grant conditional permission for the span until December, pending approval of final plans and with the stipulation that all government and military traffic be permanently exempt from tolls.[48]

A year and a half after the passage of the enabling act, members of the Bridging the Golden Gate Association could finally start enrolling counties. They selected eight counties to recruit, all with a clear interest in the bridge: San Francisco, Marin, Sonoma, Napa, Mendocino, Humboldt, Lake, and Del Norte. In just over a month Sonoma, Mendocino, and Marin had all passed ordinances to enroll. Napa joined them on April 14, and although Humboldt, Lake, and Del Norte supervisors delayed decisions on membership, they were generally enthusiastic about the proposal.[49]

Bridge boosters faced their first significant opposition in San Francisco, the bridge district keystone. From an economic and business standpoint, city leaders had relatively little to gain from the bridge. San Francisco was already a major metropolis, and any increase in real estate values resulting from the bridge would be marginal. Conservative *Chronicle* editors pointed out that there were other, more urgent projects that required attention, and that city government had a debt ceiling that limited choices: "We must finish Hetch Hetchy, which will take many millions more. We are embarked on a great school building program. We have before us extensions of the Municipal Railway urgently needed to provide for city growth. . . . We need reservoirs and firebreaks [and] are in pressing need of more sewers. . . . And we need a bridge between San Francisco and the Oakland shore."[50] When initially confronted with an application to enroll, San Francisco supervisors postponed their vote pending further study. Welch called the decision a "slap in the face."[51] Worst of all, O'Shaughnessy reversed his stance, announcing his opposition to the bridge before the Commonwealth Club in April, asserting that improvements to San Francisco's own infrastructure should take precedence.[52]

Still, San Francisco leaders were very concerned about the status of their city, which had not recovered from the destruction of the 1906 earthquake with as much vigor as they would have liked. By 1920, Los Angeles had surpassed San Francisco in population and other measures of prestige and prosperity, including number of automobiles. Almost as disturbing, Oakland, San Francisco's East Bay sibling, was gaining on the peninsular city, improving its port facilities and attracting commerce and traffic from northern California and the central valley.[53] Efforts to establish regional government or to annex new areas into San Francisco had been largely unsuccessful, but adding a new link to the north could help maintain the city's preeminence.[54]

Members of the Bridging the Golden Gate Association pointed all of this out. They appealed to city leaders' pride and ambition, promising a new empire for San Francisco. Coombs even threatened that they would consider building a bridge to Oakland if San Francisco did not join the effort. Delegates from all over northern California made the case for San Francisco's membership. They addressed the problem of debt limits by pointing out that the city would not be affected because the district had full responsibility for its own bonds—one of the most appealing aspects of special districts generally.[55] The editors of the *Examiner* enthusiastically repeated boosters' promises that the bridge would "pay for itself" and accused "obstructionist" supervisors of surreptitiously maneuvering for a "privately-built, privately-owned toll bridge."[56] They added a reference to the city's bygone glory to make their point: "If the Supervisors want to create . . . a perpetual monument that will make this city's name ring around the world and renew the magical fame which the Golden Gate enjoyed in the days of '49, they have only to vote in favor of joining the Bridge District."[57] Seduced by the promise of a glorious span, by April the San Francisco supervisors were ready to commit their support even without further studies.

San Francisco Examiner, March 27, 1925.

Just one political obstacle remained: the question of representation. San Francisco comprised 85 percent of the population and the property value of the proposed district, and its officials wanted more than a minority on its board of directors. After negotiations, Coombs amended the enabling legislation to guarantee San Francisco the right to appoint half of the directors. Finally, on April 13, 1925, San Francisco supervisors passed an ordinance to join the district.[58]

When San Francisco supervisors committed to the Golden Gate Bridge, they also joined the Redwood Highway Association. With the addition of the imperial city, the organization was renamed the Redwood Empire Association (REA) and quickly became the most influential civic organization in northern California. Bridge district contributions were the REA's largest single source of revenue once the district was incorporated in 1928. The two organizations were closely allied from the beginning and only became more intimately connected as time went on.[59]

With San Francisco finally on the future bridge district roster, bridge boosters turned their attention back to the northern counties. Unexpectedly, they discovered that opposition to the project had coalesced among rural property owners. Humboldt and Lake county farmers and timber harvesters had awakened to the prospect of new taxes and the negative implications of rising property values for industries that benefited from inexpensive land. Although the counties that had already signed on included the vast majority of the targeted property and were probably sufficient to finance the bridge, bridge backers could not just quit after San Francisco leaders agreed to join. Ordinances described the district by listing all of the counties that had been originally targeted for membership—failing to win over all eight counties could invalidate all of them.[60] In July, Humboldt County supervisors announced that they would not join, arguing that the construction of a bridge was an undertaking "properly belonging to San Francisco."[61] A *San Francisco Examiner* editor explained that "lumbermen" feared the tourists that the Redwood Highway would attract: "One of them declared . . . that the automobilists would 'get a passing glance at our great lumbering industry and go back home and call us vandals.'"[62] Indeed, the San Francisco–based "Save-the-Redwoods League" was already pressuring the timber industry. The "burned stumps and denuded lands" witnessed by motorists along the Redwood Highway inspired the league's creation in 1918.[63] Humboldt officials also contended that potential benefits of a bridge did not justify the risk of taxes. The officials of Lake County, which was not directly along the route of the Redwood Highway, also refused to enroll. Del Norte supervisors were the last to commit, passing an ordinance with a three-to-two vote in August 1926. However, without Humboldt County, Del Norte was completely detached from the rest of the district. The original enabling act required a contiguous district and had to be amended.[64]

To make matters worse for bridge boosters, members of the Mendocino County grand jury officially recommended withdrawal from the district after hearing testimony on the possibility of taxation. As soon as enough of the original petitioners signed a counterpetition to bring the total below the required 10 percent, the Mendocino supervisors rescinded their enrollment in the bridge district.[65] As a result, Secretary of State Frank C. Jordan refused to incorporate the bridge district until the California Supreme Court ruled on the question of Mendocino's membership. Mendocino representatives argued vehemently that the district was unjust and undemocratic because membership was not subject to a public vote. They also objected that the directors would be appointed, not subject to recall, and "empowered to impose an arbitrary tax rate on the various counties without giving them any say in the matter whatever."[66] However, their arguments had more political than legal weight. Harlan and Coombs asserted that the original application, ordinance, and petition for Mendocino's enrollment complied with every provision of the law, and the court ruled that membership in the bridge district was irrevocable.[67]

Though it ended with a victory for bridge advocates, this legal battle delayed the project for nearly a year. During this time, all activities on behalf of the Golden Gate Bridge had to be paid for with private contributions. Frustrated boosters also faced more legal challenges before the bridge district could be incorporated. By October 1927 northern county property owners, mostly ranchers and farmers, had filed more than two thousand protests against inclusion in the district. They were supported by agricultural and timber industry groups, as well as ferry companies.[68] Over several months, Judge C. J. Luttrell of Siskiyou County Superior Court heard them all testify that their property would not benefit from a bridge. The attorney representing them argued that amendments to the act nullified their agreement to join, and that the bridge district was unconstitutional because "it deprives citizens of their property without due process of law."[69] Judge Luttrell ignored the question of bridge district legitimacy, but he did exclude some property from the district: large swaths of timberland representing 65 percent of Mendocino's assessed valuation, and wooded hills of little value in Napa. He also confirmed that the refusal of Humboldt and Lake to join the district did not affect the membership of other counties. Based on this ruling, Jordan finally issued a certificate of incorporation for the Golden Gate Bridge and Highway District on December 4, 1928, officially establishing the boundaries of the new, autonomous government agency.[70]

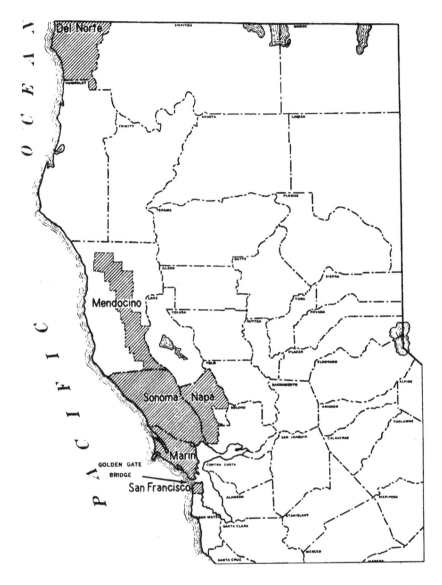

Map of the Golden Gate Bridge and Highway District. From Golden Gate Bridge and Highway District, *Long Range Planning Survey* (San Francisco, 1958, 1959).

Political Football

Almost immediately after the Golden Gate Bridge and Highway District came into being, the uneasy alliance between San Francisco progressives and northern California conservatives began to collapse. Despite the many protections from "politics" that Harlan added to the bridge district, from the conservative perspective it still had a major flaw: politicians could serve on its board of directors. To a certain extent, local business leaders could persuade county supervisors to follow their recommendations. For example, the Marin Real Estate Board endorsed Robert H. Trumbull, a leading Marin "capitalist and agriculturalist" whose long list of associations and directorships included the REA, the California Dairy Council, the Marin County Farm Bureau, the Bank of San Rafael, and the Marin County Mutual and Loan Association. Trumbull outmaneuvered Wilkins, the bridge's first important promoter. Although Wilkins was well known and popular as the mayor of San Rafael, he withdrew his name from consideration.[71] Other counties appointed directors with business credentials, as well. Sonoma supervisors appointed Doyle and Joseph A. McMinn, a member of the REA and president of the First National Bank of Healdsburg. A. R. O'Brien, owner of the *Ukiah Republican Press* and a vigorous bridge promoter, won Mendocino's seat, and Napa supervisors selected their board chairman Thomas Maxwell, who owned a nursery. Dairyman Henry Westbrook Jr. represented Del Norte as one of the county's largest landowners, with ranches encompassing more than 1,800 acres.[72]

While all of these northern county appointments were announced without much controversy, San Francisco's were bitterly contested. Shocking conservatives, the supervisors appointed three of their own, all without business experience: Warren Shannon, William P. Stanton (a prominent labor leader), and Franck P. Havenner. All had been elected in 1925, when progressives swept city elections by trumpeting public enterprise. They also appointed long-time bridge advocate Richard Welch, a career politician who was by then a U.S. congressman.

The editor of the *Chronicle* immediately attacked the appointments as "vicious," predicting that the intrusion of politicians on the board of directors would outrage northern county residents. "The bridge should not be a political undertaking but strictly business. It should be on the hands of men who will look at it from the business point of view and not the political. This indefensible self-appointment, if persisted in, will attach political stigma to the Golden Gate Bridge which, at a blow, will destroy public confidence in the project before it even starts."[73] Hotchkiss concurred, arguing that bridge promoters "owe their success largely to the fact that they desired to create and conduct a public utility free from politics, politicians, and political interference."[74] He predicted that if the San Francisco political appointments stood, the bridge bonds would never win voter approval in northern California.

To make matters worse for advocates of a nonpolitical bridge district, there were rumors of behind-the-scenes maneuvering by San Francisco's former sheriff and well-known power broker Thomas F. Finn, dubbed "Boss Finn" by the *Chronicle*. The eldest son of immigrant parents, Finn developed paternalistic instincts early in life, looking out for eleven siblings in the city's poor south-of-Market neighborhood. He caught the attention of San Francisco labor leaders by organizing the Stablemen's Union as a young man. With their support, Finn won a seat in the state assembly in 1902 on the Union Labor ticket, and joined the San Francisco Board of Supervisors in 1904. He was elected sheriff in 1909, but left the position in 1912 to serve four terms in the state senate, where his influence over the San Francisco delegation and the state Republican Party made him an important ally of Governor Hiram Johnson. Again elected sheriff in 1916, he served in that position until he was defeated in a 1927 bid for reelection. Vowing never to return to political office, Finn established an insurance business and began wielding his considerable political power from behind the scenes as a Republican Party official. He was known for helping the poor, working for prison reform, and securing jobs for his supporters. Finn helped install an impressive roster of politicians into office, including Mayor Angelo J. Rossi and Governor C. C. Young.[75]

By the late 1920s, Finn had a close friendship and business partnership with Abraham "Murphy" Hirschberg, a San Francisco real estate investor who had ties with W. N. Burkhardt, publisher of the labor-oriented *San Francisco News*.[76] *Chronicle* editors accused Finn and Hirschberg of using their influence with Shannon and Stanton to gain leverage on the bridge district and open up opportunities for patronage and graft. Assemblyman R. R. Ingalls of Mendocino introduced a last-ditch bill to dissolve the district, complaining that the San Francisco supervisors had made "a political football of the matter" by appointing elected officials.[77]

The San Francisco supervisors at first bowed to conservative pressure, calling for the resignation of all of the politicians they had appointed, with Rolph's support. Shannon and Havenner acquiesced and resigned almost immediately, but Welch and Stanton indignantly refused to step down. Shannon then changed his mind and rescinded his resignation, accusing the San Francisco papers of inventing a public outcry when there was none. The supervisors reinstated him and replaced Havenner with Francis V. Keesling, a San Francisco attorney and insurance executive with impeccable business credentials and the support of Finn and Hirschberg. San Francisco's other two appointments, insurance man C. A. Henry and William P. Filmer, the head of a printing and binding firm, were not controversial. The rapid reversals of the San Francisco supervisors on the question of political appointees suggested that, while conservatives cared deeply about preventing the bridge from falling into political hands, progressives were willing to negotiate on the specifics of representation. They did not want the bridge to end up under the control of private interests, but to them, a publicly owned bridge, whatever the form of its administration or the composition of its governing board, would still serve the interests of the people. They were willing to make concessions to quell conservatives' fear of political corruption and inefficiency.[78]

With much less fuss, the new bridge district directors elected principal officers and appointed top staff. Filmer won the position of president and Trumbull, vice president. Alan K. MacDonald, a San Francisco contractor experienced with large-scale construction projects, was named general manager. Harlan was the obvious choice for bridge district attorney. Strauss managed to win the position of chief engineer, but he had to lobby intensively to do so; he hired H. H. Meyer, a somewhat disreputable publicist, to wine, dine, and allegedly bribe bridge directors on his behalf.[79]

The first challenge facing the new bridge district officials was convincing voters to approve construction bonds. To do so, they had to address concerns about the project's feasibility—both from voters and from War Department officials, who had yet to grant final permission for the span. Strauss's appointment was extremely controversial, particularly among engineers. His bridge plans and credentials attracted derision even as he campaigned for the bridge. The Joint Council of Engineering Societies of San Francisco issued a statement critical of Strauss in 1926, and the prominent *Engineering News-Record* attacked his bridge plans in a biting editorial in 1927 that was reproduced in full in the *Chronicle*. Strauss had agreed to a low commission, just 4 percent of the cost of the bridge, which had to cover all engineering costs and salaries. This was well below the minimum 7 percent fee required by the rules of the American Society of Civil Engineers, another aggravation to Strauss's peers.[80]

To help make up for Strauss's poor professional reputation, the bridge directors appointed an official board of consulting engineers comprised of Leon S. Moisseiff and Othmar H. Ammann of the New York Port Authority, both leading suspension bridge engineers, and Charles Derleth, Jr., dean of the College of Engineering at the University of California, Berkeley. With their oversight, the bridge's design was dramatically improved and its engineering credibility resurrected. While Strauss never hesitated to take credit for all aspects of the bridge, it was actually designed by Charles A. Ellis, whom Strauss employed as an assistant, and architect Irving F. Morrow. Their plans for a graceful, all-suspension bridge replaced Strauss's hybrid bridge in 1930, reassuring many critics. Thanks to the new design, the bridge won approval from the War Department, though final permissions came through just two weeks before the vote on the construction bonds.[81]

The revised Golden Gate Bridge design was submitted in preliminary form to the directors on August 27, 1930, and released to the public in October. From Golden Gate Bridge and Highway District, *Report of the Chief Engineer with Architectural Studies,* prepared by Joseph B. Strauss (San Francisco, 1930).

In addition to engineering problems, new bridge district officials faced continuing legal challenges. In 1929, bridge district opponents argued before the California Supreme Court that the provisions for its financing were unfair and illegal. They asserted that the bridge district was essentially a special assessment district, a well-established means of financing infrastructure that required the distribution of costs according to the level of benefit for each individual property owner. Special assessment districts were based on a contract between the state and the property owners of an area defined by the range of benefit from improvements such as streets, water and sewage systems, or electricity or telephone lines. Property owners agreed to pay a tax on the expected increase in their property value resulting from the improvement: those who benefited most, paid most. In contrast, the Bridge and Highway District Act provided that all property in the district be taxed equally, and it excluded vast areas that would irrefutably benefit from the project.[82]

In a unanimous decision issued on July 31, 1929, the court determined that the Golden Gate Bridge and Highway District was not a special assessment district and did not rest on the terms of a contract between property owners and the state. Rather, it was a "quasi-municipal corporation" and its incorporation was legal despite the alterations it underwent in the process of enrolling counties. The decision, written by Justice William H. Langdon, affirmed the boundaries of the district and its ability to undertake new projects, raise funds, and acquire property—all of the things "necessary to the full exercise of its powers" and its indefinite perpetuation. The court would not consider the justice of its powers of taxation until they were actually used, wrote Langdon: "if the directors . . . have been given any unlawful powers, in a proper proceeding, when they attempt to exercise them, such exercise will be controlled or prevented by the courts."[83] The fairness of its taxing ability was separate from legitimacy of the agency, he ruled, and could only be challenged after taxes were actually imposed. This distinction had profound implications. The Golden Gate Bridge and Highway District had ongoing, permanent government functions in maintaining and administering the bridge. In finding that the bridge district was a quasi-municipal corporation, the California Supreme Court sanctioned the creation of a new government agency, endowing it with many of the powers that a city would have. Unlike special assessment districts, it was not a contract or a means to an end, and it was not limited by its function but rather its level of authority—it was a new government. The U.S. Supreme Court threw out an appeal in March 1930.[84]

With the legality of the bridge district affirmed and War Department permission for the bridge secured, leading bridge district officials agreed that there was sufficient public support to win the two-thirds' majority vote required for a bond issue. The cost estimate for the bridge had increased from the original $17 million to just over $27 million, and officials announced that a bond issue of $35 million would be on the ballot in November. It was to be the first—and only—public vote on the bridge.

However, as legal battles delayed the bridge, the concerns of San Francisco business and civic leaders multiplied. In 1928, the Bureau of Government Research, an affiliate of the chamber of commerce devoted to investigating and making recommendations on "public business," released a cautionary report on the Golden Gate Bridge.[85] While recognizing the potential economic value of a bridge, the authors of the report questioned the representational structure and powers of the proposed agency as well as the adequacy of its engineering and financial studies: "In the present incompletely-formulated stage of the Golden Gate Bridge project, no commitment can be justified beyond that of an impartial investigation of the project."[86]

In October 1928, the editor of the *New York Times* made another provocative contribution to the discussion of the Golden Gate Bridge, praising the proposed San Francisco-Oakland Bay Bridge but deriding the Golden Gate project. "It seems to have had its origin in the dream of an artist," he speculated,

certainly [it] was not inspired by any present or prospective business possibilities. . . . On one side, it is true, there is San Francisco, wealthy and populous. But stretching north of the Golden Gate is an area without a single city of more than a few thousand inhabitants, with some splendid farm and orchard land and with millions of acres of wild mountain land empty of human inhabitation except the forest ranger's cabin. The northern counties hold some very fine people . . . but 4,700 foot bridge spans cannot be suspended from moral character alone nor even from future hopes.[87]

The editor bluntly pointed out the basic flaw of the proposed bridge from a business perspective: the likelihood that it would become a major financial drain on the region. Predictably, the article inspired indignant retorts—REA spokesmen were especially vocal in refuting the contention that the area north of San Francisco was a wilderness. Executive members of the San Francisco Chamber of Commerce took these concerns more seriously, expressing doubts about the project's financial soundness, and heeding shipping executives' claim that the bridge would obstruct navigation and access to ports. They launched an investigation of the project in early 1930, and several chamber leaders testified against it at War Department hearings in July.[88]

Not only was the advisability of the bridge still questionable, but the California Toll Bridge Authority Act of June 1929 also renewed doubts about the wisdom of financing the Golden Gate Bridge with local general obligation bonds. The act made it official California policy "to acquire and own all toll bridges situated upon or along any part of the highways of the state, with the end in view of ultimately eliminating all charges thereon."[89] It established a new state agency to build and administer the San Francisco-Oakland Bay Bridge, and authorized revenue bonds to finance its construction.[90] In contrast, Golden Gate Bridge boosters were vehement about maintaining local control of the project. However, local control also meant local risk; even Coombs, the sponsor of the enabling act for the Golden Gate Bridge, remarked that its financing put a "heavy burden on the small counties."[91] Also, the Golden Gate Bridge had little chance of winning state or federal assistance because the bridge district was structured to limit its accountability to other governments. Members of the San Francisco business elite and the conservative wing of the Republican Party, represented by the *Chronicle*, the Bureau of Government Research, and the San Francisco Chamber of Commerce, suggested repositioning the project to relieve the Bay Area of direct responsibility. They argued that the burden of financing should be shifted to the state as a whole, and that bridge administration should be assigned to an entity that would be more responsive to regional business leaders and less beholden to the local boosters and provincial politicians of northern California.[92]

However convincing this argument may have been, it was too late to make much difference. Once the bridge district had been incorporated, it had power of its own and ample resources to counter its critics. Soon after the bridge directors levied their first tax, they appropriated $50,000 to fund the campaign for the bonds. They created an official bridge district information bureau headed by a full-time public relations officer and overseen by a committee on information and publicity including Filmer, Keesling, MacDonald, Harlan, and Strauss. Advertising for the bridge began to appear in local papers, on billboards, and over the radio. A volunteer speakers' bureau was made up of bridge district officials, civic leaders, and supportive engineers who shared speeches and talking points. REA leaders met with bridge directors, agreeing to take on the task of securing state funding for bridge approaches.[93]

In October, the new engineering plans for the bridge were released to the public in a three-volume report designed to win over any doubters. The directors predicted that the project would provide hundreds of local jobs, promote rapid growth and development in the North Bay, and increase the prosperity and prestige of San Francisco. Taxpayers would enjoy varied benefits, eventually including a toll-free bridge: "After the fortieth year, the bridge having retired its bonds and accumulated the substantial surplus of seventeen million-odd besides, will become free. . . . The user's tax of a toll bridge falls only upon THOSE WHO USE THE BRIDGE. Thus the visitor relieves the local taxpayer and pays his pro rata of the cost of the improvement. . . . [The bridge district] is an ASSET, and INCOME-BEARING investment, a profit-sharing public corporation, in which each taxpayer in the District is a stockholder and receives annual dividends."[94] Tolls would be more than adequate to pay for the bridge, traffic engineer Sydney W. Taylor asserted, and confidently predicted surpluses by assuming a population growth of 2.6 percent per year, the demise of ferry service, and an almost immediate increase in automobile ownership to two vehicles per family. The bridge directors repeatedly assured voters that the state could easily take over the bridge once it was constructed, and added a pledge that they would not begin construction unless the total of all contracts was less than $35 million. To address engineering concerns, the report included a letter from Ammann, Derleth, and Moisseiff endorsing the new plans for the bridge as well as positive reports from a geologist and a "regional planning engineer." The directors also continued to evoke San Francisco civic leaders' fear of losing ground in population growth and prestige, reproducing *Chronicle* editorials urging the city's leaders to take action to "keep pace" with other cities.[95]

These promises reassured many conservatives, and it was clear that the Golden Gate Bridge and Highway District was the easiest and most immediate means of building the desired span. Members of the San Francisco Chamber of Commerce Bridge Committee, many of whom had a personal or financial interest in Southern Pacific ferry operations, defied expectations and released a guarded but unanimous endorsement of the bridge on October 2. They had been convinced that "the bridge, as planned, could be operated from the start without becoming a tax burden on the public," particularly if the directors kept their pledge to act only if construction bids were within budget. The chamber officially adopted the committee report, and its president Leland W. Cutler and several other prominent members began actively campaigning for the bridge bonds.[96]

The chamber of commerce endorsement, which Cutler described as a "shock to the business community," infuriated many of its members who were still opposed to the bridge, including eight past presidents. They formed a "Taxpayer's Committee against the Golden Gate Bridge Bonds" to make a last-ditch effort to stop the project, led by John D. Galloway, a respected local engineer, and O'Shaughnessy, who was by far the most visible critic of the bridge district. Publishing ads and sponsoring speakers against the bond issue, committee members evoked the specter of unending taxes if the bridge turned out to be impossible or unprofitable, and pointed to the promise of state ownership and financing as an alternative.[97] One ad charged that the Bridge and Highway District Act "permits a self-appointed oligarchy to execute in perpetuity its own ordinances, without restriction or control," motivated solely by the prospects of "fat salaries" and "easy pickings."[98] Elsewhere, they asserted that the bridge directors were already abusing their power: "under the guise of giving out information about the project, the bridge directors [are going to spend] thousands of dollars of your tax money to exploit this promotion through expensive advertising." Committee members also objected to the "unlimited power" of the directors, pointing out that they had immense power to expand operations and that property owners would have "no recourse" but to make up for deficits with taxes.[99]

The most significant setback in the bond campaign was a California Commonwealth Club report released on October 16, 1930. Members of the club's Section on Harbor Development and State Highways agreed that while "a bridge across the Golden Gate is feasible . . . we do not feel that the project as proposed has been proven timely from the economic standpoint." They criticized the "undue haste" for a vote on the issue little more than two months after bridge plans were finalized. The report included an analysis by statistician H. P. Melinkow that contradicted bridge district financial figures. Melinkow made the point that the Golden Gate Bridge district bonds were general obligation bonds, not revenue bonds—and that this less-desirable means of financing was only necessary if there was significant risk. Despite what bridge district representatives said, Melinkow deduced, "these bonds could not be sold to the investing public because the investing public was not going to swallow any of the . . . stories about the bridge paying for itself."[100] He also questioned the credibility of bridge district traffic projections and the claim that the project would ease unemployment.

Strauss, Harlan, and Derleth all made presentations at the Commonwealth Club luncheon where this negative report was announced for the first time. Their speeches had been distributed in advance, but the report had not, and they were unprepared to refute it. They had been blindsided, and Strauss expressed his fury in an open letter to the club's president: "These men calmly undertake in thirty days to make a destructive criticism of one year's careful study and analysis by a board of four engineers. . . . The effrontery of such a procedure is no less remarkable than the unethical effort to create the impression that this project is dishonest and is to be regarded with fear and suspicion. . . . Such methods are unfortunately not unusual whenever a public enterprise runs counter to a private monopoly."[101] While the prosperous and influential members of the Commonwealth Club never officially adopted the report, they never endorsed the bridge either.

Will the Old Guard Wreck Our Bridge?　＊　＊　　*By Gregor Duncan*

San Francisco Call-Bulletin, October 27, 1930.

Bridge supporters adopted a distinctly nastier tone after this confrontation, shifting from jingoistic appeals to direct attacks on Taxpayers' Committee members. Bridge district officials accused the opposition of acting on behalf of selfish, monopolistic Bay Area ferry companies, including the notorious Southern Pacific Company. They described bond opponents as puppets: "Those whose interests lie in the preservation of outworn methods of transportation—the ferry boats—will do what they can to defeat progress, and mobilize every avenue of power, pull every string, and manipulate every wire of influence to sustain their rights and preserve their profits."[102] They dismissed concerns about bridge financing, arguing that opponents secretly still wanted a privately built bridge: "the attack on the method of financing the bridge is the last hook upon which the opposition can hang its hat . . . the argument that private capital should build the bridge is one of the very first advanced by the opposition, and its fallacy has been shown from the start. It is being revived at the eleventh hour to defeat the work of nine years."[103] San Francisco newspapers quickly labeled Taxpayers' Committee members the "Old Guard" and attributed a variety of sinister motivations to them. Alongside committee ads, editorials and cartoons ridiculed their concerns. O'Shaughnessy was the most prominent target of the papers' scorn. Even the *Chronicle*, which had been the only major paper to take his objections seriously in 1929, published a cartoon calling O'Shaughnessy's objection to potential taxes "the year's biggest joke," referencing the Hetch Hetchy cost overruns.[104]

The "Old Guard" had little hope of prevailing against the bridge district's well-funded campaign and unified Bay Area newspapers. On November 4, 1930, voters approved the bonds by a landslide in Marin, Sonoma, and Del Norte counties. In San Francisco the tally was three to one in favor. The bond issue failed to win two-thirds of the vote in Napa County, and in Mendocino County the majority voted against them. However, the measure required a two-thirds majority in the entire district, not in each county, and these counties had very small populations. The bonds passed by a comfortable margin: 145,057 to 46,954.[105]

Selling the Bonds

Loyalty, emotion, ideals, the prospect of a windfall, the promise of jobs: all of these contributed to the effort to incorporate the bridge district and to win approval for its bonds. However, they had to be sold, and the big financiers with the wherewithal to buy them were not easily convinced by promises, hope, and rhetoric. They insisted on guarantees that did not depend upon the viability of the bridge, especially as it continued to encounter engineering problems. Almost immediately after the vote, Harlan drafted legislation to improve the bonds' marketability. Two measures passed in Sacramento at the beginning of the 1931 session: one a resolution in favor of immediate construction, the other to amend the enabling act to improve the salability of the bonds. The resolution confirmed and validated the agency, its boundaries, its directorate, its bonds, and all of its actions to date. It added an argument for the urgency of the project based on expected population growth, the inadequacy of existing transportation facilities, and the promise of relieving unemployment.[106] The other measure amended the Bridge and Highway District Act to increase the financial independence of the bridge district and to buttress its authority to levy property taxes. The requirements in the original act were simple: once operations had begun, "no property taxes shall be levied except for deficits." It allowed for a sinking fund, but also required that "any surplus shall be divided . . . and apportioned to the respective counties of the district."[107] The amendments made bridge district finances considerably more complex, adding four mandatory bridge district accounts: one to pay operating expenses, one to provide for repairs and depreciation, one to pay bond interest, and another to provide a sinking fund for the bonds. All of them had minimum balances regardless of operating deficits, and the bridge district was authorized to borrow against future revenues. Harlan also added an explicit statement that bridge district taxpayers would be liable for debt whether the bridge was built or not. These amendments were introduced to the legislature as "urgency measures" necessary to "public health and safety" and the relief of unemployment. Approved on April 17, 1931, they went into effect immediately.[108] Because of these amendments, the bonds that were offered for sale were much less risky for investors and much less favorable for taxpayers than what the voters had approved.

Despite these powerful new financial guarantees, engineering problems continued to delay the sale of bonds. Questions about the foundation of the south pier caused concern, and the bridge district commissioned new borings at the site. Geologists Andrew Lawson and Allan Sedgwick of the University of California, and members of the bridge district engineering board examined the results. At Cameron's urging, San Francisco mining engineer Robert A. Kinzie also reviewed them. All of them concluded that bridge foundations were adequate except Kinzie, who characterized the rock at the south pier site as "badly decomposed and shattered serpentine," and compared it to "plum pudding." While Kinzie's objections inspired several alarmed editorials in the *Chronicle*, the directors dismissed them, arguing that the endorsements of the other, better qualified experts were more than adequate to proceed.[109] Based on revised plans submitted by Strauss in March, bridge district officials called for bids on construction contracts in June 1931, accepting low bids that combined were well under the $35 million project ceiling.[110]

In the meantime, the directors rejected a number of offers from investment groups to purchase the bonds, hoping to sell them at a premium once their legality could be conclusively established.[111] Harlan constructed a "friendly" lawsuit to bring the issue before the California Supreme Court, anticipating only a brief delay. To the dismay of bridge officials, opponents immediately entered into the fray, filing *amici curiae* briefs challenging the constitutionality of the bonds. They argued that the bridge district violated the "'inherent right' of local self-government," and therefore could not legally impose taxes. They contended that the boundaries of the district violated the original conditions of county enrollments and the principle of equal protection under the law. They also argued that the 1931 amendments substantially changing the liability of taxpayers nullified voters' approval. Prominent San Francisco lawyers filed briefs on behalf of ninety-two entities and individuals, including Southern Pacific–Golden Gate Ferries Company.[112]

The case attracted the attention of a few new bridge district allies. By 1931, California had several important agencies that were very similar to the bridge district. Both the East Bay Municipal Utility District and the Metropolitan Water District of Southern California entered opinions as *amici curiae*. A lot was riding on this decision. Not only did the legitimacy of these large and powerful metropolitan special districts depend upon the validity of public corporations, but also by that time thousands of small special districts provided services and infrastructure. The nineteenth-century system of benefit assessments had been replaced by user fees and charges supplemented by property taxes and appropriations. By 1930, there were more than eight thousand special districts in the United States—265 in California alone. This ruling could affect them all.[113] Justice Langdon, who again wrote the majority opinion, made it clear that he took the public interest into consideration: "[the bridge] will become an integral part of the Redwood Highway, linking the northern and southern parts of the state with one continuous modern avenue for traffic. . . . This court cannot lightly thrust aside a proceeding so important to the welfare of the citizens of the state."[114]

Accordingly, the court upheld the bonds' legality and the district's taxing authority once again. The lone dissenter, Justice John W. Preston, objected to the 1931 amendments as "radical and revolutionary alterations in the liability of the taxpayers of the district." He noted that "the responsibility for the bridge, its construction and perhaps for a new bond issue are all lifted from the bondholders and shifted to the shoulders of the taxpayers." Preston rebuked bridge district officials:

"progress in public improvements is laudable, but such progress should not be made at the expense of justice and fair dealing."[115] Langdon, representing the majority, disregarded these concerns, deciding that the amendments were "of a procedural character" and did not substantially affect the liability of bridge district property owners who were responsible for deficits in any case. On the question of boundaries, he pointed out that there was never any guarantee that all of the counties would join. Langdon reaffirmed the bridge district's status as a quasi-municipal

'IF IT'S A FIGHT YOU WANT!'   'By Rodger

The fighter represents "Bay Business." *San Francisco News,* December 3, 1931.

corporation, the constitutionality of its representational structure, and ability to levy property taxes.[116]

Opponents were undeterred by the clear judicial support for the bridge district in California. Lawyers of the Garland Company, a San Francisco ferry operator, and the Del Norte Company, a northern California timber firm, filed a federal appeal. Immediately, bridge supporters charged that Southern Pacific, with an interest in the existing system of ferries and railroads, was secretly bankrolling the fight against the bridge. Southern Pacific had been a political pariah in the state for decades, and protests led to a boycott. San Francisco supervisors ordered investigation of the company, whose officials denied that they were involved in the court case. Accusations of collusion were borne out in hearings when Southern Pacific executives admitted paying for the legal representation of the Garland Company. In the view of bridge boosters, this confirmed opponents' sinister associations.[117]

In July, the federal court of appeals issued its ruling, again affirming the bridge district's legitimacy as an independent government agency.[118] When Southern Pacific-Golden Gate Company executives announced that they would appeal to the U.S. Supreme Court, they were confronted with an outpouring of hostility in Bay Area newspapers. Finally bowing to pressure, they abandoned the effort in August 1932. Southern Pacific president S. P. Eastman issued a statement asserting that the bridge was "largely a promotion" and "ill founded and ill-advised," though he supported the decision to end the legal battle against it.[119] It had been costly for both sides: when the bridge district announced its dreaded third tax levy, it had a debt of more than $200,000, mostly attributable to attorneys' fees.[120] But bridge district officials reaped an important benefit in the process of fighting off their challengers: the legality of the construction bonds was virtually unassailable.

Ultimately, a syndicate headed by A. P. Giannini, president of the San Francisco–based Bank of America, funded construction. The initial $6 million bond purchase in November 1932 helped build public confidence in the wake of bank failures as part of a Bank of America "Back to Good Times" campaign that included a variety of local bond purchases. However, bridge construction bonds were also a very sound investment; Harlan arranged a special court ruling to authorize an interest rate of more than 5 percent, and initial purchases were made at a significant discount.[121]

In a newspaper editorial, Mendocino bridge director A. R. O'Brien gently teased Harlan in 1929 for claiming that the fight for the bridge "had just begun." O'Brien pointed out that the bridge district had been organized, incorporated, and legally sanctioned, and that plans for the structure were being finalized. He implied that achieving the public approval necessary to the financing was already certain, that the campaign did not represent a significant challenge: "We can no more stop the building of the bridge than we can stop the rising of the sun."[122] The ease of the bond victory suggests that he was right: the crucial moment in the battle for the Golden Gate Bridge was the incorporation of the bridge district, not the campaign for the bonds. Bridge district officials could fund operations indefinitely, both with tax levies and by incurring debt that would be covered by bond revenues later. If anything, they were in a better position to fight an extended legal battle than were the corporate executives who were challenging them, who had stockholders to rein them in. They could determine the timing of the vote on bridge bonds, and even change their terms after their approval. They could also levy taxes to fund district operations indefinitely. As long as bridge district officials could prevail in court—and every decision indicated that there was strong judicial support for their cause and for special districts in general—they were impervious to delays or expenses.

Decades later, political scientist Luther Gulick remarked that one advantage of autonomous public corporations, their ability to accomplish whatever task that they are assigned, was also a major drawback: "When you set up a function in a single authority, that single authority knows it was designated by God to do a certain job—and its work is the most important task in the world. . . . They don't care if they bankrupt the town—they're going to get their job done because that's the only job they have to do."[123] The Golden Gate Bridge and Highway District was formed to finance, build, and administer the Golden Gate Bridge, and it had the authority and the resources to carry out its mission regardless of time or expense. Although its legitimacy rested on the fulfillment of its purpose, the bridge district was much more than the means to an end. When the California Supreme Court designated it a "quasi-municipal corporation," it affirmed the bridge district as a new unit of the local state. When counties enrolled, they committed to a permanent association, not just to a single project or specific debt. They created an enduring entity led by independent officials who could act with the full authority of government.

The Golden Gate Bridge and Highway District resulted from an alliance of idealistic progressives who believed in public enterprise and pragmatic conservatives who were interested in reaping its great potential rewards. It was an autonomous agency with independent revenues and a controversial representational structure, the product of compromise between two very difference ideological factions. However, bridge supporters on both sides were disappointed as evidence of corruption began to appear soon after its incorporation, defying hope for the virtue of businesslike public administration. The remedy was unclear: the bridge district was too political for conservatives, who wanted to make sure that business interests dominated the organization and blamed "politics" for corruption. It was too secretive and not representative enough for progressives who believed its lack of public accountability made it vulnerable to abuse. During the construction period, these conflicting views led to sustained battles over bridge district operations and administration, even as its officials began to develop their own understanding of its purpose and interests.

Chapter 2

A District Divided

On February 26, 1933, an unruly crowd of 100,000 descended upon Crissy field in San Francisco to witness the groundbreaking ceremony for the Golden Gate Bridge. Police struggled to clear enough space for the bridge district president W. P. Filmer, chief engineer Joseph B. Strauss, and San Francisco Mayor Angelo J. Rossi to turn a shovelful of earth with a special golden spade. Other ceremonies were cancelled because of the unexpected throng, and a scale model of the bridge on display was badly damaged by the crush of people. Still, a grand parade managed to wind its way slowly around the crowded city, which had been inundated with visitors from throughout California. A general sense of elation muted criticism of the organizers; a decade after the passage of the California Bridge and Highway District Act, the monumental task was finally under way.[1]

The opening ceremony marked the beginning of a honeymoon period for the bridge district and the Bay Area press. Local reporters detailed construction with admiration and even awe, and public enthusiasm for the bridge combined with the natural boosterism of civic organizations to overcome residual skepticism about its viability and advisability. During construction, the bridge not only inspired local pride, but it also created many valuable jobs, from unskilled labor to highly technical work for leading engineers. The stock market crash of 1929 and its economic aftermath reverberated through the Bay Area and the country in the early 1930s. Although boosters tried to downplay its impact in West Coast cities, it was as devastating in San Francisco as it was elsewhere. In a matter of months, the rapid growth that San Franciscans had taken for granted since the Gold Rush came to a grinding halt. The construction industry was especially hard-hit, and influential labor leaders enthusiastically endorsed the Golden Gate Bridge bonds in 1930.[2] Bay Area newspaper editors, hoping to revive confidence in the region's future, covered bridge construction in detail, describing every accomplishment and setback in the most flattering light. Despite dangerous

William P. Filmer, Angelo J. Rossi, and Joseph B. Strauss (left to right) breaking ground for the Golden Gate Bridge, February 26, 1933. San Francisco History Center, San Francisco Public Library.

conditions leading to several cases of worker lead poisoning, as well as regular accidents and a dozen deaths, morale among bridge workers was generally good. The San Francisco union officials who occupied several seats on the board of directors helped maintain smooth labor relations, in part by enforcing bridge district requirements that contractors pay fair wages and hire only local residents. The Golden Gate Bridge was seen as a major boon to the Bay Area, and its construction was a source of pride and hope.

Out of the limelight and behind the front page, however, a struggle to define, shape, and ultimately control the bridge district was already taking shape. The stakes were high: construction offered potential windfalls made all the more valuable by the economic hardship and devastating unemployment of the Great Depression. Large-scale projects such as the Golden Gate Bridge not only required legions of workers but also provided a wide variety of business opportunities and many avenues for political patronage.[3] Unseemly efforts to secure the benefits of construction led to the resignation of the first general manager even before the groundbreaking ceremony, leaving a conspicuous gap in top bridge management at the event. The composition of the bridge district board of directors reflected the unlikely political alliance that created the agency, and its members battled relentlessly among themselves, competing to secure control over spending and contracts. San Francisco politicians with close ties to labor and alleged big-city bosses, including many of the self-identified progressives who resolutely supported the bridge, were interested in distributing business and favors based on a venerable tradition of patronage after political victory. Northern California directors expressed outrage at their efforts, but at the same time sought favoritism for local firms and businessmen, as did staunchly conservative San Francisco businessmen on the board. Depending on the perspective of the observer, and to some extent the specific circumstances and procedures, lucrative contracts, commissions, and jobs were either justified rewards or the spoils of corruption.[4] Struggles among the engineers working on the bridge were no less intense, as the lofty ambitions and inflated ego of the chief engineer, Joseph Strauss, collided with the realities of bridge design and construction.

The outcome of these struggles hinged on the bridge district's locus of authority. The relationship between the board of directors and the staff, particularly the district's two most important officials, the general manager and the chief engineer, determined the distribution of power within the agency. Who should be in charge was the most important question facing bridge officials during the construction period, and the answer had lasting and profound consequences for the future of the bridge district.

The Conflicting Interests of Alan MacDonald

Early on, the battle for control of the bridge district centered on the general manager, who oversaw operations and appointed all staff except the chief engineer, auditor, attorney, and secretary. The only official to report directly to the directors, the general manager controlled the agenda of meetings and the information that was presented, determined all salaries, and screened bills and claims against the bridge district. He also granted contracts and negotiated their terms with little oversight.[5] These activities provided opportunity for graft and kickbacks—not only did contractors and subcontractors have to compete for bridge work, but they also had to abide by requirements for materials and insurance.

Alan MacDonald, a San Francisco engineer with a background in large-scale construction, became the first Golden Gate Bridge general manager in April 1929.[6] The son of a prominent Kentucky architect and contractor, MacDonald graduated from the University of Louisville and went on to Cornell, where he earned advanced degrees in electrical and mechanical engineering in 1905. High strung and thin, with a ruddy complexion and light eyes, MacDonald was known for his temper.

Alan MacDonald, William W. Felt, and William P. Filmer (left to right) open bids for construction contracts on June 17, 1931. San Francisco History Center, San Francisco Public Library.

He lost fifteen consecutive jobs in less than three years, fired repeatedly for "his refusal to be a 'yes-yes' man," according to a sympathetic reporter for the *Western Construction News*.[7] Another early biographer noted his Scottish descent and described him as "hotheaded, impetuous, and opinionated."[8] In 1908 MacDonald formed an enduring partnership with fellow engineer Felix Kahn. Together they achieved prominence in San Francisco by specializing in steel-reinforced concrete, which was used for most of the city's large structures after the 1906 earthquake proved its superiority to timber and masonry. By the late 1920s, MacDonald & Kahn was one of the largest engineering firms in California, responsible for many important buildings in San Francisco and Los Angeles, including a number of skyscrapers and the striking Mark Hopkins Hotel. The firm also constructed industrial buildings, sewers, and water systems.[9]

During MacDonald's tenure at the bridge district, his company continued to expand, gaining national prominence as one of the Six Companies, Inc. A joint venture of eight construction firms (named after an influential association of Chinese immigrants), the Six Companies included some of the most powerful people in the construction business, who pooled resources and expertise to win the construction contract for the Hoover Dam in 1931. MacDonald & Kahn contributed $1 million in capital to the consortium, making it one of the largest stakeholders in the venture, second only to the Bechtel-Kaiser partnership that invested $1.5 million. Kahn served as the treasurer for the Six Companies, and MacDonald as a director and member of its purchasing committee, in addition to his duties at the bridge district. The partners were eager to expand their operations and claim a share of the massive federal public works contracts that were on the horizon in the early 1930s.[10]

By the time Hoover Dam construction began, MacDonald's position at the bridge district was already in jeopardy. Almost as soon as he became general manager, his honesty came into question. When the bridge construction bonds first went on the market, initial purchase offers were well below what bridge district officials expected. MacDonald argued vehemently in favor of accepting several rather poor bids, raising questions about his true loyalties and antagonizing members of the consortium that ultimately purchased the bonds. Francis V. Keesling, a San Francisco attorney and a leader among the directors, initially dismissed the idea that MacDonald was guilty of more than a "lack of tact," but nevertheless tracked him down on a golf course and reprimanded him for overstepping his authority.[11] Keesling and most of the other bridge directors continued to worry about his reliability, and on September 20 they secretly considered assigning a three-member construction committee to keep a closer watch on MacDonald. Somehow this leaked to the press, and MacDonald's allies denounced the discussion the next day in the *San Francisco News* as "partisan maneuvering" and even "sabotage." Mendocino County director A. R. O'Brien countered by accusing MacDonald of attempting to assume "dictatorial powers." He suggested that MacDonald was an instrument of "Boss" Tom Finn, the influential former San Francisco sheriff, and his ally and business partner Abraham "Murphy" Hirschberg. O'Brien also charged that MacDonald asked consulting geologist Robert Kinzie to alter his negative report on the bridge's foundations, promising that his fee would be raised by $11,000. *Chronicle* editors asserted that through MacDonald, Hirschberg had successfully "chiseled his way into the affairs of the Golden Gate Bridge District," and was bragging about his control over its operations.[12]

Behind the scenes, MacDonald's involvement in the Hoover Dam project also concerned the directors. Some of MacDonald's partners, including Henry J. Kaiser and Warren A. Bechtel, formed Bridge Builders, Inc. and attempted to win the entire Golden Gate Bridge job as a consolidated contract, in violation of standard construction bidding practices and stated bridge district policy. While this attempt failed, the consortium did win a $1 million contract for bridge approaches, which was assigned to Raymond Concrete Pile Company and R. J. Pomeroy, smaller firms that were also parties in Bridge Builders, Inc. Another Six Companies firm, the Pacific Bridge Company, headed by J. F. Shea and specializing in underwater construction, won nearly $4 million in bridge contracts including both bridge piers and the job of paving the roadway.[13]

While the propriety of these contracts was never questioned publicly, by the end of 1932 MacDonald faced accusations that he was using his leverage to direct insurance commissions. News broke that he was insisting that all contractors take out surety bonds with Finn's insurance company. Several Redwood Empire insurance agents who approached MacDonald to urge him to divvy up the contracts among all eligible bridge district firms were "discourteously" ejected from his office, and went to the press with their grievances. Contractors had to post large sums of money to guarantee that they would fulfill their obligations, both the work on the bridge itself and any payments due to suppliers or workers. Finn stood to make $100,000 in premiums, according to *Examiner* reporters, though "what Finn's net profit will be depends upon how generous he is with persons who assisted him in his racket."[14] Warren Shannon, a Finn ally and one of MacDonald's reliable defenders, denied these allegations. He claimed that the total premiums would not exceed $10,000 and that Finn's firm was only acting as a "clearing house" for the insurance contracts, which were then being divided among "15 or 16 firms."[15] Regardless of the details, northern California insurance agents were not getting what they considered to be a fair share of the action.

Finally, bond syndicate executives intervened and demanded Mac-Donald's removal. Bank of America president William F. Morrish sent a letter to Filmer on December 21, 1932, threatening to cancel $6 million in bond purchases unless he replaced the current "inefficient management."[16] Still, several directors remained loyal to MacDonald, including Shannon and fellow San Francisco supervisor William P. Stanton, who had nominated him for the position in 1929. Both were closely associated with Finn, and both had defied intense conservative and northern California opposition to their initial appointments as bridge directors. They insisted that the effort to oust MacDonald was unjustified and a thinly veiled power grab. According to O'Brien, Hirschberg threatened that any San Francisco director voting against MacDonald would not be reappointed.[17] The dire predictions of bridge district opponents seemed to have come true: there was strong evidence that the San Francisco politicians on the board of directors were under the influence of a political "boss," and were actively defending a corrupt general manager.

Despite the pressure from financiers, the bridge directors did not eject MacDonald outright. Instead they voted to cut his salary in half, move his office to the construction site, and require him to devote full-time to the project—he had been working just three days a week, with golf in the afternoon. MacDonald stormed out of the meeting and submitted a letter of resignation before it adjourned, refusing to "attempt any job of such magnitude at such an inadequate compensation."[18] MacDonald left the bridge district only to face more trouble; soon after his resignation, MacDonald and his partner were indicted for bribing Sidney T. Graves, chairman of the Los Angeles Board of Supervisors. They allegedly paid Graves $80,000 to help them secure a $2 million settlement from the city, compensation for their contract to build the San Gabriel Dam, which was canceled because of unsuitable rock foundations at the site. Investigation revealed that MacDonald and Kahn knew that the dam was not feasible even before they won the contract for the project, but did not disclose this information. Instead, they negotiated a "front-loaded contract" that provided for most of their payment at the beginning of construction. Graves was convicted of fraud and served time in San Quentin State Prison, but the criminal cases against Mac-Donald and Kahn were dismissed on a technicality—the prosecutor could not locate their firm's financial records before the statute of limitations expired.[19]

Immediately after MacDonald's resignation, the bridge directors reconsidered the power of the general manager. To help guard against future abuses, they created the three-man building committee that they had considered previously to preside over day-to-day decisions, appointing Stanton, George T. Cameron, and Keesling. The makeup of the committee indicated a contentious and polarized board of directors: Cameron and Stanton represented rival San Francisco political factions, and Keesling had the support of the northern California directors. Keesling quickly took a leading role on the committee, and as its chairman and most active member he was involved in daily operations, working closely with the general manager.[20]

Cameron, a conservative Republican, longtime leader of the city's chamber of commerce, and publisher of the *Chronicle*, was less active on the committee. He made his fortune by investing in California oil, in close association with San Francisco banker William H. Crocker. Cameron married Helen de Young in 1908, and her father, Michael de Young, left control of the *Chronicle* to Cameron in his will (though he divided ownership of the paper among his four daughters). Cameron embraced the responsibility and became actively engaged in its editorial policies. Charming and patrician, Cameron was known for his impeccable manners and bow tie, earning the nickname "Uncle George" among the *Chronicle* staff.[21] Despite his amiable demeanor, he had proven himself to be an aggressive and savvy capitalist, and he was willing to advance his interests and views with his newspaper. He became a leading force in the California Republican Party, and served as a delegate to the Republican national convention in 1928. Cameron also backed the San Francisco-Oakland Bay Bridge, and served as vice chairman of the Hoover-Young Commission, which made the final decision on the highly contested location of the bridge and won federal financing through the Reconstruction Finance Corporation.[22]

Stanton, the third member of the building committee, had been a San Francisco supervisor since 1925. He had also served as president of the city's Electrical Workers' Union, the San Francisco Labor Council, and the State Federation of Labor.[23] Stanton made no apologies for his association with Tom Finn, and was not popular with other bridge district directors. He was a major suspect in closed session leaks, and he had also proven that he could be petty and vindictive. As chairman of arrangements for the groundbreaking ceremony, he collaborated with Shannon to dominate the limelight during ceremonies and speeches, relegating the other directors to the sidelines or failing even to provide them with tickets.[24] Stanton lost his bid for reelection as a San Francisco supervisor in 1933 despite endorsements from both the *News* and the *Chronicle*. When Stanton's term expired in 1934, the bridge directors appointed Marin County's Harry Lutgens, publisher of the daily *San Rafael Independent*, to fill his seat on the building committee.[25]

The creation of this committee generated speculation that the directors were considering a commission-style administration, with a small group rather than a single administrator leading the bridge district, and engineers in charge of day-to-day decisions. Filmer and Keesling publicly denied this, defending the principle of a strong executive and a clear hierarchy within the staff. They insisted that the construction committee was only temporary, its members assigned to assist the next general manager with the extraordinary challenges of construction, not to replace him. Filmer hinted that growing tension between bridge management and bridge builders increased the need for an authoritative general manager: "the directors must have someone to check on the engineers and contractors."[26]

James Reed's Troubled Tenure

The backlash against MacDonald's excesses led to the selection of James Reed, a mild-mannered retired Naval officer, to succeed him as general manager.[27] Reed immediately accepted an annual salary of $12,000 (paid on a per diem basis), the same amount that provoked MacDonald's indignant resignation. Construction committee members chose Reed from a pool of seventy applicants in an atmosphere charged by MacDonald's recent digressions; Keesling publicly warned that any attempt to use political connections on behalf of a candidate for the job would only work against him. This time, he declared, they were looking for an administrator, an "office man and coordinator of all activities, rather than a construction expert."[28] Reed graduated from the Naval Academy in 1902 and then, as an officer, studied engineering and architecture at the Massachusetts Institute of Technology. During his time in the military he worked as an engineer at shipyards in Philadelphia and in the Bay Area at Mare Island in Vallejo. But he also had years of management experience; after his retirement from the Navy in 1920, Reed headed the Los Angeles Shipbuilding Company and managed the Schlage Lock Company.[29]

When Reed won the job, Keesling vehemently denied rumors that he was a "Cameron man."[30] Nevertheless, Reed was quickly embroiled in a new scandal involving Cameron's interest in cement. Hirschberg and Finn associates were not the only ones eager to benefit from the construction of the bridge—so was one of their chief conservative rivals. *Chronicle* editors had been very restrained in their criticism of MacDonald, even though during the bond campaign they had trumpeted skepticism, raising alarm about engineering issues and warning about corruption and graft. After MacDonald's resignation, a front-page commentary declared that his "high competence as a construction manager is unquestioned," and that the only problem with his administration was his limited availability due to other obligations.[31] The reason for this uncharacteristic charity soon became clear. During his tenure, MacDonald had "fought strenuously" in favor of furnishing cement, proposing that the bridge district purchase the vast quantities needed for construction and supply contractors directly rather than asking them to procure it on their own.[32] Cameron made huge profits in the cement business during the reconstruction of San Francisco after the earthquake and fire of 1906, and remained heavily invested in it, earning the moniker "the cement king."[33] Cameron hoped that his company, Santa Cruz Portland Cement, could supply all of the cement for the bridge. MacDonald helped Cameron—it seemed that he was open to suggestions on questions of administration and purchasing regardless of political affiliation.

When Cameron continued his efforts to secure an exclusive cement contract during Reed's tenure, this egregious conflict of interest came to light. Soon after MacDonald's departure, Cameron treated several bridge directors and engineers to lunch, presenting them with materials promoting Santa Cruz Portland's patented high-silica "pink" cement. This offended consulting engineer Charles Derleth, who then managed to convince a majority of the directors to leave the purchase of cement to individual contractors. Nevertheless, the issue reemerged several months later when representatives of a rival company, Pacific Portland Cement, complained that Strauss and Reed were still requiring contractors to use cement manufactured by Cameron's firm. Reed defended this policy, claiming that the rose-tinted product was superior in underwater construction and citing the opinions of consulting engineers including Derleth. A protracted debate did not produce a definitive answer to the question of which cement was best, and both companies filed lawsuits. This controversy was reported with glee in the *San Francisco News*, with indignation in the *Examiner*, and with defensive righteousness in the *Chronicle*. After three months of political heat, Cameron announced his resignation as director in November 1933. Nevertheless, Cameron's Santa Cruz Portland Cement ultimately prevailed; bridge district leaders stood by their insistence on high silica cement, and fought subsequent lawsuits.[34]

As the "pink cement" controversy raged, Finn ally Patrick McMurray quietly introduced a bill in the California Assembly to increase San Francisco's representation on the board. When conservative bridge directors got news of the measure, they immediately denounced it as another effort by "San Francisco politicians" to take control of the district. They acted quickly, soliciting and circulating statements of opposition by the leading conservative San Francisco civic groups. The bill was narrowly defeated.[35]

It became clear during the construction period that several factions were fighting for influence over bridge district affairs. The most obvious one was controlled by Finn, who had close ties with organized labor and powerful influence with the majority of the San Francisco supervisors and Mayor Rossi. Finn's interests and positions were generally represented in the *San Francisco News*. Editors of the *Chronicle*, associated with big business and traditional conservatives, were not above meddling in bridge district affairs to promote the financial interests of their boss, Cameron. Northern county directors were eager to ensure that Redwood Empire banks and insurance agents got a "fair share" of the profits from doing business with the bridge district. Finally, William Randolph Hearst's *San Francisco Examiner* was spearheading an incipient reform movement. Keesling speculated that Southern Pacific executives could be influencing *Examiner* coverage, as its editor John Francis Neylan was associated with Herbert Fleishhacker, a powerful San Francisco banker and real estate speculator. Fleishhacker was a business partner and "close personal friend" of the president of Southern Pacific, Paul Shoup.[36] Until the end of the 1930s, Southern Pacific representatives continued to fight the bridge district, and the *Examiner* featured regular exposés and vociferous editorial attacks on the bridge district. Rival bridge directors traded accusations and insults during lively board meetings.

At the storm center, Reed struggled to mediate between factions and to stave off attempts to exploit Golden Gate Bridge construction. He also began lobbying the federal Public Works Administration (PWA) for funding, applying for a $6 million bond purchase by the agency in fall 1933. At the same time, he had to solve pressing practical problems that threatened to slow or even derail construction. Rumors circulated that there were underwater canyons and a sheer cliff near the site of the south pier, aired mostly in the pages of the *Examiner*. Bridge district officials dismissed them as malicious falsehoods; in January 1934 Keesling lost his temper and called skeptics "traitors to San Francisco."[37] The editor of the *Chronicle* concurred, and added that Hearst, who by then owned newspapers around the country in addition to his flagship *San Francisco Examiner*, cared more about East Coast newspaper markets than about his hometown.[38]

Despite defensive outbursts, the reality was that bridge construction was not going very well and the south pier posed enormous engineering problems. Heavy seas, frequent storms, and extreme tides made conditions terrible for crews and equipment. After struggling to excavate with buoys and barges, in October 1933 construction crews built a large trestle to provide stable, reliable access to the construction site more than 1,000 feet offshore. This trestle was badly damaged twice and rebuilt at considerable expense, once when a steamship collided with it and again during a severe winter storm. A fifty-ton steel "guide tower," the base of which was embedded underwater in the rock at the pier site, was also completely destroyed by a storm and had to be rebuilt. In addition, the overzealous use of explosives for excavation created problems, and the pier had to be completely redesigned in December 1933, delaying its completion by nearly a year and costing more than $300,000.[39]

To calm fears and reassure PWA officials, bridge district leaders commissioned an independent investigation of the south pier foundation in January 1934. Divers descended 300 feet into the gloom at the bottom of the channel to observe the topography of the site. Andrew Lawson, consulting geologist for the bridge district, issued a statement confirming that the area could support an adequate foundation. These tests created an entirely new problem for bridge district leadership, however, by attracting the interest of Bailey Willis, a venerable Stanford geologist and engineer who had just been appointed to the earthquake safety committee of the San Francisco Junior Chamber of Commerce. After reviewing surveys of the area, on April 7, 1934, Willis wrote an alarming letter to the head of the PWA in San Francisco. He warned that a web of minor faults made the serpentine rock at its base susceptible to landslides, and recommended an independent investigation by "competent experts."[40] His letter reached the bridge directors and Bay Area newspapers the next day.

Willis had stellar credentials and could not easily be dismissed, but he was elderly and many considered him a crank. He earned degrees in mining and civil engineering from Columbia University in the 1870s, and then spent nearly three decades with the United States Geological Survey, taking leave for a variety of short-term projects around the world. He continued his far-ranging research and consulting as a professor of geology at Johns Hopkins University and later at Stanford University, publishing ten books and dozens of articles, and winning many honors and awards. After his retirement in 1922, he began advocating for stricter building codes as president of the Seismological Society. His efforts to raise awareness about earthquake danger won the ire of real estate investors and other boosters throughout the state, especially as insurance rates went up, and they did their best to discredit him. Their refusal to support stricter building codes and other safety regulations frustrated Willis, and over time his rhetoric grew extreme and his warnings dire. While Willis was credited with predicting the 1925 Santa Barbara earthquake, he crossed a line with his peers by making unsupportable, overly specific predictions of imminent disaster. Seismological Society members denounced him for exaggeration and hyperbole and forced him to resign in 1927. Nevertheless, Willis continued to work as a geologist, and his 1928 report on the collapse of the St. Francis Dam was one of the most accurate assessments of the deadly disaster, which took as many as 500 lives in Southern California.[41]

Lawson and all of the consulting engineers agreed that Willis's criticism of the south pier foundations was without merit and did not deserve serious investigation. Lawson was particularly offended, calling Willis's warning "pure buncombe" and asserting that "no reputable geologist would consider it seriously." Willis was a "professional alarmist" with a hidden political agenda, Lawson charged, and an embarrassment to geologists in general.[42]

As general manager, Reed faced the question of how to respond to Willis to minimize political and financial damage to the bridge district. Reed was torn between clearing up questions with more tests to reassure federal funders, or simply ignoring Willis's concerns to minimize damaging publicity. Frustrated, he remarked to Keesling that "if we could get a definite answer as to whether this South Pier . . . is holding up action on the [PWA] grant, or not, we would then be in a position to put the pressure [on] to get this grant approved." If concerns about the south pier foundation were not the issue, then his recommendation was clear: "we should withdraw all Federal requests immediately, rather than have this question stirred up again at a time when our financing situation is considerably improved."[43]

Faced with uncertainty, Reed chose to investigate further, and commissioned borings at the site in August and December 1934 to confirm the composition and depth of the rock. Reed also invited Willis to testify before the bridge directors and engineers. In a series of hearings in September and October 1934, Willis admitted that he had not visited the site or examined the bridge plans. He claimed that he never requested them because the bridge district's "attitude of secrecy" was well known, in contrast to the Bay Bridge, where information was "easy to obtain." The hearings revealed that the south pier site models and descriptions that Willis had presented throughout the Bay Area were based on outdated studies and that they exaggerated slope. Chamber of commerce leaders lost confidence in Willis, and informed Reed that they were willing to side publicly with the bridge district.

While the hearings may have discredited Willis, the bridge district response was not much more convincing to his peers. Building committee members submitted a report at the end of 1934 concluding that Willis's concerns were unfounded and should simply be ignored.[44] Frederick L. Ransome, professor of geology and geophysics at the California Institute of Technology, responded to the building committee report, which he asserted was "inchoate, has obvious bias, [and] does not carry conviction." He added, "Professor Willis may be wrong, but this is not the way to convince intelligent and well-informed men that he is in error as to his main contention, or to inspire confidence in those responsible for the carrying out of this great project."[45]

Despite the shortcomings of the building committee report, Reed followed its recommendations, having decided that there was little chance of federal funding. And although Willis continued his campaign against the bridge and specifically warned "potential bond buyers" that the project was untenable, bridge financiers showed no signs of concern. They may have been convinced of the pier's safety, but it was more likely that they did not care because of the ironclad legal guarantees protecting the security of the bonds even if the bridge was never built. Although bridge district officials never succeeded in securing aid from the PWA, they had no problem selling the rest of the construction bonds. Willis continued lambasting the bridge district engineers and geologists periodically, but never again got much response.[46]

The end of the construction, fittingly, was marked by a bitter power struggle that resulted in a wholesale change in bridge district leadership. It was the last time that the directors would be so deeply divided. San Francisco supervisors, allegedly under the influence of Finn and Hirschberg, made a final effort to seize control of the bridge district in 1936, just a few months before construction was complete. Throughout the construction period, Finn allies had blamed Reed personally for delays, increased construction expenses, legal problems, outside criticism, and conflict with Strauss, airing their complaints publicly and vocally.[47] Among their gripes was Reed's inability to convince San Francisco city officials, many of whom were linked to Finn, to build the approaches they had promised. Only one route through the city was ready for the opening ceremony, and promised street improvements had also been neglected.[48] The editor of the *San Francisco News* summed up Reed's administration as "careless, extravagant and downright stupid."[49] However, Reed had the solid support of a majority of the directors. Therefore it was Keesling, Reed's principal supporter and the most powerful bridge director, who became the target of a takeover attempt.

Keesling was a reformer and good government advocate, but also a conservative. He believed in operating the bridge district as a business, and abhorred the appointment of politicians as directors. He had previously pursued politics himself, running for lieutenant governor in 1910 and for governor against Hiram Johnson in 1914, and serving as the chairman of the California Republican Central Committee from 1914 to 1916, but had since settled into a private law practice. As a bridge director, Keesling applied himself wholeheartedly to his duties, and his leadership and dedication to the bridge were widely recognized. He served as the chairman of the building committee and devoted considerable time and energy to overseeing construction on a daily basis.[50] It was a very personal blow to Keesling when, without warning at a special session, the San Francisco supervisors voted to replace him. The *Examiner*

Francis V. Keesling, circa 1933. Department of Special Collections, Stanford University Library.

called it a "surprise steamroller move," the *Chronicle* referred to it as a "coup," and both immediately laid the blame on Finn and Hirschberg. Marin's *San Rafael Independent* described it as an attempt by San Francisco "political interests" to wrest control of the bridge in order to enable their "'pork barrel' and 'log-rolling' tactics."[51] The editor of the

San Francisco News was the only one to defend the decision, arguing that Reed's incompetence had been "repeatedly demonstrated" and that the present bridge management had kept itself in power to the detriment of San Francisco taxpayers. Keesling was blamed for years of bridge district "bungling" simply because he supported Reed.[52]

Keesling answered the charges against him and against Reed: "This agitation is merely a part of the program to remove the general manager and appoint someone subservient to political manipulators. When the Golden Gate Bridge has been completed, it will stand as a monument to integrity as well as efficiency."[53] San Francisco business groups came to Keesling's defense. The San Francisco Civic League of Improvement Clubs, Chamber of Commerce, and Real Estate Board took action, allying behind an unsuccessful lawsuit for his reinstatement. A majority of the San Francisco supervisors voted to appoint a Hirschberg associate, William D. Hadeler, after angry debate.[54] The *Examiner* editor accounted for the decision in no uncertain terms: "Hirschberg has been flitting through City Hall corridors gunning for Keesling . . . Hirschberg had been lining up anti-Keesling votes weeks ago by personal notification that the orders were out. 'Go see Tom,' he commanded certain Supervisors. In explanation of the orders he told members of the board: 'Finn and I can't get a thing from this fellow, Keesling. We can't get any insurance. And we can't get any jobs.'"[55]

When Hirschberg and Finn succeeded in ousting him, Keesling expressed pride at having prevented "graft and chiseling" and claimed to welcome the "relief from service." His fellow bridge directors honored Keesling by designating him the "orator of the day" at the opening ceremony in recognition of his central role in the successful construction of the bridge.[56] Reed held on to his post until the relentless attacks were too much to endure. He resigned soon after the bridge opened in 1937, complaining that his service to the bridge district had represented a "material sacrifice," and that the poor salary did not make his efforts worthwhile.[57]

The Legendary Joseph B. Strauss

As general manager, Reed was not only a target for outside interest groups competing for influence over bridge district spending and hiring, but he also had to mediate bitter internal conflict. Among his biggest problems involved the bridge district's own chief engineer, Joseph B. Strauss. From the groundbreaking ceremonies until Strauss's contract was fulfilled on opening day, relations between Strauss and the directors steadily deteriorated. A tragic incident just weeks before the completion of the bridge revealed the atmosphere of acrimony and recrimination. On February 17, 1937, a ten-ton section of scaffolding broke loose from the bridge and tore through safety nets. Eleven workers had been standing on the scaffolding, removing temporary wooden forms from concrete pavement and handing them down to two workers who were standing in the netting itself. One worker managed to cling to a bridge beam while the others fell two hundred feet into the cold waters of the bay. Several of them survived the fall only to be dragged under by the heavy hemp netting—only two men were rescued. It was a horrific accident, witnessed by dozens of workers under pressure to finish the job by the opening ceremony. Most of them returned to work the next day.[58]

State Industrial Accident Commission hearings two days after the disaster revealed a wide variety of safety violations. It immediately became clear that the Pacific Bridge Company, which had a reputation for hostile labor relations and had endured lawsuits and criticism for dangerous construction practices at Hoover Dam, was routinely ignoring safety protocols and using substandard equipment. The direct cause of the accident was the failure to install safety bolts on the mobile scaffolding, which had been used on the east section of the Bay Bridge and salvaged after it fell from that span in a separate, nonfatal accident. State inspectors who had been supervising the job had their own liability to worry about, and were eager to assign responsibility to the contractors and to Strauss, who admitted that neither he nor his employees had reviewed the scaffolding designs. The directors rejected Strauss's request that they investigate and hold their own hearings, leaving him to defend himself with no additional resources or assistance. They claimed that Strauss alone was responsible for overseeing construction and enforcing proper safety procedures.[59]

Strauss portrayed the incident as an unfortunate, entirely unforeseeable accident, and insisted that he had done all he could reasonably be expected to do to ensure worker safety. However, Strauss's version of events was not convincing enough to protect him from personal liability; the families of the victims, supported by union representatives, filed lawsuits against him and against Pacific Bridge Company. After one widow won her case and the judge awarded her the maximum amount of damages allowed by law, Strauss settled with the other families.[60] The scaffolding incident added to his bitterness and anger about his experience working on the Golden Gate Bridge.

In 1937 Strauss was sixty-seven years old and a difficult man, highly sensitive to insult, quarrelsome, and reclusive. Although he had been associated with the project since the early 1920s, he was not one of its designers and he did not take part in the everyday administration and supervision of its construction.[61] Even so, Strauss hoped that the Golden Gate Bridge would define his legacy, that it would be a glorious, crowning achievement to his long career as a prolific bridge builder. Strauss's penchant for taking credit for others' achievements is epitomized by his own account of bridge construction in the 1937 *Report of the Chief Engineer*, which was riddled with inaccuracies and exaggerated or fabricated his role in every aspect of bridge planning, financing, construction, and management. Partially because of the influence of this document, even the harshest critics of Strauss's engineering achievements portray him as a visionary and describe his efforts to sell the bridge in northern California as critical to its success. However, crediting Strauss with even this may be an exaggeration. According to observers at the time, Strauss was not an impressive or convincing speaker. Standing at about five feet with a quiet voice and a weak handshake, Strauss was less than a commanding presence and had little personal charisma. He was also an outsider, from Chicago and Jewish in a time when overt anti-Semitism was common in California, among provincial and elite residents alike.[62] While he devoted an immense amount of time and effort to promoting the Golden Gate Bridge, he was certainly not one of its most influential backers.

A more accurate story of this determined man and his involvement with the Golden Gate Bridge is one of ambition and pride beset by frustration and humiliation. Strauss grew up in Cincinnati, his father a successful portrait painter, and his mother a concert pianist. He attended the University of Cincinnati, where he was active in his fraternity and served as president of his class. He had a talent for mechanics and a penchant for poetry, perhaps an interest encouraged by his artistic parents. Two frequently repeated stories capture Strauss's youthful ambition and daring. Strauss tried out for the University of Cincinnati football team, but he was much smaller than the other players and ended up bruised and battered. He was actually confined to the infirmary for a number of days, according to accounts. One 1935 profiler suggested that the incident inspired Strauss to study engineering so that he could build big and take on great challenges that would make up for his own small physical size.[63] It may also have indicated a disregard for his own limitations, even a reckless willingness to undertake tasks that far exceeded his competence and ability. Another anecdote described Strauss's final presentation as a student. He shocked an audience by calmly reading a proposal for a railroad bridge across the Bering Strait—a fantastical scheme that was decidedly out of place among otherwise serious student presentations. Strauss's ability to ignore practical limitations later distinguished his plans and price estimate for the Golden Gate Bridge from those of other engineers. He was certainly a visionary in the sense that he was willing to make grand proposals and gamble that practical problems could be addressed later—often by other engineers with more expertise. In an era of rapid technical and theoretical advances in structural and civil engineering, this was not a poor bet. It took a decade to start building the Golden Gate Bridge, and by then Leon S. Moisseiff, one of the consulting engineers on the project, had revolutionized the knowledge and theory of suspension bridges, making them narrower, longer, more flexible, and much less expensive. The striking contrast between Strauss's original sketches and the final design of the bridge reflects these changes.[64]

Strauss earned a degree in civil engineering in 1892, and began his career with the New Jersey Steel and Iron Company. He returned to his alma mater to teach for one year in 1894.[65] He spent the next several years as an inspector and designer for the Lassig Bridge & Iron Company, and then the Sanitary District of Chicago. In 1899 Strauss joined the prominent bridge builder Ralph Modjeski's firm, working as assistant engineer and managing its Chicago office. Strauss's professional breakthrough, which allowed him to start a firm of his own, came in the field of drawbridge design. In 1902 he developed the "Strauss Trunnion Bascule Bridge," which improved the mechanism used to lift drawbridges. At the helm of his own company and an independent bridge designer a few years later, Strauss showed little interest in aesthetics—his specialty was cost-effectiveness. Strauss began substituting concrete for pig iron in bridge counterweights, which made them bulky but much less expensive. By 1930 he held more than a dozen patents for design innovations, but his bridges were not known for their beauty. He built hundreds of small, functional structures throughout the world economically and quickly, in an era when changing transportation technology and the widespread adoption of the automobile made bridge building a very lucrative enterprise.[66]

By 1922, when the idea of bridging the Golden Gate first inspired him, Strauss was a successful businessman, his Chicago-based enterprise growing and reliably profitable. But at the age of fifty-two he had not achieved the renown and status that he obviously craved. When he submitted his design for the Golden Gate Bridge to O'Shaughnessy and proceeded to promote it throughout northern California, he probably had his reputation and legacy as an engineer in mind. His time-consuming activities on behalf of a bridge that was far from a certainty suggest that glory, and not profit, was motivating him.

Because of his early campaigning, Strauss was already closely associated with the Golden Gate Bridge by the time the bridge district was incorporated in 1928. However, he was by no means assured of appointment as its chief engineer. Regardless of Strauss's contributions, the directors could choose whom they wished for the position, and in 1929 they compiled a list of candidates that included the world's top suspension bridge engineers. Strauss recognized that he needed help, that he had neither the local clout nor the diplomatic skills to be competitive for the job, so he hired a promoter and began to lobby. To win the appointment, Strauss had to agree to the oversight of three well-respected consulting engineers, an unusually low fee, and many other concessions that haunted him later.

Among Strauss's assets in competing for the job of chief engineer was the staff of his engineering firm. Although no one considered Strauss to be qualified to design a major suspension bridge, he was savvy about hiring to make up for his own shortcomings. His vice president in charge of bridge design and construction supervision, Charles A. Ellis, had stellar professional credentials. Ellis started his career as an engineer with the American Bridge Company and went on to teach at the University of Michigan. In 1914, Ellis joined the civil engineering faculty at the University of Illinois as an assistant professor. He soon built a reputation as a leading theorist, publishing frequent articles and developing a widely used textbook. In 1921 Strauss convinced Ellis to join his growing firm. By the time Ellis began work on the Golden Gate Bridge, he could claim credit for several major Strauss spans, including the Longview Bridge over the Columbia River near Portland, Oregon. When Strauss assigned Ellis the Golden Gate Bridge project in 1929, he gave him free rein to come up with an innovative design. Ellis recalled, "[Strauss] gave me some pencils and a pad of paper and told me to go to work."[67] The plans that Ellis produced in August 1930 obviously had no relationship to Strauss's earlier sketches, and were immediately recognized in the engineering community as credible and impressive.

Although Strauss must have understood the value of Ellis's skills and status to his firm, Strauss took steps to disassociate Ellis from the bridge early on. Soon after Ellis completed his plans for the bridge in August 1930 but before he could check them to his satisfaction, Strauss ordered him to leave the Bay Area and to work from Chicago. However, Ellis was still getting credit and recognition—in September 1930 he presented the theory of the bridge at the West Coast meeting of the National Academy of Sciences in Berkeley. A month later, Derleth addressed the Commonwealth Club in San Francisco. To calm concern about Strauss's competence, he emphasized that Ellis "stands high as an engineer" and was responsible for its design, confirming the prevailing opinion that Strauss knew little about suspension bridge engineering. In November, Strauss conscribed Ellis to the "Computation Division," and made him accountable to Clifford Paine, one of Ellis's former students whom Strauss had recently recruited.[68]

Despite his demotion, Ellis worked frantically on bridge specifications. His basic design was submitted to the War Department in August 1930, but much more detailed blueprints were required to solicit bids from contractors. Ellis finished them in March 1931, but he still had major concerns about the tower design. Strauss, however, was completely satisfied with the plans. As Ellis spent long hours making calculations and checking his figures, Strauss began to pressure him to stop work. It was clear that Strauss thought that Ellis was obsessed with minutiae, and he asked him to take a vacation. Ellis refused, worried about the integrity and safety of the bridge. Strauss then suspended his salary and demanded that he take a vacation, but Ellis continued to work. Finally, in December 1931, Strauss fired him outright. Still worried about the designs, Ellis asked the consulting engineers to demand his reappointment. Wanting to avoid antagonizing Strauss, they conferred and decided that Ellis was exaggerating problems with bridge plans and that it was not worth it to intervene. Instead, they recommended a limited check of critical elements of the bridge by Moisseiff's firm. After several years of unemployment, Ellis finally joined the faculty of Purdue University in 1934.[69] Ellis was never recognized for his work on the bridge by Strauss or by Paine, who later claimed to be one of the bridge's principal designers.

Other Strauss employees also contributed significantly to the project. Strauss hired architect Irving F. Morrow to consult on the job. While Morrow had no experience with bridge design specifically, he was a graduate of the well-regarded University of California, Berkeley, School of Architecture and his work was admired in the Bay Area. He was also an active member of San Francisco civic associations, including the influential Commonwealth Club. Morrow's local connections were more than matched by his talent—his art deco design and bold color scheme for the bridge was hailed as a masterpiece.[70]

Resident engineer Russell G. Cone was another major asset to the Strauss corporation. Another one of Ellis's former students, Cone graduated from the University of Illinois with a degree in civil engineering in 1922. He began work for the firm of Modjeski & Chase as assistant engineer on the Benjamin Franklin Bridge, an important early suspension span designed by Moisseiff, and spent two years as resident engineer after its completion. Cone was also in charge of construction for the Ambassador Bridge in Detroit, the world's longest suspension bridge at the time of its completion in 1929. He joined Strauss's firm in 1933 specifically to take responsibility for overseeing Golden Gate Bridge construction as resident engineer. He reported to Paine, who spent most of his time in Chicago. Cone had an active, hands-on style; for example, he donned overalls and descended to the bottom of the bay to inspect the pier foundations in 1934. He also published frequently on the practical challenges of construction, including one article describing the Golden Gate Bridge's difficult south pier construction, and another on the mechanics and equipment used in the perpetual painting

Russell G. Cone (center), 107 feet below sea level, inspecting the rock at the foundations of the south pier, accompanied by Oscar Erickson (left) and Jack Graham (right). This photograph was published in a 1934 building committee report. San Francisco History Center, San Francisco Public Library.

of the bridge. The American Society of Civil Engineers awarded him the Construction Engineering Prize in 1940.[71]

Even as his subordinates enjoyed accolades, Strauss's own work fell short of his employers' standards. The first draft of his 1930 engineer's report—a document that was critical for the bond campaign—was rejected by bridge district officials and had to be rewritten by the consulting traffic engineer, Sydney W. Taylor. Several incidents like this reflected leading directors' concern about Strauss's overall competence. Keesling and Reed were very aware that Strauss's contract gave him incentives for cutting costs. As early as 1932, Keesling noted the "unsatisfactory results and lack of accomplishment of Strauss, . . . evidence of attempts to shift responsibility [to him], and necessity of protecting against it."[72]

In February 1932, Strauss began to appeal to the bridge directors for financial assistance and a larger commission, saying that his firm stood to lose half a million dollars on the project. His pleas were firmly rebuffed; Keesling and Reed both made it clear that they would not relent on the terms of his contract. Soon after, Strauss retreated from the everyday work on the bridge and put Paine in charge of supervision and troubleshooting. Paine had a degree in civil engineering, and although he had no previous experience with suspension bridges, he carried out the day-to-day work of overseeing construction. He also became Strauss's liaison with the outside world. Strauss's health, both mental and physical, had always been precarious, and members of his staff routinely attributed his unusual behavior to the unfathomable peculiarities of genius. Apparently, the sacrifices Strauss made to win the Golden Gate Bridge job had personal consequences. He became more eccentric and irascible than ever, and he disappeared without explanation just as construction was getting underway. When Keesling tried to arrange a meeting several months later, he was informed that Strauss was recovering from a nervous breakdown at a resort in the Adirondack Mountains in New York State. Understandably, Keesling was annoyed that Strauss had left California without informing him. Even when Strauss was nearby, he did not participate in overseeing construction and rarely appeared publicly. In April 1933, Strauss again left town, citing stress and exhaustion; this time, his retreat coincided with his second marriage.[73]

As Strauss withdrew from active involvement in bridge construction, he devoted more energy to litigation. Responsibility for inspections became a major point of contention: Harlan and the bridge directors demanded that Strauss provide all inspections from his flat-rate commission. Strauss insisted that he was not responsible for them, filed a lawsuit, and began threatening to cut corners at the expense of quality if the directors did not concede the point. By September 1934, Strauss was warning his staff of possible salary delays, and a month later he asked his engineers to accept half of their normal pay. Legally, he had a good case that he should not be responsible for the cost of inspections, and he won $103,000 in December 1934 and an additional $262,500 in January 1937.[74] While contractors were able to convince bridge district officials to increase their fees when difficulties or unexpected problems arose (such as during the south pier site excavation), Keesling, Reed, and Harlan refused to make concessions to Strauss despite his unusually small budget. Their lack of sympathy probably reflected the general antagonism that they felt toward this difficult man. Certainly, they could reasonably have conceded this relatively minor issue and appropriated funds to ensure thorough and professional inspections at all critical points in the construction process. Rather, they undertook a costly legal battle that damaged the reputation of the bridge district—and Reed's critics regularly cited his legal losses as evidence of his general incompetence.

As unhappy as Strauss already may have been, in March 1935 his situation took a decisive turn for the worse. The promoter Strauss had hired in 1929, H. H. "Doc" Meyers, appeared on the scene, demanding payment from Strauss for the "publicity" work he had done to help get him the job of chief engineer. Meyers sued Strauss for 15 percent of his total commission. Strauss did not deny that he had a contract with Meyers, but claimed that he merely helped him with some social invitations, and that Meyers actually owed him money. Win or lose the lawsuit, it was embarrassing both to Strauss and to the bridge district. Reed and Harlan rushed to help Strauss settle the case, even as they continued to fight in court over the terms of his contract and payment for inspection work.[75]

When Strauss shouldered the blame for the failure of the scaffolding and the death of ten workers just before the long-anticipated opening of the bridge, he probably viewed it as another episode in a series of embarrassments and affronts. Strauss resigned soon after the completion of the span, claiming that he had made no profit whatsoever on the Golden Gate Bridge. The directors formally thanked him for "turning the bridge over to the people" and presented him with a gold pass for perpetual free crossings. They also voted to retain him as "honorary chief consulting engineer" at $1 a year.[76]

After this rather perfunctory send-off, Strauss did everything in his power to maintain his reputation and promote the idea that he was primarily responsible for the bridge. He published a lengthy meditation on the trials of great inventors in the *San Francisco News* the day after the bridge opened, comparing himself to other "pioneers in progress," including Copernicus, Galileo, and Newton: "each of man's great undertakings, as it has developed from the superhuman effort of the few, and in the face of the opposition of the many, has proved that human progress is always purchased at the price of sacrifice, but that it is irresistible."[77] The fourth stanza of Strauss's triumphant poem recounting the saga of the Golden Gate Bridge sums up his view of his experience: "Launched midst a thousand hopes and fears, / damned by a thousand hostile sneers, / yet ne'er its course was stayed; / but as of those who met the foe / who stood alone when faith was low, / ask them the price they paid." The bridge district founders expected and demanded a return on their investment of time and resources—any price they paid early on was amply rewarded. In contrast, Strauss never got what he considered to be his just rewards. Less than a year after the bridge had been completed, Strauss died of a heart attack. At his funeral, A. R. O'Brien observed that to him, the bridge had become a "mute monument of misery."[78]

As the construction period drew to a close, the bridge directors faced the task of replacing both Strauss and Reed. After a long standoff, they chose William Harrelson to succeed Reed as general manager, rejecting Cone, who had been the resident engineer since 1933 and was the obvious candidate. The elderly Harrelson, a lifelong San Francisco politician, had some experience as a contractor and civil engineer and had been a supporter of both the Golden Gate Bridge and the San Francisco-Oakland Bay Bridge in the 1920s, but more importantly, he was favored by the bridge's financiers.[79] He had recently retired as vice president in charge of real estate of the Bank of Italy (which was renamed the Bank of America in 1928). O'Brien charged that the job was a "pension" for Harrelson, and reacted to his nomination: "I don't care whether the Bank of Italy or Mussolini is interested, but just the same . . . all should have their qualifications examined. . . . I resent this being thrust down our throats."[80] O'Brien normally sided with northern California conservatives, but in this case he voted with Hirschberg allies supporting Cone. O'Brien argued that Harrelson, at the age of sixty-five, was too old for the position, and was convinced that he was secretly allied with Finn and Hirschberg anyway. Keesling helped change his mind, asserting that Harrelson was "no tottering old man" and "independent as a hog on ice."[81] With O'Brien's vote, the northern county representatives and San Francisco businessmen in favor of Harrelson prevailed.

The directors appointed Cone as bridge district "maintenance engineer." Later, Cone remembered that he accepted the position out of loyalty, despite his reluctance to work under the new general manager. Cone complained that Harrelson was a "whining, groveling politician" whose ideas were "dated by the hobble skirt" and that "unless everyone is a yes man around him they soon are either discarded or left alone."[82] Harrelson presided for just three stormy years, during which he was constantly under attack for extravagance and lax management.[83]

Despite all of the problems associated with the Golden Gate Bridge and Highway District, the agency was remarkably effective in fulfilling its primary intended purpose: building the Golden Gate Bridge. Many of the special districts created early in the twentieth century earned a reputation for efficacy, and inspired efforts across the country to reproduce their success. However, problems during the construction period revealed that neither politicians representing immigrants and labor nor business-oriented political leaders were immune to corruption. Cameron and his chamber of commerce supporters (Leland Cutler's wife insisted upon calling them a "gang") were no less opportunistic than Finn and the labor leaders who backed him, and REA members had no qualms about demanding insurance contracts as a reward for supporting the bridge district. Certain individuals, including MacDonald, stood out as particularly susceptible to corruption, but Golden Gate Bridge spoils went to a variety of interest groups.[84] While allegations of machine politics at the bridge district ceased with Tom Finn's death in

Controversial statue of Joseph B. Strauss by Frederick W. Schweigardt, unveiled at the toll plaza, May 29, 1941. Fittingly, the statue now stands on a much more modest pedestal. San Francisco History Center, San Francisco Public Library.

January 1938, charges of extravagance, no-bid contracts, and inside deals continued. The expectation that bridge district resources should benefit favored associates and supporters, even when these benefits came at a significant cost to the public, remained firmly entrenched in bridge district procedures and culture.

Other continuing bridge district problems were related to the legacies of the construction period. The bitter rift between Strauss and members of the building committee had a lasting effect on the culture and leadership of the agency, and Cone's failure to win the top management position reflected a mistrust of engineers among the directors. This mistrust was inscribed in the organizational structure of the agency, with the ascendance of the general manager and the permanent subordination of the chief engineer. Subsequently, bridge directors often treated bridge district engineers as if they were outsiders or opponents, and favored public relations over engineering in solving problems.

Strauss might have been surprised to learn that soon after his death, the bridge directors spent $10,000 to erect a larger-than-life statue of him at the toll plaza, ignoring the protests of taxpayers' advocates.[85] Despite Strauss's alienation and hostile relationship with his employers, his account of the construction period, including his consistent self-aggrandizement, provided the foundation for the institutional history and founding myth of the bridge district. Although bridge district leaders took pains to limit Strauss's authority as chief engineer and spent thousands of dollars fighting his efforts to claim compensation, after his death they cast him as a visionary tirelessly leading the fight for the bridge against sinister, greedy outsiders. This image complemented the emerging identity of the bridge district: an embattled, heroic agency fighting against relentless, covetous efforts to stop construction, and later, to exploit toll revenues and wrest control of the bridge from its rightful owners.

Chapter 3
The District and Its Enemies

On April 27, 1937, the final rivet was driven into the Golden Gate Bridge—twice. The first attempt involved a sixteen-ounce rivet fashioned from "almost 100 per cent pure gold" donated for the purpose by the vice president of the California Chamber of Commerce. Too soft and short for the task, the precious metal disintegrated under pressure, showering spectators with gold dust, breaking apart, and falling into the water below. A nimble bystander caught one two-ounce chunk. After the crowd dispersed, a steel rivet was secured in the gap. The incident foreshadowed decades of remarkable prosperity, marred by bungling, incompetence, and waste. While the Golden Gate Bridge and Highway District always had critics, once it started collecting tolls, the stakes were higher than ever. A series of threats to the agency, starting during the construction period and growing steadily more serious through the 1940s and 1950s, created a heated, defensive atmosphere at the bridge district. Each incident helped forge a steely solidarity among bridge directors and top staff.

Initially, conflict among bridge directors and officials reflected competing outside political factions: San Francisco businessmen and northern county representatives allied to fight what they considered to be efforts by corrupt politicians to seize control and exploit the bridge district. Soon, the directors' identification with the organization and interest in its success began to overcome the divisions among them and their association with outside groups. Collectively, they reinforced their alliances with other agencies, including the Redwood Empire Association (REA). They entrusted more power to staff members, and the general manager became their shield against outside assault. They further subordinated safety and maintenance to the agency's financial and political interests, firing bridge engineer Russell Cone for questioning district policy. They cracked down on dissent, enforcing a united front against bridge district critics.

After World War II there was a surge in toll revenues, and a coherent opposition to the agency emerged, spearheaded by Jack McCarthy. An

ambitious young state senator from Marin County, McCarthy was a relentless critic of the bridge district who pressured its leaders to cut costs
and lower tolls. He fought persistently to dissolve the agency and incorporate the bridge into the state highway system. In response, bridge district officials built up their fortifications, hiring James Adam as a
full-time lobbyist. Adam promoted a founding myth of heroic and righteous resistance to covetous outsiders that shaped the agency's culture,
policies, and identity. Rival directors united when the success of the
agency was at risk, and bridge district critics became enemies, at least in
the minds of its officials.

The Uncompromising Approach of the Redwood Empire Association

The first major battle that inspired the directors to overcome their differences and fight for bridge district interests involved the construction
of the Waldo Tunnel in Marin, part of the new highway that would bring
traffic to the bridge from the north. This battle also helped secure the
close relationship between the bridge district and the REA, the most influential booster organization in the region north of San Francisco.[1]
The timely completion of the tunnel through the steep, rocky slopes of
the Marin Headlands was critical to the success of the bridge. And as
part of the only route connecting the span to northern California, it
could easily become a bottleneck. If the tunnel's capacity was limited, so
would potential bridge traffic and toll revenue.

Well before bridge construction commenced, Earl Lee Kelly, director
of the California Department of Public Works, promised that the state
would build the northern approaches to the bridge, including the
Waldo Tunnel. However, Kelly's expectations for funding the tunnel
changed after the election of Franklin Delano Roosevelt as president
and the advent of the New Deal. Not only were large-scale public works
projects financed by the Reconstruction Finance Corporation (RFC)
and the Public Works Administration (PWA) important as economic
stimulus, but smaller, labor-intensive projects also provided unemployment relief. The Works Progress Administration (WPA), created in 1935,
was devoted primarily to putting people to work. The WPA funded a
wide variety of projects, including the construction of hundreds of miles
of roads and highways throughout the country.[2] The tunnel seemed to
be a perfect WPA project—excavating its 1,000-foot length would be extremely labor-intensive and building its approaches would require many
hours of grueling work to grade steep roads atop unstable rock and soil.[3]

Despite the promising employment benefits of the Waldo Tunnel and
the northern bridge approach, Kelly's application for federal work relief

funds was rejected. Thomas H. MacDonald, chief of the federal Bureau of Public Roads, had veto power over WPA road and highway projects, and personally rejected the allocation. The Golden Gate Bridge, the only destination for the tunnel, was in his view "a private bridge that is neither a Federal nor State project."[4] McDonald opposed toll bridges and turnpikes generally, insisting on the critical importance of free roads to the economic health and development of the United States. Bureau representatives demanded a guarantee that the bridge would become toll-free once its construction bonds were retired and that it would become part of the state highway system. They also demanded greater outside accountability for the bridge district in the meanwhile, including state audits. Neither the California attorney general's opinion that the Golden Gate Bridge was legally state property nor arguments that it was a crucial military route swayed federal officials.[5]

In 1935, Kelly requested that the bridge district "advance" $700,000 to initiate construction, to be reimbursed later—he assumed that the bridge directors would agree to federal requirements.[6] He was wrong. Bridge district officials flatly refused to contribute any money for the tunnel or to concede any control to advance the case for federal funding. Bridge district attorney George Harlan protested that the requirements were illegal and burdensome: "It would mean that the Bridge District could not purchase a lead pencil or accept a nickel without the consent of Earl Lee Kelly."[7] Local politicians and REA representatives supported the no-compromise stance, insisting on the tunnel as promised, with or without federal funding. Kelly pointed out that $1.7 million in relief funds were at stake, and scaled back tunnel plans to three lanes rather than four.[8] He also threatened the bridge directors: "If your Board does not see fit to enact these resolutions . . . we will go to the Legislature in 1937 and advocate that the bridge become free and that proper legislation be enacted to bring about the desired result."[9]

Kelly's belligerence garnered a swift reaction from bridge district allies. REA publicists released a scathing letter to Governor Frank F. Merriam, and Bay Area newspapers reprinted it along with a torrent of criticism aimed at Kelly personally.[10] Denying charges that he was trying to sabotage the bridge, Kelly claimed that he had "leaned over backwards" on behalf of the Golden Gate span.[11] He also threatened that if bridge district officials did not cooperate, the Redwood Empire was likely to get a "budgetary spanking" in road funding.[12] This infuriated REA and bridge district leaders, who accused Kelly of trying to "welch on the state's commitments."[13] Rumors of Kelly's impending ouster began to make Bay Area headlines. Eventually, Kelly conceded the entire issue and appropriated funds for a four-lane tunnel, citing surplus gas tax revenues and the importance of the project to the upcoming World's Fair

IF GOV. MERRIAM'S MR. KELLY HAS HIS WAY!—By Rodger

Cartoon published in the *San Francisco News,* August 25, 1935, and distributed by the Redwood Empire Association in fliers. Many *News* cartoons criticizing Kelly were reproduced in northern California papers.

in San Francisco. Thanks to the enormous public outcry against Kelly orchestrated by the REA, the bridge directors got their tunnel and approach without any concessions.[14]

The fight for the Waldo Tunnel cemented a close relationship between the REA and the bridge district that was critical to both organizations. Like the bridge district, the REA was a hybrid; the bridge district was a public agency with the structure of a business, and the REA was a booster organization with the trappings of political representation and governmental pretensions, a self-described "non-profit intercounty government instrumentality." By integrating local government representatives into its leadership structure, REA officials claimed legitimacy as policy-makers and the right to tap into public revenues. The supervisors' unit, for example, determined "highway and legislative policy . . . officially on behalf of constituent taxpayers," and always "<u>strictly</u> in the public interest." The majority of REA funding came from county appropriations, and once the bridge district began collecting tolls, it became the REA's largest single contributor and most important client. REA activities included aggressive lobbying as well as advertising to promote tourism and development. Its leaders monitored activities in Washington and Sacramento, sent representatives to testify at hearings, drafted legislation, and orchestrated letter-writing campaigns. By 1936, REA representatives took credit for winning $54 million in state and federal appropriations for Redwood Empire roads and highways.[15]

In addition to its political intervention, REA advertising promoted the Golden Gate Bridge as an iconic representation of northern California.[16] In 1937, the Golden Gate Fiesta celebrating the opening of the bridge marked another close collaboration between the two organizations. REA general manager Clyde Edmondson was one of its principal organizers. The week-long fiesta included several parades, dozens of speeches, ceremonies, luncheons, dinners, and receptions, as well as evenings of pageants, balls, and fireworks displays.[17] Two years later, the Golden Gate International Exposition took place on Treasure Island, the central anchor of the San Francisco-Oakland Bay Bridge, presenting another major opportunity for REA officials to promote the Golden Gate Bridge and Redwood Empire tourism.[18] In the decades to come, the association between the two organizations would only grow more intimate, particularly as one of the ambitious REA publicists in charge of these celebrations, James Adam, climbed the ranks of bridge district management.

Operating on an Extravagant Scale

Try as they might, in the midst of the Great Depression bridge district and REA publicists could not generate the traffic that they hoped for and counted on. A rate war with North Bay ferries in the winter of 1937 and 1938, when the directors temporarily reduced the bridge toll from 50 to 30 cents, further diminished revenues. Delays on the San

Francisco approaches also contributed to shortfalls. As the first year of operations drew to a close, bridge district staff had to draw on funds left over from construction to cover deficits.[19]

San Francisco Chamber of Commerce leaders, concerned about possible bridge district tax assessments, undertook an official inquiry into the agency's administration, budget, and finances in 1938. Frederick H. Meyer, a San Francisco architect who lived in Sausalito, Marin's primary commuter ferry port, chaired a special committee to investigate the bridge district.[20] The committee found "convincing evidence that the Golden Gate Bridge and Highway District has been operated on an extravagant scale."[21] Comparison with the San Francisco-Oakland Bay Bridge, which opened in November 1936, revealed that administrative costs were three times greater per vehicle crossing for the Golden Gate Bridge. Committee members criticized high painting and maintenance costs, advertising appropriations, and staff salaries.[22] They recommended that "only qualified persons of broad business experience who do not hold public office at the time be appointed as directors."[23] And, they called for legislation to shift responsibility for bridge maintenance to the state.

Cost in Cents per Vehicle Crossing, 1937–38

Expense Items	Golden Gate Bridge and Highway Dist.	San Francisco-Oakland Bay Bridge	Ratio of Unit Cost of Golden Gate Br. & Hwy. Dist. to San Francisco-Oakland Bay Bridge
Administrative	5.2361	1.5811	331.20%
Operating	3.3729	2.242	150.40%
Repairs, Maintenance, and Depreciation	1.8283	0.8268	221.10%
Deferred Maintenance	1.5038	None	150.10%
Total	11.9405	4.6499	256.80%

This table was originally published in San Francisco Chamber of Commerce, *Report of the Special Committee on the Golden Gate Bridge and Highway District* (San Francisco, 1938).

Bridge officials reacted to the report with unmitigated hostility, calling it "preposterous" and (turning around one of the chamber's greatest concerns) "politically inspired."[24] A. R. O'Brien remarked that "Spain had her Don Quixote, he sallied forth and fought windmills . . . San Francisco has in her Chamber of Commerce a Don Quixote who fights bridges."[25] The bridge district's official reply insinuated that competing transportation interests (that is, the Southern Pacific Company) were secretly behind the report, evoking a familiar bogey. Chamber leaders were "seeking to destroy the usefulness of this great structure . . . in order to create a demand for a return of the ferries," bridge district officials charged.[26] Apparently, they forgot that Meyer was a former REA president and longstanding Golden Gate Bridge supporter. Meyer helped convince chamber leaders to endorse the bridge during the 1930 bond campaign, and publicly sided with bridge officials in their efforts to discredit the persistent warnings of Stanford engineer Bailey Willis.[27] Certainly, he was no Southern Pacific lackey. Chamber representatives remarked that the "hostility of its reception [by the bridge directors] was surprising," and that "the Golden Gate Bridge can be operated more efficiently and more economically. . . . It is our duty, in the public interest, to talk about it."[28]

And, Meyer's concerns seemed justified. Auto ferry service between San Francisco and Marin ended in July 1938, but ferry patrons did not necessarily turn to the Golden Gate Bridge.[29] Crossings between San Francisco and Marin decreased by nearly 10 percent in the early months of 1939, compared to 1938. Although total bridge revenue did not decline because commercial vehicle tolls were raised, the bridge was losing private automobiles, the most important single revenue source. Other routes were becoming less expensive and more convenient. San Francisco-Oakland Bay Bridge approaches were being improved, its tolls were falling steadily, and its traffic rising rapidly. Tolls on the Carquinez Bridge, a link between the Sacramento Valley and the Bay Bridge, also fell.[30] And, new Sierra Nevada tourist facilities competed with Redwood Empire attractions. The bridge district suffered a net loss of $135,000 during the 1938–39 fiscal year.[31]

The San Francisco-Oakland Bay Bridge quickly became an unflattering "measuring rod" for the Golden Gate Bridge.[32] The Bay Bridge won federal financing from both the RFC and the PWA, state gas taxes provided for its upkeep, and the terms of its financing required all toll revenue to go to paying debt until its construction bonds were retired. The most glaring and obvious contrast between the two bridges was their toll rates. The basic Bay Bridge toll started at 65 cents at its 1936 opening, but dropped to 50 cents almost immediately, 40 cents in 1938, and 25 cents in 1940. The Golden Gate Bridge opened with a 50-cent toll that remained steady even as the toll on the bay span plummeted.[33] Golden Gate Bridge officials protested that their obligations and expenses were much higher than those of the state-operated bridge to the east, but that was due at least in part to their resistance to the reform that greater state or federal subsidies required. Nor could the bridge district compete with the larger state agency in the efficiency of its operations. The fact was, drivers were paying a premium to cross the Golden Gate Bridge, and its officials quickly came to loathe the inevitable comparisons.[34]

In light of disappointing Golden Gate Bridge traffic and revenues, chamber of commerce leaders extended their investigation, declaring that a tax assessment would be unavoidable "unless an earnest business-like effort is made to effect the fullest economy."[35] At the end of 1939, they recommended slashing the advertising and public relations budget and reducing meetings of the directors to one a month. They called for the elimination of four "redundant" offices and the reduction of a number of other costs, including painting, the single largest maintenance expense.[36] More than a year later, *San Francisco Examiner* investigative reporters found that the bridge directors had ignored all of these recommendations and spent three times more on operations than their counterparts at the Bay Bridge. In a three-day series, they described a bloated office staff and thousands of dollars worth of unnecessary salaries and expenditures.[37]

Hoping to avoid more scrutiny, the bridge directors initiated their own budget inquiry in 1940. O'Brien headed a committee to identify waste and recommend cutbacks. The investigation took place strictly behind closed doors, and when bridge director Richard Welch tried to discuss the directors' hotel and travel expenses at a regular meeting, he was rudely silenced by the president of the board, Warren Shannon. Offended, Welch immediately went to the press with figures showing that thousands of dollars were being spent transporting the directors to meetings and providing them with lavish meals and accommodations. To his colleagues' dismay, he pledged to oppose any federal aid until costs were reduced.[38] Welch was often absent because of his duties as a U.S. congressman, and O'Brien asserted, "Welch . . . doesn't attend enough meetings to know what is going on."[39] A few weeks later, bridge district attorney John L. McNab issued an opinion that Welch was ineligible to serve as a bridge director based on a law relating to state and federal officeholders. Welch ignored him and remained a bridge director until his death in 1949.[40]

The attempt to suppress Welch's concerns indicated that tolerance for dissent at the bridge district was waning. And indeed, O'Brien's loyalty was tested several weeks later when the other directors rejected his committee's recommendations for budget reductions, item by item. O'Brien's most controversial suggestion, cutting back on REA advertising, garnered vocal protest in the northern counties, including a front-page editorial in Santa Rosa's paper declaring that "advertising [is] an investment."[41] Soon after, O'Brien accepted appointment to the REA executive committee—Edmondson remarked jokingly that he was trying to appease his biggest opponent. The directors adopted a few cutbacks,

An Overhaul Job

San Francisco Examiner, December 16, 1940.

but these amounted to only $5,000 of the $33,000 proposed by its own committee. An *Examiner* editorial called the inquiry a "failure," and "another demonstration of the incompetence, political pettiness, and 'public be damned' spirit" of the bridge district.[42]

In 1941, bridge district officials endured yet another round of unwelcome financial scrutiny. Leland M. Kaiser, a municipal bond analyst representing a major public works finance consortium, approached the directors with a proposal for comprehensive refinancing.[43] Kaiser argued that the agency was in dire financial straits and that its fixed, non-negotiable annual bond payments made tax assessments inevitable. Moreover, Kaiser asserted that revenues would not improve after the war, and that gas rationing had little to do with the agency's problems.[44] It was the bridge district's financial structure that was faulty, too inflexible to allow for lean years or budget shortfalls. Kaiser compared the Golden Gate Bridge's financing unfavorably to that of the Bay Bridge, the Triborough Bridge, and the Holland Tunnel, all of which had more flexible terms, multiple revenue sources, or longer debt maturity. Not only would his plan allow for variation in payments, Kaiser told bridge officials and members of the press, but it would also relieve the pressure on the bridge district and result in an immediate toll reductions. Kaiser's proposal attracted considerable attention, even winning an endorsement from the San Francisco grand jury.[45]

The bridge directors denied any need for refinancing, subsidies, or taxes. One complained sarcastically that he was "inclined as I go along the streets to apologize for this poor old decrepit and broken down arthritic structure, this financial structure, that is ready for collapse, and it all stems from the desire of the bond firms in San Francisco to make $300,000 by refinancing a bridge that at this moment doesn't need refinancing."[46] Even to bridge district critics, the primary attraction of Kaiser's plan was the promise of lower tolls, and once closer analysis revealed that they were likely to remain at 50 cents, the plan lost most of its appeal.[47] The bridge district auditor pointed out that "basically the problem is one of policy—whether or not it is preferable to pay a premium in the future for the privilege of cutting tolls at this time."[48] The directors rejected refinancing with an eight-to-three vote.[49]

While Kaiser's proposal had almost no chance of success, it added to public concern about the bridge district's financial health. On December 10, 1940, the *Examiner* published a poll of San Francisco residents revealing that 85 percent supported turning the structure over to the California Toll Bridge Authority, a state agency that was managed and operated by a professional staff headed by an experienced engineer. None of its money went to advertising, public relations, or lobbying. San Francisco supervisors passed a resolution supporting the bridge's transfer, and Marvelous Marin Inc., an REA affiliate, added its support for state control. The chamber of commerce backed several bills to transfer the bridge during the 1941 legislative session, but all of them failed.[50] This became a tradition—every regular session for the next three decades featured unsuccessful legislation to bring the Golden Gate Bridge under state control.

Although reform stalled in Sacramento, critics won a minor victory on the legal front. Chamber of commerce leaders took action against the appointment of politicians as directors. At their request, the state attorney general declared in 1941 that holding dual offices was a conflict of interest. Most of the offending directors ignored this opinion, but Thomas Maxwell of Napa County did step down. A lawsuit against Marin supervisor and bridge director R. A. Thompson was decided in favor of the defendant by a Marin County judge, but in 1942 the California Superior Court reversed the ruling: "Public policy requires that when the duties of two offices are repugnant or overlap so that their exercise may require contradictory or inconsistent action, to the detriment of the public interest, their discharge by one person is incompatible with that interest."[51] Warren Shannon, the only remaining San Francisco supervisor on the board, resigned soon after the decision.

The directors responded to political and legal threats by creating a new position, hiring Adam as public relations officer in February 1941. Adam had been a political reporter and lobbyist in Sacramento in addition to his work as a REA publicist. The bridge directors voted unanimously to appoint James E. Rickets as general manager, knowing they could count on his loyalty. Rickets had been a director since 1938, and was the business representative for a number of San Francisco labor organizations, including the influential Building Trades Council.[52] These appointments marked the beginning of long-term bridge district patterns: turning to public relations in the face of criticism and staffing the organization from its own ranks and with the associates of its closest ally, the REA.

Although none of the 1941 reform bills passed, the state senate appointed a committee to scrutinize bridge district "administrative affairs, financial status and modus operandi."[53] Lengthy hearings in 1942 and 1943 included severely conflicting testimony regarding the agency's finances. On the one hand, bridge district officials testified that a toll cut was impossible, both because of wartime shortages and the use of government passes for as many as 43 percent of bridge crossings. "I don't think we can get by 1944 without an assessment," asserted president Hugo D. Newhouse in December 1942.[54] When hearings resumed in March 1943, after Leland Kaiser presented his opinion of their finances, bridge district officials changed their story. No financial crisis or tax assessments were on the horizon, claimed the new bridge district president William Hadeler: "naturally at the beginning of the gasoline rationing the outlook for the Golden Gate Bridge looked very, very bad but this has changed very, very rapidly."[55]

Close examination of the bridge district's many reserve funds revealed that its officials had been squirreling away money for years, including an "unencumbered reserve fund" of $1.5 million to cover future bond payments.[56] Hadeler announced that the district was in "the best financial condition since its opening to traffic."[57] Committee chairman John F. Shelley, a San Francisco Democrat, expressed frustration about inadequate data provided by bridge district representatives and their failure to fully cooperate with the investigation.[58] Conceding that wartime conditions made predicting the bridge district's financial future impossible, the committee recommended legislation to allow the bridge directors to "alter their financial program by whatever method they deem best under conditions existing at the time." Accordingly, a bill supported by the bridge district that increased its financial independence and incur new debt was passed unanimously by the legislature and promptly signed into law.[59]

Overall, the 1943 legislative session was a victory for the bridge district. The bridge directors responded to investigation and criticism by intensifying their public relations and lobbying activities, and were completely successful in defending their operations and shoring up their power.

Engineers as Outsiders

In the midst of financial scrutiny and political pressure, unexpected engineering problems confronted bridge district officials, increasing their sense of embattlement. This time, however, the perceived threat was coming from within the agency, from an engineer who publicly questioned the most sensitive bridge district issue: toll rates. The bridge directors reacted by consolidating power within a small group of leading officials that excluded engineers.

If the Golden Gate Bridge had a younger sibling, it would be the Tacoma Narrows Bridge, designed by Leon S. Moisseiff and completed in July 1940. Moisseiff considered the Washington State span over the waters of the Puget Sound to be his masterpiece; certainly, its construction marked the climax of his long and distinguished career. His major contributions to suspension bridges engineering were refinements to the theory of "deflection," which demonstrated that a longer bridge could be more flexible because its dead weight was greater. Long bridges could actually be narrower than shorter ones, because their overall mass makes them more resistant to movement. Moisseiff applied deflection theory as a consulting engineer on the Manhattan Bridge, the Delaware River Bridge, and many other spans, and elaborated on it at length in professional journals. His theory not only reduced costs by reducing the materials needed to build suspension bridges, but it also allowed for aesthetically desirable proportions—very narrow roadways suspended gracefully with delicate cables from slim towers resulted in elegant bridge profiles.[60] The celebrated beauty of the Golden Gate Bridge rested upon deflection theory, and the Tacoma Narrows Bridge took its application even further. Moisseiff reportedly declared the Washington span to be "the most beautiful in the world."[61] It was also the first bridge that he designed as the leading engineer. The smaller, shorter Tacoma Narrows Bridge was actually much narrower and more flexible than the Golden Gate Bridge. Its depth (determined by the height of its towers relative to its overall length) was 1:350, very shallow for a bridge. Most significantly, its width to span ratio was 1:74. The Golden Gate Bridge, with its six lanes extending 1.4 miles across the mouth of the San Francisco Bay, had a width to span ratio of 1:47, and even that was far narrower than any other bridge in existence. This made both bridges more flexible than any that had preceded them.[62]

While workers and, later, pedestrians and drivers certainly noticed that the Golden Gate Bridge bobbed and swayed in the wind, the movement was nothing compared to the wild waves on "Galloping Gertie," as the Tacoma span was immediately dubbed. Drivers complained of seasickness, and thrill-seekers made special trips to the bridge on windy days to enjoy the huge swells that moved along its roadway. It only took six months and ordinary, 42-mile per hour winds to destroy the Tacoma Narrows Bridge. On November 7, 1940, a cable snapped, and the bridge began to twist as vertical waves intensified. A team of engineers studying the bridge's movement to plan modifications were too late to prevent disaster, but caught the dramatic collapse on film. After a half hour of violent waving and twisting, the entire central roadway fell into the Puget Sound, leaving the damaged towers standing at awkward angles on either side. The bridge and Moisseiff's reputation as an engineer were both a total loss.[63]

The Tacoma Narrows Bridge destroyed, the Golden Gate Bridge was once again the narrowest suspension bridge in the world—and by a large margin. Another span shaped by Moisseiff's theory, the Bronx-Whitestone Bridge, had the next smallest width-to-span ratio of 1:34. It became immediately clear to bridge engineers that assumptions had to be examined, testing had to be done, and new theories had to be developed. If ever serious investigation into the safety and stability of the

Golden Gate Bridge was called for, it was in the wake of this major engineering disaster.

Bridge district engineer Russell Cone, respected for his work with suspension bridges, was appointed to an official investigating committee for the Washington State Department of Highways.[64] Cone went to Tacoma to inspect the failed structure, but was almost immediately called back to San Francisco to testify in yet another grand jury investigation of the bridge district. On February 27, 1941, Cone answered questions about the agency's expenses and tolls directly: to his knowledge, not only were the agency's finances sound, but he believed that with a few budget cuts and efficiency measures the bridge district could afford a toll reduction. Specifically, Cone testified, the bridge district could drop its costly insurance: a ripple effect from the Tacoma disaster had made the coverage so limited that the directors were considering canceling it anyway. Cone also suggested that annual maintenance appropriations could also be reduced, as very little of them had actually been used.[65]

One week after he testified, the bridge directors fired Cone while he was out of town, having returned to Washington State to continue his investigation. Officially the nine-to-four decision to eliminate Cone's position was an "economy measure," but no one took that explanation seriously.[66] One bridge director remarked that Cone "went behind our backs to show he knows more than the directors or the finance committee about operation of the bridge."[67] Apparently, the Golden Gate Bridge directors were under too much pressure from outsiders to be willing to tolerate such internal dissent. Cone himself expressed concern but no resentment or regret: "the Golden Gate Bridge is a public institution that should be operated for the benefit of the public. . . . If my dismissal results in bring[ing] about a toll reduction my personal sacrifice is worth the price."[68] He soon found other, more lucrative employment, taking charge of a major defense contracting firm and later returning to bridge construction as a contractor on the Richmond-San Rafael Bridge.[69]

The bridge directors refused to reinstate Cone, but he had not been silenced. The federal report on the Tacoma Narrows collapse, released in May 1941, included Cone's observations of the Golden Gate Bridge during windstorms. He witnessed violent undulations on the bridge on February 9, 1938, and reported a "wave similar to that made by cracking a whip" running down the length of the roadway at a rate of twenty to thirty vibrations per minute. Cone noted that the bridge was pushed laterally as much as ten feet from its normal position, and even recruited a witness because his observations might seem "unbelievable." Cone reported a similar event on February 7, 1941.[70] Both times, the bridge directors suppressed Cone's findings, keeping them secret to avoid bad publicity and traffic reductions, and refused to fund any further engineering investigations.

Cone's reports released a torrent of pent-up frustration from O'Brien. O'Brien was normally very outspoken, publishing frequent editorials relating to bridge district matters in his Mendocino newspaper and regularly sending critical open letters to the Bay Area press. In this case, he remained loyal to the agency and the other directors and did not "leak" their discussions about safety concerns after the Tacoma incident. Finally, he broke his uncharacteristic silence and warned the public in May 1941 to expect some news that would "curl your hair."[71] When Cone's report was released in June, O'Brien had an outraged commentary on "mismanagement" ready for distribution. He claimed that the other directors opposed hiring qualified engineers, unwilling to appropriate funding for serious study. He called for a wholesale change in administration to reorient the agency, including hiring an engineer experienced with long-span suspension bridges to replace William Harrelson. O'Brien pointed out that engineers managed most other major bridges, and that hiring an administrative general manager to oversee the bridge engineer was redundant, expensive, and even foolhardy. "I pray you do not entrust this great bridge to inexperienced hands, to neglect it by failing to provide competent engineers to study it," he pleaded, warning of its possible "destruction through a wanton lack of care."[72] The majority of the directors ignored his admonitions, choosing instead to maintain the subordinate role of the engineer that began with Strauss. As during construction, the bridge district engineer was treated like an outsider by directors who were concerned more about revenues than safety.

Golden Gate Bridge engineers Charles Derleth, Moisseiff, and even Cone issued statements assuring the public that the bridge was "as safe as ever," based on wind tunnel tests of a scale model done by Stanford engineers in March. However, they all recommended further testing.[73] Othmar Ammann was especially vehement in urging the bridge directors to initiate a thorough study by expert engineers and to be wary of "halfway measures and toy experiments."[74] The San Francisco Chamber of Commerce president Walter A. Haas urged the directors to bring in a team led by Robert A. Millikan, a renowned physicist and engineer, to investigate. The editor of the *San Francisco Call-Bulletin* remarked on the likely bridge district reaction to the suggestion: "it is so logical that we hardly dare believe that the jealousy-ridden factions comprising the bridge directorate could agree on it."[75]

Despite these and other calls for investigation, bridge directors refused to pay for any in-depth study of possible structural weakness. Nor did they replace Cone. Instead, they hired Leon H. Nishkian on an as-needed basis. Nishkian was an elderly structural engineer who had played an important role in rebuilding San Francisco after the 1906 earthquake. In 1944 he was officially added to bridge district staff as a part-time "consulting engineer."[76]

After another major windstorm years later, the issue of bridge stability was finally revisited. Winds through the Golden Gate exceeded 60 miles per hour on December 1, 1951, forcing a three-hour span closure. Recording instruments installed on the bridge for a federal study (not funded by the bridge district) documented "transverse torsional" or twisting motion in addition to six-foot vertical waves moving along the roadway. The same sort of twisting motion had been fatal to the Tacoma Narrows Bridge. Finally, the bridge directors commissioned an engineering study—a full year after Washington State officials had finished building an entirely new span over the Tacoma Narrows. In 1953, a lateral bracing system installed beneath the roadway effectively stopped the Golden Gate Bridge's dangerous twisting motion, even in high winds.[77]

Jack McCarthy: Champion of Commuters

During World War II, bridge directors counted on future revenues to bail them out of their financial and public relations conundrum. Even if they were successful in getting state or federal aid, they knew that it would come with oversight and regulation. Alternatively, if bridge district representatives waited too long to reduce tolls or were forced to levy another property tax in order to meet bond obligations, public opinion might turn against them enough to make the wholesale dissolution of the bridge district politically viable. They took a calculated risk, betting that improved postwar traffic would make up for budget deficits before they had to compromise the agency's autonomy to win subsidies. It was a gamble that paid off handsomely. The end of gasoline rationing meant a bonanza of tolls and a permanent shift in bridge district fortunes. Actual revenues surpassed projections for the very first time in fiscal year 1945–46. Traffic on the bridge went from 4.8 million vehicles in 1944–45 to 6.7 million in 1945–46, an increase of nearly 30 percent, and continued to increase every year for nearly three decades.[78] These windfalls were a mixed blessing for bridge district officials—ample toll revenues and generous expense accounts made the agency seem fat and sassy. As happy as bridge officials were to report better revenues and a comfortable surplus, bridge users were equally unhappy about high tolls.

Bridge crossings reflected rapid growth in Marin County. Until the 1950s, the bridge did not produce the development that boosters hoped for. Even with an influx of wartime shipyard workers, the county added only 33,000 residents between 1940 and 1949.[79] Then, Marin's population started to climb, increasing by nearly 70 percent in the following decade. Most growth was concentrated in the southern reaches of the county, just an easy commute away from downtown San Francisco, thanks to the Golden Gate Bridge. In the late 1940s, commuters' clubs sprang up in Marin with the explicit purpose of working for toll reductions, adding to a cacophony of complaints from taxpayers' associations, chambers of commerce, and local politicians.

Marin citizens quickly discovered that there was no effective way to influence bridge district policy. The president of the Mill Valley Commuters Club described the experience of testifying before the directors: "You identify yourself carefully and fully, make your statement and sit down. After this you might as well go home. Your statement has been listened to politely and completely ignored."[80] Frustrated commuters accused the directors of "high-handed incompetence" and an infuriating "public-be-damned" attitude.[81] Observers reported that it was impossible to obtain a record of proceedings or votes, and that all meaningful discussion was conducted behind closed doors.[82] In June 1950 the bridge district announced a long-awaited toll reduction, but it did not benefit commuters: the rate was reduced for commercial trucks but not for private automobiles and their passengers.

Protest seemed to have no impact on the appointment of bridge directors, either. Several meetings were devoted to criticizing Marin's unpopular director, Matt Graham, who was accused of being unresponsive to the public, extravagant with his expense account, and an opponent of toll reductions. According to the *Independent Journal,* the Marin supervisors received a "flood" of letters recommending other candidates for the job as his term expired in 1950.[83] Although all of Marin's newspapers opposed Graham's reappointment, the supervisors unanimously extended his service another four years. Marin's papers accused them of "turning their backs on public clamor for a change in bridge policies" and "condoning the reckless waste of public funds."[84]

Marin commuters needed a champion, a sincere and ambitious reformer willing to fight for toll reductions and against corruption and secrecy. Until 1950, their best spokesman was asemblyman Richard McCollister, who represented southern Marin. He sponsored regular bills to incorporate the bridge into the state Department of Public Works, as well as periodic resolutions encouraging lower tolls. While McCollister's persistence was undeniable, he lacked fervor and sincerity. His bills were vague and left crucial questions unanswered; an observer in Sacramento noted that he "never attempted to have them withdrawn from the committee."[85] McCollister explained his view of the prospects for bridge district reform: "If the officials in charge of the agency, on which you wish legislation, neglects or takes no part in the discussion, tries in no way to help and is on the other side of the table, it is doubtful if it would pass. It is necessary that the Bridge Directors desire a change."[86] If McCollister expected that his legislation should actually garner bridge district support, it signaled extreme naïveté. More likely, his actions were merely symbolic gestures for the benefit of his commuting constituency.

State Senator Jack McCarthy emerging from a voting booth, 1959. Courtesy of The Bancroft Library, University of California, Berkeley.

In 1950, a new arrival in Sacramento, willing to go after the bridge district in earnest, toppled McCollister from his soapbox. Marin's new state senator, Jack McCarthy, built his career on the discontent of commuters. He became the most popular politician in the county and the archenemy of the bridge district. When McCarthy took his seat he was twenty-six years old and the youngest senator ever to serve in the state senate. A resident of Kentfield, McCarthy had overseen the construction of Dominican College in San Rafael, Marin Catholic High School in Kentfield, and the reconstruction of the old San Rafael Mission as the Marin manager for his father's construction company. Robert McCarthy was an Irish immigrant and a self-made man who earned his fortune as a leading contractor for the Archdiocese of San Francisco at a time of rapid expansion. He was well connected in Sacramento, personal friends with Henry J. Kaiser, and chairman of "Democrats for [Earl] Warren," California's Republican governor.[87] By the late 1940s, he had expanded his business to Marin County, focusing on residential development and transportation infrastructure. He used his connections and resources to back his youngest son's political ambitions.

Jack McCarthy won his first election by a narrow margin in a four-way race. His main opponent, T. Fred Bagshaw, was the chairman of the county board of supervisors, former mayor of Mill Valley, and president of the supervisor's unit of the REA. Bagshaw had also served two years as a bridge director until the 1942 court ruling forced his resignation, and had recently retired as the publisher of the *Marin Journal.* Both Bagshaw and McCarthy ran as independents. Neither of the other two candidates, who had endorsements from the county's political parties, represented a serious challenge, but McCarthy's victory was a surprise and an upset. McCarthy made headlines by reporting campaign expenses of $6,375, nearly all of which was donated by his immediate family. Bagshaw spent $539.82.[88]

While McCarthy's a healthy campaign fund and extensive newspaper, radio, and billboard advertising no doubt helped make up for his lack of experience, he had other advantages as well. Marin's political landscape at the time was divided, as historian Evelyn Radford has observed. Marin's "provincial" north was dominated by agriculture, oriented around San Rafael, and socially and politically integrated with rural northern California. Residents of the "cosmopolitan" areas in the south identified more with San Francisco, and had a progressive political orientation. McCarthy had support in both communities.[89] His youth and energy probably appealed to southern Marin commuters, including many families new to the county; many local political regimes were upset as the rapid growth of the 1950s transformed the political landscape of the Bay Area.[90] At the same time, McCarthy had conservative credentials and support in the well-established Catholic communities of Marin's agricultural north.[91] McCarthy ran as a "business man" and called for "economy," but supported increased taxation for schools, highways, and hospitals. McCarthy's first, narrow political victory represented an affirmation for growth and development symbolized by the youthful son of a contractor, as well as a protest vote against the political status quo, personified by Bagshaw.

Jack joined his elder brother in Sacramento, Robert I. McCarthy, a Democrat who had been elected to the state assembly representing San Francisco two years earlier. Robert was a decorated Army officer who returned from the war to study law at the University of San Francisco and quickly became a partner in a San Francisco firm. In contrast, Jack's education was modest. He left the University of San Francisco twice, once to serve three years as a wartime merchant marine and again for professional baseball. During his time working in construction he took classes in engineering at Heald College, but never earned a degree.

Senator McCarthy was probably quite conscious of his youth, inexperience, and lack of formal education, as well as suggestions that his father bought his election.[92] His father's influence may also have been the reason that he was greeted with open arms by the Republican leadership in Sacramento and immediately assigned a choice position on the Senate Transportation Committee. He was also named chairman of the Interim Committee on Problems Concerning the Inclusion of the Golden Gate Bridge into the State Highway System. While McCarthy favored state administration of the bridge, it had not been one of his leading issues. One Sausalito resident remarked that "being for state control [of the Golden Gate Bridge] these days is a little like being against sin."[93] But McCarthy realized that in taking on the intractable and unpopular Golden Gate Bridge and Highway District he had a real chance to prove himself as a legislator and politician.

Comprised entirely of senators from bridge district counties, McCarthy's committee set out to investigate Golden Gate Bridge operations and develop recommendations to settle the disputes that had already produced so much failed legislation. McCollister complained that McCarthy was moving in on his leadership position on the issue, and it was rumored that a senate committee rather than a joint committee was created deliberately to exclude him.[94] But while McCollister may have been guilty of empty posturing, McCarthy's sincerity quickly became apparent. As chairman, McCarthy revised his committee's purpose to include assessment of the possibility of lowering tolls.[95] At hearings in February 1951, committee members questioned bridge officials about salaries, the cost of paint, and administrative expenses: the same budget items that chamber of commerce investigators had been criticizing since

1938. But these hearings also provided a forum for Marin commuters and other grassroots bridge district opponents. The Sausalito Citizens Council's chairman condemned the "flagrant disregard of good business principles and public opinion on the part of the bridge management." He also pointed out that all ninety-five people in attendance at their last meeting favored state control of the bridge: "The freedom with which public funds are spent for elaborate quarters, for self-preservation, for consultants' fees and the favoritism accorded to selected groups cannot be overlooked." Representatives of the Mill Valley Commuters' Club, Marin County Taxpayers Association, and the Associated Chambers of Commerce of Marin also condemned the bridge district. However, testimony by California legislative auditor A. Alan Post was the most provocative. Appearing at McCarthy's request, Post asserted that state control would reduce Golden Gate Bridge operational costs by nearly a million dollars annually.[96]

McCarthy eagerly asked Post to conduct a complete investigation of Golden Gate Bridge operations. The results, released a year later during McCarthy's first reelection campaign, provided credible evidence of mismanagement and revived the stale campaign for a state takeover of the bridge. Post provided detailed figures showing that the operating budget of the Golden Gate Bridge could be reduced by more than 10 percent immediately upon transfer to the California Toll Bridge Authority. The largest potential savings would be from the bridge's annual advertising appropriations, most of which went directly to the REA. The board of directors, the district secretary, and the general manager (whose duties would be assumed by a "resident engineer") could all be eliminated. Post's calculations revealed that the bridge toll, then at 40 cents, could be reduced to 25 cents even under its current management and still produce comfortable reserves. He also verified longstanding concerns about excessive paint costs, providing independent quotes from major suppliers that were more than a dollar less per gallon than the prices being paid by the bridge district.[97] The report was released soon after the directors approved an unprecedented $1.2 million operating budget, including substantial increases for public relations.[98]

While the tone of the auditor's report was subdued, its implications were inflammatory. McCarthy seized upon them with an almost gleeful enthusiasm. He launched a new campaign for state control, resolving to present his proposal in person before all bridge district county supervisors, though only Marin's agreed to hear him.[99] He excitedly reviewed the auditor's figures with them, emphasizing their reliability: "When I say to you that the representative who wrote this report . . . is a very conservative individual, I mean conservative." McCarthy claimed that surplus revenues were being distributed "arbitrarily" to various accounts, making them seem less significant than they really were, and suggested that bridge officials were exaggerating upcoming maintenance and engineering expenses to avoid toll reductions.[100]

Representing the bridge district, James Adam denounced the legislative auditor's findings, calling them "misleading" and the comparison with the Bay Bridge "unfair." He pointed out that state gas tax funds paid for Bay Bridge maintenance, and that many of its other expenses had been "absorbed by various state agencies." He claimed that the high cost of painting the Golden Gate Bridge was mostly due to labor costs, and that the conditions at the site demanded "a far different quality of paint" and more frequent coverage than those of the more sheltered Bay Bridge.[101] Adam accused McCarthy of being a "publicity seeker" who was in "absolute ignorance of the financial and legal responsibilities of the Golden Gate Bridge."[102] McCarthy responded by charging that Adam was working against economy measures because his own position as public relations officer was an unnecessary expense that should be eliminated.[103]

Marin County supervisors invited Adam to appear at their next meeting to defend the bridge district. Adam countered allegations of inefficiency and poor administration point by point, citing the results of previous investigations and the preliminary report of McCarthy's own committee. He asserted that "there has been no juggling of any reserve fund," and acknowledged that "the Bridge District today has approximately $14,000,000 in reserve . . . [but] it still owes $31,200,000 in bond principal, and it still will have to pay out, regardless of what happens, some $16,600,000 in interest alone on those bonds before they finally mature in 1971." Although Adam professed neutrality on the question of state control, he introduced the emotional appeal that was to become the cornerstone of bridge district defenses in the decades to come: "The people of Marin County and five other counties voted and had the faith and courage to vote $35,000,000 in bonds to build that bridge, a bridge [that] would cost over $100,000,000 to replace today. The people now have a voice in the operation of the Golden Gate Bridge, through their directors appointed by the Boards of Supervisors of the county." He warned that if the state "took over the bridge," higher tolls would follow, putting at risk "the taxpayers of the district, whose property, whose homes are pledged as security to the bridge." With this, Adam evoked local pride in the bridge and fear of outside encroachment and taxation. He defined the "taxpayers of the District" as property owners, *not* toll payers. He emphasized the risk that they had assumed by approving the bonds, and argued that caution and prudence precluded lower tolls. He suggested that the directors were closer and more responsive to the residents of the bridge district than state officials would be—a statement that must have infuriated many frustrated commuters. But Adam's appeal to home rule was powerful, and state control was not a welcome prospect for local politicians. He was addressing county supervisors, the group that would lose the right to appoint directors if the state took over the bridge. Although Adam won this battle, the Marin supervisors commended McCarthy for having "enough ambition . . . and enough guts to go in and fight."[104]

McCarthy's crusade for reform had just begun, and soon it was easy to see that the bridge district was facing a full-force political assault. However, bridge leaders no longer accepted criticism passively. Facing credible, determined opposition, they prepared to fight for the interests of the organization. The tone of the exchange between the youthful McCarthy and bridge district officials reflected mounting antagonism. Rickets was patronizing toward McCarthy, ridiculing him and calling him "my boy Jack," and Adam called McCarthy a "crackpot" for suggesting lower tolls in 1951.[105] McCarthy had another run-in with Adam in February 1952 when he lobbied against legislation for a state bridge from San Rafael to Contra Costa County that McCarthy had sponsored. Adam argued that the proposed span might compete with the Golden Gate Bridge for traffic and tolls. Outraged by Adams's interference, McCarthy and several of his local political allies demanded that the bridge directors rein in their lobbyist, but they were ignored.[106]

In November 1952, McCarthy's committee on the Golden Gate Bridge held another hearing San Francisco, featuring a full press contingent and a tone of thinly veiled hostility. Bridge district representatives focused on refuting the legislative auditor, and Rickets read aloud an official response to his "incomplete and erroneous" report. He rejected the notion that bridge district management was inefficient and challenged the legality of a state takeover: "nothing could be done that would impair the contractual rights of the holders of bridge bonds."[107] Rickets followed his prepared statement by charging that McCarthy's demands for toll reductions were "ignorant and uninformed." McCarthy defended himself: "to find out a 25-cent toll is feasible is not ignorance. I think it is good business."[108] An observer remarked that McCarthy "excoriated Mr. Rickets personally," and attacked him for his "expense accounts, his use of a Bridge District car from home to work . . . [and] the building up of financial reserves to huge proportions on an arbitrary basis without lowering toll."[109] Committee members also confronted Rickets and Adam about paint prices, bidding procedures, and high salaries, including their own. One committee member charged that the bridge directors were "political hacks" building up a "financial dynasty."[110]

The November hearing was a major boon to McCarthy, inspiring detailed coverage in Marin newspapers. Large photos of the young senator, with an open and innocent face, confronting Rickets and Adam, neither of whom were at all photogenic, were featured the next day in the *Independent Journal.* Rickets appeared to be a thin, hunched old man with small, closely set eyes, greasy hair, and bad teeth. Adam provided an equally unappealing counterpoint, his corpulent frame leaning back in a chair as he stared menacingly at the camera.[111] A *Sausalito News* poll revealed that 84 percent of its readers supported a state takeover, and *San Francisco Examiner* editors concluded that bridge administration was rife with "costly politics."[112]

At the start of the next legislative session, McCarthy sponsored a number of reform bills, including one that called for the incorporation of the bridge into the state highway system and the abolition of the board of directors.[113] Spurred by continuing reports of record traffic and revenues for the bridge district, McCarthy also introduced a resolution calling for the reduction of commuter tolls to 25 cents on "a trial basis," which passed easily and won endorsements in Marin and San Francisco.[114] The bridge district's own engineering consultant, Arthur C. Jenkins, reported that a 25-cent bridge toll would still leave a surplus of nearly $16 million by the time the bonds were retired, and members of the bridge district financial committee recommended lowering the toll. But the board was dominated directors from northern counties who were oblivious to bad press in San Francisco and Marin. By a vote of eight to five (with both Marin directors and three of seven San Francisco directors dissenting), the directors voted to keep the 40-cent toll. As McCarthy put it, the bridge directors told them all "to go jump in the Bay."[115] He followed the resolution with a bill requiring lower tolls. Although Adam protested that there "has been absolutely no public demand for this," it passed with twenty-three-to-four vote in the senate and fifty-five-to-four vote in the assembly. Governor Warren stopped the measure with a veto, arguing that it would set a dangerous precedent for state interference in the affairs of local government.[116]

As McCarthy agitated for toll reductions, the bridge directors approved a $3.5 million plan for strengthening the bridge developed by Clifford Paine. John G. Little, who took over for Nishkian as part-time consulting engineer in 1947, questioned the accuracy of Paine's data in a three-page report to the board. The directors promptly fired Little, saying that they could not tolerate "second guessing" on sensitive engineering issues, echoing their treatment of Cone. They did not replace him. McCarthy, knowing that even bridge safety was subject to political considerations, accused the directors of cooking up another excuse to avoid reducing tolls. He argued that the project should be reviewed by a "panel of independent engineers" before the "tremendous" expenditure was approved. McCarthy introduced a new bill in Sacramento to forcibly halt the project for further study, but it was defeated and long-overdue reinforcement measures proceeded.[117]

Fortification: Politics and Public Relations

By Adam's reckoning, thirty bills were introduced in 1953 that directly affected the bridge district, eleven of which were sponsored by McCarthy. In a major reversal of policy, the directors voted to adopt official positions on the majority of them. In the past, they always denied any involvement with lobbying activities, fearing accusations of "politics" on their agenda. This time, Adam had explicit orders to work against reform. He was joined in the effort by REA agents who presented resolutions on behalf of bridge district counties against "the state's expropriation of the Golden Gate Bridge." During the next legislative session in 1955, McCarthy tried again to incorporate the bridge district into the state Department of Public Works and to mandate a 25-cent toll, but with even less success.[118]

Still, McCarthy could take some credit for changes. In March 1953 the bridge directors accepted bids for paint for the first time, and as part of their all-out effort to defeat McCarthy's legislation approved their first significant toll reduction, voting to offer a twenty-trip ticket for $6, or 30 cents a crossing.[119] In 1955, the directors adopted a 25-cent toll, right after McCarthy dropped his legislation and before they announced a $2 million net profit for the fiscal year. There were rumors that the directors struck a deal with McCarthy to get him off their backs. And his crusade against the bridge district paid off at the polls: McCarthy retained his seat easily in 1956, and in 1960 he won more votes in Marin than any other politician. The *Independent Journal* praised his efforts to lower tolls: "The final failure of the bill dims not one sparkle of Senator McCarthy's success in pushing it through the state legislature. His achievement was phenomenal. Carried on the final bill were the names of practically every foe who had fought so bitterly his earlier gate bridge bills. He completely won over all but one of the senators in every county in the Bridge District. He reduced opposition in the Assembly to a whisper. . . . All in all it was a remarkable study in perseverance, organization, and persuasiveness."[120]

After 1955, three new causes joined bridge district reform on McCarthy's agenda: regional rapid transit, a second San Francisco-Marin crossing, and transportation planning for the greater San Francisco Bay Area. He also waged unsuccessful though strong campaigns for the chair of the Republican State Central Committee in 1954 and for president pro tem of the senate in 1955. But McCarthy never stopped wrangling with the bridge district. He began collaborating on an entirely new strategy for its reform, a full-scale assault on the bridge district in the form of a new, comprehensive Bay Area transportation agency, the Golden Gate Authority. He saw improved transportation infrastructure as the surest route to development and growth for Marin County, and he wanted to use the proposed authority to harness Golden Gate Bridge tolls to finance other projects.[121]

McCarthy built a career on his campaigns against the bridge district, but he was not the only person to do so. James Adam rose to the top of bridge district management by fending them off. Adam explained the benefits of his work: "The Golden Gate Bridge was conceived and constructed in the face of tremendous obstacles [and] selfish interests and opponents. . . . Controversy flared throughout the construction period and even after the bridge was opened to traffic, with the result that public thinking was confused, and even part of the press was hostile. . . . Public relations activities of the District over the years have definitely improved public opinion and there has been fostered and maintained a highly satisfactory relationship between the District and the press and with city, state and federal agencies."[122] While Adam's assessment of public opinion at the time may have been overly optimistic, he was articulating a new interpretation of the bridge district's past that was already shaping its policies. Adam promoted the idea that the bridge district had always been a target for unjust criticism motivated by jealousy and greed, that its representatives had a duty to protect its image, assets, and autonomy, and that they needed strong public relations and lobbying to do so. His appointment as general manager in 1954 secured an institutional transformation that he helped engineer.

At the core of the conflict between Adam and the bridge district on one side, and McCarthy and other Bay Area proponents of reform on the other, were mutually exclusive understandings of the bridge district's role and purpose. Both sides agreed that the agency should be operated on business principles, but they differed on the question of whom it should serve. McCarthy and his allies saw the toll payer, "who is, after all, the one who is paying for the Bridge," as its most important constituency, "rightfully entitled to receive some benefits of the proceeds realized through efficient and economical management."[123] In contrast, Adam and other bridge district representatives, particularly those representing northern rural counties, understood their primary responsibility to be to property owners, as expressed unambiguously in 1950: "The Bridge Board has taken the position that its <u>first</u> obligation is to the taxpayer of the District, whose property is pledged as security for the bridge's financial success. It is the taxpayer, and not the user of the bridge who would have to meet any financial deficit that would occur." He underscored his understanding of their obligations: "you can be very certain of this: the majority of the Bridge Board is NOT going to gamble with the possibility of levying an assessment against the taxpayers of Sonoma County or any other county to satisfy the selfish whims of any particular group of bridge user for lower tolls."[124] Adam's determination to protect property owners conflicted directly with McCarthy's belief that toll payers should be bridge officials' first concern. These oppositional views of the agency's rightful purpose sparked a long and nasty war over bridge district policy in which McCarthy's siege was just a single battle.

Bridge district culture was forged in the heat of escalating criticism and pressure for reform, which hardened its officials' resolve to protect its resources and autonomy. The complementary interests of the bridge district and the REA during the construction period contributed to an enduring and powerful alliance that was important to the long-term development of both organizations. Unwanted investigation of bridge district finances and expenses in the 1930s and 1940s left a lasting defensiveness and stubborn resistance to reform among the directors. Fissures within the agency between management and engineers left a legacy of disregard for safety and maintenance. Finally, the persistent criticism spurred bridge district public relations activities and political engagement. James Adam first articulated an interpretation of bridge district history that justified and explained these activities and developments and permanently shaped the identity of the agency.

While bridge district leaders laid the foundation of bridge district culture during the construction period, it was after the agency began collecting tolls that it developed powerful institutional mechanisms to protect its resources and autonomy. Probably the most important incentive for this was the dramatic reversal in bridge district fortunes. After World War II, the Golden Gate Bridge was no longer a liability—it was a very profitable asset, with toll revenue far surpassing expenses and steadily growing reserves. The directors and the county officials who appointed them had an increasingly valuable stake in the bridge district. Another impetus was Jack McCarthy. Although he never managed to reform the bridge district, McCarthy's sustained attacks, in the form of both local denunciations and legislation in Sacramento, motivated bridge district representatives to cultivate alliances with outside groups and to act aggressively against dissent within the organization. In the 1950s and 1960s, under Adam's leadership, the bridge district shifted from a defensive posture to much more active engagement in regional politics and policy.

Chapter 4
The Defeat of the Golden Gate Authority

In 1958, Jack McCarthy announced plans for a Golden Gate Authority. According to the ambitious young state senator from Marin County, the creation of this new public agency would solve Bay Area transportation problems, provide for growth and development, and establish the foundation for general regional planning. Intended to transform the region by transforming its government, the authority would consolidate responsibility for transportation policy at the metropolitan level. Industrialist Edgar F. Kaiser and members of the Bay Area Council, a civic association that represented the region's most powerful businesses, backed the proposal. They believed that the authority, which was based on a corporate business model, was vital to securing the Bay Area's future as a thriving and prosperous metropolis. However, while the authority promised jobs and profit for industry, labor, and business interests, it also threatened the existing governments of the Bay Area, particularly the Golden Gate Bridge and Highway District. Its success rested on bridge tolls; acquiring the San Francisco-Oakland Bay Bridge and the Golden Gate Bridge was the key its financing. Its creation would certainly mean the dissolution of the bridge district, one of McCarthy's primary goals since he was first elected to the state senate in 1950. Bridge district officials, led by general manager James Adam, rallied against the proposed agency, forging alliances with city and county officials who opposed the Golden Gate Authority because it threatened the independence and autonomy of local governments. Together, they took on the Bay Area civic and business elite, and won.

Never before had bridge district officials faced a challenge of this magnitude, and never had their opponents been so united and determined to achieve their goals. Much more than just the fate of the bridge district was at stake: the proposed Golden Gate Authority represented a new understanding of urban political economy, and a new philosophy of government. It was based on the idea that the metropolis had transcended cities, counties, and the fragmented collection of agencies that comprised local government, that the urban region functioned as an integrated whole, and that its government should reflect that reality.

By the end of the 1950s, the bridge district had matured as an institution; the struggle to defeat the Golden Gate Authority tested the unity and loyalty of its officials and associates. Bridge district leaders drew upon all of the resources at their disposal, demonstrating in the process the impressive flexibility, resilience, and power of a special district. Allied with city and county officials and politicians, including Berkeley Mayor Claude B. Hutchison, they fought to protect the autonomy and authority of local governments under the rubric of "home rule." One result of the battle was the creation of the Association of Bay Area Governments in 1962, an organization designed to step into the void of authority and to preclude meaningful regional planning. This virtually powerless council of governments took the place of metropolitan government *without* filling the vacuum of power created by new regional problems. The defeat of the Golden Gate Authority reveals the influence of local government in shaping Bay Area policy. The institutional imperatives of existing governments—the most fundamental of which are power and autonomy—proved compelling.

Metropolitan Problems

As bridge district surpluses grew during the post–World War II boom, so did the intensity and ambition of its critics. Jack McCarthy's failed attempts to dissolve the agency and incorporate it into the California Department of Transportation contributed to a general mood of frustration about Bay Area transportation problems. Even after repeated setbacks, McCarthy persisted, and indeed, he raised the stakes. Appointed chair of the Senate Interim Committee on Bay Area Problems in 1957, McCarthy used the opportunity to propose a financially independent regional agency to take over the Golden Gate Bridge. The officials of this new agency would coordinate the entire region and encourage growth by building infrastructure. While the Bay Area already had several large multicounty special districts limited to specific functions, McCarthy had in mind an agency that would be considerably more powerful.[1] He looked to the Port of New York Authority (which had recently inspired the creation of the Port of Massachusetts Authority and the Delaware River Port Authority) as a model of efficient centralized administration, planning, and financing. Committee members toured its facilities in October, accompanied by several other interested Bay Area officials, including Adam representing the bridge district.

Early in 1958, McCarthy's committee released a preliminary report outlining the characteristics of the Golden Gate Authority, an independent, self-supporting agency that would take charge of all Bay Area bridges, airports, and harbors. Its officials would initiate and carry out policy, specifically the construction of new infrastructure. Most importantly for McCarthy, they would be able to put the assets and ever-increasing revenues of six local toll bridges, including the Golden Gate Bridge, to use in financing new projects. McCarthy turned to Bay Area business leaders for support, recruiting dozens of developers and industrialists from Oakland and San Francisco to raise funds and campaign for his proposal.[2]

McCarthy's focus on transportation not only reflected his interests as the representative of a peninsular county with limited access to the urban core, but also his desire to accommodate rapid suburban growth throughout the Bay Area. As in many metropolitan areas, postwar prosperity came with side effects, including an escalating traffic crisis. Between 1940 and 1960, the population of the Bay Area more than doubled, and the number of private automobiles more than tripled. Although state highway engineers were building miles of new freeways with state and federal gas-tax funds, local opposition delayed many of these projects, including a number of new bridges. At the same time, San Francisco remained the economic hub of the region; commuters packed both the Bay Bridge and the Golden Gate Bridge, and by the late 1950s engineers warned that both were nearing capacity. The abandonment of trolleys, transit railroads, and ferries after World War II compounded traffic problems, and while a regional commuter rail system was in the planning stages, its construction would take decades to complete. Moreover, interregional and international transportation was being squeezed. Three uncoordinated airports suffered from congestion, five public ports competed for traffic, and all of them were undercapitalized and out of date.[3] As early as 1952, state analysts concluded that "the development of the San Francisco Bay Area is now being seriously retarded by the lack of a proper agency to provide more adequate transportation facilities."[4]

McCarthy was the latest of many Bay Area leaders to call for better transportation infrastructure and planning. Members of the Commonwealth Club of San Francisco studied the possibility of a regional "harbor district" in 1912, but dismissed it as politically impractical; the idea was revived in 1934 as a "regional port authority," but again it went nowhere.[5] A unified Bay Area transportation system had been a central goal of both the "Greater San Francisco movement" backed by the San Francisco Chamber of Commerce, as well as the short-lived San Francisco Regional Plan Association in the 1920s. The ambitious 1942 Reber

Plan described a number of massive structures designed to accommodate traffic and shipping and to provide ample fresh water for large-scale industry and development, attracting attention but never significant support.[6] A 1935 effort to institute comprehensive county-based planning failed, as did a 1941 proposal for a Bay Area Regional Planning Commission backed by the State Planning Board.[7]

In 1945, leading Bay Area business executives (Francis V. Keesling among them) attempted to improve upon these efforts by creating the Bay Area Council (BAC).[8] The BAC quickly became the region's most powerful civic association, representing big business and industry and including more than one hundred labor leaders.[9] Its mission emphasized some of the same goals that the Golden Gate Authority was intended to achieve. The BAC was established to "coordinate and unify the efforts of public and private agencies leading to the successful completion of bay area development activities . . . [and] to analyze and take action on recommended projects that will further the economic, industrial, commercial, civic or cultural growth of the area."[10] Six firms contributed more than a third of the BAC's initial funding: the Bank of America, the American Trust Company, Standard Oil of California, Pacific Gas and Electric, United States Steel Corporation, and Bechtel Corporation.[11] Its members espoused a corporatist ideology that supported partnership between government, business, and labor, based on the idea that growth benefited everyone and should be rationally planned and actively promoted.[12]

When McCarthy proposed the Golden Gate Authority, the BAC's newly elected president Edgar Kaiser immediately recognized its potential as a regional planning agency. Kaiser was already a Bay Area celebrity; in 1956 he took the helm of the billion-dollar empire built by his father, Henry J. Kaiser.[13] The Golden Gate Authority idea appealed to Edgar Kaiser as a businessman, a self-styled reformer, and a new industrialist eager to make his mark. As a young man, Kaiser was groomed to advocate for public enterprise. From the early twentieth century, his father won contracts for some of the largest and most lucrative public works projects in the American West, including roads, freeways, bridges, dams, and ships. Vertically integrated, Kaiser Industries Corporation provided everything from the raw materials (cement, concrete, sand, gravel, and steel) to administrative and technical expertise. He launched his career during the New Deal, cutting his administrative teeth as shovel foreman on the Hoover Dam in 1930. Moving up the ranks in his father's expanding empire, Kaiser led crews on the Bonneville Dam and served as the general manager of Grand Coulee Dam construction. During World War II, he oversaw Kaiser shipyards in Portland, Oregon. He then took control of Kaiser automobile manufacturing enterprises, compounding his interest in transportation policy. In keeping with a venerable Bay Area tradition of business-oriented Progressivism, he supported public-sector promotion of economic development and growth.[14] And, like many of his colleagues in the BAC, Kaiser had both financial and ideological interests in improved infrastructure.

Together, Kaiser and McCarthy constituted a formidable coalition—a rising political star teamed up with a leader of industry, business, and labor. Kaiser initiated a study of the authority proposal through the BAC even before he met with McCarthy for the first time in July 1958. They decided to introduce legislation no later than February 1959, before an anticipated reapportionment of the state legislature reduced northern California's influence.[15] McCarthy would spearhead the effort in Sacramento, and under Kaiser, the BAC would coordinate and finance it, commissioning a major study of the Golden Gate Authority proposal, providing legal advice and publicity, and securing corporate support.[16]

A Metropolitan Solution

On Kaiser's recommendation, BAC trustees conferred $60,000 for a study of the Golden Gate Authority proposal by Coverdale & Colpitts, a nationally known transportation planning and engineering firm based in New York. Directed to document the need for metropolitan-level coordination in the Bay Area, the report's authors described the nine counties as "essentially [one] economic unit" that "as a whole has suffered from the lack of cohesion and regional planning brought about by its division into a multitude of independent agencies."[17] Building upon McCarthy's initial concept, they described an agency that would base its finances on bridge toll revenues, coordinate and upgrade the region's ports and airports for more efficient operation, develop new transportation facilities, and "plan for the further development of the Bay Area, not only upon economic and industrial lines, but . . . to provide residential, recreational and social facilities of value to all the citizens of the community."[18] Kaiser later downplayed the expectation that the Golden Gate Authority would evolve into a comprehensive planning agency, but privately he made it clear that he expected that the authority would not only "automatically" develop a master plan, but would also be a critical "start toward metropolitan government."[19] This was a key element of the authority's appeal to Kaiser and other BAC leaders, who believed that regional planning would not only rationalize and regulate growth, but also facilitate large-scale infrastructure and development projects.

The authority described in the Coverdale & Colpitts report would coordinate and administer ports at San Francisco, Oakland, Redwood City, Richmond, and Stockton, encouraging mutually beneficial development and the pooling of resources instead of the prevailing cutthroat competition. Unified management of the airports at San Francisco and Oakland would help accommodate rapidly increasing air traffic and reduce capital expenditures. Intraregional competition, redundancy, and waste would diminish, "strengthen[ing] the local competitive position with respect to other metropolitan areas," one of the primary goals of the BAC.[20] The authors of the report also considered the possibility of incorporating the Bay Area Rapid Transit (BART) District into the authority. Coverdale & Colpitts analysts estimated that the authority could take on the task of building a regional commuter rail system even without public subsidies, but ruled this out because of high costs and political difficulties. Instead, they recommended close coordination with BART officials and an eventual merger of the two agencies.[21]

In order to ensure its close association with big business and industry and its independence from local politicians, the authority would have a corporate management structure, giving "a business administration to what are essentially business functions."[22] Local chambers of commerce would formally nominate candidates for appointment to its board by county supervisors. The authority had to be "protected" from political pressures and avoid partisan politics. Local elected officials, with an inherent conflict of interest in representing the region as a whole, would be ineligible to serve on its board of directors. The authority would have a professional, expert staff that would be accountable only to its directors. But, the critical element of its administration was financial independence, as the authors of the Coverdale & Colpitts report explained: "The moment an Authority finds the need to rely on subsidies from political bodies, it finds itself subject to political considerations and its value as a businesslike concern disappears."[23]

Bay Area bridges were the key to the proposed Golden Gate Authority's finances. Bridge tolls could secure bonded debt for new transportation infrastructure, just as the bridge and tunnel tolls of the New York authority underwrote and subsidized less lucrative ventures. By the end of the 1950s, both the Golden Gate Bridge and the San Francisco-Oakland Bay Bridge (which Kaiser dubbed the "Great Fat Golden Cow") were generating large surpluses, and traffic was increasing steadily.[24] Bay Bridge toll revenue was ample enough to retire its $73 million in construction bonds in 1952, eighteen years ahead of schedule. Golden Gate Bridge revenues made it a strong second in net income, despite ongoing debt service: the terms of its bonds precluded early retirement. The report showed Bay Bridge and the Golden Gate Bridge earnings in 1957 to be $8.6 million and $2.6 million, respectively, and predicted increases for both. The tolls of the two bridges constituted nearly 80 percent of the net income of all of the targeted facilities. The Golden Gate Bridge and Highway District was estimated to have assets totaling $58 million (including the bridge itself and the district's considerable reserve funds), and the Bay Bridge, $103 million. The value of all Bay Area bridges (including the Dumbarton Bridge, the Carquinez Straights Bridge, and the Richmond–San Rafael Bridge) totaled $225 million dollars in 1957, nearly 60 percent of the value of all facilities slated for the authority.[25] All but one of the bridges in the Bay Area were under the control of the California Toll Bridge Authority, a state agency that was subject to a legislature and governor amenable to turning over these assets in the name of regional transportation planning. The only exception was the Golden Gate Bridge, the operation and administration of which was the sole function and purpose of the Golden Gate Bridge and Highway District.

When BAC trustees met to discuss the authority proposal in December 1958, Kaiser urged them to endorse it and accept their "proper leadership role" based on the idea that industry and business should be at the helm of regional government.[26] They adopted the Coverdale & Colpitts report unanimously, embarking upon a campaign not only to restructure the administration of transportation to promote growth and prosperity, but also to realize a corporatist vision of business-government association.[27] Once the Golden Gate Authority was established, it would have little outside accountability, but its processes would be streamlined and efficient. The transportation infrastructure necessary for sustained growth would be planned and financed without additional subsidies, difficult political negotiations, time-consuming public hearings, or the interference of state or federal agencies. BAC leaders envisioned day-to-day management in the hands of planners and economists guided by the "facts" of growth. They wanted to exclude the politicians who they saw as wasteful, arrogant, and inept, and whose petty schemes stood in the path of solid growth for the region as a whole and BAC members in particular. No longer would big business have to negotiate with small-town officials; instead, they could go directly to the business- and growth-oriented officials of the Golden Gate Authority.

BAC leaders launched an intensive, well-funded campaign for the authority, what Kaiser's assistant described as "an old-fashioned, six-month political slugfest."[28] They issued the Coverdale & Colpitts report publicly with a press release announcing the unanimous endorsement of the BAC trustees and board of governors, whose members represented "the who's who of Bay Area business," and its secondary board of governors, composed of Bay Area labor leaders. On December 10, 1958, Kaiser enthusiastically called for the Bay Area to "sweep away its cobwebs with this plan and move forward boldly and profitably . . . resolving the transportation problems which until now have threatened to stifle and choke

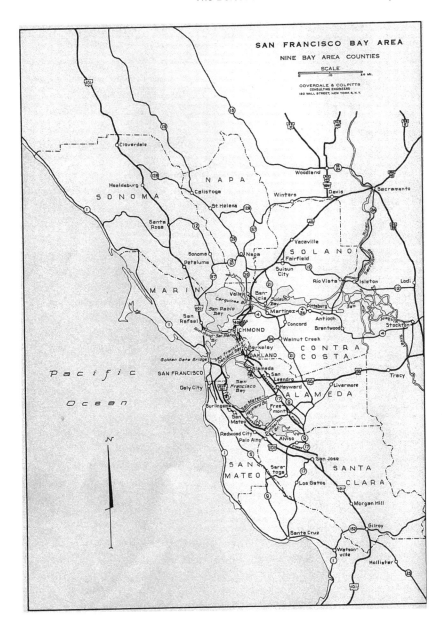

Map of the nine-county San Francisco Bay Area. From San Francisco Bay Area Council, *Report on a Proposed Public Authority for the Bay Area,* prepared by Coverdale & Colpitts (San Francisco, 1958).

off its economic greatness." He also anticipated the opposition of local governments: "a sensible halt is being called to the economic Balkanization of the Bay Area."[29] There was an imperative for regional action, Kaiser argued, and unless the authority was created, the state would intervene directly in Bay Area affairs. "We need economic home rule in this area. And that is what the Golden Gate Authority will provide."[30] Well-known BAC members spoke before business and civic groups around the Bay Area, and both Kaiser and McCarthy stumped relentlessly. Kaiser met with the editors and publishers of major Bay Area newspapers, who got behind the proposal immediately. He also maintained close contact with labor leaders, and personally led the lobbying effort in Sacramento.[31]

Working closely with Kaiser and BAC legal advisors, McCarthy introduced legislation to create the Golden Gate Authority in February 1959. McCarthy provided for the rapid acquisition of transportation facilities, with the transfer of the San Francisco-Oakland Bay Bridge and Golden Gate Bridge on July 1, 1960. Other Bay Area bridges would be turned over as soon as their debt could be refinanced, and the transfer, lease, or sale of regional ports and airports would be negotiated individually. The proposed authority's jurisdiction included all nine Bay Area counties: Alameda, Contra Costa, Marin, Napa, San Francisco, San Mateo, Santa Clara, Solano, and Sonoma.[32]

The Opposition

Golden Gate Authority proponents could rally behind the leadership of Kaiser and McCarthy, who set up a structured campaign with a clear chain of command. In contrast, their foes were relatively unorganized as the struggle commenced in 1959. Despite a lack of coordination, Golden Gate Authority opposition was well defined, arising almost exclusively from local government. Citing the intrinsic value of "home rule," elected officials, bureaucrats, and associates of cities, counties, and special districts, whose power, autonomy, and jurisdiction were threatened, immediately began fighting the proposal.

Hutchison and Wesley McClure, city manager of San Leandro, were among the first local officials to respond to the proposal. Hutchison embarked upon a political career after his retirement as dean of the University of California, Berkeley, College of Agriculture.[33] He took on the task of organizing local governments against the authority as the mayor of Berkeley, with the support of an activist city council, including T. J. Kent, founder of the University's Department of City and Regional Planning.[34] McClure, a career administrator, had already established himself as an active defender of "home rule," having successfully campaigned for the Bay Area Air Pollution Control District to be organized as a federation of local governments with city and county officials in control.[35] Hutchison and McClure turned to the League of California Cities to develop a list of specific objections to the authority. The league's executive director, Richard L. Carpenter, composed a "Statement of Principles." This document set out guidelines for judging proposed metropolitan agencies, emphasizing the protection of "local self-determination" by requiring that they be "responsible to the cities and counties within the district." Carpenter denounced the authority's capacity to develop a master plan for the area, the exclusion of county and city officials from its governing board, and the lack of "protections . . . for the governmental agencies which will be a part of the authority."[36] The statement asserted the sovereignty of municipal and county governments and flatly rejected the idea that metropolitan government should be independent of local politics or local government. It precluded the BAC goals of business-like government and comprehensive planning that were at the heart of the Golden Gate Authority proposal.

Hutchison distributed the "Statement of Principles" and called a meeting discuss the Golden Gate Authority in Berkeley on March 20, 1959. Kaiser anticipated his most significant opponents would be there, and was ready to present an impassioned speech to win their support.[37] He was never heard. Instead, McClure delivered a scathing report denouncing the authority to a receptive audience of mayors, councilmen, and city managers representing forty-two Bay Area cities. "[This] ill conceived and only partially matured proposal is now in the process of being sold to the general public and local government officials in an apparently well-financed and well-organized crash program of 'sweetness and light' publicity and personal visitations," McClure asserted. "It is ironical that the State Legislature is being asked to adopt not merely a monster, but a financially healthy monster, which, with built-in financing from all the lucrative revenue producing facilities of the area, can independently go its merry way . . . without regard to local government."[38] The assembled officials passed resolutions, one to request that the legislature defer the bill for further study, and another to form an area-wide council to study and oppose the authority. The resulting Planning Committee on Metropolitan Bay Area Problems met regularly over the next several months, its members working to create an alternative to the authority. It was from this seed of reaction that the Bay Area's council of governments grew.

Even as local government officials organized to protect "home rule," threatened Golden Gate Bridge and Highway District leaders worked to derail the Golden Gate Authority. In March, the bridge directors resolved unanimously to fight the proposal. Accordingly, Adam launched

Trouble brewing in the Balkans

San Francisco Chronicle, February 11, 1959.

a well-funded campaign to defend the bridge district. Already practiced in fending off legislation thanks to McCarthy's previous efforts, he did not waste any time in countering the BAC's publicity. Letters to county supervisors went out urging resolutions, and by the end of the month, the supervisors of Sonoma, Mendocino, Napa, Del Norte, Lake, and Humboldt counties were all on record against the authority.[39]

Bridge directors addressed political and civic groups around the Bay Area, describing McCarthy's proposed Golden Gate Authority as a self-interested political gambit aimed at boosting his own power. Director Matt A. Graham broadcast their objections over Marin County radio station KTIM. He also played the district's best card, the issue of tolls. Previous attempts to dissolve the bridge district had always relied heavily on the promise that under state administration Golden Gate Bridge tolls would be reduced or eliminated. Proponents of the Golden Gate Authority could offer no such promise, as bridge revenues were critical to their financing plans. Graham promised that "a substantial reduction in tolls on the Golden Gate Bridge can be made in the not too distant future if traffic continues to increase and as our bonded debt goes down," but he pointed out that "under McCarthy's bill, tolls on the Golden Gate Bridge could be increased . . . [and] diverted to other projects."[40] Understandably, Marin commuters would not want to bear a disproportionate burden for financing the entire region's infrastructure. But McCarthy believed that their best option was to free the toll proceeds that were locked in bridge district coffers and to use at least some of them to develop North Bay infrastructure. Although it was clear that the county was divided, some of the most powerful Marin organizations favored the authority. Marin County had always been the epicenter for bridge district criticism, and support for eliminating the bridge district outweighed concern about perpetual tolls.[41]

Realizing that they faced an uphill battle in Marin, bridge district representatives turned their attention to San Francisco supervisors, who had not taken an official stance on the bill. Bridge director Dan E. London addressed them twice, asserting that the Golden Gate Authority was unconstitutional and violated the rights of the district's bondholders.[42] Dion R. Holm, city attorney and staunch ally of the bridge district, also issued a statement questioning the legality of the measure. He pointed out that San Francisco would have a smaller proportion of representatives in the authority than they did on the bridge board (half of the fourteen bridge directors were from San Francisco).[43] Kaiser met with Holm and other San Francisco officials to address their concerns, but to no avail. He called the legal objections "extremely disturbing," pointing out that a large team of legal experts had been working on the project for months under the auspices of the BAC.[44]

Not only did bridge district officials have the resources to launch a publicity campaign, but they also had the funds and connections to counter BAC lobbying efforts. In anticipation of the fight, Adam hired a new assistant to cover his duties while he lobbied unofficially in Sacramento. Later, auditors revealed that he spent thousands of dollars gleaned from various bridge district accounts on unspecified incidentals, including $10,000 from a canceled engineering contract.[45] The district also retained Gordon Garland, former speaker of the California Assembly, as a full-time lobbyist with an unlimited expense account.[46] Like the proposed Golden Gate Authority, the bridge district had independent revenue and finances that Adam and the rest of its staff could easily mobilize to defend its interests.

By the time hearings began on the Golden Gate Authority in Sacramento in 1959, lists of resolutions both for and against the authority were growing long. Besides the northern bridge district counties, the cities of Fairfield and Ukiah officially opposed the takeover of the

Golden Gate Bridge, as did the Marin and Sonoma County Taxpayer's Associations, the Redwood Empire Association, the California Automobile Association, and the Sonoma Chamber of Commerce. Most Marin County labor leaders were against the authority, knowing that Golden Gate Bridge and Highway District contracts were much more likely to go to Marin workers than they would be if a region-wide agency was taking bids. In contrast, East Bay union leaders, bitterly antagonistic toward the anti-labor Oakland Port Commission, had nothing to lose and a lot to gain. BAC leaders advocated a mutually beneficial partnership between industrial leaders and labor representatives. Kaiser actively courted labor leaders and won the balance of their support.

The intensity of campaigning on both sides was reflected by the attention devoted to the issue by the press. Local radio stations broadcast regular programs discussing the authority proposal, and newspapers featured frequent front-page coverage and passionate editorials on the issue. This was the leading Bay Area story from its introduction in late 1958 until its final defeat in 1961. The next big story was the referendum on the massive regional rapid transit bond issue of 1962. Transportation problems were on the top of the regional agenda.

Over the course of the 1959 legislative session, amendments to the Golden Gate Authority bill answered almost all objections. By the end of March, legislators had removed all mandatory acquisitions of locally controlled transportation facilities except the Golden Gate Bridge, which McCarthy would never concede. They also changed the bill to allow for gubernatorial appointments in the hopes of quieting bickering over representation, but this only fanned the flames of local opposition.[47] These and many other alterations began to undermine the credibility of the proposal while doing little to reduce opposition. Nevertheless, supporters of the bill remained hopeful until the San Francisco supervisors passed a unanimous resolution against the bill. They called for nine amendments, including a guarantee of at least half of the authority's directors—the same representation that San Francisco had on the Golden Gate Bridge board.[48] This demand was a deal-killer; Alameda County had about the same population as San Francisco, and its leaders would never agree to let San Francisco dominate the authority.

Soon after San Francisco's negative resolution, Governor Edmund G. "Pat" Brown, who had recently made addressing metropolitan area problems an official priority of his administration,[49] went on record in favor of creating the authority, and the sooner the better: "Reasons can be found for delaying anything, but I am not so much afraid of getting ahead of ourselves as of falling behind."[50] It was too late. After six months of debate the Golden Gate Authority bill had been amended more than one hundred times, and the proposed agency's independence, power, and scale had been eroded dramatically. Editors of the *San Francisco Chronicle,* who had been enthusiastic supporters, commented that "the demise of the Authority proposal—as amended and re-amended by the Legislature—may prove a mercy killing. . . . [It] was so thoroughly emasculated in terms of representation, of power, function and duty, that enactment might have created more problems than it solved."[51]

Regional Home Rule: The ABAG Alternative

At end of the 1959 legislative session, McCarthy revamped the original bill to create and fund a temporary study group, the Golden Gate Authority Commission. The commission was made up of authority supporters appointed by the governor, including Kaiser and the state director of public works Robert Bradford. They were charged with developing a new bill for the 1961 legislative session.[52] They held twelve public hearings throughout the San Francisco Bay Area between February and August 1960, which were primarily dedicated to negotiating the acquisition of individual facilities.

The first two hearings focused on state toll bridges, and testimony indicated that state representatives would not oppose the authority. Bradford, whose department included the California Toll Bridge Authority, made it clear that he believed that the authority's jurisdiction should not be compromised by petty local protests. He remarked, "if the Golden Gate Authority idea is a good one for the Bay Bridge, it is a good one for the Carquinez Strait bridges; if it is a good one for those bridges, it is good for the San Mateo Bridge, and it is a good one for the Golden Gate Bridge."[53]

Hearings also revealed that most locally controlled transportation facilities would be transferred without opposition if the governments with an interest in them were either compensated or relieved of a financial burden. The Port of San Francisco could easily be incorporated as long as its bonded indebtedness was taken over. The Port of Richmond, owned by the City of Richmond but leased to private shipping companies, would also pose little problem as long as the leases were renegotiated favorably (profits from the facility were negligible). Redwood City's port, in contrast, netted the city $700,000 during the previous year, and its representatives wanted its full market value plus a public vote before turning it over to the authority. The city of San Jose, whose municipal airport was slated for expansion in the decade to come, raised concerns about adequate representation, but expected that the authority would relieve its financial burden. Representatives of the City of Vallejo and

Solano and Napa counties opposed the inclusion of the Carquinez Bridge because of tolls, but that facility was state owned and there was little they could do about it.[54]

The Oakland Port Commission presented a greater challenge. Both Oakland's port and airport were run by five commissioners who were nominated by the mayor and appointed by the city council, serving without compensation for six-year terms. An executive director and chief engineer oversaw operations. The commissioners maintained their own legal and public relations departments.[55] The Alameda Labor Council voiced strong support for the authority, as did executives of several important shipping companies, the powerful Bechtel Corporation, and the Oakland Chamber of Commerce. However, the executive director of the Port of Oakland, Dudley Frost, presented a list of twelve demands, including equal representation for Alameda and San Francisco counties, the oversight and approval of port commissioners on all negotiations for the takeover, the simultaneous transfer of the San Francisco and Oakland airports. He also wanted the elimination of collective bargaining provisions. Most of these conditions were met by the new legislation. In January 1961, both the Port of Oakland and the Oakland City Council endorsed the Golden Gate Authority.[56]

The Golden Gate Bridge was the only facility that merited two hearings, one in San Rafael in May and an October hearing in San Francisco. Closely watched by the region's press, both hearings embarrassed the defenders of the Golden Gate Bridge by highlighting the problems with bridge district administration. George P. Anderson, an elderly director from Mendocino County who had promoted the bridge in the 1920s, spoke for the bridge district in San Rafael. Anderson read a lengthy statement against the authority, citing the rights of bridge bondholders, the prospect of perpetual tolls, and the lack of representation for the northern bridge district counties. However, he was nearly defenseless against the inquiry that followed, which resembled a hostile cross-examination by commission members. Anderson faced questions the bridge district's large staff, legal team, well-paid director and chief engineer, and high maintenance costs. He protested that other state-operated bridges had high "hidden costs," which increased "the further away you get from local control." Commission members pointed out that the bridge district had reserve funds and high tolls, but that its directors unwilling to spend them on transportation improvements. Anderson denied this, but could not cite any specific plans. Bridge director Leland S. Murphy responded to questions about district's public relations and lobbying expenses by pointing out that McCarthy had spent equivalent amounts on promoting the bill. The response by William S. Downing, Kaiser's personal representative, was quick and forceful. He pointed out that "not one penny" of public money had been spent on behalf of the authority, but that all of the promotional efforts were conducted by the BAC with private funds. The Golden Gate Bridge's advertising and lobbying money was public.[57]

Golden Gate Authority Commission members made it clear at the May hearing that they saw bridge district policy as flagrantly defying the public interest, but they were even less sympathetic at the San Francisco hearing in October 1960. This time, bridge district heavy hitters, including Adam and consulting engineer Arthur Jenkins, accompanied Anderson. The hearing started with testimony in favor of including the Golden Gate Bridge. A representative of the state attorney general offered the opinion that the bridge was legally the property of California. This produced emotional testimony from Anderson: "The Golden Gate Bridge belongs to the people of the District whose property is mortgaged to pay those bonds . . . we claim, and we hold, that the Golden Gate Bridge belongs to the Golden Gate Bridge and Highway District."[58] Finally, the commissioners presented Adam with a list of hostile questions regarding bridge district finances.[59] Anderson complained about being humiliated during the previous hearing in San Rafael, and both the commissioners and the bridge district representatives accused the other of having preconceived, unjustified prejudices. By the end of the hearing, it was clear that the commissioners would fight to the end to dissolve the bridge district and take over the bridge, and that bridge district officials would oppose the authority with their dying breath.

Immediately following the hearings on the Golden Gate Bridge, the *San Francisco Examiner* featured a three-day investigative series lambasting the bridge district. Detailing extravagant spending and waste, it concluded with a strong editorial call for state legislators to dissolve the bridge district by passing the Golden Gate Authority bill.[60] Undeterred by negative publicity, bridge district officials continued working against it. A San Francisco radio commentator remarked: "It seems likely that the district directors feel that they have built up a tidy little empire and, by gum, they don't want to let it go."[61]

Golden Gate Authority Commission hearings included the introduction of a new organizational opponent to the Golden Gate Authority, in addition to the Golden Gate Bridge and Highway District. The local officials who had been working to protect their autonomy from the authority finally had their answer to demands for a regional planning agency: the Association of Bay Area Governments (ABAG). Hutchison first described ABAG at the June hearing in Berkeley on the subject of "Governmental Aspects of a Regional Bay Area Authority." Although it was still just an idea, Hutchison described ABAG as an alternative to the authority, which he asserted was not in the region's best interests because it was not "politically responsible to the existing cities and counties."[62] ABAG would be a voluntary organization made up of a single representative of each city and county in the Bay Area. Its members would discuss and develop recommendations on metropolitan area problems, but would have no power to act on them. Hutchison suggested that more "single-purpose metropolitan-type districts . . . appointed by the elective officials of the cities and counties" could continue to fill the gaps in local government and actually carry out limited regional policy.[63] The Golden Gate Bridge and Highway District was one such agency. It was not the corporate form, regional scale, or independent financing of the proposed Golden Gate Authority that local government officials objected to—it was its capacity for authoritative regional planning, and with it the potential to impose policy or restrict the options of local governments.

Commission members were immediately antagonistic to the concept of ABAG. They suggested that the city and county representatives were opposing regional "supergovernment" while at the same time proposing to administer one themselves. Thomas Lantos, an economist at San Francisco State University testifying in favor of the authority, pointed out frankly that the authority was "an attempt to curb the [influence] of cities and counties in regional matters," and opposed their demands that mayors and city council members be allowed to sit on its board. "One doesn't ask a dying man to prescribe his own cure. He would have done so long before, if he could have."[64] Commission members pointedly observed that ABAG representation would have no relationship to population whatsoever, suggesting that the claim that it would be closer to the people was specious. In response, Hutchison asserted that ABAG's lack of power made representation immaterial: "This Association of Bay Area Governments has no authority. All it can do is recommend. . . . We would hope that once it got started it would command some respect from the Legislature of the State of California, and we might want to make recommendations to the Legislature."[65] The large but toothless proposed agency garnered ridicule from commissioners, but Hutchison was undaunted and began the effort to enroll members.

Overall, the hearings were successful from the perspective of the authority's proponents. The region's press covered them in detail, and although the testimony included plenty of opposition, there was an obvious pattern of general support with specific objections. A technical report released in December reviewed the financial status of the facilities to be included in the proposal and concluded that a regional transportation authority was politically viable and urgently needed.[66] The commission's final report outlined recommendations for new legislation, which was expected to pass easily. The counties of Alameda, Contra Costa, Marin, San Francisco, San Mateo, and Solano would be immediately included, all on record as supporting the proposal.[67] Sonoma and Napa counties, loyal to the bridge district, were excluded, as was Santa Clara County, due to concerns about perpetual tolls on the Carquinez Bridge. All of these facilities could be brought into the new agency later with a petition. The composition of the governing board fully answered demands for representation of and accountability to local governments. It would have eighteen members, for the most part appointed by county supervisors: three from San Francisco (one to be appointed by the mayor), three from Alameda (one appointed by the Oakland City Council), two from San Mateo, two from Contra Costa, one from Marin, and one from Solano. The director of the state department of public works would also serve on the board, and the governor would appoint at-large representatives from the "West Bay" and the "East Bay," as well as a bridge district representative until its construction bonds were retired in 1971.[68] Local officials would be allowed on the board, though this was "permissive rather than mandatory, since . . . lay members are likely to feel more freedom from local commitments and view the region more objectively."[69] This revised proposal maintained the power and scope of the agency while making concessions to local government in an attempt to re-cast the Golden Gate Authority as "an extension of local government rather than a superimposed level of authority."[70]

Nevertheless, local government officials led by Hutchison continued to work frantically behind the scenes to stave off the authority. Regardless of the composition of its governing board, they were opposed to its potential power. They used the California Joint Exercise of Powers Act, which was passed in 1921 during an earlier period of interest in regional government, to create ABAG. The act allowed existing governments to form a new agency—with the approval of a majority of the cities and counties in its proposed jurisdiction—to take over functions that they were already authorized to perform individually. When San Mateo supervisors voted to ally with the counties of Alameda, Contra Costa, Marin, and Santa Clara, ABAG finally had the membership it needed to become a legal entity (despite the conspicuous absence of San Francisco and Oakland). Hutchison presided over its first formal meeting in February 1961 as its new chairman.[71] Organized and united at last, local politicians opposing regional planning could argue that metropolitan planning could take place through ABAG, making a Golden Gate Authority unnecessary.

Still, by all indications public opinion and a majority of state legislators supported the Golden Gate Authority. Editors of all the major Bay Area newspapers supported it, including the *San Francisco Examiner*, the

San Francisco Chronicle, the *Oakland Tribune,* and the *Marin Independent Journal.* Jenkins remarked on their wholehearted endorsements: "Obviously, the heavy contributors of advertising will have the advantage. . . . All one needs to do is look at the personalities behind the Golden Gate Authority to draw a conclusion from where the advertising money most freely flows."[72] Golden Gate Bridge officials compiled a long list of resolutions against the proposed authority, but mostly from minor civic associations and small cities and counties outside of the Bay Area. The most populous counties, prosperous chambers of commerce, and powerful civic groups supported the authority. The senate bill to create it, introduced on March 2, 1961, had twenty-five authors (out of forty senators), including the majority of Bay Area senators.[73]

One Marin County commentator predicted that, because the effort for a regional transportation agency was obviously gaining momentum, "the bridge folks will come out swinging."[74] True to form, the bridge district campaign against the authority intensified. Adam sent a copy of the new bill to all of the bridge directors and district counties and state representatives, followed by a detailed and highly critical "summary digest" prepared by bridge district attorneys. The directors passed another unanimous resolution that was mailed to counties, congressmen, and city councils all over the Bay Area. On the same day, the bridge district president Matt Graham addressed the San Francisco supervisors, stressing the financial interest and potential tax liability that San Francisco had in the Golden Gate Bridge. Marin's two bridge directors, Graham and Murphy, spoke before the Marin County supervisors on April 18, finally winning over this last bastion of resistance. One concurring supervisor remarked, "the directors have made some errors, have had some criticisms, but have made money for the people of the six counties and have decreased tolls. I think we'd be very foolish to slap them in the face, and also this bill smacks of super-government."[75] By a vote of three to two, Marin supervisors condemned the authority proposal. In early May, the text of a speech by Graham to the Sausalito City Council was mailed to cities around the Bay Area. Bridge district officials sent yet another resolution condemning the assembly version of the bill to Bay Area county supervisors, the governor and other officials in Sacramento, all state assembly members from the region, and Senator Randolph Collier.[76] No one could deny their determination to protect the bridge district.

The Senate Transportation Committee had to approve the bill before it could go to the legislature for a vote. At this critical juncture, the behind-the-scenes influence of bridge district allies came into play. Collier, who represented Del Norte, the smallest, northernmost bridge district county, chaired the committee. Known as the "silver fox," Collier built his power base in rural northern California by advocating state highway construction.[77] One reporter described him as a "shaggy, white-maned power in Sacramento who is called the 'father of the freeway system.'"[78] He was certainly a leader in California transportation policy, and had a real stake in maintaining control over state bridges. Collier pointed out the measure would "take millions of dollars of state property and turn it over to a commission and gives no one in the rest of the state any voice in the matter at all."[79] His political interest in supporting the Golden Gate Bridge and Highway District was even more immediate. Not only was a bridge district directorship a rare sinecure for Collier's small rural district, but the district paid thousands of dollars a year to the Redwood Empire Association as its largest contributor, and REA members won a large proportion of its half-million-dollar annual advertising budget.[80] REA members were among Collier's most important constituents. Later, a former director recalled that he was the "godfather of the bridge district, he was the watchdog."[81]

When Senate Transportation Committee hearings commenced, Collier welcomed a parade of bridge defenders testifying against the authority. Anderson, representing both the REA and the bridge district as its newly appointed president, acted as the facilitator for the case against the bill, calling witnesses whose testimony touched on every possible criticism. Collier introduced Anderson as an "old title man like myself, a friend of many, many years for the last 40 at least."[82] Collier refused to limit the length of presentations against the bill or to allow hostile questioning; he repeatedly interrupted and cut off McCarthy, who was a member of the committee and was obviously infuriated. Collier extended hearings on the bill several times to allow more testimony against it. Some witnesses in favor of the bill had to appear three times before they were heard, and many never spoke at all. When they finally got the floor, proponents of the authority could only summarize their case. They cited public opinion, listed resolutions, and described the twelve Bay Area hearings, but had definitely been upstaged by the opposition.

After two weeks of testimony, a six-to-six vote of the committee effectively killed the authority bill. This outcome suggested careful orchestration: if the bill had been defeated outright, it could have been reintroduced through another committee during that session. Instead, more hearings were scheduled before another vote of Collier's committee. An assembly version of the bill passed easily by a vote of fifty-four to fourteen—only two of the eighteen Bay Area assemblymen opposed it. It obviously had sufficient support to pass it in the senate as well, but it would never make it to the floor for a vote because of Collier's opposition. The editors of both the *San Francisco Examiner* and the *San Francisco Chronicle* blamed Senator Collier and the "imperial directors of the

Golden Gate Bridge and Highway District" for the defeat of the authority.[83] *Examiner* editors pointed out that the three senators on Collier's committee who voted against the bill represented only 900,000 people, while its supporters spoke for nearly nine million.[84] They vented their rage: "Senators dominated by rural thinking and suspicions act[ed] in concert to defeat a measure necessary to the orderly growth of a metropolitan area . . . the most promising of all the efforts made through the years to unify the Bay Area economically, and to lay the foundations for a form of metropolitan government."[85] Kaiser answered for the bill's loss to BAC trustees, attributing its defeat to Collier's influence and the bridge district's "well-financed lobbying campaign against the bill."[86] McCarthy, in a Marin radio interview, remarked that he was "very sentimental" about the defeat of the measure, and explained circumstances that Collier was also aware of: "Chairman Collier . . . is very close to the Golden Gate Bridge and Highway District. They spent I would say sixteen to seventeen thousand dollars on lobbying. They had many counties to the north . . . concerned with the $25,000 [annual contribution to] the Redwood Empire Association. Their public relations man and the staff worked very hard to create this feeling. It was a wrong way to spend funds to create that emotional feeling."[87] McCarthy launched a fresh set of attacks on the Golden Gate Bridge and Highway District. In 1962, he announced eight major charges against the agency, a grand jury investigation, and new legislation for its dissolution and state control of the bridge.[88] But he alone was no match for the bridge district—this was the closest McCarthy would come to slaying his dragon.

The bridge district honored Collier after the close of the 1961 session with a special "victory dinner," where he described and explained his efforts against the Golden Gate Authority to the directors and top staff. Collier also received warm thank-you notes from several district officials, including an invitation to stay at San Francisco's St. Francis Hotel as the guest of the hotel manager, bridge director Dan E. London.[89] Collier had been a willing agent of local government, effectively using his senatorial committee to defeat a popular proposal supported by the ruling elite in both Sacramento and the Bay Area. The state legislature, always a blunt instrument, could much more easily obstruct change than initiate it. The senate, heavily overrepresenting rural areas, could be reliably manipulated to favor "home rule" and "local control" in defiance of urban or metropolitan area interests.

Abandoning hope for a regional transportation authority, BAC leaders conceded defeat in 1961.[90] They chose Stephen D. Bechtel, the head of another Bay Area corporate giant invested in the construction of transportation infrastructure and public works, to succeed Kaiser as BAC president.[91] In his abdication speech, Kaiser cited public support for the

The Jolly undertakers

San Francisco Chronicle, June 11, 1961.

Golden Gate Authority as evidence that regional cooperation could still prevail. He also announced BAC support for ABAG. Kaiser and the other pragmatic BAC leaders knew that ABAG, specifically designed to undermine regional planning, had become the most viable organization to perform that function.[92]

Local officials who opposed regional planning and government designed ABAG, and its structure and rules reflected their views and priorities. Any city or county could withdraw its membership at any time, and ABAG had no means of enforcing its planning recommendations.[93] Population determined its dues but not its representation, which heavily favored small political entities. All ABAG recommendations required a majority vote of both the county and the municipal representatives of its general assembly, which was composed of one representative from each member county and city and met only twice a year. The executive council, which drafted recommendations assisted by a five-member professional staff, met four times a year and included a representative of each county and one mayor or city councilman from within each county. Seven standing committees met informally to discuss specific regional problems. ABAG's stated purposes were to "review governmental proposals" and to "study metropolitan area problems." It had no mechanisms for developing policy or taking action. ABAG generated discussion and debate—and little else.[94]

As intended, ABAG's very limited powers and awkward structure prevented its development into an effective planning body: the entities that most opposed regional planning, small cities and counties, controlled the agency. Ten years after its creation, when the political climate was even more favorable to regional planning, several attempts to expand ABAG's authority failed. The organization would probably not have survived very long if it were not for new federal planning requirements in 1966. Yet, its existence thwarted attempts to create a new, more authoritative entity. Once it had been formed, proposed regional agencies not only had to overcome the inevitable resistance of local officials, but they also had to compete against ABAG. Despite its crippling structural limitations, ABAG officials fought to maintain its status as the region's principal planning agency.

At the time of its creation, ABAG was just one of seven councils of governments (COGs) in the nation, but by 1972 there were three hundred with regional planning responsibilities. Like ABAG, many were created specifically to prevent a more authoritative agency from infringing upon the sovereignty of local governments, but unlike ABAG, they were also usually created in response to federal regional planning requirements. The Demonstration Cities and Metropolitan Development Act of 1966 required the review of federal grants by an areawide agency; ABAG won that designation and federal funding along with it, as did COGs throughout the country. The 1968 Intergovernmental Coordination Act and the Office of Management and Budget circular A-95 further empowered COGs, and many also fulfilled federal transportation planning requirements in the 1970s and 1980s.[95] Among planning advocates, they became notorious obstacles to meaningful governmental coordination: COGs represented local interests and served as bulwarks protecting a decentralized, federalist system of government. One political scientist remarked in 1981 that "no COG has solved a major problem."[96] Their lack of power was fundamental to their purpose.

The proposed Golden Gate Authority, ironically, shared many of the characteristics that made the Golden Gate Bridge and Highway District such a formidable opponent. Both bridge district officials and authority advocates embraced a business model of public administration and held financial independence to be paramount. Arthur Jenkins stated this principle clearly in a 1959 bridge district planning survey: "Although the Golden Gate bridge is publicly owned and operated, and is a nonprofit entity, it is essentially parallel to a private corporation as to its functional mission. . . . Operation and administration of the Golden Gate Bridge is big business and must be conducted as such if the interests of the public are to be fully protected."[97] Bridge district officials frequently cited budget surpluses as evidence of its success and legitimacy—the same surpluses that toll payers saw as evidence of abuse. The only facilities that were never exempted from the proposed authority or transportation commission were those that generated significant revenue: bridges. Both agencies were intentionally insulated from political pressure and oversight. State legislators created the bridge district with broad powers and almost no accountability, and its officials could use toll revenues as they saw fit. A Golden Gate Authority would have had even greater autonomy, with independent revenue and almost unlimited capacity to build new facilities and expand its jurisdiction. While any new bridge district bonds required public approval, the Golden Gate Authority could issue bonds at its officials' discretion. The bridge district faced possible dissolution with the retirement of its debt in 1971, but Golden Gate Authority officials could have taken on new projects and new responsibilities indefinitely.

Had the Golden Gate Authority come into being, the San Francisco Bay Area would be a very different place. The authority would be a powerful engine for growth and development: self-financing, independent, and inherently interested in expanding. It was to be a public agency that would have a corporate outlook and would pursue business objectives, including expansion to maximize profits. Many more bridges and transportation routes would link the city to the greater Bay Area, which would probably be much denser with more industrial development. But, this account is not intended to speculate on fates avoided or opportunities missed. Instead, it describes what actually *did* come out of the struggle over the authority, including the formation of ABAG and the continued decentralization of transportation administration and policy-making. The defeat of the Golden Gate Authority represented a remarkable triumph of local government officials acting to protect their autonomy and power. It demonstrates how metropolitan area governmental fragmentation was self-perpetuating; growing numbers of special districts supported "home rule," allying with local governments. This dynamic turned out to be crucial in determining the outcome of efforts to achieve regional government and planning in the late 1960s.

The success of bridge district officials in opposing the Golden Gate Authority is a testament to the power of special districts. They were up against the Bay Area growth machine on a grand scale, and the very survival of their agency was at stake. Their success was all the more impressive because they were fighting another threat to the institutional integrity of the bridge district at the same time, in the form of rapid transit to Marin. The defeat of the Golden Gate Authority was a major victory for the bridge district, but it was also a prelude to a larger struggle against comprehensive regional government in the decade to come. In the San Francisco Bay Area and throughout the country, regionalism was crushed by the collective weight of existing local governments.

Chapter 5

Rapid Transit Versus the Golden Gate Bridge

Until 1962, there was every reason to expect that Marin County would be included in the Bay Area Rapid Transit (BART) system. Plans for the regional rail system released both in 1953 and in 1956 included a line extending across the bay to the north via the Golden Gate Bridge, to be built during the first stage of construction. Engineering studies confirmed the feasibility of adding rails to the bridge. Marin County civic and business leaders enthusiastically supported bringing BART to the North Bay, anticipating a windfall of development, increased property values, and general economic growth. Local politicians applauded Jack McCarthy, a leading proponent of BART in the state senate, for his efforts on behalf of the system. It was not until Golden Gate Bridge and Highway District officials decided to oppose BART plans that rapid transit for Marin County came into question. Guided by the analysis and strategy of bridge district engineer Arthur C. Jenkins, they waged a covert campaign to stop the BART district from competing for toll revenues or infringing on bridge district autonomy.

Efforts to thwart plans for BART to Marin pitted bridge district officials against their most loyal constituents, North Bay boosters and real estate investors. Politically, bridge directors could not directly oppose BART and hope to keep their appointments, and a significant minority among them openly favored rapid transit. Nevertheless, they were well aware that the prospect of a rail system on the bridge posed a direct threat to bridge district autonomy by introducing a rival public agency into its jurisdiction, one that could potentially reduce toll revenues, or even worse, make a claim on surplus toll revenue for subsidies. In addition, Jenkins, general manager James Adam, and influential directors questioned the advisability and desirability of rapid transit for the bridge district in general. While Jenkins and his allies could do little to prevent regional rapid transit for the rest of the Bay Area, they could and did mobilize the resources of the bridge district against its extension to the North Bay. Bridge district officials used the expert authority of engineers to ensure that Marin was excluded from the BART district before its bonds went before voters in November 1962, and manipulated engineering studies to secure an "authoritative 'no'" on the feasibility of running BART trains on the bridge. Their success illustrates the power of special district officials acting behind the scenes to influence public policy, taking advantage of the resources, independence, and protection from public accountability of a well-funded, autonomous special district.

Marin County and Mass Transportation

The original backers of the Golden Gate Bridge expected it to stimulate growth and development in the North Bay. Marin boosters envisioned their county's transformation from a largely rural area with a predominantly agricultural economy to an important suburban extension of the San Francisco metropolitan area. They saw the bridge as just one element of the varied and extensive system that was needed to adequately connect suburb and city. During the bond campaign of 1930, Golden Gate Bridge promoters promised voters that streetcar lines would run across the bridge.[1] Nevertheless, after the bridge was funded and approved, transit plans were ruled out, though not because of engineering or safety concerns. Mass transportation was in a precipitous decline across the country, and bridge engineers unanimously favored an all-automobile bridge because "it was useless to provide surface tracks in view of the non-existence of facilities on either side to connect with them," and predicted that the only feasible future service would be provided with "modern buses." However, as consulting engineer Charles Derleth noted, "the people are clamoring."[2] Marin boosters, unconvinced that automobiles would take over completely, still wanted trains to run from San Francisco to the North Bay. Bridge engineers assured them that "the future addition of rapid transit tracks" was still possible.[3]

Twenty years later, Marin boosters were again clamoring for trains from San Francisco to Marin across the Golden Gate Bridge. McCarthy, who was assigned to the Senate Interim Committee on San Francisco Bay Area Metropolitan Rapid Transit (in addition to heading a senate committee investigating the Golden Gate Bridge), helped establish the Bay Area Rapid Transit Commission in 1951, working closely with some of the same Bay Area Council members who supported the Golden Gate Authority. Stephen D. Bechtel, the founder and first president of the BAC, was probably its leading individual backer. Other prominent and wealthy BART advocates included Edgar F. Kaiser, banker Mortimer Fleishhacker, James D. Zellerbach, Bank of America executive Carl F.

Wente, and Arthur Dolan of the investment banking firm Blythe & Company. The chairman of the BART commission, Allan Browne, was Bank of America vice president in charge of municipal bonds, and the first BART district president, Adrien J. Falk, was a member of the BAC executive board and president of the California Chamber of Commerce. Critics have charged that self-interested bankers and industrialists conceived the system, hoping to "Manhattanize" San Francisco for their own profit and glory. Certainly BART's major sponsors did not apologize for their vision of a great, centralized metropolitan region, integrated and unified through transportation infrastructure. Nor did they disguise their interest in maintaining the global prominence, vitality, and absolute centrality of San Francisco's downtown—a goal that later worked against BART leaders as they sought support from business and civic leaders of smaller, competing downtown areas.[4]

Marin fit into this vision as a suburban tributary, benefiting from traffic relief and increased property values while shoring up the financial base of the BART system. A 1953 BART commission report noted that Highway 101 was "the county's only means of ingress and egress" and that if predictions were correct, before long "five highways of the capacity of U.S. Highway 101 would be required to accommodate traffic."[5] Pacific Greyhound buses served some Marin commuters, and although they provided the only mass transportation service to the North Bay, patronage was dropping steadily. The company lost $1.5 million on its Marin lines in 1950, with passenger trips declining from 7.3 million in 1947 to 5.2 million in 1951.[6] A fare increase, approved by the Public Utilities Commission in March 1956, brought ridership even lower, and soon Greyhound was looking for a way to end its service.[7] The authors of the BART commission report asserted that "the expected growth of Marin County poses a transportation problem that is insolvable except by some system of mass transit." They predicted that the high quality and convenience of rapid rail transit would appeal to the affluent commuters who eschewed Greyhound buses, particularly as traffic congestion on the Golden Gate Bridge made driving increasingly difficult.

The question of the engineering feasibility of the Marin line first arose in 1955. Local boosters and politicians were dismayed by an unexpected announcement that Marin would not be included in the first stage of BART construction. BART representatives cited the high probable costs of construction as well as the doubts of bridge district officials about the bridge's structural capacity to accommodate them.[8] An uproar ensued both north and south of the Golden Gate, as San Francisco and Marin newspaper editors proclaimed the planned northern BART line to be vital and irreplaceable. Almost immediately, Marin was reinstated, pending further investigation.[9] A few months later, BART engineers confidently reported the results of their study, concluding that rails could be easily and safely installed below the deck of the Golden Gate Bridge. Prudence required rebuilding sidewalks, roadways and railings to reduce weight, but the engineers found that a "considerable reserve capacity exists in the Golden Gate Bridge."[10]

The first comprehensive plans for BART, released in a colorful, over-

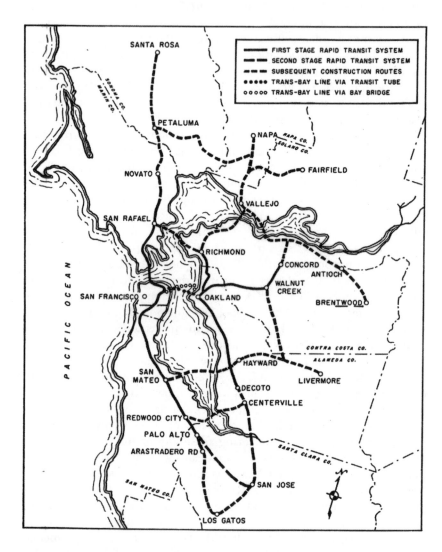

Map of proposed BART routes, from San Francisco Bay Area Rapid Transit Commission, *Proposed Bay Area Rapid Transit System,* prepared by Parsons, Brincker-hoff, Hall, and MacDonald, Engineers (Sacramento, 1956).

sized report designed to win public support in 1956, detailed a three-phase plan for a nine-county transit system.[11] A Marin County line, traversing the Golden Gate Bridge and extending through San Rafael nearly to the northern border of the county, was included in the first-phase "minimum plan." According to BART engineers, none of the required bridge alterations would be particularly difficult, interfere with traffic, or diminish its structural strength.[12] However, all of the financial tables at the end of the report included subtotals for the first phase of the project excluding Marin County. The reasons for leaving Marin out this time had nothing to do with engineering—they were entirely financial. Property taxes would secure BART's initial bonds and help pay for its construction, capital costs, and operation. Of all of the counties included in initial plans, Marin had by far the lowest assessed value, $135,000 in 1956. The next lowest was San Mateo at $520,000, and both San Francisco and Alameda topped $1 million. Marin County property comprised only 3 percent of the assessed value of all Bay Area counties, and only 4 percent of the value of the five counties to be included in the first phase of construction.[13] Moreover, even with toll revenue from the Golden Gate Bridge subsidizing construction, extending BART to Marin would be very expensive. Estimated construction costs for the Marin line alone ranged from $122 million to $137 million in 1956, more than 20 percent of the budget for the entire project.[14] The editor of Marin's daily *Independent Journal* warned of the danger of Marin's last-minute exclusion: "In the tabulation of costs the bookkeepers have handily added up a subtotal excluding Marin, [and] the consultants have made it easy, almost suggested, that Marin be eliminated from the first step."[15] Despite this, Marin demographics promised high ridership; the county's median income was second only to San Mateo's among the counties to be served by the system, which was designed to attract exactly the sort of well-paid, professional workers that Marin County exported on a daily basis. As chairman of the Senate Interim Committee on BART, McCarthy ensured that when state legislators approved the Bay Area Rapid Transit District in 1957, it included all five original counties: Alameda, Contra Costa, San Francisco, San Mateo, *and* Marin.[16]

As an organization, the new BART district had striking similarities to the bridge district. It was authorized to issue general obligation bonds, it had the power of eminent domain, and it had minimal requirements for public accountability or oversight. Like their Golden Gate Bridge counterparts nearly three decades before, new BART officials, including president Adrien Falk, general manager John M. Pierce, and chief engineer Kenneth M. Hoover, had to win voter approval for its financing. To achieve the required majority, Marin voters had to be convinced that rails would actually reach the North Bay.

Survival Through Rubber Tires

Though they did not know it, BART officials had a formidable opponent in bridge district engineer Arthur C. Jenkins. "The Bay Area is still young enough," the authors of the 1965 BART report claimed, "for its over-all economic development to be purposefully molded into a desired pattern, according to the long-range needs and desires of its population."[17] Jenkins disagreed—he saw mass transportation as an enterprise that was no longer viable, and BART as folly. And, he was willing to do whatever he could to protect the public and the bridge district from its perils.

Jenkins's professional life had been intertwined with the decline of mass transportation in California. After graduating with a degree in engineering from the University of California, Berkeley in 1931, Jenkins began his career as a civil engineer, rising steadily through the ranks of the California Public Utilities Commission. From a rare vantage point, Jenkins witnessed first-hand the downfall of private transit companies as they suffered cascading financial disaster. He handled the applications of franchise holders to increase fares, cut back routes, or end service entirely, all of which required state permission. He recalled that "in each instance where abandonment of a rail line was proposed by the transit companies, there was great opposition by public and city officials, and in some cases the counties and the state. Long series of hearings were held before the State Public Utilities Commission . . . the same was true with respect to substitution of buses for rail lines in the interest of economy. Throughout this process of transformation, the public as individuals indicated its choice by shifting to the automobile."[18] While recognizing that there was strong political support for mass transportation, Jenkins interpreted this as a more compelling message from consumers, who chose private automobiles and supported subsidies for roads and highways to accommodate them.

While working for the Public Utilities Commission, Jenkins helped shape transportation policy in both the Bay Area and Los Angeles.[19] Early on, he supported the replacement of streetcars and rails with buses. In 1939 he delivered an address on "The Future of Urban and Interurban Transportation" at the University of Southern California. "The rubber-tired trackless vehicle has established itself permanently in the field of passenger transit and its continued growth and development can be expected," Jenkins predicted, "not only in providing service to new areas but [also in the] replacement of existing rail service. Due to its rapid development during recent years and the traditional place in society occupied by the rail car, the motor coach has not met with full public approval, but when the masses are acquainted with its desirable

Arthur C. Jenkins, circa 1945. Family photograph collection of Wende Mintz.

features and the strides being made in engineering and research in an attempt to develop a vehicle which will afford the maximum comfort, speed, safety, durability, and adequacy of service, the existing resentment will be for the most part dispelled."[20] Jenkins believed that prolonging the life of older technologies was merely delaying the inevitable at the expense of both private companies and taxpayers.

During World War II, Jenkins left the Public Utilities Commission to take command of automotive and passenger transit operations for the Twelfth Naval District, which was headquartered in the Bay Area and included California, Nevada, Utah, and Colorado. After the war, he was licensed as a mechanical and electrical engineer, and received further training in industrial relations, military law, and public relations as a Naval reserve officer. Jenkins served briefly as transportation manager for the Key System Transit Lines in Oakland, which operated an extensive though rapidly declining streetcar system in the East Bay.[21] Jenkins also influenced the development of San Francisco's transit system as a consultant to the city. In 1949 he declared a proposed subway to be unnecessary and expensive, advising instead that express buses and traffic control techniques be adopted to alleviate traffic problems. The subway was rejected.[22]

At the time, transit companies all over the country, many of which were created to support land speculation and development schemes rather than as independent profit-making ventures, had already succumbed to the automobile or were in the process of going out of business. Overcapitalization, poor management, neglected equipment, onerous fare regulations, labor problems, and public antagonism, as well as a rapid loss of riders to private automobiles, all contributed to transit's financial ruin.[23] Private companies were begging to be released from the obligations of their charters. Over the next decade, while working part-time for the bridge district, Jenkins helped clear the ruins of streetcar lines and railways and replace them with bus systems in San Diego, Fresno, Phoenix, Long Beach, Los Angeles, San Francisco, and Oakland. He also advised the failing Pacific Greyhound Lines, which provided bus service between San Francisco and the North Bay after the ferries went out of business.[24]

Jenkins played an important role in the famous transformation of the Pacific Electric Railway into a bus system in the Los Angeles metropolitan area, working on the case as a state official in the 1930s, and in the 1940s and 1950s as a private consultant.[25] In 1949 Jenkins developed a "modernization plan" for the complete elimination of rails, and expressed his frustration about public opposition: "The theory so often propounded that retention of rail lines enhances public values and adds intrinsic importance to the community it serves is as obsolete as the rail equipment itself." He observed that there was no other industry "so persistently beset with militant opposition in its efforts to follow the natural course that good business judgment dictates, in attempting to maintain a reasonable margin between revenue and cost of providing service. It is inconceivable that anyone could advocate the preservation of outmoded facilities whose cost of operation far exceeds the revenues earned and insist upon further heavy capital investment to insure the preservation of such a losing project."[26] Jenkins firmly believed that the only reasonable option for mass transportation—whether public or private—was "survival through rubber tires," or the adoption of an all-bus system.[27] Jenkins appealed to municipal, state, and federal regulating bodies on behalf of Pacific Electric for permission to abandon rail lines and replace them with bus service by arguing that it was clearly in the public interest.[28]

Jenkins began working as a consultant for the bridge district in 1948 and was simultaneously elected to the executive committee of the Redwood Empire Association (REA). Taking over as the occasional consulting engineer after the death of Leon Nishkian in 1947, Jenkins devoted more and more of his time to the bridge district and developed a close working relationship with Adam, the bridge district general manager. By the mid-1950s he was, for all practical purposes, the acting chief engineer. Jenkins's years in management and public administration and experience dealing with the political conundrums of the Public Utilities Commission made him an adept policy-maker. He had a deep understanding of the dynamics of public bureaucracies, the importance of financial considerations, and the conflicting pressures of public opinion. As an expert not subject to political or public pressure, Jenkins believed that he was able to make much better decisions on behalf of the agency than its directors were. And, he was not above covert maneuvering to achieve the outcomes that he believed served the interests of the public and of the bridge district, regardless of their unpopularity.

Jenkins reviewed the 1956 BART engineering study on the installation of rails on the Golden Gate Bridge and concluded that technically, it was probably possible. But he pointed out to the bridge directors that engineering feasibility was not enough, that they should consider its potential consequences for the agency and its constituents. In particular, he was concerned about "the financial obligations of the district and the . . . interests of [bridge district residents] who are tax-bound to carry out any deficit burden that might arise."[29] In a ten-point preliminary argument against rails, Jenkins asserted that the project would never be self-sustaining, citing the dismal financial history of similar ventures. Jenkins also argued that "the human aspects involved in such a project are of great importance and perhaps more so than the purely technical and engineering elements." The directors needed to maintain an awareness of their larger obligations: "the responsibility for safe-guarding the financial integrity of the District and the safety of the patrons making use of the bridge, as well as the safety of the prospective rapid transit passengers, is a burden that would fall squarely upon the District. . . . This responsibility is not one of a temporary nature that can be brushed off upon submission of a technical report."[30] Jenkins had spent years trying to free other agencies from transit obligations, and he was not about to let the bridge district entangle itself in their treacherous financial web.

Jenkins reiterated this assessment of rapid transit in his extensive *Long Range Planning Survey*, which was commissioned by the bridge district in 1957 and completed in 1959.[31] The survey was intended as a demonstration that the district could plan for and meet the transportation problems of the North Bay without outside intervention or assistance. It also included discussion of possibilities for expansion and new activities, and an assessment of emerging threats to bridge district autonomy and revenues. He suggested installing a second deck for automobile use, noting that some sort of "corrective measures" would have to be taken to avoid severe traffic congestion in the near future.[32] And, the agency's interests demanded that measures be taken by the bridge district itself, not some potential competitor. Jenkins described BART plans at length, noting that their engineering feasibility should be "carefully checked."[33] However, his objections to the proposed system primarily emphasized its expense: "Unless conditions should change radically to show concrete evidence of a tendency for the public to shift back to mass transit from private automobiles, there appears to be little prospect of a rapid rail transit line . . . being operated within the foreseeable future, on a self-sustaining basis financially."[34] Because of the subsidies that it would require, Jenkins opposed involvement in BART or any form of mass transportation. True to the ideological foundations of the bridge district, Jenkins argued that business principles and consideration of its financial well-being should determine its policies.

In a 1960 letter to bridge director Charles W. Reinking, Jenkins claimed that he was not "antagonistic toward rail rapid transit per se," but had spent the last twenty-nine years observing its decline and failure. Jenkins explained the connection between real-estate interests and transit operations early in the twentieth century: "In those days the rail lines came into existence first and then the population and residential development followed." However, the automobile and state-supported roads and highways changed the development patterns of cities in California by providing individual, flexible long-distance transportation at a relatively small cost: "Population distribution is widely dispersed. Commercial activities [have] followed population. Shopping centers and commercial enterprises have sprung up in many outlying areas to meet the convenience demand of dispersed population. This pattern is difficult to serve with rail transportation. . . . Bus lines can come much closer to meeting this requirement due to their flexibility and ease of maneuvering over existing streets, roads and highways." Jenkins described the abandonment of rails on the San Francisco-Oakland Bay Bridge after public officials took over the failing system, only to let it deteriorate further: "the public, which had the means at hand for at least partially solving the mass transit problem, did nothing whatsoever in a constructive way." Because rail facilities had been abandoned wholesale rather than rehabilitated by local governments while they were still intact and operational, according to Jenkins, the opportunity was entirely lost for viable rail systems. Bad public policy decisions were being followed by worse: "The next illogical step of our public officials is . . . reconstructing an entire new rail rapid transit system superimposing its routes upon essentially the same trunk lines as formerly existed under the old rail system. Instead of the population and commercial activities being controlled by rail lines, there has been a mass dispersal patterned after the convenience of the private automobile."[35]

Jenkins believed that the only hope for solvent rapid transit would be entirely new development along its route, supported by traffic and congestion that was bad enough to make high-density living appealing to middle-class commuters—which Jenkins viewed as highly unlikely. He predicted that eventually population would shift back into cities, but not quickly enough to justify the high costs of the proposed BART system. He described BART as the misguided pet project of naïve public officials, adding that "persons appointed to transportation and traffic committees, commissions and boards are likewise, in general, completely uninformed as to the problems with which they are confronted . . . [and] unfortunately become influenced unduly by political pressures and local influences."[36] He saw rapid transit as fundamentally irrational given the land-use patterns of the Bay Area, and as a boondoggle and a massive waste of money.

The Bridge District Responds

Publicly, bridge district officials' reaction to the prospect of rapid transit on the bridge was neutral and measured. Even as Jenkins was privately making his case against rails behind the scenes, agency representatives insisted that they were open-minded about the proposal and would cooperate fully with BART officials. Informal negotiations between the two large special districts began in 1959 and, on the whole, relations were cordial. One BART official reported that "we received a very warm welcome from the Directors of the Bridge District and I am sure we can look forward to full cooperation from them."[37]

In May 1959 John C. Beckett, one of Marin's BART directors, presented the basic case for rapid transit over the Golden Gate Bridge at a

joint meeting of both agencies: "We see our job as being one of full partnership with all of the other agencies dealing with transportation problems in the Bay Area—city and county planners, Bridge Districts,
parking authorities, private transportation concerns, the State Division
of Highways, and others," he said magnanimously.[38] BART district officials also appealed directly to Marin County officials, meeting with local
politicians in Sausalito, Mill Valley, Corte Madera, Larkspur, and San
Rafael—all of the Marin cities on the proposed North Bay route.[39]
Marin BART director Thorpe J. DeLasaux addressed members of the
REA in October, warning that rapid transit plans would require bridge
district cooperation: "we believe Marin and the other North Bay counties should be linked to the remainder of the regional rapid transit system. We are convinced that it is feasible and possible to use the present
bridge for rapid transit purposes, and we believe nothing should deter
whatever further studies are deemed necessary to convince the officials
of the Bridge District."[40] Although the REA took no official stand, *Independent Journal* editors urged the bridge directors to support BART.[41]
They also announced the positive results of a poll in August showing
that 87.7 percent of Marin residents with an opinion on the project favored it.[42] The bridge district harbored the only significant opposition
to BART in Marin County.

As BART supporters campaigned in Marin, at the bridge district alarm
was rising. The directors realized that they could not oppose BART directly without facing withering public criticism, but that the proposal
presented an enormous threat to their agency's autonomy and financial
security. Already, the district was unpopular in Marin, its finances and
tolls under close scrutiny, and its legitimacy under relentless attack by
McCarthy. Their outright refusal to accommodate rapid transit in the
bridge would only rally the public behind BART and provide fodder for
bridge district enemies.

Jenkins developed a close working relationship with Adam, acting as the
chief strategist in their covert war against BART.[43] His politically astute advice won Adam's confidence and the respect of many directors, despite
the bridge district structure and culture that subordinated engineers.
Through detailed daily correspondence and meetings, Adam kept Jenkins
informed of every new development relating to the bridge district, and
Jenkins provided Adam with analysis, strategy, and policy in return. Adam
kept a tight grip on bridge district operations and had an immense personal influence over the directors, but he trusted Jenkins and followed his
advice without hesitation. Jenkins was the brains behind the operation of
the bridge, and some of his influence no doubt resulted from his ability
to anticipate the opinions and desires of his boss. They were a closely coordinated team, and their partnership lasted for two decades.

Jenkins described Adam's options shortly after the official request from BART officials to run trains on the bridge: "It appears to me that the Bridge District is in a vulnerable position if it maintains a policy of complete 'hands off' with respect to this controversial subject. . . . The District, of course, retains the ultimate decision as to whether or not the bridge should be made available for rail rapid transit, even if technical studies indicate the engineering feasibility thereof. It would also retain the right to render an adverse decision based upon conditions other than purely the structural balance of stresses and strains."[44] Jenkins questioned the motives of BART officials in publicly emphasizing the issue of engineering feasibility: "If the Transit District is conclusively convinced that the Golden Gate Bridge can accommodate rapid transit, then why should they make such an issue of it? If the big issue in this controversy can be established by the Transit District as hinging around the decision of the bridge directors, then whatever weaknesses exist in their position and in the engineering surveys thus far developed can be hidden behind the cloak of attack upon the Bridge District."[45] Of course, at this point it was bridge officials who were making "such an issue" of engineering feasibility, but Jenkins described a siege upon the district, framing the issue as a battle between two opposing agencies.

On November 5, Adam and Jenkins met informally with the BART district general manager John M. Pierce and chief engineer Kenneth M. Hoover. It quickly became obvious that Pierce and Hoover were making a bid for the support of bridge management before formally presenting their case to the board of directors, as Jenkins noted: "Mr. Pierce expressed his desire that the technical matters and procedural aspects be thoroughly discussed at staff level before preparing a suggested letter of reply . . . [and] that a draft of the letter be reviewed by Mr. Adam before its final submission."[46] Adam rebuffed their presumptuous suggestion, repeatedly asserting that his responsibility was to the bridge district "and the public it represents." Jenkins was more direct, voicing his principal reservations: that alterations would not be feasible from an engineering standpoint, that BART would hurt the bridge district financially, and that it would be too difficult to negotiate a power-sharing agreement between the two organizations for joint decisions.[47] Although the first objection was the only one that they made publicly, it was really the last two points that most concerned Jenkins and Adam. The financial and administrative elements of the proposal were crucial to the bridge district, and its leading officials had already demonstrated their commitment to maintaining its autonomy and independence. These were concerns that BART district representatives could do nothing to address.

Nevertheless, Adam and Jenkins agreed to an independent study to determine engineering feasibility. The BART district would pay for a mutually agreeable engineering firm that had experience with suspension bridges. After three BART district nominations were rejected, they settled on the bridge district's choice, a firm headed by D. B. Steinman. BART officials made it clear that "so far as it is concerned, feasibility of rails on the Golden Gate Bridge has been established conclusively by its own engineers, and that the only reason for further consideration is an attempt to convince the Bridge & Highway District of such feasibility."[48]

Jenkins commented on the situation facing the bridge directors: "Obviously, there is no valid reason for lack of cooperation of the bridge district . . . in developing the essential features of rail rapid transit as related to the Golden Gate Bridge."[49] However, they needed to develop a politically acceptable reason for denying permission for rails on the bridge, and Jenkins knew that engineering feasibility was the most vulnerable part of the proposal. The financial and institutional drawbacks that he believed were the most important disadvantages would not even persuade the majority of the directors. "It therefore can only be concluded that the bridge district must approach the problems on a more carefully planned basis aimed at the engineering problems involved rather than general policy." The independent study would buy them time to develop credible engineering objections of their own. "When considering this aspect of the problem," Jenkins explained, "it should be recognized that the Transit District is equipped with three major engineering firms, whereas the Bridge District has no engineering organization. The matter becomes . . . an issue involving the matching magnitude of engineering organizations."[50] Jenkins believed that they already knew whether BART should run on the bridge—they just needed to justify their decision.

Closely following this agreement came a disturbing revelation regarding plans for a rapid transit connection to Marin. John C. Beckett, one of Marin's two BART appointees, made it clear at a BART board meeting that he expected tolls to pay for the installation of rails on the Golden Gate Bridge. With subsidies covering the costs of the alterations "the remainder of the Marin rapid transit line can be logically financed by the resources of the area directly served."[51] As far as BART leaders were concerned, the problems of the Marin line were solved. The finances added up, and they were confident that the Steinman study would definitively answer all engineering questions. Beckett pointed out that "the Golden Gate Bridge is a tremendous asset belonging to the people living within the bridge district. It is this asset that offers our best hope of area improvement at the least cost to the people."[52] Once again, bridge tolls were being targeted to support new transportation infrastructure, just as with the Golden Gate Authority proposal.

The Gronquist Report

As expected, the results of Steinman's study were affirmative. He found the installation of rails on the bridge to be "feasible and practical," although he recommended further aerodynamic tests. Echoing previous studies, Steinman pointed out that "design loadings and allowable stresses adopted were conservative, understandably so in view of the pioneering nature of the structure. . . . By present-day standards, therefore, there is considerable reserve strength in the bridge."[53] BART officials wasted no time in promoting Steinman's findings in Marin County with radio features and public presentations.[54] Falk asserted that "the Marin plan depends on the bridge . . . the country's very best engineering brains have studied the use of the bridge for transit and all indications to date point to the feasibility of carrying trains under the present highway deck."[55] As studies continued, BART officials canvassed Marin County, keeping *Independent Journal* reporters and receptive civic leaders current on engineering developments.

C. H. Gronquist, a partner in Steinman's firm, conducted wind tunnel tests that confirmed these findings. Gronquist concluded in his report that rapid transit on the bridge was clearly "feasible and practical," but recommended that the sidewalk be modified to reduce overall weight as a precaution, and suggested that the bridge's pylons be reinforced.[56] He predicted that the installation of rails on the bridge would cost around $9 million, slightly less than previous estimates. These findings were received enthusiastically in San Francisco and Marin, and immediately a bill was introduced in Sacramento to authorize the use of Golden Gate Bridge tolls to subsidize the North Bay BART line.[57]

However, bridge district officials were finally ready to answer Gronquist and the BART engineers with their own study. Clifford E. Paine appeared on the scene from retirement in Michigan to refute Gronquist's findings. Although bridge officials touted his credentials one of Joseph Strauss's original team of engineers, Paine lacked professional credibility. He was seventy-three years old, and Jenkins mentioned that there was some "inference . . . that the age of Mr. Paine is such as to cast some shadow of doubt upon the reliability of his findings."[58] Even during the construction period, Paine was "a detail man, an organizer and administrator . . . not a theorician," as bridge chronicler John van der Zee described him.[59] In 1941, bridge district engineer Russell G. Cone marveled that Paine's amateur engineering reports were approved by the consulting engineers and accepted by the directors.[60]

Paine's first and principal objection to the BART proposal was that it would lower the center of the bridge below the "navigation clearance line" required by the original War Department permit. Gronquist had already suggested that the BART district apply for an amendment to the original permit, but Paine ridiculed this idea. "Does anyone think that the Department of the Army is going to establish clearances and say that 'now and then these clearances may be reduced'[?]"[61] Neither shipping industry representatives nor military spokesmen had expressed any concern about adding rails to the bridge, and the political climate in Washington was very favorable toward mass transportation. Nevertheless, Paine's judgment was firm: "This infringement on clearance is not permissible and cannot be remedied. It is a prime consideration, and it alone rules out any possibility of carrying rapid transit trains over the Golden Gate Bridge."[62]

Although he agreed with Gronquist's calculations for the most part, Paine insisted that his safety standards were too lax: "The size and importance of the Golden Gate Bridge demand that its design loads and unit stresses be conservative."[63] Paine rejected the alteration of sidewalk areas and the replacement of the concrete roadway with open grating to reduce the weight of the bridge "because the reconstruction involved would interfere with traffic . . . [and] because riding over long lanes of open grating is obnoxious to automobile drivers and passengers."[64] The sidewalk was used for maintenance, and its ample width "avoids the necessity of using a much needed traffic lane for the purpose." Paine also pointed out that high-heeled shoes might get caught in an open-grating sidewalk.[65] He objected to any alteration to the pylons: "such mutilation of these excellent structures might be condoned only in an emergency," and "the margin of safety built into the bridge should not be whittled away."[66] Paine observed, "The plan may seem feasible and simple on paper, but it will be difficult to carry out. All work must be done without interference with traffic. It is certain that even under the closest, expert supervision the structural integrity of the pylon would never be restored."[67]

Gronquist dismissed Paine's objections, refused to modify any of his original conclusions, and insisted that adding rails would in no way compromise the beauty or safety of the span: "The Golden Gate Bridge when built almost thirty years ago, was, and is today, the outstanding suspension span of the world." Gronquist wrote in a brief response, "The magnitude of span and height of towers, in its majestic appearance and in the excellence of its design, this bridge demands universal respect. To impair its life, its present usefulness or its appearance would be unthinkable." Gronquist presented his rebuttal before skeptical directors on August 25, and Paine made it clear that his opposition to the alteration was steadfast.[68]

Shortly after Paine's exchange with Gronquist, Napa bridge director Peter Gasser asked Jenkins for background and analysis of the issue. Jenkins provided a lengthy discussion of the political and economic as well as engineering issues involved. Jenkins suggested that the engineering studies that had already been done were so thorough that no new revelations would be made. He made it clear that the important considerations were not related to engineering feasibility, pointing out that even Paine had agreed that technically, "the added load could be carried within the design limits of the structure." Instead, Jenkins suggested that the question had "gone beyond the stage of better engineering logic as relating to stresses and strains and loading characteristics of all, which are subject to calculation and predictions based upon accepted formula. In this instance it is my opinion that [we] must go beyond the pure mathematics of engineering design and contemplate the human side of engineering."[69]

Despite the engineering stalemate, the bridge directors passed a resolution on September 5 adopting Paine's findings by a vote of nine to four, citing safety concerns. They also rejected the possibility of further studies: "a joint engineering board of review to pass upon the Gronquist and Paine reports would not resolve or reconcile any differences of opinions expressed in these reports."[70] BART officials were informed that the bridge directors had made their final decision and that there would be no further negotiations. Falk's good faith efforts to negotiate had been rebuffed, and he reported the negative decision to the BART directors in tones of frustration and anger: "If the difference of opinion between engineers that existed back in the 1930's had been treated in the same manner, the Golden Gate Bridge would not link San Francisco and Marin today. We certainly are not, as some bridge directors glibly and erroneously charged Tuesday, asking anyone to 'gamble' with lives or with the safety of the bridge. Such comments . . . have one purpose; to divert attention from the main issue—to inject an emotional and inflammatory element into a decision that should have been based only on engineering facts and figures and determination to fulfill the public trust." Falk made it clear that he believed that the bridge directors had betrayed that trust, and that they were to blame for the "amputation" of the North Bay from the BART system.[71] Falk recommended that Marin and San Francisco supervisors appoint a new, impartial board of engineers to review the two reports, to be paid by the BART district.

The next day, San Francisco newspapers quoted "the usually mild-mannered" Falk angrily accusing James Adam of a "Machiavellian plot" and asserting that "somewhere along the line there was a lot of by-play in this action that was not open, frank and full." Adam had manipulated the vote by asking the bridge insurance agents if the trains would "affect the insurability" of the bridge, Falk contended, and then exaggerated the significance of the affirmative answer to intimidate the majority of the bridge directors into voting against trains.[72]

San Francisco Chronicle, September 13, 1961.

Falk was not the only one expressing dismay. Letters and resolutions flooded the bridge district offices from dozens of local civic associations as well as individual citizens, all demanding that the directors reconsider and agree to another independent engineering study. Editorials appeared in all of the Bay Area newspapers condemning the directors' decision as hasty and arbitrary.[73] To make matters worse, Cone, who had been dismissed for questioning bridge district policy in 1941, provided the *San Francisco Examiner* with some embarrassing documents from the construction period that undermined Paine's credibility—Strauss himself had promised that the bridge would have ample capacity to accommodate trains if the need or demand for them ever arose.[74]

In response to public outrage and pressure from San Francisco and Marin supervisors, the bridge directors voted to revisit the issue of engineering feasibility of BART on the bridge, adding it to the agenda of their October meeting in San Francisco. Gasser took the opportunity to make a case against trains using arguments and information provided by Jenkins. He described in detail the effects of a fire, a high wind, and the "panic, the hysteria, the conditions that would exist on the lower deck of this bridge if a ten-car train should meet with a major accident."[75] Attempting to sway undecided directors, Gasser argued that one important consideration in evaluating Paine's report should be his "years of closest association with this bridge in its design." Reopening the question to discussion would be an insult to Paine and to the memory of Strauss, as well as a waste of time and public money:

In their wisdom these original designers incorporated a factor of safety into this bridge . . . how can we now, merely in the light of subsequent design practices, say that these engineer designers were wasteful in specifying more steel than was necessary to carry the load. I personally do not believe that their judgment was poor. I think it was good. . . . [W]e should place more reliance upon the personal judgment of the man who participated in the original design of this bridge and at that time carried on his shoulders the full responsibility for the successful performance of the structure. . . . Can you say today, that in the light of the responsibility that has fallen upon this man, that he would look lightly upon the tampering with the bridge in any way that might possibly, even by one iota, reflect upon the safety margin as it now stands? The main question now facing us, gentlemen, is whether or not the decision of this Board is going to hinge around, first, the cold and impersonal features of engineering design and mathematics, and secondly, mere majority numbers of engineers. Gentlemen, you have heard of the term intuition. Although it might seem out of place in a discussion of engineering design and feasibility, I would like to caution you that the responsibility you will be taking upon your shoulders is one that should be guided by the human aspects of engineering as well as the engineering handbook aspects.[76]

As Gasser unintentionally suggested, Paine's association with the bridge district created a conflict of interest and made his analysis of rapid transit problematic. And, the directors knew that the case against rapid transit was less than definitive: few engineers would agree that "intuition" should trump scientific calculation and rational analysis.

Despite Gasser's impassioned appeal, the bridge directors were not completely immune to public pressure. They retreated from their stance of loyal support for Paine and agreed to a new, impartial engineering study on the question of BART feasibility, as Falk had suggested in September. However, this change of heart came too late for BART officials. In 1959, McCarthy managed to pass a bill to authorize the use of toll revenue from the San Francisco-Oakland Bay Bridge to pay for the construction of the expensive underwater tube that would carry BART trains between Oakland and San Francisco. This bill had a deadline, however, and would expire if at least $500 million in BART bonds for the rest of the system did not win voter approval by November 30, 1962.[77] Since the bridge directors' vote against rails in September 1961, BART officials had been more concerned about this looming deadline and less concerned about the North Bay. Already, bridge district opposition had delayed the public referendum on BART, and cost estimates for the system were rising quickly. BART officials had to finalize plans to ensure that the November ballot measure would be viable. Despite the popularity of BART in Marin, voters there could not be expected to support the bonds if rapid transit would never actually reach the North Bay. Their opposition could put the entire project in jeopardy. As soon as Paine's findings were announced, BART engineers and consultants went to work on a four-county system excluding Marin. At the end of October 1961, despite the an announcement that the bridge directors would allow yet another engineering study, BART directors officially adopted a revised plan that eliminated the North Bay line from first-phase construction. Although BART officials promised that Marin would be reinstated if an engineering review proved favorable, they proceeded at full speed with the presentations and public hearings that were required to get the construction bonds on the ballot.[78]

An Authoritative No

Although the delays caused by bridge district recalcitrance had already effectively eliminated the threat of rails on the Golden Gate Bridge, appearances and public relations demanded one final engineering study. Once again, the Golden Gate Bridge and BART officials agreed on a panel of independent engineers to study the question of rapid transit on the bridge. This time the bridge directors went to great lengths to take the initiative, providing a list of recommendations for candidate engineers, and paying all of their expenses and fees.[79] Ben Lerer of San Francisco described discussions on the best way to select and pay for an "impartial engineering board" that would provide the desired result: "Perhaps if we paid for it, we would feel better that we can select . . . the engineers and they would have no obligation to anyone in this matter. If the Rapid Transit District pays for it, they may feel some sort of an obligation to them. . . . We discussed it and we thought that we should pay for it."[80] Apparently, this strategy was effective: while the engineers may not have felt an obligation to the bridge district, the outcome of their study certainly suggested that they felt none to the BART district. The three engineers selected by the bridge district were Othmar Ammann, Frank M. Masters, and N. M. Newmark. Ammann was one of the original consulting engineers for bridge construction, and his firm carried out the reinforcement of the bridge in 1953 after its vulnerability to wind damage became undeniable. Masters was a junior engineer in Ammann's firm. Newmark, who later joined Ammann's firm, was a leading structural engineer, but his specialty was earthquake safety, not bridges.[81]

For this fourth study, Ammann, Masters, and Newmark submitted a "proposed scope of investigations" to the bridge directors in February 1962, developed "in accordance with the understanding arrived at between the Golden Gate Bridge and Highway District and ourselves" at an informal meeting held in San Francisco in January. Later in 1962, James Adam's former assistant asserted that the engineers had been "thoroughly brief[ed], screened, and interviewed" before they were hired for the review.[82] The purpose of the study was carefully defined to encourage a negative decision: "[It] is the prime concern of the Board of Directors that, whatever changes and additions are contemplated, the bridge must be preserved in a first class condition, with a conservative margin of safety, to serve highway traffic for which it was intended and designed. The question as to what constitutes a conservative margin of safety is a very complex one. . . . Any increase in the adopted permissible primary stresses may mean encroachment on the margin of safety."[83] Not surprisingly, the final report, issued in April well after the BART district had officially adopted its four-county plan, was negative. As reported in the *Independent Journal,* the bridge district had finally achieved an "authoritative 'no.'"[84]

The bridge directors voted to accept the report and proclaim that trains would never run across the bridge, but there were dissenters.[85] Two of Marin's directors, the newly appointed DeLasaux and M. J. Lamperti, expressed their opinion clearly as to the outcome of the latest engineering study. DeLasaux quoted fellow Marin director Leland Murphy as asserting that "we are going to pay for the review because we want to control what's in that report."[86] At the next board meeting, Murphy angrily denied saying this, and threatened to sue DeLasaux and Lamperti. Another director remarked on the vocal dissent of the Marin representatives: "forgive them for they know not what they say."[87]

Well before the final engineering report was released, it was obvious that Marin County missed its chance to be part of the first-stage plans. Because of the dim prospects for a North Bay line, Marin voters were likely to balk at the prospect of taxes to support the rest of the system, and BART officials wanted them out of the district completely. In May 1962 Marin County supervisors reluctantly succumbed to pressure and withdrew their membership. A week later, they changed their minds in a somewhat pathetic attempt to recover some of the taxes that they had already paid to the BART district. They also hoped that by staying in the BART district they could ensure their inclusion in second-phase construction. But it was too late: BART officials rejected their petition, adamant about excluding Marin voters from the public referendum.[88]

Once it was irrefutable that rapid transit would never reach the North Bay, *Independent Journal* editors lamented that "we need transportation;

nobody's planning for it." Two large-scale regional efforts to alleviate transportation problems had been decisively defeated by the bridge district.[89] Ironically, bridge district policies worked against the original intentions of the boosters who had created it. Rather than facilitating growth and development, the bridge became a transportation bottleneck, its officials actively opposing any competing transportation facilities within its jurisdiction.

After Marin was eliminated from first-phase plans, BART officials confronted a new problem: San Mateo County supervisors voted to withdraw from the district in January 1962, arguing that the system favored San Francisco's downtown at the expense of San Mateo commercial interests and was not worth the price of increased property taxes. The elimination of San Mateo was a financial blow that reduced BART's tax base and required yet another revision of the rapid transit system plan.[90] Nevertheless, six years of campaigning and careful strategizing paid off for BART officials in November 1962, when a three-county regional rapid transit system got a resounding public endorsement. San Francisco voters were particularly enthusiastic, passing the measure by 66.9 percent. Along with Alameda County's respectable 60 percent affirmation, it more than offset the 54.5 percent vote in Contra Costa. Marin probably could have stayed in the district without the disaster of defeat. But, BART officials were under more time pressure than bridge district leaders had been during their bond campaign—they could not risk a loss at the polls, nor could they continue campaigning without losing valuable Bay Bridge subsidies for the transbay tube.[91]

As popular as the idea of rapid transit may have been among Bay Area voters, the reality of BART administration immediately began generating controversy. One week after the bond vote, the BART directors faced their first taxpayers' lawsuit, charging them with illegally using public funds to influence the vote, challenging the fairness of contracts with engineering firms, and questioning staff salaries. Though the BART district prevailed, the court fight cost millions of dollars and delayed construction more than six months. Once construction finally commenced, it became clear that the BART district's relatively weak board of directors and staff, dominated by businessmen with close ties to the engineering firms working for the district, were failing to oversee and manage construction adequately. Consulting engineers had almost unfettered control over decision-making, and their fees were based on a percentage of total costs, giving them a disincentive to economize. Consequently, there was a sudden shift in public sentiment about BART, as federal analysts described: "There was a dramatic contrast in BARTD's relationship with the Bay Area community before and after the referendum. [Its] honeymoon with the voters was over within weeks of the election. With few exceptions, the media, political leadership, and most organized groups supported BART before the election, but not afterward. After the election, BARTD seems to many to have become a well-funded, powerful, independent organization with relatively little accountability."[92]

Public relations continued to worsen for the BART district. During construction, the agency garnered local opposition because of engineers' unwillingness to modify station plans or routing based on community preferences. Conflict between contractors working on the project highlighted BART officials' lack of responsibility and the power of its consulting engineers, particularly those of the Bechtel Corporation. Moreover, BART leaders, engineers, and contractors were accused of racism in hiring and in route selection during construction. Later, labor relations became a persistent problem for the agency.[93]

Despite all of this, BART depended heavily on state and federal subsidies, and its leaders had to maintain the good graces of politicians and the public. The BART system was too capital intensive and its operational costs too great to come close to covering its costs with rider fares. The BART district never had the autonomy that the bridge district achieved with its toll revenue. And, some reform efforts aimed at improving its public accountability were successful: starting in 1974, its directors were elected rather than appointed. In any case, the BART district always had much more of its institutional interests riding on positive public relations than did the bridge district. Fortunately for its officials, the popularity of rapid transit endured in the Bay Area despite problems with its administration.

To some extent, public perceptions were also a concern to bridge district officials. The Golden Gate Authority had been defeated only a few months earlier, the continuing existence of the bridge district was still uncertain, and opposition to trains on the span was exactly the sort of policy that made it unpopular. However, Jenkins, Adam, and leading directors agreed that sharing the span with the BART district would have compromised the financial integrity and independence of the bridge district, creating an unacceptable threat to its power and autonomy. Any boost in public opinion that accommodating rapid transit might have created for the bridge district would have been fleeting, and many years would pass before any trains would run. Whether or not they ever made it to Marin, it was doubtful that cooperation would mollify bridge district critics in the meantime.

The successful effort to stop BART by bridge district officials working against public opinion suggests that the organization developed interests as an institution that were distinct from those of even its closest allies and most loyal supporters. Of course, these interests were interpreted and defined by its officials, who saw them through the lens of their own ideology. Nevertheless, they consistently pursued goals and policies that promoted the integrity and security of the organization as a whole. Special districts were intentionally designed to take decision-making out of the political sphere and put it in the hands of expert administrators and technocrats; Jenkins was so influential in defining policy because they empower their administrative staff and at the same time insulate them from political pressures or public scrutiny.

Jenkins's view of mass transportation was shaped during a period when it was largely a private enterprise, and he judged its prospects in the Bay Area based on its financial bottom line. However, financial considerations were not motivating the Bay Area residents who voted to approve BART construction bonds in 1962. Jenkins ignored the many social, economic, and environmental benefits of mass transportation (not to mention traffic relief) that are not reflected in fare revenues, benefits that make it a vital public service in cities and metropolitan areas throughout the United States. In a way, however, history vindicated Jenkins. Marin avoided having to pay for enormous cost overruns and high operating subsidies that other BART counties and East Bay toll payers had to contend with. The bridge district maintained its authority and integrity, eventually taking over all Golden Gate bus and ferry lines itself. While the installation of rails on the Golden Gate Bridge was reconsidered in the late 1960s and the 1980s, it was never financially or politically viable again.

Chapter 6
James Adam, Boss of the Golden Gate Bridge

After its officials waged successful campaigns against the Golden Gate Authority and the Bay Area Rapid Transit District, the Golden Gate Bridge and Highway District descended into the worst period of scandal and public antipathy in its history. While bridge district policies continued to generate controversy in the late 1950s, it was the questionable accounting, expenses, and administrative practices of its management that tarnished the agency's reputation the most. Accusers laid the blame on the bridge district's most unpopular general manager, James Adam, who was appointed to the position in 1954. Irascible and authoritarian, Adam maintained nearly absolute control over the agency. As its top official, the autonomy and resources of the bridge district allowed him to avoid personal consequences for mismanagement and questionable, unpopular policies. By the time Adam was forced into retirement in 1968, his administration had sunk the bridge district into a mire of notoriety and scandal, but he remained determined to defend its independence and interests. He believed in the right of bridge district leaders to collect tolls and to make policy without interference—he defended bridge district power for its own sake.

Adam took control of the bridge district at the cusp of a period of turmoil, in the Bay Area and nationwide. Expertise and professionalism no longer seemed as compelling or as dependable as they had when bridge district founders structured the agency to empower its top officials and insulate them from political interference. A wide variety of national and global developments in the 1950s and 1960s threw the wisdom of authority figures into question, and bridge district management contributed in its own small way to widespread disillusionment. This chapter traces the story of how bridge district officials, under Adam's leadership, were forced to confront the issue of racism for the first time. It highlights the power of special districts, particularly when exploited by a savvy and ruthless bureaucrat like Adam, who was willing to defy the law, flout public opinion, and weather the most scathing criticism. Adam was adept at using the resilient structure and assets of the bridge district to protect himself and the agency's interests as he understood them. Adam's refusal to compromise led to damning California Fair Employment Practice Commission hearings for racial discrimination, but even they were not enough to end his reign as general manager. Removing Adam from power required significant opposition from within the bridge district, combined with timing and luck.

James Adam, circa 1958. San Francisco History Center, San Francisco Public Library.

From Public Relations to General Manager

Adam started his career as a newspaperman, working as a reporter for the *San Francisco Examiner,* the *Oakland Tribune,* and the *San Francisco Chronicle.* In 1932, Adam ran as a Republican for the state assembly as a resident of Berkeley. Although he was defeated, he became a leading member of the local Republican Central Committee. By 1939, he was living in San Francisco's Marina District and serving as president of the neighborhood Home Owners' Protective Association. Around that time, Adam secured the job of chief political writer for the *San Francisco Call-Bulletin,* which he held through the end of World War II. Adam's first job for the bridge district was as the publicity director for the Opening Day Fiesta in 1937, and he was hired part-time as its public relations officer in 1941. He served a brief stint as warden at Folsom State Prison, winning the position in 1943 through bridge district connections. Bridge director A. R. O'Brien was also a member of the state board of prison directors when a scandal forced the Folsom warden to resign. Although Adam won praise as "the finest warden material," he returned to public relations work after a few months. Adam joined the bridge district staff full-time in 1948.[1]

Adam's role at the bridge district was always controversial. In 1950, *Examiner* editors noted that his salary as a "part time public relations man and part time lobbyist" was another example of bridge district extravagance.[2] San Francisco director Jesse C. Coleman pointed out in 1952 that his expenses exceeded $400 for a single month in Sacramento and called for the elimination of his position: "This is an absolutely unnecessary expenditure of the bridge district's money. . . . It makes it look like we can't get any consideration in the legislature without Adam. . . . We don't need to hold cocktail parties and take the legislature to dinner to get their help. It's wrong."[3] Nevertheless, a record $1.2 million administrative budget for the bridge district passed that year with only two dissenting votes. It included a raise for Adam and an overall increase in public relations appropriations. Adam made sure that the directors had no illusions about the importance of good representation in Sacramento.

However, Coleman was not alone in opposing lobbying activities by the bridge district or other public agencies. At the time, California lobbyists were under severe scrutiny due to a recent nationwide scandal generated by the notorious Sacramento power broker, Artie Samish. Reforms intended to reduce the strength of political parties in California during the Progressive Era vastly increased the influence of private interest groups and their representatives: individual legislators were essentially free agents, able to wield their power to the best advantage, regardless of the interests or goals of party leadership. However, they had small salaries and almost no party fundraising support. Lobbyists were the main source of funding for many campaigns, and also provided entertainment, political favors, and everyday expenses for many legislators, including food and lodging. This situation undermined the power

of parties even further, and meant that private interests could easily secure alliances across party lines and push favored legislation through
with little resistance (unless it conflicted with the interests of another
well-represented group). In 1949, Samish bragged of his power as a lobbyist to a reporter from *Collier's* magazine. Samish was a skilled behind-
the-scenes manipulator, using a network of informants to keep a close
watch on everything that was going on in the legislature. He described
frequent parties, sumptuous dinners, free-flowing liquor, and large cash
campaign contributions, all generously underwritten by his clients, the
most prominent of which was the California State Brewers' Association.
The issue of *Collier's* with Samish's profile featured a cover photo of him
with a dummy on his lap that he called "Mr. Legislature." The image
shook the Sacramento establishment to its foundations. In 1950 the legislature voted to require that all lobbyists register and file annual expense reports, and in 1953 Samish was imprisoned for tax evasion.
Although salaries and conditions improved for legislators in the 1950s,
the "third house" retained much of its influence. Adam and other
bridge district lobbyists were more discreet and probably less powerful
than Samish, but they no doubt used many of the same strategies to fight
off State Senator Jack McCarthy's efforts for bridge district reform and
to promote the interests of the agency in Sacramento.[4]

When James Rickets, who was nearing the mandatory retirement age
of seventy, announced his intention to resign as general manager in
1953, Adam was the favorite candidate to replace him. But as the bridge
directors were considering the appointment, they were embroiled in a
debate over expenses and cost-cutting. The negative publicity stirred up
by McCarthy and scandal about lobbying in Sacramento attracted attention to the bridge district's fleet of Cadillacs, advertising appropriations,
REA contributions, and other expenses. In 1953, the bridge district
spent at least $33,000 for advertising, and Adam was paid a $16,000
salary in addition to expenses. To make matters worse, Rickets was involved in a traffic accident while using a bridge district car for personal
business, and when he billed the district for damages, it made front-page
news.[5]

In the midst of these problems, Adam was appointed as general manager by the directors with a ten-to-three vote. The dissenting directors
wanted to solicit applications from other candidates, particularly from
qualified engineers. Phil Davies of San Francisco complained the appointment was "a framed deal, worked out in advance."[6] The *Independent
Journal* suggested that Adam won support from an emerging "economy
bloc" of newly-appointed bridge directors by promising to eliminate the
position of public relations director once he was general manager.[7] The
vote in favor of Adam affirmed a heavy-handed approach to defending

the interests of the organization as well as the continued subordination of engineering to politics and public relations. At the start of the following legislative session in 1955, notwithstanding any understanding that he may have had with the directors at the time of his appointment, Adam managed to secure permission to hire a new lobbyist. One director explained that it would "reflect upon the prestige of the general manager if he registered as a lobbyist."[8] Gerald O'Gara, a former state senator from San Francisco, was tapped for the position; reportedly he had "pulled [out] all the stops" in fighting against McCarthy's bill for bridge district dissolution in 1953.[9] O'Gara was succeeded as bridge district lobbyist by Gordon Garland, a former speaker of the assembly, in 1959.[10]

Adam's understanding of his role as general manager was informed by his experience in public relations. In a 1955 presentation before the American Bridge, Tunnel and Turnpike Association, Adam equated the operation of the bridge district to that of a private corporation, emphasizing its business orientation and priorities. While the bridge district did not face significant competition for its services, he argued that, unlike most commercial enterprises, it did face important political challenges. Adam emphasized the wide variety of responsibilities assigned to the general manager, describing public relations work as the most important among them: "each person paying a toll at the bridge plaza is a potential friend or enemy and it is a highly essential function of administrative management to exert every effort through all means at his disposal to make friends and favorably influence people."[11]

Almost immediately after becoming general manager, Adam was accused of misrepresenting bridge district finances. Less than a month after he took the helm, he presented a report to the directors claiming that the bridge district had suffered an operating loss of $169,634 in the previous year, despite record traffic and an increase in overall revenues. Adam explained that the loss was due to a major maintenance project. However, *Independent Journal* reporters cried foul, noting that the bridge district auditor's annual report showed a profit of $164,000. Adam had manipulated the figures, they charged: "Why? The reason is obvious. Bridge directors are setting the stage to once again refuse realistic requests for a cut in the cash toll. . . . General Manager James Adam emphasized an 'operating loss' in his semi-monthly report to the board. Differences between operating income and net income is interest and profits the district receives from investments, deposits and other sources other than tolls. Last year this difference totaled more than $330,000, enough to turn the 'operating loss' into a profit."[12] Bridge district revenues continued to improve, its reserves grew steadily, and pressure for a toll cut increased. By the end of 1954, the directors finally agreed to lower tolls, offering a 60-cent round-trip despite Adam's opposition. A year later, they set the one-way toll at 25 cents, on par with the San Francisco-Oakland Bay Bridge toll for the first time. However, Marin County commuters had many other things to complain about—and not only bridge district policies that resulted in the rejection of BART trains or the defeat of the Golden Gate Authority. Before long, Adam himself was at the center of scandal, his management and administration the subject of investigation and condemnation.

In 1956, Adam's dictatorial management style made the news. Ruth Dow, who had worked for the agency for nineteen years and had been its secretary for eleven, was fired. Adam did not actually have the authority to discharge Dow himself. While he had control over the rest of the bridge district employees, who numbered approximately 150 at the time, the secretary and attorney were both formally hired by and accountable directly to the board of directors. Ignoring rules and procedure, Adam changed the locks on Dow's office door and the combination of the district vault after she wrote a letter to the directors criticizing him. Two months later in a closed meeting, the directors officially dismissed Dow, citing "general incompatibility." Adam claimed that it was a unanimous decision, but several directors told reporters that there were four dissenting votes until it was agreed to give Dow an additional six months' pay. After reporters were allowed to return to the meeting, one director snapped: "Adam is not Mr. Golden Gate Bridge . . . he is just an employee."[13] After the fact, the directors approved detailed minutes drafted by Adam that indicated that they had originally given Dow notice. Dow hired an attorney, but never sued or discussed her side of the story with the press—no doubt, she struck a deal with Adam and the directors.[14]

A 2 A.M. incident a few months later indicated the level of Adam's personal commitment to the bridge district. News of a four-car pileup on the span prompted Adam to rush to the scene to help police. When he started setting flares to divert traffic near a large pool of gasoline, he was ordered to leave. He objected loudly and was eventually given a four-man escort off of the bridge. Apparently, this was not Adam's only run-in with police; the car provided to him by the bridge district had been stripped of its siren after reports that he was using it to speed across the bridge a few months before.[15] Adam might well have considered himself "Mr. Golden Gate Bridge."

Bridge of Gold

As general manager, Adam perpetuated the policies that led to accusations of inefficiency and extravagance early in the 1950s and that inspired McCarthy's first crusade for dissolution and toll reductions. A *San Francisco Examiner* exposé, titled "A Bridge of Gold," decried lavish bridge district spending and high salaries under Adam's direction in 1960. Among other things, it pointed out the directors' habit of enjoying gourmet meals at district expense at the St. Francis Hotel in San Francisco, which was managed by bridge district president Dan London. Adam's salary, according to the report, was more than $21,000, plus another $3,149 for expenses; his counterpart at the California Toll Bridge Authority, who was an engineer, had no expenses and earned just $15,876 per year.[16] The familiar comparison was still unflattering for the bridge district, and the series made a new case for a state takeover just as legislation for the Golden Gate Authority was being prepared in Sacramento. Unruffled, Adam won approval for a new staff position a few months later and appointed William Hendricks of San Rafael as assistant to the general manager, with a salary of $12,000. Among Hendricks's duties was to fill in for Adam while he was in Sacramento unofficially putting pressure on bridge district allies and opponents in the legislature.[17]

In 1962, just in time for the bridge's twenty-fifth anniversary celebration, *Chronicle* reporters made more accusations against bridge management in another series, "Our Plush Gate Bridge." This time, the charges of extravagance and waste were much more serious, and included significant undocumented expenses and dubious accounting practices. Adam could only produce receipts for $1,993 in personal expenses, but claimed a total of $13,340. Many of his other expenses were not included in this total. For example, he charged airfare for a trip to the East Coast to a different bridge district account. He also withdrew $1,104 in cash from a revolving fund. The *Chronicle* reported that Frank M. Masters of the engineering firm Ammann & Whitney, one of the engineers who had done the final independent review of rapid transit trains on the bridge, had been hosted by the district at the St. Francis Hotel while vacationing in San Francisco with his wife, even though he conducted no business on the trip. Reporters also detailed various means of extra compensation for directors beyond the legislated allowances, including routine travel compensation and entertainment expenses. Each director received full medical benefits and $10,000 life insurance policies, while employees, including those with hazardous work such as painters, were provided with only $2,500 policies. In addition, they questioned the propriety of providing deluxe travel accommodations for a seven-week trip to Europe for Adam and two directors in 1958, ostensibly to negotiate insurance from Lloyd's of London. The final article in the series revealed that bridge district officials spent $625,591 on unspecified advertising in the previous year, even as the bridge suffered from traffic congestion. Bay Bridge managers, in contrast, had spent a total of $2,772 for advertising in twenty-five years. It also pointed out that the district's annual financial reports were significantly abbreviated in the late 1950s, and no breakdown of expenses was available to the public.[18]

An outraged *Chronicle* editorial followed the exposé, calling for investigation of bridge district officials' "free spending," and particularly of Adam's "sizeable checks to pay expense accounts that were curiously uninformative." The bridge directors were running the agency as if it were "their own private little principality," the editor remarked. "If gravy were being ladled out in the form of payments and perquisites, no higher authority felt called upon to notice the spots on the neckties."[19] Members of the Marin County grand jury initiated their own investigation of the bridge district, announcing that they were "extremely shocked. . . . We as taxpayers feel that a complete investigation into the unchecked and unaccounted for spending of public funds is mandatory and at this point long overdue."[20]

Jack McCarthy, who was campaigning for lieutenant governor at the time, also rose to the challenge of reining in bridge district spending. He was probably still smarting from recent defeats on rapid transit and the Golden Gate Authority at the hands of the bridge district. McCarthy had a new ally in Hendricks, who resigned from his position as assistant to the general manager after two years. In a press conference called by McCarthy, Hendricks claimed that he left "as a matter of self-respect and integrity."[21] He accused Adam of keeping information from the directors, refusing them access to bridge district reports, and asking him to disseminate "misinformation" to the public. Hendricks described the "mess at the Bridge District" as "an iceberg, with only a small portion showing above the muddy water." He claimed that Adam denied him any direct contact with the directors, and "since there was no way of reaching [them], I felt it was my responsibility as a citizen to do something about it."[22] Hendricks claimed that Adam installed a system to eavesdrop on employee conversations. He offered many other details, describing a decision by the directors to reject the low bid on commuter tickets and their failure to entertain any bids on other important contracts. He also explained how Adam gained $10,000 to use at his discretion by misappropriating engineering funds, and pointed out the close relationship between the accounting firm that did annual audits and the bridge district, including their common legal counsel. "The capper was when the board spent the afternoon at the races at the Sonoma County Fair," Hendricks recalled, "At lunch, they entertained 50 'friends of the District' at the Flamingo Hotel. All the guests were told the two Sonoma County members of the board were paying the bill. But it just wasn't so. The bill came to the bridge auditor from the Flamingo, and it was promptly paid." McCarthy followed Hendricks's allegations with an inventory of eight serious and familiar charges: irregular audits, misappropriation of funds, excessive fees and expenses, secret meetings, and "gross misuse of public funds for lobbying."[23] He concluded the presentation with a call for Adam's dismissal.

Adam accused Hendricks of "personal vindictiveness" and claimed that he had been fired for "incompetence and neglect of duty."[24] President Dan London refuted the charges point by point, denouncing McCarthy's "campaign of continuous public abuse and harassment," his "intemperate and violent attacks to undermine the confidence in Board management actions," and his "willful and personal vilification [of] the Bridge District."[25] London asserted that the directors were fully in control of administration, management, and policy. In his official response to McCarthy, London called his demand for Adam's dismissal "unstatesmanlike," adding that Adam was "one of the most capable executives I have known—one of the hardest working men I have known."[26] The bridge directors voted to commission a complete report on accounting procedures, but they hired the same firm that had been responsible for bridge district financial reports and auditing since 1937, Arthur Young & Co. Predictably, the auditors found "no evidence of any irregularities in the accounting procedures," but did recommend that the bridge district stop paying a flat fee for travel expenses to meetings and start requiring receipts.[27]

The Marin County grand jury investigation involved hearings over the course of nearly a year, which were faithfully reported in the press. It was the first major probe of the internal affairs and day-to-day operations of the bridge district going beyond accounting procedures and expenses. In the course of testimony, it came out that in 1947 and 1949 Adam successfully lobbied for legislation that eliminated the requirement that the bridge district return surplus funds to the member counties. He also succeeded in making the bridge district auditor accountable to the general manager rather than the board of directors. Among those called to testify were Adam, the bridge district auditor, and several of its directors. Ruth Dow also appeared before the grand jury, but refused to discuss her testimony with the press.[28]

Grand jury members concluded that, though criminal charges could not be justified, "many of the past and present procedures of the bridge district warrant severe censure."[29] They criticized the "lax attitude" of the bridge directors. The power structure and the decision-making process of the district was severely off balance, they asserted: the board should share responsibility equally with the general manager for its "proper management," and should not abdicate its authority.[30] The harshest criticism in the grand jury report was reserved for Adam.

Investigation confirmed that his personal expense accounts, more than
$5,000 per year, were "approved with cursory examination and insuffi-
cient substantiation."[31] Jury members questioned the propriety of
Adam's "public relations expenses," totaling more than $4,000 in 1961,
especially in light of the fact that the bridge district had a lobbyist on the
payroll. Adam's honesty as an administrator came into question as well,
with charges that he failed to report important information and edited
the minutes of meetings after the fact without authorization. Jury members had "ample evidence . . . that the general manager has, at times, al-
tered official documents, e.g., personnel records, and has acted in
violation of board rules and policies with respect to invoices."[32] They
also criticized the "free and easy" attitude toward public money at the
bridge district, calling for an end to "luncheons and dinners not essential to bridge business, paid hotel bills offered as gratuities, excessive legislative costs and large sums spent for advertising."[33]

The grand jury findings created a stir at the bridge district. Newly
elected president Ben K. Lerer of San Francisco demanded that the district auditing committee start "hold[ing] its meetings in the open—
instead of in an anteroom off general manager James Adam's private
office."[34] He managed to convince the other directors to pass a resolution to limit lobbying expenses. The directors questioned an extremely
uncomfortable and reluctant auditor from Arthur Young & Co. at their
next meeting, whose testimony had been an important source of information for the grand jury. When asked repeatedly whether he had en-
countered any "dishonesty," he was either aggressively interrupted by a
director or refused to answer: "My duty is a legal duty, and the interpretation of dishonesty is a moral one. I can see there are various interpretations on what constitutes dishonesty. I have nothing to say on the
matter."[35] A few months later the hapless auditor was forced to resign.[36]

The investigations generated an enormous amount of coverage in
Marin and San Francisco newspapers, and the public scrutiny did make
a difference. The *Chronicle* reported smugly when the bridge district annual report was released in July that its officials had a "tough year."
Adam's personal expenses dropped from more than $13,000 the previ-
ous year to $1,984, and he had receipts. His incidental expenses and
"once lively" revolving account claims were reduced to next to nothing.[37] In addition, McCarthy introduced a new series of reform
measures in the 1963 legislative session based on grand jury recommendations. One bill reinstated the requirement that the district return ex-
cess profits to member counties, and another made the bridge district
auditor accountable to the board rather than the general manager.
McCarthy also tried to institute a term limit for the directors and a requirement that they submit annual reports to county supervisors. A

fourth bill, which observers agreed had the best chance of passage, called for a regular outside audit. The bridge directors passed resolutions opposing all of McCarthy's legislation; one director remarked that an outside audit was "an insult to the board. . . . I don't know why we have to have a nursemaid."[38] Despite his best efforts and his increasing influence in the legislature (he was elected senate minority leader in 1961), none of McCarthy's bills made it out of committee—the bridge district too had increased its sway in Sacramento.

As in previous years, bridge district officials responded to public criticism by bolstering their political fortifications. In addition to their effort to clean up accounts at the bridge district, they also moved to strengthen their public relations and lobbying in the wake of investigation. The district's lobbyist in Sacramento, Gordon Garland, was experienced and savvy. A solid majority of directors were willing to increase his salary to make up for new restrictions on his expense account. Leland Murphy, one of Marin's directors, made it clear that he felt McCarthy was responsible for creating the need for these expenses: "We have a senator now that has done nothing but slur the directors and try to abolish the district. . . . [The] people that built the bridge would have been swindled out of it. We have kept the district alive."[39] Adam could depend on the loyalty and support of the directors, many of whom had been members since the construction period. They were used to public criticism, and expressed pride in the organization and loyalty to its staff. Admitting that the agency was poorly administered or even corrupt would be admitting to their incompetence as its leadership, or even worse, compliance in the abuse of its resources and funds.

The bridge district had several advantages. Its reserves were growing steadily, and its auditors reported a net profit of $2.7 million at the end of the 1964 fiscal year.[40] McCarthy could no longer wave the red flag of high tolls; the Golden Gate commuter toll was actually less than that of the Bay Bridge. Support for the bridge district remained strong in the northern counties. Only in Marin and San Francisco were the investigations and accusations against its management taken very seriously. Sonoma's *Press Democrat* expressed the typical northern county attitude: "The return of robins is accepted as the first harbinger of Spring—and whenever State Senator Jack McCarthy hits the headlines with a bunch of charges about the way the Golden Gate Bridge is operated it's an infallible reminder that the California Legislature will begin another session within a few weeks. The gentleman from Marin County is the legislative front man for those who want to get the state's hooks on the multi-million dollar reserves."[41] Bridge district operations were consistently praised in the northern counties and its financial solvency and growing reserves applauded.

Even so, the bridge district moved to reinforce its political alliances in rural northern California through its reliable organizational partner, the Redwood Empire Association (REA). By the end of the 1950s, REA had an aging membership and its influence was waning; its relationship with the bridge district had become less symbiotic and more dependent. However, largely because of its association with the bridge district, the REA was revitalized under the leadership of Carney J. Campion, who was appointed as its general manager in 1961. Not only did the bridge district continue to pay REA dues, but it also remained its biggest advertising client.[42] Even as promoting the bridge became more difficult to justify as it neared its traffic capacity, the bridge district began employing REA officers and public relations agents. Starting in 1964, an REA officer attended all of the bridge directors' general meetings and most of their committee meetings to "assist in reporting and interpreting actions of the Board of Directors and their resultant decisions on policy and programs that are of general interest." The REA released almost daily announcements of "bridge anniversaries; emergency service; toll collectors plight; traffic oddities, etc."[43] This effort to court the press may have been an attempt to deflect some of the scrutiny of San Francisco and Marin newspapers, but it was more likely meant to encourage coverage of bridge district operations in small northern county newspapers, which had sympathetic editors but no regular correspondents. Campion developed a comprehensive press release mailing list that included all northern California newspapers and television and radio stations, as well as national press services.[44]

After the 1963 investigations, McCarthy turned his attention away from the bridge district. Always an advocate for development, he devoted himself to supporting the construction of a second crossing from San Francisco to Marin. He even relaxed his enmity momentarily to offer an endorsement for a plan to add an additional deck to the bridge in 1965. McCarthy was attempting to move up in the GOP hierarchy; in addition to his duties as senate minority leader, he was busy campaigning for the position of lieutenant governor. He made a well-publicized trip to Washington with Richard Nixon and there was speculation that he was considering a bid for governor or U.S. senator. In 1966 he was at the peak of his popularity, winning by a two–to-one margin in Marin County against a well-known challenger.[45]

Racism at the Bridge District

Even without McCarthy's criticism, Adam was not out of trouble for long. In 1966 he faced charges that were more serious than ever, and a new round of investigations and accusations brought bridge district labor relations into the limelight. In July 1965, Adam refused to hire James Haugabook, an African American painter, after requesting candidates from Local 4 of the Painters' Union of San Francisco. Adam did hire the white painters who applied for the job at the same time, several of whom were less experienced than Haugabook.[46] Haugabook had been a union journeyman painter for six years, and had even worked as a foreman. He had experience working at heights painting structural steel on scaffolding similar to that used on the bridge.[47] Union officials accused Adam and the district of racial discrimination, bringing their case to the California Fair Employment Practice Commission (FEPC). After five months of investigation, the FEPC demanded that the bridge district hire Haugabook and "compensate him for time lost due to discrimination."[48] In an unusual move, Adam refused to comply or to negotiate a settlement, initiating a rare FEPC hearing that took place in March 1966. After just one day of embarrassing testimony, the directors ordered him to settle the matter. Adam agreed to hire Haugabook without admitting any liability, and the directors pledged to adopt an official nondiscrimination policy.[49]

However, charges of racism continued. Almost immediately after Haugabook was hired, another painter, Jimmie Lee Wilkins, filed a complaint against Adam and the bridge district with the FEPC. Wilkins was the first African American skilled worker on the bridge, winning the job just days after Haugabook's first complaint. Wilkins was mentioned as an example of the bridge district's fair hiring practices during the 1966 hearing.[50] Harry Bigarani, a high-level painters' union official and San Francisco housing commissioner, testified that he had recommended Wilkins for the job and that he had worked with him in 1949. Wilkins himself never appeared at Haugabook's hearing. Instead, an incident at the bridge district offices led to his dismissal. Wilkins was called off of the bridge to discuss the hearing in a meeting with Adam and the bridge district attorney on the day that he was supposed to testify.[51] When he arrived, Wilkins informed them that he did not have any experience as a painter before he started working at the bridge and was not willing to lie to the FEPC. At the request of the bridge district attorney, Wilkins signed a statement admitting to falsifying his original application. Wilkins offered to resign to "save any embarrassment to the bridge and to . . . the other people involved who were trying to help me."[52] Wilkins was told to go on vacation while the hearings proceeded. Two days later he was fired with a letter that was hand-delivered to him along with his last paycheck at 11:50 P.M. It was the day before the end of Wilkins's six-month probationary period, when it was customary for painters to go on permanent status with medical benefits and paid leave.[53]

Soon after his dismissal, Wilkins had a change of heart and submitted a formal complaint to the bridge directors. He charged that bridge district officials "who wanted him hired to mitigate Haugabook's charges of discrimination" had instructed him to lie about his experience and told him what to write.[54] Representatives of the National Association for the Advancement of Colored People held a press conference to call attention to the obvious contradictions between Wilkins's confession and Bigarani's testimony under oath before the FEPC. They accused Bigarani and Adam of "perpetuat[ing] racially discriminatory employment practices," and pointed out that Wilkins was fifteen years old and attending high school in Tennessee at the time Bigarani said he was working with him.[55] Local 4 secretary Morris Evenson, a longtime critic of Adam, also supported Wilkins's complaint. Evenson contended that Adam hired Wilkins expressly because he did not have previous experience, and that Adam and Bigarini conspired to bypass the union hiring hall to make it easier to fire him later.[56]

Wilkins was rehired, and along with Haugabook, worked on the bridge for another year. However, they were under intense surveillance and faced difficult working conditions. Haugabook recalled his first day as a Golden Gate Bridge painter:

My first day on the bridge I was assigned to work with the sandblasting crew . . . with Paul Powell. Mr. Powell was sandblasting underneath the roadway, on occasions work was done on a swing stage 500 feet above the bay underneath the roadway. At the time I had no clue in terms of work replacement. I found out later that the bridge never placed a new employee in such an advanced working condition. There are 4 rolling scaffolds that roll on tracks under the roadway, which is relative[ly] safe. This is where new employees are assigned on their first tour of duty. Two things were going on here with my assignment with Paul Powell. Number one, Mr. Powell was a union shop steward, and I discovered later that he did not side with the bridge on race issues. That explains why he was working the most difficult area on the bridge. Secondly, since . . . I was an experienced painter before I went to work, I suppose they wanted me to prove it right off the bat.[57]

Paul Powell was a steward for the Painters' Union, and one of the first people to befriend Haugabook. He had complained to one of the foremen that Haugabook and Wilkins had not been granted permanent status after more than a year on the job, and also testified to safety violations on the bridge at the one-day hearing in January 1966.[58]

The first time Wilkins attempted the difficult job of sandblasting, no effort was made to show him how to do it, either. He remembered that his foreman "just put the helmet on me and he said, 'Blast this section here.' And that was it."[59] Supervisors were required to fill out regular performance evaluations on every painter for the first time, as well.[60] Wilkins noted that "they started keeping work sheets, on a day to day basis. And I found out that they never did that to anybody else."[61] His work was also being scrutinized: "There was a little spot left on a—on a knee brace out there. . . . It was just a spot that wasn't painted. It had been cleaned for painting but it had been left. . . . And so the Paint Superintendent came out and we were told in front of witnesses that he demanded that the foreman write this down—that he write all this stuff down."[62]

Despite various warning signs, Wilkins and Haugabook were surprised when Adam terminated them both in March 1967. At the same time, he fired Powell.[63] "I am one of the alleged 'incompetent' painters recently fired from the Golden Gate Bridge," Powell recounted bitterly:

After five years of alleged "incompetence" I was appointed union shop steward. In the discharge of my duties, I continued showing my "incompetence" by urging the bridge district management to accord fair and equal treatment to the two Negro painters they were forced to hire in 1966 under an FEPC ruling. . . . I testified to the whole truth in an Industrial Accident Commission hearing on behalf of a bridge painter seriously injured in a fall . . . damag[ing] the case that the management had built up against the injured painter. . . . Management can only take so much "incompetence" so I was fired on April 28 along with my two Negro union brothers. . . . The moral: "Don't be so incompetent that you try to stick up for your fellow man."[64]

Powell's lawyers charged that Adam fired him to show that "he didn't just fire Negros."[65] Union officials also contended that Powell "had an unblemished record until he spoke out as a citizen against the racial policy of James Adam."[66]

NAACP representatives and union officials began to protest bridge district racism, and appeared before the directors at several heated bridge district meetings to demand Adam's dismissal. Nevertheless, at a meeting in April 1967, during which TV coverage and "any discussion of racial discrimination" were expressly forbidden by the bridge district president, the directors voted twelve to two to uphold Adam's authority to fire employees at his discretion, refusing to entertain any further debate on the matter.[67] San Francisco attorney John E. Dearman, who became the first African American director in 1966, called the other directors "cowards" for shirking their responsibilities, and urged them "not to let Mr. Adam dictate the way to run this bridge." Newly-appointed San Francisco director Stephan C. Leonoudakis, who cast the other dissenting vote, called the meeting "one of the ugliest scenes I have ever attended and a disgrace to all of us."[68] The ensuing uproar coincided with the thirtieth anniversary of the bridge's opening. Local politicians declared their intention to boycott bridge district parties and luncheons, which were all cancelled. Bay Area papers instead covered angry denunciations of the agency and calls for Adam's dismissal. A protest march across the bridge was the only public event to mark the end of its third decade.[69]

Leading this march were (left to right) Jimmie Lee Wilkins, James Haugabook, and Paul Powell. This photo was printed by the *San Francisco Chronicle* on May 26, 1967, a day before the thirtieth anniversary of the opening of the bridge.

Haugabook and Wilkins filed a new complaint against Adam and the bridge district with the FEPC in July 1967, initiating another investigation. Once again, the commissioners called for reparations, and once again Adam refused to concede, leading to public hearings on the complaint. Commissioner C. L. Dellums, a well-known and respected Bay Area civil rights leader, expressed dismay at the bridge directors' refusal to negotiate a settlement: "they made it crystal clear that their minds are closed . . . they said the men were fired and were going to stay fired, and they didn't want to talk about it."[70] Dellums noted that there was ample evidence of discrimination and remarked that it was "almost unbelievable that it was a public agency that was the first employer to flatly refuse to cooperate with an FEPC representative." Adam was "guilty of serious abuse of his office," according to Dellums.[71] The attorney representing Adam, George Bahrs, took the position that the California Bridge and Highway District Act specified that the general manager had "complete control over the personnel and the operations of the bridge" and that the directors' hands were tied in the matter: they could not influence his decisions or reprimand him in any way short of dismissing him.[72] Dellums responded by pointing out that the "only remedy [for the district] would be for the directors to fire Adam."[73] However, the directors were clearly unwilling to consider that.

Another full-scale FEPC hearing commenced, taking place over the course of two weeks in September and November 1968. Before a large audience and a television crew, Wilkins described the circumstances of his application. He had been working in a car wash in Oakland when Bigarani approached him and asked if he was afraid of heights. When he replied in the negative, Bigarani told him to go out to the bridge and apply for a job.[74] When he turned in his application, Adam informed him that the position was temporary. "You might work a year or two years," Wilkins remembered him saying.[75] Wilkins caught on quickly despite his lack of experience. One of his foremen remembered, "I could see that he had not done this type of work before. . . . He said there is a lot of difference between this and washing cars. Jim is a willing worker and works hard at it. At the last he was keeping right along with the rest of the crew."[76]

Haugabook got less glowing reports. Repeatedly, painters called to testify by bridge district attorneys claimed that he was slow and inconsistent and that he failed to operate equipment correctly, resulting in damage and losses. Several of Haugabook's coworkers remembered him ignoring safety procedures, and a bridge district attorney cross-examining him suggested that he was caught sleeping on a scaffold. Perplexingly, other bridge district witnesses testified that Haugabook's obvious fear of heights also hindered his performance and indicated a lack of experience.[77] However, six painters were willing to assert under oath that both Wilkins's and Haugabook's work was as good as any of their peers.[78] When Adam testified, he claimed that all three painters were fired mainly because of poor workmanship. When daily evaluations were entered into evidence, the lawyer for Wilkins and Haugabook protested: "They set up a system here to try to catch these painters [and] make a record for the basis of their subsequent dismissal of them."[79] Evaluation reports on painters stopped immediately after the three were fired. Adam also claimed that the final straw in the decision to fire Haugabook was an investigation revealing that some of the experience listed on his original application was fabricated. When questioned further, however, Adam admitted that he knew that some of the white painters had also falsified their applications, but had not taken any action against them.[80]

The FEPC found Adam guilty of discriminating against Wilkins but absolved the bridge directors of any responsibility. With a split vote, the three-member panel that was hearing the case dismissed Haugabook's complaint completely.[81] Adam said that he was "disappointed" with the decision, insisting that "there is no discrimination whatsoever in employment procedures at the Golden Gate Bridge."[82] Union officials protested the decision: "The FEPC is a farce, used only to dull the militancy of those who believe in constitutional government."[83] And indeed, the FEPC had only very limited enforcement authority and was dominated by white, pro-business appointees.[84] The decision was subject to court review, but the directors conferred in a private meeting and decided to end the public spectacle by re-hiring Wilkins.[85] However, they insisted that only Adam had the authority to reinstate Haugabook or Powell, despite efforts by Leonoudakis and Dearman to "suspend the rules" on the matter.[86] Union officials appealed to the NAACP for funding to continue Haugabook's legal campaign for reinstatement, but ultimately abandoned his case. The FEPC refused to consider a complaint from Powell that he was also the victim of discrimination, but he filed a separate lawsuit that was settled quietly by bridge district lawyers out of court.[87]

The hearings revealed that the bridge district failed to adopt the nondiscrimination policy as they promised in the 1966 settlement with the FEPC and Haugabook. The third African American skilled laborer to be hired, Maurice Harris, began work as a "painter's helper" just before the hearings. Union representatives charged that he was another token and held another demonstration on the bridge. One protestor commented that "Adam believes he's God and he owns the bridge."[88] After the 1967 hearings, the directors hired a consulting firm to do a thorough study of bridge district hiring practices and to recommend changes. The result was a condemnation of bridge district procedures— the report revealed that each department of the district had different hours, promotion guidelines, and evaluations, and even these were often ignored. The directors adopted an employee appraisal form and agreed to start using examinations for promotions, but failed to adopt an official nondiscrimination policy or a formal grievance procedure.[89] In 1968, when Dearman presented a plan to give summer jobs to six black youths as a gesture of atonement and a community service, the directors voted it down.[90]

Smooth and Smother

A secondary outcome of the FEPC hearing was the emergence of new concerns about Adam's management of the bridge itself, particularly neglect of engineering and maintenance. A number of painters testified that sloppy methods for painting were encouraged by foremen. Instead of carefully removing all rust before applying a new coat of paint, they claimed, they were regularly urged to "smooth and smother" rust in problem areas to keep up their pace.[91] One painter called the bridge a "rust bucket," and another remarked that it was "absolutely a mess up there."[92] Bridge district lawyers used this contention to try to prove the incompetence of the discharged workers, even transporting the commissioners, witnesses, and court reporters to the bridge to view poorly painted sections.[93] However, they ended up encouraging more damaging questions about the condition of the bridge and adequacy of maintenance operations. According to several witnesses, badly designed suspender boxes where the vertical cables attached were impossible to properly clear of rust. All that could be done was simply to cover them with paint, and they were deteriorating rapidly beneath it. "This Golden Gate Bridge . . . is supposed to be like a tooth," one painter reflected, "well I sure as heck hate to have my tooth done that way."[94] The problems were exacerbated by painting procedures, but probably originated during the construction period, when the directors decided against sandblasting the structure before painting it in order to save limited construction bond funds, planning to redress the problem once they had toll revenue to spend.[95] A full inspection of the bridge, which the directors commissioned during the FEPC hearings, revealed that the painters' assessment of the bridge's condition was accurate. In 1969, engineers recommended $200,000 worth of repairs and urged the bridge district to replace the faulty cable boxes immediately.[96]

Painters also testified before the FEPC that the bridge district provided inadequate safety equipment, some of it as old as the bridge itself. In the midst of the FEPC hearings, a worker fell to his death while painting the bridge when his safety line snapped six feet from his belt. An official REA press release announced that it was the first accidental death on the bridge since its opening, but further investigation uncovered another death in 1958 and serious injuries from falls in 1961 and 1965. Union officials claimed that Adam had been ignoring their concerns about safety on the bridge for years, and demanded his dismissal.[97] The "senseless death . . . is an extreme example of Mr. Adam's arrogant disregard for human life and the community we live in," they claimed.[98] Though a state investigation revealed no "gross" safety violations and determined the death to be accidental, it added considerably to the district's ongoing public relations disaster. After the fall, the bridge district adopted formal safety procedures for the first time.[99]

Only the Names Have Changed

Even in the midst of all the bad press and intense scrutiny, the directors voted to approve several questionable expenditures. They added a new Cadillac limousine to the district fleet and spent more than a half a million dollars to remodel bridge district offices and purchase luxurious new furnishings for the board room. They increased their life insurance policies from $10,000 to $100,000.[100] And bridge management continued to refuse to entertain bids for many contracts and purchases, asserting that district rules required bidding on construction or repairs only, not on maintenance. Adam was paying a premium for paint, arguing that it could not be purchased competitively because "it is very necessary to use the best material."[101] Paul Peterzell of the *Independent Journal* observed that "all that glitters is gold when the Bridge District buys."[102] The Marin County grand jury called for legislation to "close the loophole" that allowed the bridge district to avoid competitive bids. Regardless, the directors voted nine to four to ratify their existing contract for paint without calling for bids.[103]

The inspection following the FEPC hearings was carried out by the New York engineering firm Ammann & Whitney, the favored bridge district contractor. After conducting the inspection, the firm won another $320,000 no-bid contract for repairs and reconstruction. Legally, the bridge district was required to open all repair contracts for more than $5,000 to bids, but Adam argued that this work was actually an extension of the inspection. Leonoudakis, the lone dissenter among the directors, protested vehemently: "there have been some strange maneuverings, but this one has to rank as the worst and the squirreliest yet."[104] In less than a year, Ammann & Whitney were paid $680,000 in fees without ever having to compete with other firms.[105] Clearly, reform had to be forced on the agency.

Year after year, bridge district leaders had been charged with a lack of accountability, inefficiency, poor management, and general extravagance. Adam was at the locus of controversy, subject to regular denunciation for dishonesty and arrogance. After the FEPC hearings he was ravaged by the regional press, and by the late 1960s, he had become a pariah. A *San Francisco Examiner* editorial described his career at the bridge district:

The inner workings of the Golden Gate Bridge and Highway District—Ye Feudal Fief—are so determinedly despotic that they have a certain charm, the charm of consistency . . . Jim Adam, who went from press agent to lobbyist to manager-lobbyist, to manager WITH lobbyist, has come as close as anybody to owning and operating the Golden Gate Bridge as a private preserve. And in most consistent fashion, Jim is properly feudal about the whole highhanded business. It can be said in general that EVERYBODY connected with the Golden Gate Bridge, and most especially Jim Adam, gets paid more by far than anybody connected with any similar operation in the state. That's in straight salaries. The perquisites of a fiefdom, the happy extras, are even more lavish.[106]

Similarly, *Chronicle* editors noted that the bridge district had "under Adam's tutelage shown consistent disregard for public opinion, for public policy and for the public good."[107] But criticism was not limited to Adam; one commentator remarked that the directors' consistent position was that "their general manager, Mr. Adam, can do no wrong."[108] In 1968, the editor of the *Independent Journal* described a 1940 incident when a director was ruled out of order for attempting to discuss excessive spending during a board meeting, noting that the same thing was still going on at the bridge district: "only the names have changed in the last forty years."[109] Dick Nolan, a regular editorialist for the *Examiner*, made a sarcastic assessment of the state of the bridge district and the mental health of its officials:

Nowhere in all this broad land is there a public agency whose neuroses are so lacerated as those of the Golden Gate Bridge & Highway District. . . . The income rises, inexorably. A silver tide of two-bitses chokes the toll gates and inundates the board room. Try as they will (and as they must) the management and the directors cannot boost expenditures to meet income. Failing in their natural function as bureaucrats, they are haggard, haunted men. It is a shattering thing. Weakened by years of shoveling quarters, they are at last reduced to sitting hopelessly on the board, flipping mere spoonfuls and sobbing hysterically. After you have exhausted your imagination on absolutely astonishing salaries, expense accounts, elaborate headquarters and furnishings, limousines, a parade of the most expensive engineering consultants available, plots, charts, studies, reports, paperwork beyond belief—well, you have done your best, and your best is not good enough. There drifts the damnable surplus, mocking, inexhaustible. So you go mad. That's what you do. Mad, do you hear? Ah-ha-ha-ha-ha! Mad! And you hire a lobbyist.[110]

Nolan's assessment reflected the level of outrage that Adam's administration had generated. The directors approved a new lobbying budget in time for the 1969 session of the state legislature, and Garland maintained his $16,000 salary and unlimited expense account, to which he had previously charged more than $30,000 in a single year.[111] By that time, facing the retirement of construction bonds in 1971, the directors had much more to worry about than spending surpluses, redeeming their public image, or keeping the abuses of the general manager in check: the threat of the agency's dissolution was more serious than ever before.

Those who remember Adam uniformly describe him as an uncompromising, iron-fisted boss who maintained absolute control over the bridge district. During Adam's watch there was an obvious pattern of lax oversight, loose spending, and cozy relations with contractors and politicians. Adam may have been zealous about protecting his personal authority, but he saw his role at the bridge district as more than just its ruler. While personal obstinacy and refusal to compromise harmed his own reputation and exposed him to prosecution and public condemnation, Adam worked doggedly to defend the interests of the bridge district as he understood them, even when they seemed to conflict with his immediate, personal interests. His long and stubborn struggle against the FEPC was no doubt motivated primarily by bigotry and racism, but Adam also considered his authority as general manager and bridge district independence to be important values. In asserting his power to determine personnel policies, to hire and fire employees at his discretion, Adam was also defending bridge district autonomy.

Though the source of his authority was very different, in many ways Adam had as much discretion and personal power as the nineteenth-century urban bosses who were the targets of progressive reformers. Special districts were intentionally removed from the pressures of public opinion and electoral politics, partially to reduce the influence of party machines, but also to prevent graft and reduce opportunities for patronage. In theory, their expert, professional administrators would promote the public interest, free from pressure from less than honorable politicians. However, special districts also enabled officials like Adam to avoid accountability for their actions and policies. It was an ironic consequence of the institutional structure of special districts that their officials were also susceptible to corruption. The abuses that special districts were designed to eliminate could be actually facilitated by their autonomy, independent revenues, hierarchical structure, and lack of political accountability. That the agency survived Adam's administration essentially unscathed by reform is more evidence for its durability and enormous power as an independent special district.

Chapter 7
Regionalism, Transportation, and Perpetual Tolls

At the end of the 1960s, the abolition of the Golden Gate Bridge and Highway District seemed imminent. The agency descended into disrepute under the leadership of James Adam, and its construction bonds, its raison d'être, would be retired in 1971. No longer would its leaders be able to use legal obligations to bondholders as a shield against their critics. Nevertheless, defying increased pressure for reform or dissolution, the agency underwent a dramatic rebirth, its operations expanded to include mass transportation. This apparent paradox—that the bridge district took on new obligations and thereby guaranteed its perpetuation just as its reputation reached a nadir—can only be understood in the context of regional politics and policy. A momentous power struggle over regional planning and government engulfed the San Francisco Bay Area. The bridge district survived because it filled a gap left open by the failure of regionalism.[1]

Several Bay Area agencies already had limited regional planning authority or regulatory responsibility by the 1960s. In 1957, state legislators established the Bay Area Rapid Transit (BART) District and the Bay Area Air Pollution Control District. After the defeat of the Golden Gate Authority, appointed members of the Bay Area Transportation Study (BATS) Commission took on the task of developing a regional transportation plan in 1963. Planning advocates added two more ostensibly temporary bodies to the list of regional agencies in 1965: the San Francisco Bay Conservation and Development Commission (BCDC), and the San Francisco Bay-Delta Water Quality Control Program, a collaboration between state Water Quality Control Board leaders and local officials.[2] In April 1966, Melvin B. Lane, chairman of the BCDC, addressed a letter on the subject of "governing the Bay Area" to the leaders of these five regional entities. Lane spelled out the decision facing all of them: whether they should fight for the continuation of their separate programs, or support the creation of a single, centralized regional government. "The question is no longer *whether* there should be regional government in the Bay Area; the fact that several regional agencies exist has already answered that question. The real problem we face is this: what *form* should regional government take in the future . . . [and] whether this system of fragmented responsibility will be adequate in the coming years of intensive population growth in the Bay Area."[3]

Lane rightly assumed that the leaders of these regional agencies would have a role in this decision. Ultimately, they sided with the home rule faction spearheaded by the Association of Bay Area Governments (ABAG), which opposed regional government and supported the status quo of local government autonomy and decentralization. However, they faced formidable challengers: the business and labor interests represented by the Bay Area Council (BAC) had the weight of expertise and public opinion on their side, in favor of authoritative, comprehensive regional government. A new growth control movement, made up of an increasingly powerful coalition of environmentalists, conservationists, and neighborhood activists opposed to continued unchecked development, tipped the balance of power in favor of home rule. By the end of the decade, a decentralized network of limited-purpose special agencies, including a newly reorganized and even more powerful Golden Gate Bridge, Highway and Transportation District, took permanent responsibility for regional coordination and planning. The bridge district was only a minor player in this titanic political struggle, but its survival as an agency depended on the outcome.

Reconsidering Regionalism

Efforts to instate Bay Area regional planning were driven by dramatic, sustained growth that began during World War II and was expected to continue for decades to come. In the Bay Area, most of the increase in population occurred in small cities or unincorporated areas, compounding its impact on traffic. During the 1950s, the South Bay, especially Santa Clara and San Mateo counties, experienced the fastest growth. The North Bay was not far behind: Marin's rate of growth ranked third among Bay Area counties. Its total population increased by nearly 70 percent, going from 87,700 in 1950 to 148,800 in 1960; Marin and Sonoma together added more than 100,000 new residents. And by 1963, 40 percent of Marin's residents left the county for work every day—more and more of them in private automobiles. In the 1950s, traffic on the Golden Gate Bridge increased beyond even the most optimistic predictions of its original promoters. The 9.4 million crossings of 1950 was nearly double the annual total that financial planners projected in 1930.[4]

Even more traffic was on the horizon. Two major studies predicted continued intensive development and an urgent need for improved transportation infrastructure. In 1956, the BART Commission presented high and low growth projections, estimating that the region could more than double its population in the next thirty years, from three million residents to seven million in 1990.[5] Three years later, the Army Corps of Engineers forecast even faster growth, depicting a region about to undergo a wholesale transformation. According to their analysis, the population of the nine-county Bay Area would nearly double by 1990 and double again in the thirty years after that, going from 3.8 million in 1960 to 14.4 million in 2020. The North Bay, including the counties of Marin, Sonoma, and Napa, would grow by 172 percent, adding nearly a million new residents by 1990. Agricultural acreage would decline and industrial areas would expand, but most new development would be residential and commercial, turning the North Bay into "a dormitory for San Francisco." Existing and future state highways provided the "skeleton" of the plan, determining the location and timing of development. In short, planners for the Army Corps of Engineers expected the communities north of the Golden Gate to swell with automobile commuters.[6] Through the end of the 1960s, these projections were generally accurate and inspired urgent and persistent efforts to establish metropolitan government and regional planning in order to accommodate and manage growth.

Although it was seldom acknowledged at the time, the relationship between transportation infrastructure and development was a two-way street. Until 1959, transportation policy consistently supported predictions of rapid, decentralized growth; state and federal road and freeway construction was backed by ample funding and eagerly sought by local politicians. In 1947, the Collier-Burns Act provided state gas taxes specifically earmarked for road and highway construction, and included a special commitment to construction in metropolitan areas. When Congress passed the Federal-Aid Highway Act in 1956, launching the Interstate and Defense Highway System, California's politicians and public works officials were poised to tap into federal subsidies. They consolidated existing plans in a highly ambitious, comprehensive *California Freeway and Expressway Plan*, which the legislature officially adopted in 1959. It made urban areas the main targets of state construction, and included an entirely new freeway system to open the Pacific coastline of Marin to recreation and residential development.[7] The BART system was expected to give the Bay Area another boost. Other initiatives, including a new bridge south of the San Francisco-Oakland Bay Bridge and a second crossing from San Francisco to Marin via Angel Island, were "in the pipeline," promised state engineers.[8]

However, these plans for transportation infrastructure were increasingly at odds with local politics. Two decades of rapid growth degraded both the environment and standards of living in the Bay Area, generating a widespread backlash. In 1959, San Francisco supervisors put a sudden halt to the construction of all freeways in the city with their famous "freeway revolt." They voted unanimously to deny permission for street closures, which was required under California law, hoping to negotiate less destructive street improvements or state subsidies for the construction of a tunnel instead. Several federally funded interstate projects were ultimately scrapped, much to the dismay of pro-growth state officials and businessmen. With less fanfare, local dissent stopped transportation projects elsewhere in the Bay Area. Opposition to a second Marin-San Francisco crossing thwarted state efforts to build it in 1957 and again in 1961. Public protest also prevented the construction of two east-west freeways in Marin and a major expansion of the Shoreline Highway along the Pacific coast. In Napa County, local activists determined to protect agricultural land from suburbanization also blocked a new freeway. Dissent in Santa Clara County resulted in its exclusion from the BART district in the early planning phase, and San Mateo County residents stopped three planned freeways.[9]

These incidents heralded the emergence of a new coalition of environmentalists, conservationists, and growth-control advocates. A powerful movement took shape in the Bay Area, reflected in public protest against the construction of new transportation infrastructure and supported by members of the social and intellectual elite. The San Francisco freeway revolt left in its wake an enduring network of activists, various neighborhood associations, and a secure growth- and traffic-control majority on the board of supervisors. It also encouraged other critics of growth, including park and open space advocates, whose accomplishments included the creation of the Point Reyes National Seashore in 1962 and a major expansion of parkland in the East Bay. Dorothy Erskine and T. J. (Jack) Kent were among the first Citizens for Regional Recreation and Parks, which was formed in 1958 and later renamed People for Open Space and then Greenbelt Alliance. Its members participated in the development of the ABAG regional plan as well as various local planning and zoning measures. The Marin chapter of the Audubon Society, which included Martin Griffin, opposed subdivisions along the bay in the 1960s. The Committee for Green Foothills on the Peninsula began pursuing similar goals in San Francisco and San Mateo Counties in 1962. These and other newly minted organizations joined forces with more venerable entities such as the League of Women Voters and the Sierra Club in agitating for environmental regulations and planning, not only to rein in growth and establish guidelines for new development, but also to focus attention on repairing some of the damage to the region's environment and landscape. Increasingly, local politicians in the Bay Area were elected because of their record on growth control. In Marin, a coalition of traditional conservationists and more radical environmentalists challenged the longstanding pro-growth establishment, eventually taking control of county-level government. San Francisco leaders remained solidly committed to controlling traffic and staving off freeways.[10]

This movement upset the balance of power in the Bay Area, resulting in shifting coalitions, new local political regimes, and transformed regional politics. Efforts for regional government and planning were newly controversial, and their purpose was thrown into question. The two basic camps for and against regionalism remained the same, with the local government officials of ABAG facing off against big business and industry, represented by the BAC, but now a third power group had emerged that could not be ignored by either side. And indeed, growth-control advocates recognized that regional planning could promote their goals as well as those of industry and business. With the creation of the Bay Conservation and Development Commission, conservationists and environmentalists mobilized some of the same strategies and institutional tools that pro-growth interests had refined. In 1961, Kay Kerr, Sylvia McLaughlin, and Esther Gulick, all well-connected, well-educated women married to leading UC Berkeley professors and administrators, formed the Save the Bay Association. The 1959 Army Corps of Engineers plan describing miles of bay fill that would reduce the bay to a narrow "deep water ship channel" by 2020 horrified them. They drafted and lobbied for the 1965 McAteer-Petris Act, which created the BCDC to study environmental and development issues and gave its commissioners four years to develop a long-term regional plan for the bay. The state legislature also created the San Francisco Bay Delta Water Quality Control Program in 1965, requiring that the state Water Quality Control Board work with other agencies (including the BCDC) to study regional water pollution, and to develop recommendations for transferring planning, administration, construction, and financing responsibilities for water facilities from state and local entities to the regional level.[11]

Jack Kent, a high-profile Bay Area planner, conservationist, and environmental activist, was probably the single most influential proponent of a new sort of regionalism to promote environmentalist goals. The son of a San Francisco architect, as a youth Kent witnessed efforts for regional planning that stalled in the 1930s. After graduating with a degree in architecture from UC Berkeley and completing a fellowship with Lewis Mumford in 1939, Kent began his career at the Berkeley office of the federal National Resources Planning Board. He also joined "Telesis," a group of young and ambitious Berkeley planners. He completed his master's degree at the Massachusetts Institute of Technology in 1944 and, after spending two years in the Army, quickly rose to the position of director of planning for San Francisco. He was recruited to teach as a professor at UC Berkeley and, with several other leading scholars, founded the Department of City and Regional Planning in 1948. In the following decades, he served on the Berkeley City Planning Commission, the Berkeley City Council, and the governing boards of many Bay Area conservationist organizations.[12]

Like his mentor Mumford and most of his peers, Kent saw an imperative need for meaningful regional planning to manage urban and suburban growth.[13] He was also well aware of the potential for local government opposition to derail regional efforts, as he had observed first-hand during a 1941 effort to establish a Bay Area Regional Planning Commission. He supported the formation of ABAG in 1958, helped draft its constitution and bylaws, and served on its executive committee. Kent hoped that ABAG would not only defeat the pro-business, pro-growth regionalism expressed in plans for a Golden Gate Authority, but would also promote a new sort of regional planning by getting local government officials directly involved. While convinced that regional planning was necessary, Kent believed that it had to be structured and implemented to preserve open space and environmental quality rather than simply accommodate growth. He saw its potential as a powerful tool for reining in the very business interests that had, until then, been its biggest proponents (e.g., Edgar Kaiser and BAC leaders). He explained his views in 1963:

Without a regional plan, the so-called "natural" forces of economic development will overwhelm the best efforts of local governments to control them. . . . Speculative land development forces now operate on a metropolitanwide basis. They are commanded by men of great enterprise and ability. These men—the builders and doers of today—will wipe out the vineyards of the upper Napa Valley and fill it with suburban tracts; they will overrun the Livermore Valley; they will mop up Stinson Beach, Bolinas, and the Olema Valley. They will spread to the northeast, beyond Vallejo and Fairfield toward Sacramento; to the south, below San Jose to Hollister; and to the west, beyond Santa Rosa to Sebastopol and the Pacific Ocean. . . . Freeways will precede the initial wave of surging growth, and more freeways will follow. Predictably inadequate bridges for trucks and automobiles will be constructed [and] tidelands will be filled. The central districts of San Francisco, Oakland, and San Jose will become inaccessible, and will decay.[14]

During the 1960s, Kent worked ceaselessly to forge an alliance between ABAG and Bay Area growth-control advocates. It was an unlikely partnership, between largely conservative home-rule defenders and sometimes radical environmentalists and conservationists, but Kent hoped that ABAG could evolve into a regional planning agency that would serve growth-control and environmentalist goals. After all, the two interest groups faced a well-defined common enemy: the pro-growth establishment, manifested in the BAC, which had dominated regional planning efforts since 1944. Success for Kent's program required redefining the purpose of regional planning as well as transforming the attitude of ABAG members, most of whom were still stalwart supporters of growth and development. Certainly, the shifting currents of Bay Area politics favored this course.

In the meanwhile, traditional, pro-growth regionalists worked to recover from the defeat of the Golden Gate Authority and to forge a new plan for meaningful, authoritative metropolitan government. State Senator J. Eugene McAteer of San Francisco led the effort in Sacramento, working closely with BAC leaders and a cadre of political scientists at the UC Berkeley Institute of Governmental Studies including Eugene Lee, John C. Bollens, Victor Jones, and Stanley Scott. They agreed that providing for economic development and managing growth required unprecedented governmental coordination and a massive commitment of public resources, particularly in the field of transportation. Scores of conferences, studies, and committee meetings to meet the challenge of providing regional government and planning for the Bay Area were held in the 1960s. Major business and labor groups supported regional planning to accommodate and encourage development through a single, multi-purpose organization—unitary, coordinated, and incisive. They favored state-level appointees or direct election for its leadership, and the exclusion of local politicians.[15]

Early on, the outlook seemed to favor the same pro-growth regionalism that inspired the Golden Gate Authority proposal in the 1950s. Not only did the most powerful Bay Area businessmen still support the cause, but the political establishment in Sacramento, led by Governor Edmund "Pat" Brown, also continued to favor metropolitan regional planning. In 1959 the State Office of Planning was created within the Department of Finance to advise and coordinate planning efforts, its officials charged with dividing the state into regional planning districts. Brown appointed the Governor's Commission on Metropolitan Area Problems to make recommendations on transportation infrastructure, housing, pollution, and local governmental structure. He also appointed an industry-led Coordinating Council on Urban Problems, whose members agreed on the need for a single, multifunction regional government, to develop planning legislation.[16]

However, even before the alliance between ABAG and the growth-control coalition that Kent envisioned began to materialize, pro-growth regional planning advocates suffered a series of setbacks, starting with the defeat of the Golden Gate Authority. In 1963, a bill to create a state commission to oversee and encourage comprehensive metropolitan area planning was narrowly defeated. Instead, the Knox-Nisbet Act, a rival proposal officially supported by ABAG officials, required counties to develop and adopt comprehensive plans, but left the substance and enforcement of these plans to local governments. Knox-Nisbet also created weak, county-level Local Agency Formation Commissions (LAFCOs) to coordinate annexation, incorporation, and special district formation. Pro-growth regional planning suffered another blow when ABAG won federal sanction in 1966, designated as the agency responsible for review of grant applications for the Demonstration Cities and Development Act. In addition, both the BCDC and the Bay-Delta Water Quality Control Program were viewed as potential obstacles to a comprehensive regional agency. Regional needs were being addressed on a piecemeal basis through new agencies with limited authority and jurisdiction, and BAC leaders and their allies could see that their cause no longer had as much urgency.[17]

However, advocates of pro-growth regionalism did achieve a few victories in the early 1960s. Rapid transit won a resounding endorsement at the polls in 1962 when a large majority of Alameda, San Francisco, and Contra Costa County voters approved BART construction bonds. The temporary BATS Commission, created in part to fulfill the planning requirements of the Federal-Aid Highway Act of 1962, also represented a small victory for pro-growth planning. It provided an opportunity to restart efforts for Bay Area bridge and freeway construction that had been put on hold by local opposition and the defeat of the Golden Gate Authority. The commission was comprised of seven at-large members appointed by the governor, eighteen representatives of Bay Area counties and cities, and twelve representatives of other organizations, including the Golden Gate Bridge district, ABAG, and BART. BATS commissioners released a prospectus in 1962 that argued that a clear and compelling regional transportation plan was the key to winning back public support for a pro-growth agenda. Adopting the high growth projections of the 1956 BART study as a starting point for transportation planning, they undertook a comprehensive review of all existing economic and land use plans and studies.[18] BATS commissioners set out to recommend a means by which its regional plan could be refined and updated and the function of regional transportation planning continued indefinitely, and its members favored the creation of a unified, comprehensive regional agency. But the future structure of regional government remained uncertain. Could the BATS Commission and its functions be incorporated into a new multipurpose Bay Area government as pro-growth regionalists wanted? Or would a limited-purpose agency devoted to transportation join those already managing regional functions in the Bay Area? The future of the bridge district and other regional special districts depended on the answers to these questions.

The Golden Gate Corridor

Efforts for Bay Area regional planning provided the context for the metamorphosis of the bridge district, as bridge officials did their best to maneuver into a position of power and make their agency indispensable. As rush hour grew longer and congestion worse, Marin commuters, who had always been vociferous bridge district critics, suffered the most. The traffic crisis offered a compelling reason to expand operations and to undertake new projects and responsibilities that could overcome the agency's unpopularity and record of questionable administration and make it less vulnerable to dissolution.

Growth in the North Bay continued to exceed expectations in the 1960s. Improvements to Highway 101 in the 1950s encouraged residential construction along its route. As the wealth of North Bay residents increased steadily, so did their preference for private automobiles. Automobile ferry service between San Francisco and Marin ended in 1941, leaving only a few decrepit Greyhound buses and a once-daily commuter ferry.[19] And, the Golden Gate Bridge was nearing its maximum capacity. Bridge district engineer Arthur Jenkins noted that 17.5 million crossings in 1959 tested the structure's limits. Annual crossings surpassed 25 million in 1965, five years earlier than forecast. In 1966, Jenkins warned that within a few years "southbound traffic in the morning and northbound traffic in the evening maximum rush hours [will] reach a grand total of 6,000 vehicles. This total is equal to and probably more than the practical capacity of four lanes in a single direction."[20] He recommended a $10 million "modernization program" that involved updating the design of approaches, replacing obsolete toll facilities, and installing new traffic safety and control devices. Although these improvements could allow as many as 25 percent more crossings, even so he predicted that bridge traffic would reach its "maximum potential" by 1970.[21]

The bridge directors acted on many of Jenkins's recommendations. They adopted a system to reverse the direction of the central lane to accommodate lopsided rush hour traffic in 1962, and built more efficient toll collection facilities in 1964. They also worked with embattled state highway engineers and provided funds to widen several bridge approaches. However, these projects put just a small dent in bridge district accounts; only a major, capital-intensive project that justified significant new debt could ensure bridge district survival. The best prospects for that were the construction of a new Golden Gate crossing or the addition of a second automobile deck to the bridge. Both possibilities were discussed at length in Jenkins's 1958 *Long Range Planning Survey*, the aim of which was to ensure the "preservation of the district's financial integrity."[22] Building a second crossing—another bridge or tunnel from San Francisco to Marin—would be a defensive effort. Marin County representatives had been agitating for a second crossing from San Francisco to Marin since the 1940s, and new San Francisco-Marin bridge via Angel Island seemed likely. Jenkins pointed out that competition from a state-operated Angel Island span would be a financial disaster for the bridge district, inevitably reducing its revenue and undermining its ability to finance new projects. The best solution would be to delay the "necessity" of a new crossing by accommodating more traffic on the existing bridge.[23] If that was not enough to stop it, Jenkins argued, the bridge district had to maintain control over the Golden Gate corridor by taking on the project itself.

In 1956, Angel Island bridge plans developed by state engineers won federal approval. Jack McCarthy, a member of the Senate Transportation Committee, was their primary backer. However, the bridge district was not the only interest that was threatened by the prospect of a new state-owned bridge. Grassroots growth control and neighborhood groups generated an outpouring of public vitriol against the proposal. No one wanted bridge traffic to cut through their neighborhood, and influential residents on both sides of the bay, in the wealthy Marina District of San Francisco and the exclusive Tiburon peninsula in Marin, staged protests and organized committees and action groups. The editors of the *Chronicle*, spearheading the movement to stop freeway construction in San Francisco, announced their opposition to a second crossing with a series of highly critical editorials. State parks officials and conservationists, including philanthropist Caroline Livermore, supported a plan to make Angel Island a state park, and argued that a bridge landing would ruin the island's potential for recreational use. McCarthy risked his popularity with the residents of southern Marin by continuing to fight for the bridge, but despite his efforts, funding for the span was rescinded.[24]

Despite determined opposition in the Bay Area, McCarthy and other supporters of a second Golden Gate crossing persevered. In 1965, there was a face-off over yet another San Francisco-Marin bridge study. Two bills were introduced to continue the effort for an Angel Island bridge. One bill provided funding for a "full study of the San Francisco-Marin traffic problem," specifically including the "feasibility of rapid transit," by the Department of Public Works; another bill, introduced just a few days later by Senator Randolph Collier and coauthored by McCarthy,

The surveyor and the planner are standing on a San Francisco pier examining Marin County, represented by the hills in the distance. *San Francisco Chronicle,* September 25, 1961.

would have made the project entirely the responsibility of the bridge district.[25] McCarthy's desire to make Golden Gate Bridge tolls available for new transportation infrastructure briefly overrode his aversion to bridge district administration. The measure allowed the bridge district to issue new bonds for the purpose without a public referendum. Both bills passed, but Governor Brown refused to entrust the bridge district with any new responsibility and vetoed Collier's bill. *Examiner* editors accused Collier and bridge district officials of "devious tactics," remarking that they had been "caught once again trying to expand their limited domain into a perpetual empire."[26]

Although their overture to build a second crossing was rebuffed, bridge district officials had little reason to fear a new state-controlled bridge. San Francisco supervisors reaffirmed their rejection of freeways in March 1966, including the proposed Golden Gate Freeway that was to be the primary route into the city for traffic from the Angel Island span. Without this connecting freeway, the idea of a new bridge dumping traffic onto the crowded streets of downtown San Francisco was ludicrous. Accordingly, a third state report on the proposed San Francisco-Marin crossing, released in May 1967, deemphasized plans for a new bridge. Instead, state engineers recommended a two-phase approach to expanding traffic capacity between San Francisco and Marin, starting with a second deck on the Golden Gate Bridge.[27]

Adam's Second Deck

This state endorsement for a second deck represented a major victory for bridge district leaders in staving off competition in the Golden Gate corridor. The prospect of expanding bridge capacity was much more attractive to them than building another bridge. A second deck would be less expensive than a new bridge, but it would be expensive enough to require new debt that would ensure the continued need for tolls. And, the district's enabling legislation clearly provided the authority to undertake the second deck, which could be financed as an improvement to the existing bridge without a public vote or the approval of the legislature.[28]

Although they hoped it would relieve traffic problems and soften criticism of their opposition to BART on the bridge, the second deck proposal ultimately added to the bridge directors' public relations problems. McCarthy touched upon its main attractions—and glaring flaws: "The board could perpetuate its existence and block progress for another 50 years if allowed to build and operate another bridge. . . . And where would the cars go at each end of a double-decked Golden Gate Bridge?"[29] Similar denunciations followed: growth and infrastructure advocates including McCarthy accused bridge district officials of deliberately undermining state efforts for a second crossing with their proposals for a second deck.[30] For different reasons, traffic opponents in San Francisco and growth-control advocates in Marin also opposed the second deck.

Soon after refusing to allow BART trains on the bridge, the directors commissioned a second deck feasibility study from the New York engineering firm Ammann & Whitney. The same three engineers who provided the "authoritative 'no'" for the bridge district in its efforts to stop BART were paid $30,000 to study the possibility of adding a second deck for automobiles. They sketched a plan in a spare thirteen-page report, which they presented to the directors in August 1964. They promised bridge directors that adding four new lanes would require "only moderate changes in the existing structure." O. H. Ammann himself explained that the difference between automobiles versus trains crossing the bridge was analogous to "a group of elephants running full speed across the bridge" as opposed to a "group of gazelles."[31]

Despite these assurances, one newly appointed director was willing to point out the elephant in the room. San Francisco attorney Stephan C. Leonoudakis angrily observed that the actual numbers suggested that a second deck for automobiles would be only slightly less burdensome than a deck for rails. "If a second deck was wrong two years ago, then it's wrong today," he shouted to unresponsive colleagues.[32] Leonoudakis had environmentalist leanings and refused to support any measure that would add more traffic to San Francisco streets. With a penchant for attracting attention, he immediately became a maverick member of the board, willing to ignore pressure from Adam and to question his colleagues' honesty and competence.[33]

Ignoring Leonoudakis, the directors officially adopted plans for a second deck with a vote of eleven to two. Adam mobilized to promote the project, dedicating funds for lobbying, distributing fliers at the toll booths, issuing a call for support to all associates and employees, and soliciting endorsements from civic associations and local governments.[34] Forging ahead, bridge district officials offered the construction contract to Ammann & Whitney without a general call for engineering proposals.[35] Nevertheless, Norman C. Raab, a structural engineer who had worked on the design of several Bay Area bridges, submitted an unsolicited design for the second deck in 1965.[36] Raab's proposal drew attention to the fact that Ammann & Whitney was effectively getting another no-bid contract, generating complaints (from Leonoudakis, among others) and questions about the overall quality of their design.

To address these concerns, the directors voted to commission another full study of the second deck from Raab's firm, the prominent San Francisco-based Tudor Engineering Company.[37] They asked retired bridge district engineer Clifford Paine to analyze the two competing proposals. Predictably, Paine backed Ammann & Whitney, questioning the credibility of Tudor cost estimates and criticizing various details of their design.[38] However, the Ammann & Whitney design garnered outside criticism, particularly because it failed to meet current freeway safety standards and exceeded the weight limits that Paine himself had outlined previously. Tudor engineers proposed replacing the current decks with steel grating and lightweight concrete that would actually reduce the total weight of the bridge. They provided for wider lanes, separation of opposing traffic, and the addition of a suicide barrier. Ammann & Whitney's heavier addition had reversible lanes on both decks and would flatten the span's arch. Ammann & Whitney engineers insisted that the Tudor proposal would cost three times more than theirs, despite Tudor's lower initial estimate.[39] After examining the Ammann & Whitney plan, independent Bay Area bridge engineer Francis J. Murphy called it "so ridiculous that it actually defies my imagination." Murphy charged that "the second deck idea is not now being given an engineering evaluation, but a political evaluation." He contended that the addition of a second deck was feasible, even advantageous from an engineering perspective, but that the New York firm had submitted a "makeshift, jerrybuilt design."[40]

While the seemingly cozy relationship between Ammann & Whitney and the bridge district raised eyebrows, the perceived purpose of the second deck generated much more criticism. In April 1966 a *Chronicle* reporter noted that "directors of the Golden Gate bridge district, debating a second deck, discovered yesterday that if they don't spend more money on something by 1971 the district might be dissolved."[41] McCarthy spelled out their dilemma in less flattering terms, accusing the bridge directors of "empire building" in their efforts to build a second deck or a parallel crossing, motivated by the desire to "prevent the district from having enough money to pay off its obligations and go out of business. They will spend to survive."[42] The financial estimates for the second deck, released in October 1967, seemed to confirm this. Bridge district officials planned to borrow the entire $45 million for the project, even though its reserves were approaching $30 million at the time, not including sinking funds. The district auditor estimated that, with

Revenues threaten to sink the leaky boat labeled "Golden Gate Bridge District's Legal Existence." *San Francisco Chronicle,* August 30, 1966.

modest fare increases, new debt for the second deck would take twenty-six years to repay.[43]

Despite Adam's determination to pursue second decking plans, a showdown was imminent. Controversy and scandal eroded the loyalist majority on the board of directors; Leonoudakis led a growing faction of newly appointed directors critical of Adam and of second deck plans. Longtime Marin director Matt Graham was replaced in 1962 with Thomas D. Hardcastle, a steamship company executive who favored bridge district dissolution and comprehensive regional government. San Francisco director Daniel F. Del Carlo lost his seat in 1962 after two decades at the bridge district. Marin director Leland Murphy, who had criticized bridge district spending in the 1950s but had since sided with Adam, was replaced with former Marin County planning commissioner and growth-control advocate George Ludy in 1964. In 1966, San Francisco supervisors replaced Joseph Diviny, a San Francisco labor leader who had been on the bridge board since 1950, and banker Alvin Derre, both of whom sought reappointment. Contractor Chris D. McKeon and John E. Dearman, who explicitly supported the dissolution of the bridge district after the retirement of its bonds, took their places.[44]

In 1967 another vote on the second deck finally forced a confrontation between Adam loyalists and the new appointees. On July 28, three San Francisco directors did not make it to a board meeting in Santa Rosa. Despite, or perhaps because of their absence, the directors voted ten to two to commission final engineering plans from Ammann & Whitney. A year before, when the release of the two engineering studies for the second deck created an uproar in San Francisco, bridge district officials assured city supervisors that they would seek their approval before they took any further action on second deck construction.[45] The unexpected decision was a slap in the face to San Francisco. The *Chronicle* summed up the situation:

With their customary enthusiasm for any scheme that might prolong the life of their cozy little principality, directors of the Golden Gate Bridge and Highway District have almost unanimously [voted] to spend $265,000 of accumulated toll revenues for an engineering and cost study of a second deck for their bridge. San Francisco's supervisors are irritated at what they call the "typical headlong manner" in which the directors thus set out to augment the capacity of a bridge [that] is already carrying peak-hour traffic that overtaxes and clogs its approaches at both ends. "Maybe," says Supervisor Terry Francois, "they have plans for all the traffic a second deck would create—but we haven't."[46]

Anger in San Francisco increased when bridge district officials finalized the contract with Ammann & Whitney a week later. According to the bridge district secretary Helen Jack, Adam signed it following a regular meeting of the board, but only after all of the directors had left the building: "I don't know why." Bridge district president John E. Nelson of Mendocino County commented that "maybe this . . . will cause the San Francisco Supervisors to quit playing politics, get off their duffs and get something done about freeway approaches."[47]

Nelson could not have made a more inflammatory remark. The second deck project had the support of the California Division of Highways and there were suggestions that bridge district representatives were conspiring with state engineers to impose traffic on an unwilling San Francisco. Certainly, Nelson was not the first to suggest that the second deck would increase pressure to build freeways in San Francisco.[48] Second deck opponents began marching alongside the labor protestors who were picketing meetings to support the fired painters. San Francisco neighborhood groups fighting freeway construction also banded together to oppose the second deck.[49] Southern Marin property owners formed the Marin Transportation Action Committee to "prevent overdependence on the automobile from destroying the amenities of life in Marin County."[50] Dozens of Marin and San Francisco organizations passed resolutions against the project, and the objections of their representatives dominated hearings in November 1967.[51] San Francisco Mayor-elect Joseph L. Alioto, who campaigned on a platform of traffic control, urged the directors to abandon the second deck in favor of a bus- and ferry-based transportation system, as did Marin supervisor and conservationist Peter Behr. Marin County supervisors reversed their position on the second deck, voting three to two against it. San Francisco supervisors unanimously condemned the project, urged the directors to cancel the Ammann & Whitney contract, and promised to remove any directors who voted for it. Most importantly, by the end of 1967 new appointments to the bridge district board finally resulted in a slim majority willing to oppose Adam. On November 24, 1967, Leonoudakis introduced a resolution to cancel second deck plans in favor of a system of mass transit.[52] Nine Marin and San Francisco directors voted for the resolution as a bloc against four northern county directors. The *Chronicle* called the decision "one of the worst setbacks ever sustained" by James Adam.[53]

The rejection of second deck plans forced all bridge district officials, even the remaining cadre of longtime directors, to reexamine their strategies for protecting the bridge district. Mass transportation suddenly became the obvious route for the agency's perpetuation—the bridge directors could no longer beat the growth-control coalition, so they joined it. After the split vote against the second deck, on December 15, 1967, the directors voted unanimously to begin planning for a bus and ferry system to be owned, operated, and subsidized by the bridge district.[54]

Mass Transportation

Marin's difficult transportation and traffic problems provided a critical opportunity to make the bridge district indispensable, despite its past and reputation. The only thing that the county's environmentalist growth-control advocates and its pro-development establishment could agree on was the need for improved mass transportation. However, in order to take advantage of the situation, bridge district officials had to elbow aside another potential competitor, the newly formed Marin County Transportation District (MCTD).

In 1963, soon after they were forced out of the BART District, Marin supervisors voted to create their own transit agency. At their request, the state legislature passed enabling legislation for a county transportation district with a governing board composed of county supervisors and city councilmen. Much to the dismay of Marin's beleaguered mass transit supporters, Governor Brown refused to sign the bill, arguing that a new local district might present an obstacle to a future regional transportation agency.[55] In 1964, as the situation in Marin worsened and public pressure for action increased, the governor acquiesced to the agency as an "interim solution to the transit problem."[56] In the next election, 80 percent of Marin voters endorsed the MCTD.

The county supervisors plus two city representatives directed the MCTD. Their primary goal was to revitalize the county's bus system, both local service and intercounty commuter lines. At the time, Greyhound was petitioning the state for permission for fare increases and service cutbacks in the North Bay to help reduce its annual $500,000 losses. After considering several alternatives, including the continuation of Greyhound service with new subsidies, MCTD leaders resolved to develop an entirely new, publicly owned and operated bus system.[57] From the beginning, attracting riders was a concern. Poor service and aging, uncomfortable coaches were major reasons for Greyhound's decline. Marin transportation planners wanted to ensure that the quality of service was adequate to lure even affluent patrons, but that would require an enormous capital investment in new buses and stations. MCTD officials hoped to tap into federal Urban Mass Transportation Act (UMTA) funds. They also resolved to "persuade the Golden Gate Bridge and Highway District to pay at least a fourth of the county's share."[58]

At first, bridge district officials supported MCTD plans and promised funding for intercounty bus service. In 1963 they agreed to join a "Tripartite Transportation Committee," including representatives from Marin, San Francisco, and the bridge district, dedicated to promoting interagency cooperation. In 1965, at the directors' request, the bridge district attorney confirmed that toll revenues could legally subsidize MCTD bus operations.[59] However, the bridge directors' attitude changed dramatically after they voted to take on mass transportation themselves at the end of 1967. Suddenly, the MCTD was a competitor.

When the Tripartite Committee met in February 1968, tensions were already high. San Francisco representatives opposed buses because of traffic concerns, but enthusiastically supported an expanded ferry system for tourists as well as commuters. Marin officials challenged ferries, arguing that they were inefficient, expensive, and could never meet commuter demand. Instead, they fervently wanted toll subsidies for buses, but they made it clear that they did not trust the bridge district to operate mass transit honestly and efficiently. Bridge district representatives were amenable to both ferries and buses, but insisted that only they should operate them, questioning the competence and business sense of the elected officials on the MCTD board. The only point of agreement achieved at the meeting was expressed in the committee's first and only resolution, which declared that toll surpluses should subsidize mass transportation exclusively in the Golden Gate corridor. This statement was intended to oppose any new region-wide transportation agency. All of the other pressing questions remained unanswered as committee meetings quickly deteriorated into a forum for recrimination. Thomas T. Storer expressed the sentiment of the Marin representatives, calling the bridge district a "virtually an unmovable obstacle in the path of achieving any realistic, meaningful solutions to the Marin-San Francisco transportation problem."[60] Marin and San Francisco committee members overruled bridge district representatives and called for a review of the 1962 decision against BART.[61] Outraged, bridge directors William Hadeler and Lowell Edington denounced the "unwarranted, vicious and cheap political attacks upon the Golden Gate Bridge Board" and resigned from the committee in protest.[62]

At this point, everything seemed to indicate dissolution for the bridge district. In 1967 the state legislative analyst reported that "the present organization and authority of the Golden Gate Bridge and Highway district is inconsistent with solution to the corridor problem," and recommended that its revenues "be made subject to the appropriating power of an agency with a broader responsibility."[63] In 1965, reapportionment of the state legislature reduced the representation of rural northern California, where the bridge district had the most support. Although McCarthy's influence began to wane as power shifted, his name still topped a bipartisan roster of bridge district critics, including McAteer in the state senate and William T. Bagley and John F. Foran in the assembly. Like McCarthy, Bagley was a Marin County Republican; he won his first election in 1960. Foran, who was first elected as a San Francisco Democrat in 1962 and was appointed chair of the Assembly Transportation Committee in 1967, advocated for labor and championed mass transportation, including BART.[64] McAteer, a leading regional planning advocate with close ties to San Francisco labor interests, called the bridge district a "luxury we cannot afford" in 1966.[65]

In 1968 Bagley revived the idea of a Golden Gate Authority with Assembly Bill 855, coauthored by McCarthy and George Moscone of San Francisco. As in the past, the Golden Gate Bridge was one of its main targets. At the same time, Bagley introduced another bill that would create a much smaller agency to take over the operation of the Golden Gate Bridge, a San Francisco-Marin Transportation District. He declared that "the Golden Gate bridge District board has parted company with the public's patience—and mine. . . . Apparently inherent in the present bridge district set-up is an unresponsiveness to the public and a tendency to defer to the more northerly counties which think they own the bridge."[66] Bagley acknowledged that neither bill had much chance of success, but explained that they were intended to put pressure on the bridge district. He hoped to "haul [the bridge directors] back into the realm of reality" and establish a position in Sacramento from which to negotiate reform.[67]

Bagley achieved his goal. After months of revision and maneuvering, he managed to get AB 855 through the state legislature. The bill added four new directors to the bridge district, two from San Francisco and one each from Marin and Sonoma counties. It negated the 1942 superior court decision that made county supervisors ineligible to serve on the board and required that nearly half of the directors be elected officials.[68] The bill also required a competitive bidding process on all contracts over $5,000, not only for construction and repair, but also for maintenance, alteration, and inspection. Bridge district lobbyist Gordon Garland worked feverishly against the bill, and Collier tried to have it transferred to his transportation committee where it could be quashed. Collier also introduced milder reform bills, hoping to divert support. Despite their efforts, members of both houses approved Bagley's measure by large margins. It was signed into law on August 30, 1968 by Governor Ronald Reagan, who ignored last-ditch bridge district appeals for a veto. The reorganization and reform ensured that a solid majority of bridge directors would support mass transportation and oppose a second deck, and propelled Leonoudakis into a leadership position.[69]

Another profound change for the bridge district took place at about the same time. After nearly three decades on its staff and fifteen years as its general manager, James Adam finally left the bridge district. Shortly after the FEPC found Adam guilty of racial discrimination in December 1967, Leonoudakis found the leverage to oust him, discovering that official bridge district policy required employees to retire at the age of seventy. In March 1968 Adam announced that he would retire on his birthday in July. Adam tried to convince the directors to replace him with Robert F. Shields, who had been loyal to Adam since he began as a project engineer in 1961. Rumors also circulated that Adam wanted the job of bridge district lobbyist. Ultimately, the directors rejected Adam's advice and hired Dale W. Luehring, a "soft-spoken," charming, and politically astute military man who had also worked as an automobile salesman. An Air Force colonel, Luehring retired from his post in Oakland as chief of staff of the Military Traffic Management and Terminal Services for the West Coast and took on the job of resurrecting the bridge district's image and transforming it into a comprehensive transportation agency.[70] One of his first moves as general manager was to implement a one-way toll system, an idea that Adam had opposed for years. The change resulted in an immediate improvement in traffic flow.[71]

Despite Bagley's reform and changes in leadership, the bridge district retained its fundamental characteristics. Certainly, its new leaders had their own stake in ensuring its survival and independence—having gained control, they were not about to let the agency die. Even Leonoudakis, once a vociferous critic, quickly became a loyal bridge district partisan and one of its most vocal promoters. Leonoudakis explained the directors' new duties: "we are not there just to paint the bridge every year . . . the first priority of the district is not to the auto, but to mass transit."[72] While the bridge district underwent a shift in orientation that reflected its changing political and ideological context, the foundations of its power remained intact: tolls, surpluses, and autonomy. Even though it faced redundancy and its power in Sacramento was at a nadir, the bridge district had the capacity to solve local transportation problems easily and quickly—and its new leaders took advantage of its resources and flexibility to ensure its survival.

Still, bridge district officials had to make a compelling case that they were a better choice for the job than their competitors at the MCTD. Jenkins, returning to work as a consulting engineer, argued for expanding bridge district operations to include mass transportation in a March 1968 report. He pointed out that the agency already had the staff, experience, financial resources, and initiative that were required for the successful development of a new system, all of which the MCTD lacked. Jenkins emphasized the bridge district's independent ability to set toll rates and, potentially, bus fares. Its reserve funds could pay for initial investments, including new facilities and equipment, and its toll revenues would make the system "comfortably self-sustaining."[73] He estimated that a mass transportation system would require $8.5 million initially and $1.4 million in subsidies annually, which could come entirely from bridge tolls. He also pointed out that federal UMTA funds were available for capital investments, but required matching funds and assurance that operations would be supported locally—MCTD leaders had no plans to raise any of this money other than from bridge tolls anyway. Jenkins argued that a decision had to be made quickly, and the bridge district was ready to act. This could be the "last year of decision" for Marin and San Francisco, Jenkins asserted. If they did not choose a course of action, some regional government might take on the task, and the bridge district surplus would "go down the drain somewhere else and the Golden Gate corridor will lose its ability to solve its own problem."[74]

It was difficult to dispute Jenkins's reasoning, given the pragmatic goal of establishing mass transportation. And, new bridge district leadership and recent reform kindled hope for bridge district redemption even among jaded Marin County officials. The promise of immediate action to address the Golden Gate corridor transportation problem, backed by the enormous financial resources of the bridge district, was too compelling for them to resist. In February 1969 MCTD directors reversed their position on bridge district dissolution, unanimously endorsing Jenkins's transportation plan.[75] Assured by Tripartite Committee members that the bridge district would also commit resources to establishing a new ferry system, the San Francisco supervisors rescinded their support for bridge district dissolution as well, and voted to back its transformation into a mass transportation agency.

Regional Governance

Even as the specifics of Golden Gate corridor transportation were being negotiated locally, the ongoing struggle over regional government paved the way for the bridge district's move into mass transportation. Changing attitudes undermined support for pro-growth regionalism, and environmentalists, conservationists, and property owners allied to form a powerful new political bloc in the Bay Area. The alliance foretold by Jack Kent in 1963 became a reality; local officials represented by ABAG came together with the emerging growth-control coalition to oppose comprehensive regional government as it had been envisioned by BAC executives and other proponents of development.[76] In 1971, Kent's rhetoric was very different than it had been in 1963. Rather than emphasizing the danger of a lack of planning, he stressed the importance of local control and decentralization, reflecting his support for the ABAG/growth-control alliance:

People will turn to their local governments more and more to protect themselves and their communities from unwanted, predictably destructive, large scale public works, such as freeways and projects required by the seemingly never ending expansion. . . . They will make use of their local governments also to bring about modifications in the plans for clearly necessary and beneficial regional projects where such plans have failed to give sufficient consideration to community values and local environmental conditions. Thus, stronger local governments will be needed and will develop to check the natural tendencies of regional agencies to continually expand their range of authority and to automatically defend their already authorized projects, some of which as initially proposed will, when reconsideration is compelled, be shown to be as harmful as they are well intentioned.[77]

Not only did the rhetoric of growth control reflect its leaders' embrace of home rule, but changes in ABAG regional plans also indicated the influence of growth-control principles. In 1966, ABAG's *Preliminary Regional Plan*, developed in close association with the predominantly pro-growth BATS Commission, presented a future of population increases, expanding suburbs, and rapid regional development. The *Regional Plan 1970–1990* was very different. Drafted by James Hickey with significant input from Kent and other members of People for Open Space, it included radically reduced population projections, earmarked large swaths of permanent open space where development had been envisioned, and eliminated several planned bridges and freeways.[78] The ABAG plan was entirely advisory—it was officially "approved" rather than "adopted" by its general council. But it did provide guidelines for activists working for local growth-control measures and to stop the expensive, large-scale public works projects (such as urban freeways and new bridges) that made powerful regional government necessary in the first place. And, it proved that home rule and growth control could be complementary.

As pro-growth regionalists feared, existing regional agencies also became obstacles to centralized, unified Bay Area government. The BCDC and the Bay-Delta Water Quality Control Program, which were both temporary agencies, issued final reports in 1969 arguing for new regional but not comprehensive agencies to take over their planning and administrative functions. Their officials supported a system of complementary, limited-purpose agencies working on a cooperative basis—essentially, the perpetuation of the status quo. They argued that waiting for more ambitious regional government was impractical and emphasized that the state should not be allowed to take over their functions. BATS commissioners, more sympathetic to the pro-growth regional planning cause from the beginning, argued that a "multi-purpose regional organization" would be the best solution, but acknowledged that the creation of a single-purpose regional agency responsible only for transportation planning functions was a much more likely outcome.[79]

In the meantime, ABAG leaders and administrators worked to develop relationships with existing regional agencies, creating a special "cooperating member" status for special districts in 1966. ABAG represented the local governments whose leaders successfully defeated the Golden Gate Authority, and the same local officials now hoped to minimize the impositions of regional planning by securing control over it. ABAG adopted a report in 1967 calling for the creation of a "regional home rule council" made up of local elected officials appointed by their peers; essentially, it was a proposal to make ABAG a weak regional government overseeing a collection of limited-purpose regional planning agencies, rather than simply an advisory board with federal sanction.[80]

The 1969 session of the state legislature turned out to be decisive on the question of regional planning and government. The effort to create a new comprehensive government for the San Francisco Bay Area was spearheaded by John T. Knox, who took over the chairmanship of the Joint Committee on Bay Area Regional Organization (BARO) after McAteer's sudden death in 1967. Knox introduced Assembly Bill 711 to establish a democratically elected, multipurpose regional government that would take over many of the functions of existing agencies and wield comprehensive planning authority. While this was what pro-growth regionalists had been working for since the end of World War II, Knox's ideas about its purpose were different than those of his predecessors—he was an avowed environmentalist, and hoped that regional government would help control sprawl and reduce environmental degradation as well as promote economic development and prosperity. That both regionalists and home rule defenders were courting the support of environmentalists and conservationists reflected the enormous power that they had already achieved in the Bay Area by the late 1960s.

However, Knox's approach to regionalism came too late. By that time members of the Bay Area growth-control coalition were siding with ABAG and local government, following Kent's lead. Regional planning was too closely associated with big business, industry, and rapid, destructive development to be credible. Bagley sponsored a measure devised by ABAG to compete with Knox's bill that would extend and reshape ABAG into a "regional home rule agency," headed by city and county officials.[81] The rival proposals sparked a paralyzing debate on the issue of representation. Supporters of Bagley's proposal argued that Knox's agency amounted to a "takeover" of local resources; Knox's supporters argued that any regional government should be democratically elected, not appointed by counties and cities as ABAG allies wanted. The chances for Bagley's measure were hurt considerably by scandal in 1968, when the assistant to ABAG's executive director was caught embezzling nearly $500,000 in federal funds.[82] Neither bill made it out of committee, and both were strongly opposed by existing agencies and attacked by advocates of regional government as either misguided in terms of representation or too weak to carry out effective planning.

During the next legislative session, Knox tried again, but his bill again stalled in committee despite support for the measure in the legislature as a whole. This time one of the critical opponents was Marin County representative Peter Behr, a well-known environmentalist who won McCarthy's seat in the state senate when he retired from politics in 1970.[83] The 1971 defeat was a final, crushing blow for pro-growth regionalism in California, and its advocates resigned themselves to pursuing their planning goals on a piecemeal basis through existing single-purpose regional agencies. Accordingly, Knox himself co-sponsored a bill to make the BCDC a permanent agency with broad powers to regulate development near the bay shore. The San Francisco Bay Water Quality Group took over for the temporary Bay-Delta Water Quality Control Program. Legislation also passed to require Napa, Solano, and Sonoma Counties to join the Bay Area Air Pollution Control District, counties that had refused membership when it was created in 1955. These measures reduced the need for a new general-purpose regional agency and reinforced the existing, fragmented structure of Bay Area government.[84]

ABAG leaders and other home rule advocates had the status quo and time on their side—no decision was a victory for them. The existing system of *regional governance,* carried out by a variety of limited agencies, prevailed over the effort to create a single *regional government.* The formation of the Metropolitan Transportation Commission (MTC) was an indication of their victory. The BATS Commission final report, released in 1969, had two major elements: a general plan for transportation infrastructure and recommendations for an institution to continue the task of regional transportation planning. In keeping with the commission's pro-growth orientation, the report presented an ambitious program for expanding transportation infrastructure and generated considerable opposition.[85] But its other major recommendation, that a new, permanent regional agency be created to continue to plan for the Bay Area's transportation needs, was a given. Federal requirements made regional transportation planning imperative, but by the end of the 1969 session, it was easy to see that the chances for a comprehensive regional government, or even an "umbrella agency" to coordinate and oversee the functions of existing regional agencies, were remote.[86] Assemblyman John Foran, who supported Knox and his efforts for regional government in principle but whose first priority was improving Bay Area transportation, remembered that he finally reached the conclusion that "the pure politics of the situation would not permit a regional, multipurpose authority to come into being."[87] Foran's bill to create the MTC passed in 1971.

The MTC was designed above all to minimize opposition, in deference to the Bay Area home rule faction. Existing regional transportation agencies also had a lot of collective sway; the BART District, the Alameda–Contra Costa Transit District (AC Transit), San Francisco's Municipal Railway (MUNI), and the newly expanded Golden Gate Bridge, Highway and Transportation District all opposed any agency with significant authority. The goal for the MTC was to avoid imposing on existing agencies while meeting federal requirements for regional planning. Analysts observed that it was "created with just enough authority to fill the vacuum of planning responsibility in the gaps between agencies but not enough to mold the outcome of implementation or to command the operation of local authorities."[88] Of its nineteen commissioners, fourteen were appointed by various local Bay Area governments, one by ABAG directly, and one by the BCDC. Three nonvoting members represented the state Business and Transportation Agency, the Department of Transportation, and the federal Department of Housing and Urban Development. The MTC had the capacity to plan, to make recommendations, and to approve projects by other agencies that were requesting federal funding, but it did not have the authority to initiate or operate any transportation programs. It was strictly an advisory body, and had no independent source of revenue or power to tax. The agency depended entirely on state and federal subsidies to pay for its planning functions. MTC officials were required to submit a comprehensive regional transportation plan for the Bay Area to the state legislature by 1973. While they could draw upon the BATS study and data for this task, the limited timeframe imposed by the legislature was another indication of what was expected of the MTC: not much.[89]

In 1971, the same year that the MTC was created, the state legislature disbanded Knox's BARO committee. Efforts for comprehensive, multifunction regional government in the Bay Area quickly lost momentum, and by the end of the decade had been entirely abandoned.[90] ABAG's status as the Bay Area's metropolitan planning organization, recognized at the federal level since 1966, was reaffirmed in 1968 when it won federal funding. For better or for worse, the fate of Bay Area regional government had been decided in favor of a decentralized network of limited-purpose special districts.

Perpetual Tolls

In 1969, the new leaders of the bridge district were in an excellent position to take advantage of the conflict over regional government in Sacramento to win approval for mass transportation. Although the original California Bridge and Highway District Act authorized the agency to establish and operate "railroads, streetcars [or] interurban lines," new legislation was needed for a bridge district ferry system. Senator Collier introduced a bill to give the bridge directors full discretion over their mass transportation operations and the authority to issue new bonds without public approval. However, the bridge district still had too many enemies to dictate its own terms. Collier's bill was defeated in favor of a compromise measure sponsored by Foran, who wanted a pragmatic, workable solution to transportation problems, and also had personal connections with the new bridge district leadership. He was satisfied with the 1968 reform of the agency and had confidence that his friend and law partner Leonoudakis would ensure its honest and competent administration in the future. Signed into law on August 22, 1969, by Governor Reagan, Foran's measure officially created the "Golden Gate Bridge, Highway and Transportation District." It gave the bridge district new authority to "study, construct, acquire, improve, maintain, and operate any and all modes of transportation."[91] The act included several restrictions and requirements: only a limited percentage of toll revenues and reserves could be spent on transportation, no further studies of a second deck would be allowed at least until 1972, and the bridge district had to submit a long-term plan to the legislature for approval by 1971, as well as regular reports on its operations. Despite these caveats, it was a decisive victory for the bridge district in the battle for mass transportation and the war for its survival, and effectively halted all efforts for dissolution.

Bridge district leaders took immediate action. Ferries were controversial because of the expensive port facilities they required and their high operational costs, which were nearly double those of buses per passenger. The northern county directors resolutely opposed them, as did the Marin directors who were concerned about toll hikes. However, Bagley's reorganization had increased San Francisco's representation on the board of directors. Leonoudakis, who was later nicknamed "the Admiral," passionately wanted to bring ferries back to the bay, and he had the backing of the San Francisco supervisors as well as of Marin County environmentalists. The directors voted to commission plans and cost estimates for dock facilities and an entire fleet of state-of-the-art, first-class ferries from a Seattle naval architecture firm. The bridge district's first operation as a transportation agency was to charter a single ferry between Tiburon and San Francisco while its private operator was negotiating with striking workers in November 1969. The effort garnered enormous attention, particularly in San Francisco, and even yielded a small profit for the bridge district. The next spring, the directors purchased their first boat, a used San Diego vessel to be remodeled at a cost of more than $700,000. The MV *Golden Gate* started service between Sausalito and San Francisco in August 1970. Foreshadowing problems to come, the cost of remodeling it was nearly twice what was originally estimated. Despite having been completely overhauled, the *Golden Gate* broke down on the first day of regular commuter service and required a week of high-profile repairs. Nevertheless, the directors remained enthusiastic about ferries, crediting the small operation with reducing bridge traffic congestion.[92]

Winning approval for buses took longer—the issue pitted San Francisco representatives against northern county directors, particularly those from Marin. San Francisco bridge directors announced their "unequivocal opposition" to any buses into the city, and refused to back down. Convinced that they would lose their appointments if they voted for bus operations, they stalled the project for months. One observer remarked that "James Adam at his most adamant could not have been more blindly stubborn than these San Francisco directors" and that the board of directors was "no longer a quiet gentlemen's club."[93] Nevertheless, both bridge district and MCTD officials pleaded that an improved commuter bus system was the most cost effective and immediate means of alleviating the Golden Gate corridor traffic crisis. Finally, a guarantee that the bridge district would establish a full-scale ferry system (at twice the estimated cost of the proposed bus system) won over reluctant San Francisco representatives by the end of 1969.[94]

The reality of a bridge district bus system turned the tables on negotiations with Marin leaders. Now, MCTD officials had to use their limited financial resources as leverage to influence bridge district transportation policies. Making the best of the situation for Marin meant getting the maximum benefit from the bridge district's new enterprise. Despite lingering hostility, MCTD representatives entered into talks with bridge district officials, hoping to convince them to take responsibility for local as well as intercounty bus service. MCTD officials had the authority to contract through other agencies and potentially, the power to levy property taxes, and could offer crucial support for federal funding. After a year of difficult negotiations, the MCTD, the county, and the bridge district adopted a formal agreement. Bridge district representatives would follow the detailed bus plan that the MCTD had developed for local service in Marin, and maintain all routes and high bus frequencies.[95] Both the MCTD and Marin County agreed to make annual payments to the bridge district to cover the operating costs of local service that were not covered by fares. Calculating the total amount of deficit incurred by local operations was difficult, in part because much of the service was to be provided on buses that were ultimately destined for San Francisco, but a formula was adopted to determine Marin's contribution. The bridge district took complete responsibility for transbay operations, agreeing to provide all necessary subsidies for both ferry and bus service. As part of the deal, the MCTD directors officially endorsed the bridge district's application for UMTA funding for both buses and ferries, effectively renouncing any claim on federal funds. The bridge district became Marin's official mass transportation operator.

Even as they negotiated the final agreement with MCTD, bridge district officials proceeded with interim bus operations. As promised, they backed their plans with cash. In 1969, capital costs for the system were estimated to be between $4 and $6 million, and annual deficits were projected to be more than $10 million. Reserves that had been building up for decades would cover much of the initial costs. Arthur Jenkins had been arguing from the beginning that significant investments for high quality service were essential to success: "A modern bus system with first-class, new equipment and extended service routing, with moderate passenger fares that are competitive with the cost of operating personal autos, will without question capture a substantial portion of present peak-hour auto passengers. It must be a model operation."[96] Accordingly, bridge district officials ensured that their purchases were up to that standard, paying a premium for two buses to provide ferry feeder service. Local bus operations began in Marin County with seven deluxe new coaches. The directors voted to extend bus operations to Santa Rosa and add local service in Sonoma as well. By 1971, the capital costs of the system were estimated at $9.3 million (buses plus three bus terminals and depot facilities). Bridge district officials applied for a UMTA grant to cover two-thirds of this, but in the meanwhile they tapped into their reserves. By the end of the year, the bridge district owned 132 new General Motors buses. On January 1, 1972, it took over all of Greyhound's existing lines, which at the time were serving 4,000 commuters a day. Almost immediately, the number of transbay bus riders exceeded expectations, and after only two months of service, bridge district officials began calling for a bigger fleet. Even more luxurious vehicles replaced 20 old Greyhound buses to complete the 152-bus fleet called for in the MCTD plan. By the end of 1972, federal officials granted the bridge district nearly $8 million to offset the cost of initial purchases and to add an additional 30 buses.[97]

After the bridge district reorganization and Adam's retirement, civic leaders in both Marin and San Francisco seemed ready to give new bridge officials a chance to redeem the organization. Marin commuter groups endorsed Jenkins's plan for bridge district transportation at a meeting in San Rafael in 1969.[98] Luehring's early performance as general manager, particularly his willingness to act quickly to develop transportation operations, earned him glowing reviews from San Francisco reporters, who dubbed the "new" bridge district an "action agency."[99]

Even Bagley, who briefly took on the role of bridge district nemesis after McCarthy retired in 1969, commented that he would support empowering the bridge district to solve transportation problems if it could "operate in a businesslike manner and gain public confidence."[100]

In Marin, however, this optimism faded quickly. Even as bridge directors hammered out an agreement with the MCTD and negotiated their celebrated transformation into a transportation agency, Jack Craemer, the editor and publisher of the *Independent Journal*, concluded that "you can't teach an old bridge board new tricks."[101] Craemer opposed the bridge district ferries, claiming that they were an inefficient way to move people and a waste of money. To make matters worse, the projected cost of the ferry system began to increase rapidly before negotiations on the size of the bus system could even begin. Primed for a toll-free bridge, or at least a toll reduction, after years of anticipating the retirement of construction bonds, Marin motorists instead faced a series of hefty toll hikes.[102] As a result, the bridge district retained its villainous reputation in the minds of most Marin residents despite changes in its leadership and mission.

Because bridge district leaders knew that hostile Marin voters would never authorize a bond issue for ferries, they set up a subsidiary non-profit corporation that could finance the ferry system without public approval. Donald Van Dyke, head of the Marin County Taxpayers' Association, complained that bridge leaders had exercised "raw political power" to achieve the agency's conversion while ignoring public opinion: "the issuance of 'non-profit corporation bonds' rather than voter approval bonds constitute some of the more recent examples of [a] total lack of regard for what the people want."[103] Van Dyke, a municipal financing consultant who had advised California Toll Bridge Authority officials, asserted that by going into mass transit the bridge district was risking property taxes without public authorization. He published a series of full-page ads in the *Independent Journal* criticizing the cost of the bridge district's transportation enterprises, and commuters responded at the largest public hearing in Marin County history. In February 1970, more than 700 people attended a board meeting to express their fury about bridge district hubris. One unsympathetic observer described the crowd as a "rough, uninformed, obstreperous segment of the Marin populace, expressing its outrage at the recent hike in commute tolls."[104] Disregarding the outrage of Marin commuters, the directors issued $10 million in revenue bonds for the ferry system through its subsidiary.[105]

Bridge district officials could look forward to a future of guaranteed financial liabilities. In addition to the cost of establishing and operating mass transportation, they expected several big engineering expenses for the bridge. A study of its "major structural units" that was commissioned

"Bless your sweet, crowded, profitable, paid-for heart . . . I think I'll keep you"

San Francisco Chronicle, May 16, 1971.

from Ammann & Whitney in the midst of the uproar over hiring practices was released publicly in January 1970, along with estimates that the bridge required $10 million worth of repairs, including a complete replacement of vertical suspension cables. The long-range plan that they submitted to the legislature in 1971 included $301.5 million in new transportation projects and a $3.3 million toll plaza modernization. Over the course of the following decade, bridge district officials planned to establish a system of exclusive bus right-of-ways, to build underground busways in San Francisco, and to revive plans for a second deck, this time devoted exclusively to transit. While most of these proposals never came to fruition, they made it easy to argue for the importance of preserving the Golden Gate Bridge, Highway and Transportation District and its tolls.[106]

When the last of the Golden Gate Bridge construction bonds were paid off in 1971 and the bridge district continued to collect tolls, the *Chronicle* announced that it represented "vindication today, tomorrow, and presumably forever for the skeptical motorists who refused over the years to believe the old promise that the bridge would be toll-free once its bonds were paid off."[107] Before taking on mass transportation, the bridge district was a small organization with a clearly defined purpose, fewer than two hundred employees, and a very cohesive leadership. Suddenly, it became an expansive bureaucracy with three major departments. The bridge district added a bus manager in 1971 and a ferry manager in 1972, plus consulting engineers and a full office staff for both departments.[108] The directors were more removed from day-to-day operations than ever, and the general manager, now one of very few officials in a position to view the overall status of its operations, had more power and even less oversight and accountability. A bitter editorial ran in the *San Francisco Examiner* in 1970, soon after the first major toll hike to support mass transportation: "the Bridge Directors have one goal. It is the same goal that they have always had, ever since it was discovered what a bonanza there was in owning the only toll bridge between San Francisco and Marin, astride the main route north. They want to serve forever."[109]

By itself, the bridge district was not a major player in the struggle over regionalism in the late 1960s, but it was part of an alliance of regional agencies and local governments whose influence was decisive in preserving status quo and fighting off efforts for authoritative regional government. A variety of multicounty or area-wide special districts in the Bay Area maintained their function and jurisdiction as participants in a voluntary system of regional coordination based on association and cooperation. This was a necessary prerequisite for the transformation and perpetuation of the bridge district. It and other limited-purpose special districts took over imperative regional functions in the Bay Area and met the federal regional planning requirements that were not fulfilled by ABAG.

In decades following World War II, efforts to establish regional government and planning in metropolitan areas got underway nationwide. Policy analysts proposed various means of regional coordination, including city-county consolidation, regional federations, and large-scale, multi-function government corporations. These measures had the support of industry and business, represented by civic associations, business councils and chambers of commerce, and national advocacy groups. The federal government stepped in with new requirements for regional planning, starting with housing and transportation programs.[110] Despite a concerted, multi-level effort, by the mid-1970s, it was widely agreed that the results of two decades of efforts for metropolitan political integration or regional planning were abysmal. One analyst observed in 1976 that the metropolitan reform movement had an "almost unblemished record of failure."[111] An important reason for this change was the proliferation of limited-purpose special districts; as in the San Francisco Bay Area, these agencies actively opposed the creation of comprehensive regional government, defending their institutional interests and autonomy. In addition, special districts always presented a compelling, low-risk, and easy alternative for addressing regional problems. They were an extremely effective means of providing services, realizing public works projects, and enforcing regulations on a limited, circumscribed basis.

Intellectual support for metropolitan government and planning expired in the 1970s. Academics began to extol the virtues of decentralized government, applying the principle of free market competition and questioning the idea that centralized, multipurpose government or comprehensive regional planning was necessary to manage metropolitan area problems. Public choice theory gained prominence, both with local defenders of home rule who had always resisted planning and governmental centralization, and with federal policy-makers. Scholars argued that a decentralized state structure was not detrimental; rather, it encouraged healthy competition among localities and government agencies, making them more responsive to the needs and desires of citizens.[112] Most federal programs designed to encourage comprehensive regional planning were abandoned by the 1980s, replaced by a "new federalism" that funneled resources directly to individual cities, increasing their power. Special districts enjoyed a renewed legitimacy and continued to proliferate and evolve, and weak councils of governments similar to ABAG took responsibility for meeting regional planning throughout the country.[113] The devolution that occurred in the wake of regionalism's decline was as much a reflection of the power of a decentralized local state, including large numbers of special districts, as it was the result of ineffective federal policy.[114]

In the 1990s, the negative consequences of governmental fragmentation in metropolitan areas became one of the primary concerns of urban policy analysts and federal officials once again. Proponents of a "new regionalism" urged greater governmental coordination for metropolitan areas, but with much more emphasis on voluntary cooperation, giving up on the goal of consolidating planning authority in any sort of centralized, general-purpose agency. Scholars and policy-makers including David Rusk, Myron Orfield, Henry Cisneros, and Anthony Downs argued that regional coordination could promote social justice and a more equitable distribution of resources, and help metropolitan areas compete in a global economy.[115] However, as political scientist Donald F. Norris recently explained, "while regional cooperation is almost certainly better than conflict, cooperation is the weakest of all institutional responses to metropolitan problems."[116] Even modest goals for communication and coordination may be too ambitious. Ultimately, regionalism cannot succeed without authority, something that existing governments—including special districts—refuse to compromise.

Conclusion
Subsidies, Suicides, and Sensitivity

From the moment of its incorporation in 1928, the Golden Gate Bridge and Highway District had the autonomy and resources to effectively pursue an agenda independent of outside political, social, or economic interest groups. Over time, the bridge district developed a compelling culture that shaped the goals and priorities of its officials and determined what they considered to be appropriate action on its behalf. Bridge district representatives engaged in battles to defend the agency's autonomy, and even its very existence, starting with the campaign for construction bond approval in 1930 and continuing through its move into mass transportation in 1969. The conflict and scandal surrounding the bridge district reflected its ability to pursue its own goals and to define and protect its purpose and interests. Its officials were willing to use all of the resources at their disposal to defend the bridge district, regardless of public censure or even the opposition of the agency's traditional allies. They consistently worked to maximize the power and influence of the organization and to fend off threats to its integrity and security.

Initially, bridge district officials had a mandate to fulfill the primary objective of the agency. President William P. Filmer, chief engineer Joseph B. Strauss, and general manager Alan K. MacDonald all had very different reasons for supporting the construction of the Golden Gate Bridge and sometimes had conflicting ideological and personal agendas, but they shared a clear stake in the survival and success of the bridge district. San Francisco engineer Michael M. O'Shaughnessy and other early critics questioned the wisdom of its skewed representational structure, which favored rural northern California. They also worried that bridge district officials were subject to very little oversight and had almost no outside accountability, leaving the agency vulnerable to abuse and corruption. These concerns went unheeded. Although by 1929 there were other viable means of bridging the Golden Gate, a special district had already been created, and its leaders had ample resources and initiative to fend off criticism. Bridge district officials met their opponents with a powerful, well-funded political campaign, and they could decide the timing of the vote for the bonds. They could develop and promote bridge plans on their own schedule, and had the authority to modify the terms of the bonds, even after voter approval, to ensure their sale. The construction of the Golden Gate Bridge was virtually inevitable from the moment the bridge district came into existence.

Public enthusiasm for the bold, striking span during the construction period masked vicious, behind-the-scenes battles for control of the bridge district that erupted even before work commenced. As James Reed, Francis V. Keesling, and other bridge district leaders struggled to overcome engineering problems and build the bridge, the diverse coalition that backed the bridge district early on began to break apart. Deep fissures appeared within the agency as Strauss battled with top management. MacDonald, Keesling, George T. Cameron, and Russell G. Cone were all forced out of high-level positions as various outside groups put pressure on the agency. However, each new threat helped to unify bridge district officials and build solidarity within the organization. Its structure began to coalesce and harden as its officials adopted formal procedures, established lines of authority and accountability, and defined the purpose and orientation of the agency. Engineering concerns took second place to political considerations as the bridge district began to develop internal cohesiveness and a unique organizational culture and identity. This process accelerated as the agency faced increasingly vocal critics, including members of the San Francisco Chamber of Commerce and later, State Senator Jack McCarthy.

The disadvantages of special districts, many of which were built into the structure of the bridge district, became even more apparent after the agency began to collect tolls in 1937, and in the period after World War II, to accumulate large surpluses. Its financial independence and business values translated into high tolls in the late 1940s and the 1950s. Bridge district officials enjoyed almost total budgetary discretion, and although their expenses and indulgences were occasionally exposed to public scrutiny, they often violated ethical standards and tested the limits of legality. They began defending unpopular policies with controversial lobbying, advertising, and public relations activities.

James Adam was instrumental in interpreting the history of the bridge district to bolster its legitimacy, and in articulating its identity and purpose. Though there was a crescendo of criticism and public outrage about bridge district policies and administration in the 1950s and 1960s, the unity and power of its officials grew steadily, and there was little hope for meaningful reform. Adam's ascent to the position of general manager in 1953 represented the worst-case scenario for the insulated power of special district administration, and under his leadership, charges of mismanagement and corruption escalated. The California Fair Employment Practice Commission found Adam guilty of racial discrimination, and held public hearings that uncovered years of negligent bridge maintenance and structural deterioration. Nevertheless, Adam remained impervious, protected by powerful fortifications against outside interference that he helped construct.

Some of the unforeseen and unintended consequences of the creation of the bridge district for the Bay Area emerged in the 1950s and 1960s as the agency accumulated power and exercised its growing capacity to engage in policy-making and politics. Not only did the bridge itself shape the landscape and physical development of the region, but bridge district policies also shaped its government. Bridge district engineer Arthur C. Jenkins worked behind the scenes to prevent rapid transit to the North Bay from competing against the bridge, even against the wishes of the most loyal bridge district constituents, northern California boosters and real estate investors. Adam, State Senator Randolph Collier, and Redwood Empire Association boosters effectively prevented legislation to create a Golden Gate Authority from passing in Sacramento, defying Edgar F. Kaiser and other members of the Bay Area Council, including some of California's most powerful businessmen. The financial autonomy and political independence of the bridge district enabled its representatives to wage aggressive campaigns, both covert and overt, to influence regional policy. By the end of the 1950s, the bridge district became an obstacle to growth and the bridge a major traffic bottleneck. This was ironic in light of its original purpose: the organization that was intended to promote the development of northern California prevented the construction of new transportation infrastructure required for continued growth, jealously defending its toll revenues, jurisdiction, and autonomy.

Ultimately, the flexibility, resources, and toll revenue of the bridge district ensured its indispensability and survival despite its unpopularity. The changing politics of the Bay Area finally resulted in new bridge district leadership in 1968. Leading bridge director Stephan C. Leonoudakis and general manager Dale W. Luehring changed the outlook and purpose of the agency to reflect the environmentalist, growth-control politics that was emerging in the Bay Area in the late 1960s, particularly in San Francisco and Marin. With the consent of home-rule advocates, including T. J. Kent, William T. Bagley, and members of the Association of Bay Area Governments, they convinced state legislators that a reformed bridge district could be trusted with new responsibilities. Staving off likely dissolution with the retirement of bridge construction bonds in 1971, an expanded Golden Gate Bridge, Highway and Transportation District inaugurated a bus and ferry system. The investments and operating subsidies required for mass transportation guaranteed an indefinite need for tolls. With its transformation into a multi-purpose transportation agency, the bridge district reached maturity as an institution, fulfilling its first imperative: survival.

Political scientist Annmarie Hauck Walsh describes the dynamic that makes special districts and other government corporations so enduring: "Public authorities show a strong will to survive and expand . . . over time, sponsors, board members, and the community that created the corporation give way to professionalized management and operating routines. When the corporation has developed its own financial resources, its professional staff takes control of policy initiation and defends the organization from outside intrusion."[1] The officials of other special districts protect them with just as much ingenuity and dedication as did bridge district leaders. However, the structure of special districts, intentionally designed to shield decision-making and policy from public scrutiny and interference, makes them all too easy to overlook. John C. Bollens, another leading scholar of special districts, observes that the "phantom-like quality" of these agencies "does not diminish their collective and sometimes individual importance. It merely increases the difficulty of comprehending [them]."[2] While high-profile elected leaders take well-publicized positions on the issues of the day in the upper echelons of traditional government hierarchies, the officials of special districts make deliberately discreet but often immensely significant decisions from within a complex tangle of local and regional agencies.

Special districts continued to multiply through the end of the twentieth century and into the twenty-first. In 1982 the U.S. Census Bureau counted 28,078 special districts, in 1992 there were 31,555, and ten years later they numbered 35,052. In the meanwhile, the number of other local governments remained fairly static, and by 2002 special districts comprised 40 percent of all local governments.[3] New criticism of special district administration appears periodically from intellectuals, policy analysts, and would-be reformers, who consistently emphasize how little is known about these "shadow governments."[4] While they contribute to a critique that dates back to the 1930s, their observations have largely been ignored because the pragmatic political advantages and usefulness of special districts continue to override their many disadvantages.

Democratic values have always been contested and qualified in the United States. The amount of power residing with the electorate has waxed and waned over the course of American history, and the rights of people have frequently taken second place to the rights of subnational governments or property owners. Special districts undermine democracy—they remove the decision-making process from public scrutiny and participation for the sake of expediency and efficiency. They empower professional bureaucrats and reduce the authority of elected officials, but expertise and professionalism do not preclude corruption and abuse. Once oversight and accountability are eliminated, they are difficult, if not impossible, to reinstate. Although no decision-making process is foolproof, the history of the Golden Gate Bridge and Highway District and many similar agencies suggests that removing it too far from voters can be disastrous. Its record of mismanagement and corruption, immunity to censure, and resistance to reform reflect problems inherent to its corporate form and bureaucratic structure as a special district.

The implications of the emergence and proliferation of special districts are not limited to issues of administration and accountability. The collective weight of thousands of independent authorities, commissions, and districts helped tip the balance in favor of federalism at a crucial juncture in American history. Typically, scholars cite longstanding intellectual traditions to account for the decentralized, fragmented government of American metropolitan areas: the influence of federalist ideologies at the foundation of American government and the enduring legal and political sanctity of home rule. They point to the "new federalism" and the rise of public choice theory to explain the failure of regional planning measures in the 1970s. Certainly, these intellectual trends and traditions contributed to local control. However, decentralization is no longer the product of any rational political philosophy or policy decision when it becomes a self-perpetuating pattern, and the interests of bureaucratic organizations, including cities and counties as well as public corporations, become obstacles to reform. The story of the Golden Gate Bridge helps explain why the fragmentation of local government endures, despite major efforts to consolidate and coordinate regional policy-making and planning. Agencies like the bridge district can change and adapt to their political context while defending their fundamental interests. Over the course of the twentieth century, special districts became a large, powerful, and permanent sector of government in the United States.

The history of the bridge district since its move into mass transportation provides a telling epilogue to the story of its institutional coming of age. The organizational culture that developed early in its history has persisted, as have its officials' insensitivity to public opinion and opposition to reform. What have changed are the major problems its leaders face: since 1971, they have had to grapple with persistent budget deficits and other financial difficulties. When the Golden Gate Bridge, Highway and Transportation District initiated its new mass transportation operations, it had been in the black since the end of World War II, adding to its reserve funds every year. Despite the initial popularity of bus operations and high hopes for the new ferry system, they both turned out to be financial disasters. Bridge district officials knew that transportation operations would lose money—part of their original appeal was that they would provide a justification to continue to collect tolls after the bridge construction bonds were retired. But cost overruns quickly exceeded the wildest predictions of the most parsimonious taxpayers' advocate. While the bridge district managed to win millions in state and federal subsidies to establish its new system, little money was available to support day-to-day operations, and fares did not come close to covering their costs. The difference had to come from tolls.

As always, Marin commuters were the most directly affected by bridge district policies, and bore the brunt of its shortcomings. Although its buses never lacked for riders, the task of financing and subsidizing them was contentious and complicated. In taking responsibility for local service in addition to its new transbay operations, the bridge district was stepping into a political and financial quagmire. From the first year of operations, Marin County Transportation District (MCTD) leaders objected to the formula used to calculate their share of operational expenses. In 1969 it seemed to Marin officials that letting the bridge district take over local bus service was a good deal, but the federal and state subsidies that they forfeited far exceeded their original expectations. In 1971, the California Transportation Development Act (TDA) made state funds available for local transit, and Marin's allocation went directly to the bridge district. Not only that, but the bridge district also received $55 million in federal money to cover mass transportation capital costs that was designated for Marin County. Although Marin representatives agreed to forgo most federal transportation subsidies in 1970, they thought it only fair that the bridge district make up for any unexpected operating deficits. They were keenly aware that Marin residents had always paid the majority of tolls, and felt entitled to their use to support local bus service. Their payments to the bridge district consistently fell short of the amount that was required by their original agreement for local bus operations.[5]

However, ferries created the biggest financial problems for the bridge district. The initial cost estimate for a four-terminal system was $14 to $17 million for equipment and facilities along with an annual $2 million in subsidies. The system was slated for full operation in 1974. As high as these figures seemed at the time, cost overruns and delays began almost immediately. By 1972, when UMTA officials approved a grant of $12.6 million, the estimated total was $19 million.[6] Four separate studies of the proposed ferry operations between 1969 and 1974 all severely underestimated the cost of equipment and docking facilities.[7] Ultimately, bridge district officials settled for a scaled-back system with three terminals and four ferries for $51.4 million—more than twice the projected cost of their original four-terminal, seven-vessel plan. A federal investigation of ferry operations in 1975 suggested that inflationary pressures were the least of several reasons for the inaccurate estimates. More significant were "poor initial estimates," the exclusion of several essential expenses, and changes in ferry boat specifications (they were upgraded several times for maximum comfort and speed).[8] More than two-thirds of the federal capital grants that went to the bridge district were spent on the ferry system, even though it had the potential to serve only a small fraction of the riders of the bus system. In addition, ferries required nearly twice the subsidies per passenger, 70 cents per trip as opposed to 44 cents for bus passengers in 1974.[9] Marin officials argued that the ferry system was a luxury and an enormous unnecessary expense that primarily served tourists and did little to relieve traffic congestion or enhance the North Bay economy.[10]

In the mid-1970s, the full implications of bridge district transportation operations began to emerge. In 1969, bridge district reserves stood at $27.4 million, but by 1974, they were down to $17.7 million; that year, bus operations incurred a deficit of $5.9 million, and the ferries $800,000. At first, the bridge district officials tried to offset these losses with toll increases. Commuter discounts were eliminated and one-way tolls were raised from 50 to 75 cents in 1974.[11] Marin officials felt little sympathy and no obligation to assist the bridge district when its officials were sinking so much money into ferries. Marin voters got a chance to express their opinion on bridge district operations in 1975, when they resoundingly defeated a ballot measure to increase the local sales tax to improve the bus system. Marin residents wanted better bus service, but opponents argued convincingly that it was unwise to entrust bridge district officials with more money.[12] Bridge district responded with major cutbacks in local service. By 1979, mass transportation had completely drained bridge district reserves, and the agency faced a large budget deficit. That deficit worsened in the decades to come.

Although bridge district finances were probably the most worrisome issue for its officials, and certainly they concerned commuters, not all criticism was coming from Marin. In addition to its controversial and expensive mass transportation operations, a slew of other problems plagued the agency, some of which originated well before the expansion of its operations. Bridge district spending and public relations activities continued to garner criticism. Despite traffic congestion, the bridge district faithfully made large annual contributions to the REA and the San Francisco Visitors' and Convention Bureau. One analyst noted in 1974 that it was the only "district entity" paying dues to the REA, and its second largest contributor.[13] Even after the end of Adam's regime and the purge of old boys in the late 1960s, the northern counties maintained their disproportionate influence on the board. The strongest indication of this was the appointment of bridge district secretary Carney J. Campion as general manager in 1984, over the objections of San Francisco directors. Like Adam, Campion was a publicist who had worked closely with the bridge district for many years, particularly after he took over as the director of the REA in 1961.

Labor problems continued to plague the bridge district, including a three-month bus driver strike in 1976 and a similar confrontation with ferry workers in 1979. Bridge officials faced more accusations of discrimination in hiring in 1975 and in 1981. And in 1988, a major reconstruction and repair project revealed that bridge officials routinely deferred maintenance to solve short-term budget problems.[14] In that year's annual report, bridge district president Carol Ruth Silver complained about the "unremitting and unjustified barrage of bad press" and denounced efforts to restructure the bridge district, echoing her predecessors.[15] And indeed, while attempts to dissolve or reform the agency continued, they were no more successful than before. Even Willie Brown, the powerful speaker of the assembly who led campaigns to clean up the bridge district in 1981 and 1988, was no match for the "well-connected lawyers, lobbyists, and legislators" defending the agency.[16]

Frequent suicides were another persistent problem that reflected the culture of the bridge district, and helped perpetuate its reputation for imperviousness and insensitivity. The first known disconsolate jumper ended his life in August 1937. By 1940, the deadly appeal of the Golden Gate Bridge was attracting national attention, and the bridge directors considered installing a "suicide net," but ruled it out as too expensive.[17] Since then, they have regularly discussed prevention measures, but have only occasionally taken steps to reduce fatalities. In 1951 the directors made their first meaningful, albeit temporary, effort by instituting a 24-hour patrol. Three years later, they erected a suicide fence test model, only to reject it because it might hinder bridge painters. In 1964, members of a bridge district suicide prevention committee called for a media blackout on suicide coverage, arguing that attention encouraged jumpers. Bridge directors installed a television monitoring system to speed help to potential leapers in 1970 and commissioned a full-scale engineering study of a suicide barrier. They selected one of several barrier designs proposed during the study, but concern that it would compromise the bridge aesthetic prevailed in 1974.[18] In 1980 the directors considered installing a suicide barrier as part of a major maintenance project, but decided that it could undermine their case for historic landmark designation.[19] Bridge district officials considered the patented "Z-clip" fence system in 1998, spending $50,000 for a full demonstration.

This time, attorneys warned that they could be liable for deaths if it was not completely effective, and tests showed that a determined, athletic climber could scale the fence. Indeed, without a barrier the bridge district prevailed in court against grieving relatives—certainly, its officials were under no legal obligation to intervene in what many of them understood as a personal decision and a private responsibility.[20]

Public opinion on a suicide barrier has always been divided. At hearings in 1977, opponents outnumbered proponents by four to one, although an *Examiner* poll the same year suggested that San Francisco readers were evenly split on the question.[21] Since then, many of the common arguments against a suicide barrier have been discredited. According to studies by Richard Seiden, more than 90 percent of surviving jumpers regretted their act and did not attempt suicide again— significantly more than the members of a control group.[22] Psychologists weighing in on the question agree that the bridge is an "attractive nuisance," seeming to offer an easy, appealing, even glamorous death to many who would not otherwise end their lives. A sharp increase in suicides from the bridge in the 1990s generated renewed concern about the issue. The annual fatality rate tripled between 1990 and 1994, and Bay Area newspapers reported the one thousandth death in 1995.[23]

The most recent bridge district study of suicide deterrence followed a run of bad publicity. In 2003 Tad Friend published a lengthy piece on Golden Gate Bridge suicides in the *New Yorker*, which made bridge district officials seem callous and inept. The *San Francisco Chronicle* followed with a seven-part series on suicides in fall 2005. Filmmaker Eric Steel captured twenty-three deaths on film over the course of a year and included the footage in his controversial 2006 documentary film *The Bridge*, much to the horror of bridge district officials.[24] Some of the worst years on record were 2006 and 2007, with twenty-nine and thirty-five confirmed deaths, respectively. An understood agreement among public officials and the press not to discuss bridge suicides broke down as advocates began to publicize the issue. Marin County Coroner Ken Holmes was among those who were willing to break the silence, arguing that the potential for greater public awareness to spur action on a barrier outweighed concern about mimicry.[25] And indeed, at the end of 2006 the bridge directors agreed to a two-year, $2 million feasibility study as long as it was funded entirely from outside sources. The Metropolitan Transportation Commission came through with $1.9 million from state and federal funds slated for Bay Area transportation projects. The rest came from local government and private donations. The only commitment that bridge directors made to the project was a promise to consider further action when the study was complete. The final report was scheduled for release by the end of 2008.[26]

While bridge district policy regarding suicides may reflect public ambivalence about the issue, in 1997 another tragic fall from the bridge evoked larger questions of safety and responsibility. That year, a toddler fell to her death, slipping through the gap between sidewalk and the bridge roadway. While small children had lost their lives on the bridge before, this was the first entirely accidental death. The 9 1/2-inch opening, which had been created during a 1985 bridge modification, violated state safety regulations.[27] The incident linked the suicide barrier debate to the issue of bridge safety in general. For decades, horrific head-on collisions occurred regularly on the bridge. Activists, including former bridge director and State Senator Quentin Kopp, spent years campaigning unsuccessfully for a central traffic divider on the bridge. In 1988, one commentator called crossing the bridge "San Francisco roulette."[28] The bridge's most dangerous approach, Doyle Drive in San Francisco, has been dubbed "blood alley."[29] Improvements to the thoroughfare have been stalled for decades by bickering over the design of a new roadway and whether the bridge district, San Francisco, or the state should pay for them.[30]

Not only did these issues call into question the sensitivity and responsibility of bridge district officials, but their overall competence also continued to generate doubt. One of the most spectacular foreseeable disasters in Golden Gate Bridge history was its fiftieth anniversary celebration in 1987. A throng of as many as 800,000 people attended the dawn bridge walk. Inadequate planning meant that those who managed to get onto the bridge were stranded for hours, unable to move in any direction. The weight of the densely packed crowd caused the normally arched roadbed to sag visibly in the middle, raising the question of structural damage. The nonprofit organization formed by three bridge directors to organize and pay for the celebration failed to raise enough money, and the district ended up contributing more than $1 million to retire its debt, despite promises made earlier that public money would not be spent on festivities. Later investigation revealed that organizers also failed to obtain liability insurance as they had promised. The bridge district hired a new, permanent public relations officer to handle the aftermath of the fiasco.[31]

In 1991, the Golden Gate Bridge toll was raised to $3, triple that of other California toll bridges. Nevertheless, in 2002 bridge district officials announced that the agency was facing a financial crisis, its debt mounting rapidly and its budget deficit at a critical $454 million. A number of major maintenance projects, including bridge roadway resurfacing and earthquake retrofitting, added to unexpectedly large bus and ferry deficits, representatives explained. Costs associated with the terrorist attacks of 2001 and a slumping economy exacerbated financial problems.[32]

To reduce shortfalls, tolls were raised to $5, despite loud public protest. In response, Kenneth Garcia penned an editorial: "You don't need to be a native to look out at the Golden Gate and see for whom the bridge tolls. It tolls for the Golden Gate Bridge, Highway and Transportation District, a quaint, insular agency that seems more than content to keep itself wrapped permanently in a fog. At the district, bridge tolls are the coin of the realm, a fast pass to longevity and comfort for a transit authority unlike any other in the West. And the years have proved one thing beyond doubt—few agencies are better at taking commuters for a ride."[33]

The $5 toll did not resolve the district's budget crisis, nor did donation boxes installed a few months later to encourage visitors to help out.[34] In 2003 bridge district officials reduced bus service by more than 30 percent, weakening the already anemic North Bay mass transportation system. At least two hundred regular riders were left with no transit alternative and ninety-seven drivers lost their jobs. Bridge district officials also eliminated commuter discounts and declared that an $8 toll was on the horizon.[35] In 2006, facing an $87 million deficit, the directors sought corporate sponsors for the bridge, spending $90,000 to hire a consultant who promised that the right deal could actually improve the "overall bridge experience."[36] The prospect of advertisements on bridge district property inspired an upwelling of dismay, and the secrecy with which it was developed and presented to the directors also garnered criticism. In 2008, bridge district officials announced that they were adding another $1 to the regular toll, in addition to an unspecified congestion fee during peak traffic periods.[37]

Accusations against bridge district management and objections to its policies ranged from trivial to serious, but regardless of their validity they had little influence on its policies or decision-making. Through the end of twentieth century and into the twenty-first, the bridge district remained largely oblivious to protests, public hearings, outraged editorials, and even legislation. Obviously, its invulnerability was not due to a lack of persistence or determination on the part of its foes. The basic qualities of the bridge district resulted both from its organizational structure and from the influential and persistent culture that it developed over time. The history of its policies suggests that its officials consistently served the interests of the agency rather than the public. Marin commuters and residents of the entire San Francisco Bay Area paid a heavy toll for the ambition of Northern California boosters and the naïveté of progressive reformers. The many unintended products of this single, relatively modest special district culminated in its transformation into an intractable, untouchable organization whose overriding purpose was its own perpetuation. In the shadow of the beautiful bridge is an agency that may well endure as long as the structure it was created to build.

Notes

When I made my first request to view records of the Golden Gate Bridge, Highway and Transportation District, an unknown quantity of boxes was in the District Secretary's vault in the basement of the toll plaza offices or stored in a damp paint tunnel in or near the bridge itself, according to bridge district representatives. Many of these records were moved to an Iron Mountain private records storage facility in South San Francisco sometime in 1998. For lack of a better system, I refer to the location of the boxes at the time of my research in citations. That location was the basis for provisional indexes created by the bridge district archives coordinator in 1999, which were identified as "Inventory of 94 Boxes from Paint Tunnel," and "District Secretary's Files in Vault, List #1, List #2." Many of the official reports and other publications that I first discovered in bridge district files I later located elsewhere. Occasionally, I found duplicate copies even of unpublished materials and correspondence in one of the many archival collections related to bridge district history. I cite the most readily accessible location.

The following abbreviations for archival collections and bridge district storage locations are used in the notes:

Bagley Papers	William T. Bagley Legislative Papers, BANC MSS 77/109 c, The Bancroft Library, University of California, Berkeley
California DPW Files	California Director of Public Works Files—Director's Office, California State Archives, Office of the Secretary of State, Sacramento, Calif.
Collier Papers	Randolph Collier Papers, LP 229 California State Archives, Sacramento, Calif.
Derleth Papers	Charles Derleth Papers, DERLETH, Water Resources Center Archives, University of California, Berkeley

DS Vault	District Secretary's Vault, Golden Gate Bridge, Highway, and Transportation District, San Francisco
E. F. Kaiser Papers	Edgar F. Kaiser Papers, The Bancroft Library, University of California, Berkeley
Galloway Papers	John Debo Galloway Papers, GALLOWAY, The Water Resources Center, Archives, University of California, Berkeley
GGAC Papers	Golden Gate Authority Commission Papers, California State Archives, Sacramento, Calif.
IM facility	Iron Mountain Records Storage Facility, San Francisco
Jenkins Papers	Arthur C. Jenkins Papers, Harmer E. Davis Transportation Library, Institute of Transportation Studies, University of California, Berkeley
Keesling Papers, M0100	Francis V. Keesling Papers, M0100, Department of Special Collections, Stanford University Libraries, Stanford, Calif.
Keesling Papers, M1146	Francis V. Keesling Papers, M1146, Department of Special Collections, Stanford University Libraries, Stanford, Calif.
REA Records	Redwood Empire Association Records, The Bancroft Library, University of California, Berkeley
Reed Papers	James Reed Papers, JL012, Department of Special Collections, Stanford University Libraries, Stanford, Calif.

Introduction. "Agency Run Amok"

1. *San Francisco Chronicle,* July 6, 1994.

2. John E. Fraser of Del Norte County took over his father's seat in 1987.

3. Two former employees tipped off law enforcement officials, accusing bridge district officials of misappropriating federal mass transportation funds, among other things. No charges resulted from the investigations, but one of the former employees pleaded guilty to the theft of $60,000 in bridge district funds and property. *Marin Independent Journal,* Nov. 17, 1992; *San Francisco Chronicle,* Feb. 6, 1992, Jan. 29, 1993, Feb. 18, 1993.

4. *San Francisco Chronicle,* July 6, 1994.

5. While a variety of books and documentary films describe the construction

of the bridge, its politics and its subsequent history have escaped scholarly scrutiny until now. Richard Loomis's 1958 dissertation is one of the few documented studies of early bridge history, but it was written with the possibility of publication by the bridge district in mind and therefore avoids controversy. Many Golden Gate Bridge histories rely heavily on Allen Brown's 1965 book, a generally reliable though undocumented overview of its early history. John van der Zee's critical study of bridge engineering contrasts with several laudatory accounts of the construction period. Van der Zee examined archives of the New York engineering firm of Ammann & Whitney prior to their destruction on September 11, 2001, and also unearthed the personal papers of several engineers and architects. Richard Thomas Loomis, "The History of the Building of the Golden Gate Bridge," Ph.D. diss., Stanford University, 1958; Allen Brown, *Golden Gate: Biography of a Bridge* (Garden City, N.Y.: Doubleday, 1965); John van der Zee, *The Gate: The True Story of the Design and Construction of the Golden Gate Bridge* (New York: Simon and Schuster, 1986). Other books and films chronicling Golden Gate Bridge construction include Stephen Cassady, *Baron Wolman Presents Spanning the Gate* (Mill Valley, Calif.: Squarebooks, 1979, 1986); Tom Horton and Baron Wolman, *Superspan: The Golden Gate Bridge* (San Francisco: Chronicle Books, 1983); Richard H. Dillon, *High Steel: Building the Bridges Across San Francisco Bay* (Millbrae, Calif.: Celestial Arts, 1979); Henry Petroski, *Engineers of Dreams: Great Bridge Building and the Spanning of America* (New York: Knopf, 1995); Charles F. Adams, *Heroes of the Golden Gate* (Palo Alto, Calif.: Pacific Books, 1987); Andy Thomas, director, *Modern Marvels: Golden Gate Bridge* (New York: A&E Television Network, 1994), film; Ben Loeterman, director, *American Experience: Golden Gate Bridge* (Boston: WGBH, 2004), film.

6. The California Public Records Act was written in 1968 with the bridge district in mind by Assemblyman William T. Bagley, who became the first successful bridge district reformer the same year when he passed a bill modifying the make-up of the board of directors (see Chapter 7). The act significantly increased the accountability of all government agencies in the state. In 1973 Bagley introduced amendments identifying several agencies by name, including the Golden Gate Bridge and Highway District, and requiring them to "adopt guidelines for accessibility of their records to the public" and post them in their headquarters. William T. Bagley, interview with the author, tape recording, San Francisco, March 7, 2002; carton 15, William T. Bagley Legislative Papers, BANC MSS 77/109 c, The Bancroft Library, University of California, Berkeley. For more information on the act and advice on accessing the records of California public agencies see Stephen Levine and Barbara T. Newcombe, *Paper Trails: A Guide to Public Records in California*, 2nd ed. (Sacramento: California Newspapers Association, 1996).

7. These requirements were outlined in a series of telephone conversations followed by a formal meeting with public relations officer Mary Currie, district services director Lori Murray, and newly appointed archives coordinator Trubee Schock on April 7, 1999. Currie summarized the requirements in a March 29, 1999, letter to the author, and in an undated document, "Preliminary Guidelines for Access to Unprocessed Archives of the Golden Gate Bridge, Highway and Transportation District," that was enclosed with that letter.

8. Bridge district leaders have considered several proposals for a museum near the toll plaza. A $5 million "restricted museum reserve fund" was earmarked for the preservation of bridge history in 1972, but plans were suspended and the project assigned the district's lowest priority rating. Some of this money was used

for the restoration and conversion of the Roundhouse Restaurant at the toll plaza from a restaurant to a gift shop for the fiftieth anniversary celebration in 1987. Although the storage and management of records presents an ongoing problem for district administrators, the prospect of a museum is still cited as a reason not to donate them to an established archive. Minutes of the Committee on Public Information—Governmental Affairs, Jan. 4, 1974, Golden Gate Bridge Highway and Transportation District, District Secretary's Vault, San Francisco (hereafter cited as DS Vault); Clyde Winters Design, "Proposal for: Golden Gate Bridge Museum," Golden Gate Bridge and Highway District, Dec. 9, 1977; Carney Campion to Roger Boas, Feb. 10, 1978, DS Vault; California Office of the Auditor General, *A Review of the Golden Gate Bridge, Highway and Transportation District and the 50th Anniversary Celebration of the Golden Gate Bridge: Report* (Sacramento, 1987), 52; *Marin Independent Journal*, Aug. 28, 2000; Carney J. Campion, interview with the author, tape recording, San Rafael, Calif., July 30, 2002.

9. This analysis draws upon organizational theory as well as ideas associated with "historical institutionalism" in political science and sociology. Philip Selznick was influential in defining the basic principles of organizational theory. He describes institutionalization as a process that all formal organizations undergo to some extent. According to Selznick, "as an organization acquires a self, a distinctive identity, it becomes an institution." It is "infused with value" and can become, in effect, a "responsive, adaptive organism." As this happens, its leaders and associates come to identify with the organization and will defend its interests and integrity as well as the values they associate with it. Organizational culture is a product of institutionalization that becomes more distinctive and more powerful over time, increasing the capacity of organizations to develop and promote their own independent interests and agenda. The idea that organizations develop independent agency as they go through a process of institutionalization has important implications for "historical institutionalism" in political science and sociology. Many scholars recognize that as structures, government institutions can determine the agenda and constrain the options of policy-makers, and thereby shape outcome of decisions. However, understanding that governmental agencies can and do engage in the policy-making process as collective actors with independent agency takes institutional theory beyond structure. As James G. March and Johan P. Olsen observe, "Most of the major actors in modern economic and political systems are formal organizations. [They are] collections of standard operating procedures and structures that define and defend interests. They are political actors in their own right." Philip Selznick, *Leadership in Administration: A Sociological Interpretation* (New York: Harper and Row, 1957), 16–22; James G. March and Johan P. Olsen, "The New Institutionalism: Organizational Factors in Political Life," *American Political Science Review* 78 (1983), 738. Theda Skocpol's 1985 essay, which called for recognition of the independent influence of government organizations and the enduring effects of institutional structures, was a keystone of historical institutionalism. "Bringing the State Back In: Strategies of Analysis in Current Research," in *Bringing the State Back In*, ed. Peter B. Evans, Dietrich Rueschemeyer, and Theda Skocpol (Cambridge: Cambridge University Press, 1985), 3–37. Discussions of historical institutionalism include Sven Steinmo, Kathleen Ann Thelen, and Frank Longstreth, *Structuring Politics: Historical Institutionalism in Comparative Analysis* (Cambridge: Cambridge University Press, 1992); Colin Hay and Daniel Wincott, "Structure, Agency and Historical Institutionalism," *Political Studies* 46 (1998), 951–57; Ellen M. Immergut, "The Theoretical Core of the New Institutionalism," *Politics and Society* 26 (1998),

5–34; Ira Katznelson, "The Doleful Dance of Politics and Policy: Can Historical Institutionalism Make a Difference?" *American Political Science Review* 92 (1998), 191–98; B. Guy Peters, *Institutional Theory in Political Science: The New Institutionalism,* 2nd ed. (New York: Continuum, 2005). The relationship between institutionalism and organizational theory is discussed in Paul DiMaggio and Walter W. Powell, "Introduction," in DiMaggio and Powell, eds., *The New Institutionalism in Organizational Analysis* (Chicago: University of Chicago Press, 1991); James G. March and Johan P. Olsen, *Rediscovering Institutions: The Organizational Basis of Politics* (New York: Free Press, 1989); Johan P. Olsen, "Political Science and Organization Theory: Parallel Agendas but Mutual Disregard," in *Institutions and Political Choice: On the Limits of Rationality,* ed. Hans Keman (Amsterdam: VU University Press, 1996); Donald D. Searing, "Roles, Rules, and Rationality in the New Institutionalism," *American Political Science Review* 85 (1991), 1239–60; W. Richard Scott, *Institutions and Organizations,* 2nd ed. (Thousand Oaks, Calif.: Sage Publications, 2001).

10. United States Census Bureau, *Governments in the United States in 1952* (Washington, D.C., 1953), 4, 6. The Census Bureau has used the same basic criteria for identifying special districts since 1952. According to this definition, special districts have a "governmental function" and possess corporate powers including "perpetual succession, the right to sue and be sued, have a name, make contracts, acquire and dispose of property," as well as "substantial autonomy" including "considerable fiscal and administrative independence." I use this definition because of its emphasis on autonomy. Other scholars use different terms and criteria to define their subject, reflecting their emphasis and interpretation. Annmarie Hauck Walsh focuses on "public corporations," a broader category that includes entities that do not meet census criteria for political autonomy but are legally and financially distinct from other government agencies; often they are instrumental rather than autonomous. Kathryn Foster emphasizes function, using the term "special-purpose governments" to distinguish these agencies from traditional, "general-purpose" governments including cities, counties, and states. Another major question in defining special districts is the significance of financing, and whether authorities, which rely exclusively on revenue to secure debt, are fundamentally different from special districts that are authorized to levy property taxes. The Census categorizes authorities that meet requirements for political, fiscal, and administrative independence as special districts. The Golden Gate Bridge and Highway District funded its initial operations secured its construction bonds with property taxes, but lost the ability to tax property when it won authorization for mass transportation operations in 1969, thereby evolving from a traditional special district into an authority. Annmarie Hauck Walsh, *The Public's Business: the Politics and Practices of Government Corporations* (Cambridge, Mass.: MIT Press, 1978); Kathryn Ann Foster, *The Political Economy of Special-Purpose Government* (Washington, D.C.: Georgetown University Press, 1997). For a brief overview of competing definitions see James Leighland, "Public Authorities and Determinants of Their Use by State and Local Governments," *Journal of Public Administration Research and Theory* 4 (1994), 521–44.

11. In rural areas with weak or nonexistent local government, special districts carried out tasks that were vital to promoting economic activity but were too large and expensive for all but the wealthiest individuals or largest private corporations. In cities, special districts financed major infrastructure projects, taking advantage of new technologies that offered better sanitation, cleaner water,

electricity, and improved transportation. While many traditional governments were restricted by debt ceilings and balanced budget amendments imposed in the nineteenth century, special districts were limited in their financing only by the market for their bonds. In California, the first general legislation enabling special districts was the Wright Act, passed in 1887. The Massachusetts Metropolitan Water Board, which was formed in 1895, was a model for many special districts, including the Golden Gate Bridge and Highway District. In Illinois, consistently a leader in special district government, the Chicago Sanitary District was created in 1889 to serve both the city and surrounding communities. Chicago special districts constructed miles of parkways in the 1890s, and park districts appeared throughout the country in the 1910s and 1920s. The Passaic Valley Sewage District was incorporated in 1902 to serve 100 square miles of New Jersey. Special districts took over many ports in the United States, including the Port of New Orleans in 1890, the Port of Seattle in 1913, and the Port of New York in 1921. The Golden Gate Bridge and Highway District shared many basic characteristics with dozens of small California water districts and larger entities, including the East Bay Municipal Utility District, created in the 1923, and the Metropolitan Water District of Southern California, incorporated in 1928. Surveys of these and other early special districts include Eric H. Monkkonen, *The Local State: Public Money and American Cities* (Stanford, Calif.: Stanford University Press, 1995); Nancy Burns, *The Formation of American Local Governments: Private Values in Public Institutions* (New York: Oxford University Press, 1994); Alberta M. Sbragia, *Debt Wish: Entrepreneurial Cities, U.S. Federalism, and Economic Development* (Pittsburgh: University of Pittsburgh Press, 1996); Norris Hundley, *The Great Thirst: Californians and Water, a History*, rev. ed. (Berkeley: University of California Press, 2001), 99–103; Gordon Miller, "Shaping California Water Law, 1871 to 1928," *Southern California Quarterly* 55 (1973), 9–42; Donald J. Pisani, *From the Family Farm to Agribusiness: The Irrigation Crusade in California and the West, 1850–1931* (Berkeley: University of California Press, 1984); Jon C. Teaford, *City and Suburb: The Political Fragmentation of Metropolitan America, 1850–1970* (Baltimore: Johns Hopkins University Press, 1979); John C. Bollens, *Special District Governments in the United States* (Berkeley: University of California Press, 1957); Paul Studenski, *The Government of Metropolitan Areas in the United States* (New York: National Municipal League, 1930).

12. Most scholars point to the practical, functional advantages of special districts to explain their early popularity, either as a "palliative" for the "failure" of local government or as a "triumph" of pragmatic problem-solving. However, special districts also had significant ideological appeal. Public enterprise was genuinely popular in the early twentieth century, and their creation was an expedient means of achieving public ownership and active government. In addition, special district proponents shaped them to promote good government and scientific administration. Progressive era theorists such as Woodrow Wilson and Herbert Croly blamed corruption on flawed governmental structures and organizations that allowed economic and individual interests to dominate politics. The sponsors of special districts believed that incentives for efficiency and entrepreneurial leadership could be built into a streamlined, hierarchical corporate structure that was adapted to serve the public interest, just as it served the pursuit of profit in the private sector. Functionalist interpretations of the origins of special districts include Walsh, *The Public's Business*, 16; Bollens, *Special District Governments*, 256; Ernest S. Griffith, *A History of American City Government: The Progressive Years and Their Aftermath, 1900–1920* (New York: Praeger, 1974), 297; Grif-

fith, *A History of American City Government: The Conspicuous Failure, 1870–1900* (New York Praeger, 1974), 297; Teaford, *City and Suburb;* Teaford, *The Unheralded Triumph: City Government in America, 1870–1900* (Baltimore: Johns Hopkins University Press, 1984). On the ideological appeal of special districts see Gail Radford, "From Municipal Socialism to Public Authorities: Institutional Factors in the Shaping of American Public Enterprise," *Journal of American History* 90 (2003), 863–90; Radford, "William Gibbs McAdoo, the Emergency Fleet Corporation, and the Origins of the Public-Authority Model of Government Action," *Journal of Policy History* 11 (1999), 59–88; Susan Tenenbaum, "The Progressive Legacy and the Public Corporation: Entrepreneurship and Public Virtue," *Journal of Policy History* 3 (1991), 309–30; Jameson W. Doig, "'If I See a Murderous Fellow Sharpening a Knife Cleverly': The Wilsonian Dichotomy and the Public Authority Tradition," *Public Administration Review* 43 (1983), 292–304.

13. Although there was no systematic nationwide count of special districts until 1942, their rapid increase during the first three decades of the twentieth century was unmistakable. The United States Census provided limited data on the debt and revenue of governments that indicated their ascendance. Eight states reported more than $1 million in special district debt in 1913. By 1922, sixteen states had at least that much, and some much more: California reported $102 million, Arkansas $77 million, and Illinois $58 million in special district debt. At least forty states had special districts by 1932, and every state and the District of Columbia reported special district debt in 1942. United States Bureau of the Census, *Wealth, Debt and Taxation 1913* (Washington, D.C., 1915), 446; United States Bureau of the Census, *Wealth, Public Debt, and Taxation: 1922* (Washington, D.C., 1924), 180; United States Bureau of the Census, *Financial Statistics of State and Local Governments: 1932* (Washington, D.C., 1934); United States Bureau of the Census, *Governmental Units in the United States 1942* (Washington, D.C., 1944); William Anderson, *The Units of Government in the United States, an Enumeration and Analysis*, 1949 rev. ed. (Chicago: Public Administration Service, 1934, 1949).

14. Studenski, *The Government of Metropolitan Areas*, 29, 340; Victor Jones, *Metropolitan Government* (Chicago: University of Chicago Press, 1942); Bollens, *Special District Governments*, 255. For discussion see G. Ross Stephens and Nelson Wikstrom, *Metropolitan Government and Governance: Theoretical Perspectives, Empirical Analysis, and the Future* (New York: Oxford University Press, 2000), 29–50.

15. The modern special district originated at the local level, and that is where it has had the most powerful, lasting appeal. However, federal policy has also spurred the creation of special districts. As Susan Tenenbaum notes, several temporary federal public corporations that were created during World War I to assist with the war effort helped bolster the legitimacy of special districts in general. During the Great Depression, a series of federal agencies modeled after local special districts also promoted them with subsidies and support, starting with the Reconstruction Finance Corporation, created at the behest of Herbert Hoover in 1932. A variety of similar corporate entities followed, including the Public Works Administration (PWA). One New Deal official later called them "'spin-offs' from an RFC prototype." Many of them were short-lived and did not have sufficient autonomy to qualify as special districts by the census definition, but they did have a feedback effect on local policy. For example, PWA officials explicitly encouraged states to authorize the creation of special districts to undertake large public works projects, and cities created housing authorities throughout the United States to tap into federal subsidies for public housing

construction. Franklin Delano Roosevelt intended the Tennessee Valley Authority, which he praised as "clothed with the power of government but possessed of the flexibility and initiative of private enterprise," to serve as a model for the creation of large, multipurpose special districts around the country. In 1934 he issued a letter to United States governors urging them to sponsor them, and later offered legal assistance and model legislation. Tenenbaum, "Progressive Legacy"; Thomas G. Corcoran quoted in Arthur M. Schlesinger, *The Age of Roosevelt: The Politics of Upheaval* (Boston: Houghton Mifflin, 1960), 228; Franklin Delano Roosevelt quoted in Philip Selznick, *TVA and the Grass Roots*, 5; Robert G. Smith, *Public Authorities, Special Districts, and Local Government* (Washington, D.C.: National Association of Counties Research Foundation, 1964), 88; Doig, "Murderous Fellow," 295; Council of State Governments, *Public Authorities in the States: A Report to the Governors' Conference* (Chicago: Council of State Governments, 1953), 26; Gail Radford, *Modern Housing for America: Policy Struggles in the New Deal Era* (Chicago: University of Chicago Press, 1996); Robert Gerwig, "Public Authorities in the United States," *Law and Contemporary Problems* 26 (1961), 591–618. See also Chapter 2, n. 3.

16. Victor Jones, "Regional Councils and Regional Governments in the United States," paper presented at the National Conference of the American Society for Public Administration, Detroit, 1981, 10–11.

17. Since the 1940s, authorities have accounted for much of the increase in special district numbers and scale. Robert G. Smith, discussing them in 1964, remarked on the disproportionate interest in the largest organizations and asserted that the numerous smaller, single-purpose "municipal corporations" were much more important to understanding their structure, function, and proliferation in the 1950s and 1960s. Historical scholarship on special districts reflects this orientation as well; exceptionally large, high-profile agencies such as the New York Port Authority, the Tennessee Valley Authority, and the Metropolitan Water District of Southern California have inspired numerous studies. Hopefully, this book will draw attention to a vast, diffuse sector of government made up of thousands of smaller special districts with a pervasive influence on everyday life. Robert G. Smith, *Public Authorities, Special Districts, and Local Government* (Washington, D.C.: National Association of Counties Research Foundation, 1964), 9–13. Studies of large-scale entities include Jameson W. Doig, *Empire on the Hudson: Entrepreneurial Vision and Political Power at the Port of New York Authority* (New York: Columbia University Press, 2001); Stephen Erie, *Beyond Chinatown: the Metropolitan Waste District, Growth, and the Environment in Southern California* (Palo Alto, Calif.: Stanford University Press, 2006); Robert Caro, *The Power Broker: Robert Moses and the Fall of New York* (New York: Vintage Books, 1979); Robert Gottlieb and Margaret FitzSimmons, *Thirst for Growth: Water Agencies as Hidden Government in California* (Tuscon: University of Arizona Press, 1991); Robert Gottlieb, *A Life of Its Own: The Politics and Power of Water* (San Diego: Harcourt Brace Jovanovich, 1988); Erwin C. Hargrove, *Prisoners of Myth: Leadership of the Tennessee Valley Authority, 1933–1990* (Knoxville: University of Tennessee Press, 2001); Elkind, *Bay Cities and Water Politics.*

18. By 1982 there were 28,078 special districts in the United States. Alberta Sbragia estimates that their debt accounted for half of all long-term public borrowing by 1986. In 2002 the census of governments counted 35,356 special districts nationwide. These figures do not include increasing numbers of authorities that are legally and financially independent but are governed by ex officio boards and are therefore not counted by the census. United States Bu-

reau of the Census, *1972 Census of Governments* (Washington, D.C., 1973), 23; Sbragia, *Debt Wish*, 167.

19. Max A. Pock, *Independent Special Districts: A Solution to Metropolitan Area Problems* (Ann Arbor: University of Michigan Law School, 1962), 1.

20. On special district corruption and abuses, see Diana B. Henriques, *Machinery of Greed: Public Authority Abuse and What to Do About It* (Lexington, Mass.: Lexington Books, 1986); Donald Axelrod, *Shadow Government: The Hidden World of Public Authorities—and How They Control $1 Trillion of Your Money* (New York: Wiley, 1992). Scholarly analysis of the drawbacks of special district decision-making include Walsh, *The Public's Business*; Foster, *The Political Economy of Special-Purpose Government*; Sbaria, *Debt Wish*; Jerry Mitchell, *The American Experience with Government Corporations* (Armonk, N.Y.: M. E. Sharpe, 1999); Sara C. Galvan, "Wrestling with MUDs to Pin Down the Truth about Special Districts," *Fordham Law Review* 75 (2007), 3041–80; James T. Bennett and Thomas H. DiLorenzo, *Underground Government: The Off-Budget Public Sector* (Washington, D.C.: Cato Institute, 1983).

21. Max Weber, "Bureaucracy and Political Leadership," in *Economy and Society*, ed. Guenther Roth and Claus Wittich, vol. 2 (Berkeley: University of California Press, 1978).

Chapter 1. A Bridge to Prosperity

1. Doyle was a consummate booster. He started his career working as a clerk in the Santa Rosa Exchange Bank, which was founded by his father Manville Doyle in 1890, and ascended quickly. He was active in promoting and financing reconstruction after the 1906 earthquake, which had an even more devastating effect on Santa Rosa than it did on San Francisco. Later in life, Doyle contributed generously to many Sonoma institutions and endowed a major scholarship fund for Santa Rosa Junior College. *Press Democrat,* March 29, 1987, July 5, 1992, May 23, 1999; *History of a Partnership: Exchange Bank Santa Rosa* ([Santa Rosa, Calif.], n.d.), Sonoma State University Library—North Bay Digital Collections, Gaye LeBaron Digital Collection, http://northbaydigital.sonoma.edu (accessed Nov. 2007).

2. *Marin Journal,* Jan. 18, 1923; *Santa Rosa Press Democrat,* Jan. 14, Feb. 26, 1925; Honoria Tuomey, *History of Sonoma County, California* (Chicago: S. J. Clark Publishing, 1926).

3. Historical analysis of the Good Roads Movement in the United States evokes the larger debate on the origins and meaning of Progressivism; both had many manifestations and constituencies. Scholars including John B. Rae and James J. Flink argue that the movement was spurred by the undeniable technological advantages of the automobile. Bruce E. Seely emphasizes the power of bureaucrats and engineers in promoting construction and defining road policy; Howard Lawrence Preston demonstrates the appeal of roads to opportunistic small businessmen, who enthusiastically backed the cause. Owen D. Gutfreund has argued that it was a top-down movement controlled by representatives of big business manipulating naïve politicians and voters. John B. Rae, *The Road and Car in American Life* (Cambridge, Mass.: MIT Press, 1971); James J. Flink, *America Adopts the Automobile, 1895–1910* (Cambridge, Mass.: MIT Press, 1970), 202–13; Bruce E. Seely, *Building the American Highway System: Engineers as Policy Makers* (Philadelphia: Temple University Press, 1987), 11–65; Howard Lawrence Preston, *Dirt*

Roads to Dixie: Accessibility and Modernization in the South, 1885–1935 (Knoxville: University of Tennessee Press, 1991); Owen D. Gutfreund, *Twentieth Century Sprawl: Highways and the Reshaping of the American Landscape* (New York: Oxford University Press, 2004). See also U.S. Federal Highway Administration, *America's Highways, 1776–1976* (Washington, D.C., 1976), 64–123.

4. In 1909 the California legislature funded highways with $18 million in general obligation bonds, following a nationwide trend. By 1917, every state in the nation was funding roads. State-imposed gasoline taxes and other user fees became very popular during the 1920s; Oregon adopted the first gas tax in 1919 and other states quickly followed its lead, including California in 1923. Federal subsidies began with the 1916 Federal Aid Road Act, whereby Congress created the Bureau of Public Roads and appropriated $75 million to fund road construction throughout the country. A 1921 act established an annual federal appropriation, designated an official national highway system, and increased requirements for state matching funds and maintenance programs. Richard M. Zettel, *An Analysis of Taxation for Highway Purposes in California, 1895–1946* (Sacramento, 1946), 16–24; Seely, *Building the American Highway System,* 46–87; John Chynoweth Burnham, "The Gasoline Tax and the Automobile Revolution," *Mississippi Valley Historical Review* 48 (Dec. 1961), 435–59; U.S. Department of Transportation, *America's Highways,* 80–110.

5. Clyde McIntyre Edmondson, [Resumé], carton 49, Redwood Empire Association Records, The Bancroft Library, University of California, Berkeley (hereafter cited as REA Records).

6. Redwood Empire Association, *Brief History of the Redwood Empire Association* ([San Francisco: Redwood Empire Association, 1936]); Ted Wurm and Alvin C. Graves, *The Crookedest Railroad in the World: A History of the Mount Tamalpais Railroad and Muir Woods Railroad of California,* rev. ed. (Glendale, Calif.: Trans-Anglo Books, 1983).

7. Frank Anthony Speth, "A History of Agricultural Labor in Sonoma County, California," M.A. thesis, University of California, Berkeley, 1938; Ernest P. Peninou, *History of the Sonoma Viticultural District: The Grape Growers, the Wine Makers and the Vineyards* (Santa Rosa, Calif.: Nomis Press, 1998); Simone Wilson, *Sonoma County: River of Time* (Chatsworth, Calif.: Windsor Publications, 1990).

8. James Michael Buckley, "Building the Redwood Region: The Redwood Lumber Industry and the Landscape of Northern California, 1850–1929," Ph.D. diss., University of California, Berkeley, 2000.

9. *San Francisco News,* Feb. 17, 1932.

10. Redwood Highway Association, *Redwood Highway Empire* (San Francisco: Redwood Empire Association, 1926).

11. John Robinson, *The Redwood Highway . . . Its Origins and Development* (Sacramento: California Office of State Printing, 1964), 5.

12. Katherine M. Johnson points out that, despite what these boosters claimed, they consistently won significantly greater state road subsidies per capita than their Southern California counterparts because of the disproportionate power of northern California in the legislature and the rural orientation of federal road programs. Katherine M. Johnson, "Captain Blake Versus the Highwaymen, or How San Francisco Won the Freeway Revolt," paper presented at the Conference of the American Association of Geographers, San Francisco, 2007.

13. Redwood Empire Association, *Brief History.*

14. The Good Roads Movement built upon a tradition of cutthroat competition between the leaders of rival cities and towns to attract railroads. The close

collaboration between local business interests and politicians for the sake of transportation infrastructure was not new, but in this era of association, clubs and civic groups like the Redwood Highway Association achieved unprecedented influence over local policy and government. Noteworthy studies of nineteenth- and early twentieth-century boosterism include Daniel Boorstein, *The Americans: The National Experience* (New York: Random House, 1965); Wyatt Belcher, *The Economic Rivalry Between St. Louis and Chicago, 1850–1880* (New York: AMS Press, 1968); Carl Abbott, *Boosters and Businessmen: Popular Economic Thought and Economic Growth in the Antebellum Middle West* (Westport, Conn.: Greenwood Press, 1981); William Cronon, *Nature's Metropolis: Chicago and the Great West* (New York: W. W. Norton, 1991); John Logan and Harvey Molotch, *Urban Fortunes: The Political Economy of Place* (Berkeley: University of California Press, 1992).

15. Terrence McDonald makes a convincing case that the San Francisco delegation had enough power in Sacramento to ensure the effective autonomy of city fiscal policy. The disproportionate influence of San Francisco and northern California persisted for decades, despite its relative decline in population. In 1930 the state senate was reorganized on a federalist model, with representation based on counties rather than population, which reinforced and increased the imbalance between north and south. In 1965 court-ordered reapportionment of the state legislature reduced the inequity (see Chapter 4, n. 16). Terrence J. McDonald, *The Parameters of Urban Fiscal Policy: Socioeconomic Change and Political Culture in San Francisco, 1860–1906* (Berkeley: University of California Press, 1986), 24–32; Don Allen, *Legislative Sourcebook: California Legislature and Reapportionment, 1849–1965* (Sacramento, [1965]), 5–68.

16. *San Francisco Bulletin*, Aug. 26, 1916.

17. Ibid.; Richard Thomas Loomis, "The History of the Building of the Golden Gate Bridge," Ph.D. diss., Stanford University, 1958, 9–10.

18. Loomis, "History of the Building of the Golden Gate Bridge," 11–17; *Marin Journal*, July 24, Aug. 7, 14, 1919, April 28, July 14, 1921. For a profile of Kent, see Anne F. Hyde, "William Kent: The Puzzle of Progressive Conservationists," in William Deverell and Tom Sitton, eds., *California Progressivism Revisited* (Berkeley: University of California Press, 1994), 34–56.

19. Classical historical studies of Progressive Era politics emphasizing the importance of governmental structures generally and municipal reform specifically (though diverging on what motivated it and who controlled it) include Samuel P. Hays, "The Politics of Reform in the Progressive Era," *Pacific Northwest Quarterly* (1964), 157–69; Hays, "The Changing Political Structure of the City in Industrial America," *Journal of Urban History* 1 (1974), 3–68; Robert H. Wiebe, *The Search for Order, 1877–1920* (New York: Hill and Wang, 1967); James Weinstein, *The Corporate Ideal in the Liberal State, 1900–1918* (Boston: Beacon Press, 1968). Also see Martin J. Schiesl, *The Politics of Efficiency: Municipal Administration and Reform in America, 1800–1920* (Berkley: University of California Press, 1977); Kenneth Fox, *Better City Government: Innovation in American Urban Politics, 1850–1937* (Philadelphia: Temple University Press, 1977); Bradley Robert Rice, *Progressive Cities: The Commission Government Movement in America, 1901–1920* (Austin: University of Texas Press, 1977); Kenneth Finegold, *Experts and Politicians: Reform Challenges to Machine Politics in New York, Cleveland and Chicago* (Princeton, N.J.: Princeton University Press, 1995); Amy Bridges, *Morning Glories: Municipal Reform in the Southwest* (Princeton, N.J.: Princeton University Press, 1997).

20. On Phelan and the Hetch Hetchy project, see Robert W. Righter, *The Bat-*

tle Over Hetch Hetchy: America's Most Controversial Dam and the Birth of Environmentalism (New York: Oxford University Press, 2005); Warren Hanson, *San Francisco Water and Power: A History of the Municipal Water Department and Hetch Hetchy System* (San Francisco: San Francisco Public Utilities Commission, 1985); Gray Brechin, *Imperial San Francisco: Urban Power, Earthly Ruin* (Berkeley: University of California Press, 1999), 100–117; William Issel and Robert Cherney, *San Francisco, 1865–1932: Politics, Power and Urban Development* (Berkeley: University of California Press, 1986), 174–76, 82–84. On San Francisco progressivism and reform from the late nineteenth century through the 1920s see Philip J. Ethington, *The Public City: The Political Construction of Urban Life in San Francisco, 1850–1900* (New York: Cambridge University Press, 1994); William Issel, "Business Power and Political Culture in San Francisco, 1900–1940," *Journal of Urban History* 16 (1989), 52–77; Issel and Cherney, *San Francisco, 1865–1932;* Judd Kahn, *Imperial San Francisco: Politics and Planning in an American City, 1897–1906* (Lincoln: University of Nebraska Press, 1979); McDonald, *The Parameters of Urban Fiscal Policy;* Mansel G. Blackford, *The Lost Dream: Businessmen and City Planning on the Pacific Coast, 1890–1920* (Columbus: Ohio State University Press, 1993).

21. Kevin Starr, *Endangered Dreams: The Great Depression in California* (New York: Oxford University Press, 1996), 84–89, 276.

22. E.g., *San Francisco Chronicle,* Jan. 12, 1929; Issel and Cherney, *San Francisco, 1865–1932,* 81–82, 172–74; Anthony Perles, *The People's Railway: The History of the Municipal Railway of San Francisco* (Glendale, Calif.: Interurban Press, 1981).

23. Democrats had little clout in San Francisco or in California from early in the century through the election of 1934, and even the Republican Party was unusually weak in the state relative to political factions or interest groups. For an overview of California party politics in this period, see Carey McWilliams, *California: The Great Exception* (New York: Current Books, 1949), 171–213. See also Michael Paul Rogin and John L. Shover, *Political Change in California: Critical Elections and Social Movements, 1890–1966* (Westport, Conn.: Greenwood Publishing, 1970); Stephanie Sabine Pincetl, *Transforming California: A Political History of Land Use and Development* (Baltimore: Johns Hopkins University Press, 1999), 25–131; Richard B. Harvey, *The Dynamics of California Government and Politics* (Belmont, Calif.: Wadsworth, 1969).

24. Roger W. Lotchin, "John Francisco Neylan: San Francisco Irish Progressive," in James P. Walsh, ed., *The San Francisco Irish, 1850–1976* (San Francisco: Irish Literary and Historical Society, 1978), 86–110.

25. Issel and Cherney, *San Francisco, 1865–1932,* 182–84. For a lively discussion of the politics of San Francisco newspapers and details about the dynasties that controlled them, see Brechin, *Imperial San Francisco,* 171–241.

26. San Francisco Board of Supervisors, Resolution No. 16,241, Nov. 12, 1918. The prevailing practice at the time was for local governments to grant private companies franchises to build bridges, with the right to collect tolls and limited competition to make their investments worthwhile. In 1923 the American Toll Bridge Company was granted a franchise for a span over the Carquinez Strait, which was completed in 1927. The same company built the Antioch Bridge across the mouth of the San Joaquin River at the bay's inland extreme, which opened to traffic in 1926. In 1927, the Dumbarton Bridge Company completed the first transbay bridge to accommodate automobiles, located twenty-six miles south of San Francisco. Frank M. Cortelyou, "The Dumbarton Bridge," *Transactions of the Commonwealth Club of California* 20 (1925), 251–54; *San Francisco Chron-*

icle, Dec. 17, 27, 1926, Jan. 4, July 29, Sept. 20, 1927, April 6, July 9, 1928; *San Francisco News,* June 20, 1927; *San Francisco Bulletin,* June 21, 1928.

27. *San Francisco News,* Sept. 21, 1927; *San Francisco Examiner,* Aug. 11, Dec. 18, 1926, July 31, 1928, Aug. 2, 1928; *San Francisco News,* July 28–29, 1927, Sept. 21, 1927, July 31, Aug. 1, 1928; *San Francisco Chronicle,* Aug. 9, 1927; *San Francisco Call and Post,* July 28, 1928; *San Francisco Business,* March 9, 1927.

28. Allen Brown, *Golden Gate: Biography of a Bridge* (Garden City, N.Y.: Doubleday, 1965), 13; Loomis, "History of the Building of the Golden Gate Bridge," 14; Golden Gate Bridge and Highway District, *Report of the Chief Engineer with Architectural Studies,* prepared by Joseph B. Strauss, vol. 3, *The Golden Gate Bridge at San Francisco, California* (San Francisco, 1930), 27.

29. O'Shaughnessy wrote to "four or five distinguished engineers, including Mr. Gustav Lindenthal of New York, who is the most experienced engineer in the country of long span construction, Mr. Ralph Modjeski, who has the largest bridge experience of any engineer in the United States and is the recognized leader on all large span construction, Francis C. McMath, president of the Canadian Bridge and Iron Company, Detroit, and Joseph B. Strauss, with whom I had previous experience on a short span bridge. Mr. Strauss has considerable experience with short span bascule bridges, but never to my knowledge attempted previously any design over a 700-foot length span. I received replies from all of those gentlemen. Mr. Lindenthal wrote a most exhaustive letter to me on June 22, 1920, in which he estimated the cost of the bridge within $56,000,000 without cost of rights of way and without interest during construction." Michael M. O'Shaughnessy, "Statement by M. M. O'Shaughnessy, City Engineer, on Golden Gate Bridge," Oct. 11, 1930, box 8, John Debo Galloway Papers, The Water Resources Center Archives, University of California, Berkeley (hereafter cited as Galloway Papers).

30. Brown, *Golden Gate,* 13, 226. Strauss's credentials are discussed in Chapter 2.

31. O'Shaughnessy, "Statement on Golden Gate Bridge." Allen Brown, in his mostly laudatory history of Strauss and the bridge, described these initial plans: "It was a hybrid bridge, a mongrel bridge, an ugly bridge. . . . It looked as if it were supported in the mouths of two grotesque beetles crawling out from either shore, and those beetle-shaped supports for the cantilever sections were so weighty, so ponderous, so view-blocking that Strauss felt it necessary to justify his design." Brown, *Golden Gate,* 14.

32. Loomis, "History of the Building of the Golden Gate Bridge," 19; Brown, *Golden Gate,* 14–15; Henry Petroski, *Engineers of Dreams: Great Bridge Builders and the Spanning of America* (New York: Knopf, 1995), 276.

33. James Herbert Madden, quoted in Brown, *Golden Gate,* 15.

34. *Marin Journal,* Jan. 18, 1923; *Santa Rosa Press Democrat,* Jan. 14, Feb. 26, 1925.

35. According to Harlan, the Boston area Metropolitan Water and Sewer District, part of the first wave of metropolitan area special districts, inspired the 1911 Municipal Water District Act. However, its most obvious California precedents were the irrigation districts authorized by the 1887 Wright Act. George H. Harlan to Francis V. Keesling, Sept. 13, 1929, box 61, Francis V. Keesling Papers, M0100, Department of Special Collections, Stanford University Libraries, Stanford, Calif. (hereafter cited as Keesling Papers, M0100); Marin Municipal Water District, *Story of the Marin Municipal Water District,* by Leo L. Stanley and Thomas T. Kent ([Novato, Calif.], 1960); Marin Municipal Water District, *Marin Munici-*

pal Water District, by John Burt ([Novato, Calif.], 1931); Clifford Flack, *Marin Chronology 1880–1930* (n.p., [1961]), 452, Anne T. Kent History Room, Marin County Free Library Civic Center Branch, San Rafael; Marin Municipal Water District, "An Historical Summary of the Marin Municipal Water District," ([Novato, Calif.], 1972); Marin Municipal Water District Board of Directors, *Report* (n.p., 1916). On the Wright Act, see Donald J. Pisani, *From the Family Farm to Agribusiness: The Irrigation Crusade in California and the West, 1850–1931* (Berkeley: University of California Press, 1984); Hundley, *The Great Thirst,* 99–103; Gordon Miller, "Shaping California Water Law, 1871 to 1928," *Southern California Quarterly* 55 (1973), 9–42.

36. George Harlan to Francis V. Keesling, Sept. 13, 1929, box 61, Keesling Papers, M0100; Golden Gate Bridge and Highway District, *Report of the Chief Engineer with Architectural Studies,* 22.

37. If all eight counties originally slated for bridge district membership had enrolled, there would have been thirteen directors. Each county would have had one representative except Sonoma with two and San Francisco with five. *Statutes of California* 39th reg. sess. (1911) ch. 671, 1290–1302; Marin Municipal Water District Board of Directors, *Report* (1916).

38. George H. Harlan to W. J. Hotchkiss, June 27, 1923, box 80, Golden Gate Bridge Highway and Transportation District, Iron Mountain Storage Facility, South San Francisco (hereafter cited as IM facility).

39. *Statutes of California* 45th reg. sess. (1923) ch. 228, 452–64.

40. *Statutes of California* 45th reg. sess. (1923) ch. 228, 452–64.

41. Ibid.

42. Loomis, "History of the Building of the Golden Gate Bridge," 30; Brown, *Golden Gate,* 16; *San Francisco Bulletin,* June 26, 1923; *Statutes of California* 45th reg. sess. (1923) ch. 228, 452–64; A.J.R. 2, 45th reg. sess. (Ca. 1923).

43. *San Francisco Examiner,* June 24, 1923.

44. *Marin Journal,* June 14, 1923; *San Francisco Chronicle,* March 16, June 24, 1923; C. H. Purcell, Charles E. Andrew, and Glenn B. Woodruff, *Designing and Building the San Francisco-Oakland Bay Bridge* (New York: Engineering News-Record, [1937]), 2.

45. *Marin Journal,* June 14, 1923.

46. Golden Gate Bridge and Highway District, *Report of the Chief Engineer with Architectural Studies,* 29.

47. "Bay Bridges," *The Commonwealth* 1 (1925), 272–77; Petroski, *Engineers of Dreams,* 294–308.

48. One *Chronicle* reporter counted several hundred representatives of northern California counties and civic associations in attendance at the War Department hearing, but "not one with a voice against spanning of the Gate." *San Francisco Chronicle,* May 17, 1924. Secretary of War John W. Weeks to Chairman, Commercial Development and Trans-Bay Bridge Committee, Board of Supervisors of the City and County of San Francisco, Dec. 20, 1924, in Golden Gate Bridge and Highway District, *Report of the Chief Engineer with Architectural Studies,* 93-G.

49. George H. Harlan to W. J. Hotchkiss, June 27, 1923, box 80, IM facility; Golden Gate Bridge and Highway District, *Legislative Chronology* (San Francisco, [1937]), box 66, Keesling Papers, M0100.

50. *San Francisco Chronicle,* April 4, 1925.

51. *San Francisco Chronicle,* Feb. 12, 1925.

52. *San Francisco Chronicle,* April 3, 1925.

53. The population of San Francisco increased 22 percent between 1910 and

1920, growing from 416,912 to 506,676. At the same time, the population of Los Angeles went from 319,198 to 576,673, an 81 percent gain, and Oakland grew by 43 percent, its population increasing from 150,746 to 216,261. For discussion of the status anxiety of San Francisco's civic elite in the face of its relative decline, see Kahn, *Imperial San Francisco*, 5–27, 57–79, 154–76; Blackford, *The Lost Dream*, 13–62; Roger Lotchin, "The Darwinian City: The Politics of Urbanization in San Francisco Between the World Wars," *Pacific Historical Review* 48 (1979), 357–81.

54. Efforts to revive San Francisco and to protect its status after the 1906 fire spurred the formation of a number of regionalist organizations, including the Greater San Francisco Association and the San Francisco Regional Plan Association. The Commonwealth Club was especially active in promoting regional planning and large-scale public enterprise. Leaders of these organizations helped win approval for the Hetch Hetchy project, spearheaded several annexation efforts, and developed a proposal for organizing the Bay Area into boroughs. Efforts to consolidate or coordinate San Francisco and East Bay government failed and generally intensified antagonism and rivalry. The formation of the Golden Gate Bridge and Highway District was one of the few successful efforts to unite on a regional level for a common purpose. I. M. Barlow, *Metropolitan Government* (New York: Routledge, 1991), 237–49; Kahn, *Imperial San Francisco*; Mel Scott, *The San Francisco Bay Area: Metropolis in Perspective*, 2nd ed. (Berkeley: University of California Press, 1985).

55. *San Francisco Chronicle*, Jan. 27, 1931, Jan. 31, Feb. 14, 1925; *San Francisco Examiner*, Jan. 17, 1925.

56. *San Francisco Examiner*, March 25, 1925; Brown, *Golden Gate*, 24–25.

57. *San Francisco Examiner*, March 24, 1925.

58. The Bridge and Highway District Act was amended on May 23, 1925, to read: "[for] any county or city and county having a population of more than five hundred thousand the number of directors appointed shall be equal to the total number of directors appointed from all of the counties or cities and counties within the district having a population of less than five hundred thousand." *Statutes of California* 46th reg. sess. (1925) ch. 387, 714–22; *San Francisco Chronicle*, April 6, 1925; San Francisco Bureau of Governmental Research, "The Proposed Golden Gate Bridge," *The City*, Jan. 25, 1928.

59. For discussion of the REA, see Chapter 4. Clyde Edmondson, *Building the Redwood Empire . . . An Epoch of the Adventurous West* (San Francisco: Redwood Empire Association, 1937), carton 49, REA Records; Edmondson, [Resumé], (1942), carton 49, REA Records; [Edmondson], Summary References— Redwood Empire Association (1942), carton 49, REA Records.

60. Harlan explained their dilemma: "In my opinion the failure of the County of Humboldt to join the district would not invalidate the formation of the district if the provisions of the act are otherwise complied with. . . . This does not relieve the sponsors of the district from the necessity of applying to the Board of Supervisors in every county named in the original ordinances passed in Marin and Sonoma counties, and proceedings must be started in Humboldt, Del Norte, Lake, Napa and Mendocino and either terminated by the lapse of time above provided for or favorably passed." George H. Harlan to W. J. Hotchkiss, June 6, 1925, box 80, DS Vault.

61. *San Francisco Examiner*, July 25, 1925.

62. *San Francisco Examiner*, Sept. 3, 1925.

63. In the 1920s, promoting roads and facilities to allow for easy access to the redwood groves for automobile tourists was an important strategy to win public

support creating parks and preserves. Susan R. Schrepfer, *The Fight to Save the Redwoods: A History of Environmental Reform, 1917–1978* (Madison: University of Wisconsin Press, 1983), 20; Paul S. Sutter, *Driven Wild: How the Fight Against the Automobile Launched the Modern Wilderness Movement* (Seattle: University of Washington Press, 2002).

64. Financial analysts later pointed out that the owners of timberland in Del Norte County already had a very high rate of tax delinquency, so had little to lose. Blythe & Co. Inc., *Golden Gate Bridge and Highway District California* (New York, Chicago, and Los Angeles, 1934), 13; *Statutes of California* 46th reg. sess. (1925) ch. 387, 714–22.

65. *Ukiah Republican Press,* Aug. 7, 1929; Golden Gate Bridge and Highway District, *Report of the Chief Engineer with Architectural Studies,* 10.

66. *San Francisco Chronicle,* April 10, 1925.

67. *Doyle v. Jordan,* 200 Cal. 170 (1926).

68. *Wheatley v. Superior Court of Napa County,* 207 Cal. 723 (1929); Harlan to W. J. Hotchkiss, June 6, 1925, box 80, Golden Gate Bridge Highway and Transportation District, DS Vault; Brown, *Golden Gate,* 26.

69. *San Francisco Chronicle,* Oct. 25–26, 1927, Feb. 2, 1928.

70. *San Francisco Chronicle,* Nov. 4, Dec. 5, 1928; *San Francisco Call-Bulletin,* Nov. 7, 1928; *San Francisco Examiner,* Dec. 4, 1928; *Statutes of California* 49th reg. sess. (1931) ch. 70, 77–80. For a physical description of the district, see Blythe & Co., *Golden Gate Bridge and Highway District.*

71. *San Rafael Daily Independent,* Dec. 12, 15, 27, 1928; *Marin Journal,* Dec. 27, 1928, Jan. 24, 1929; Leo L. Stanley and Thomas T. Kent, *Story of the Marin Municipal Water District* (San Rafael, Calif., 1960); Golden Gate Bridge and Highway District, *Report of the Chief Engineer with Architectural Studies,* 10.

72. *San Francisco Chronicle,* Jan. 1, 1929; *San Rafael Daily Independent,* Dec. 24, 1928, Jan. 3, 22, 25, 28, Feb. 4, 1929; *San Francisco Chronicle,* Jan. 25, 1929; Loomis, "History of the Building of the Golden Gate Bridge," 163–64; Golden Gate Bridge and Highway District, *Report of the Chief Engineer with Architectural Studies,* 10–11.

73. *San Francisco Chronicle,* Dec. 28, 1928.

74. *San Rafael Daily Independent,* Dec. 26, 1928.

75. Frank C. Jordan, *California Blue Book or State Roster 1913–1915* (Sacramento, 1915), 499–500; *San Francisco Chronicle,* Jan. 8–14, 1938; *San Francisco News,* Jan. 6, 1938. See also Walton Bean, *Boss Ruef's San Francisco: The Story of the Union Labor Party, Big Business, and the Graft Prosecution* (Berkeley: University of California Press, 1972).

76. Francis V. Keesling, a leading bridge director from 1929 to 1936 (see Chapter 2), noted in his personal log that Burkhardt was a "valiant supporter of the bridge" but was "dominated" by Hirschberg and Finn. He also believed that Warren Shannon, W. P. Stanton, and Richard Welch were under their influence. Francis V. Keesling to A. R. O'Brien, Jan. 13, 1933, box 65, Francis V. Keesling Papers, M1146, Department of Special Collections, Stanford University Libraries, Stanford, Calif. (hereafter cited as Keesling Papers, M1146); Francis V. Keesling, *Daily Calendar* (1929–1937), 2–3, Keesling Papers, M1146; Issel and Cherney, *San Francisco, 1865–1932,* 185.

77. *San Rafael Daily Independent,* Jan. 27, 1929; *San Francisco Chronicle,* Dec. 28, 1928, March 6, 1929.

78. *San Francisco Chronicle,* Jan. 1, 25, 1929; *San Rafael Daily Independent,* Dec.

24, 1928, Jan. 3, 22, 25, 28, Feb. 4, 1929. The *Independent* was the only paper to print Shannon's statement on the matter.

79. Loomis, "History of the Building of the Golden Gate Bridge," 55–57; John van der Zee, *The Gate: The True Story of the Design and Construction of the Golden Gate Bridge* (New York: Simon and Schuster, 1986), 76–77, 226–27; *San Francisco Examiner,* March 29, 1935; Keesling, *Daily Calendar,* 99.

80. *San Francisco Bulletin,* Aug. 16, 1929; *San Francisco Chronicle,* Aug. 16, 1929.

81. San Francisco Bureau of Governmental Research, "The Proposed Golden Gate Bridge," 21–22; Loomis, "History of the Building of the Golden Gate Bridge," 60; *Engineering News-Record,* Dec. 1, 1927; *San Francisco Bulletin,* Aug. 16, 1929; *San Francisco Chronicle,* Aug. 16, Oct. 18, 29, 1929; *San Rafael Daily Independent,* Oct. 16, 1929; *San Francisco Examiner,* May 15, 1930; *Ukiah Republican Press,* May 21, June 25, July 9, 1930.

82. *San Francisco Chronicle,* Aug. 1, 1929; *San Rafael Daily Independent,* Aug. 1, 1929. On the history of special assessments see Robin L. Einhorn, *Property Rules: Political Economy in Chicago, 1833–1872* (Chicago: University of Chicago Press, 1991); Stephen Diamond, "The Death and Transfiguration of Benefit Taxation: Special Assessments in Nineteenth-Century America," *Journal of Legal Studies* 201 (1983), 201–40; Alberta M. Sbragia, *Debt Wish: Entrepreneurial Cities, U.S. Federalism, and Economic Development* (Pittsburgh: University of Pittsburgh Press, 1996), 62–79; Victor Rosewater, *Special Assessments: A Study in Municipal Finance* (1893; New York: AMS Press, 1998).

83. *Wheatley v. Superior Court of Napa.*

84. For analysis of the decision, see *Golden Gate Bridge and Highway District v. Felt,* 214 Cal. 170 (1931); George H. Harlan to Francis V. Keesling, Feb. 16, 1943; Senate Interim Committee on Problems Concerning the Inclusion of the Golden Gate Bridge into the State Highway System, *Final Report* (Sacramento, 1953), 13–17.

85. Issel, "Business Power and Political Culture in San Francisco, 1900–1940," 53–55.

86. San Francisco Bureau of Governmental Research, "The Proposed Golden Gate Bridge," 39.

87. *New York Times,* Oct. 27, 1929.

88. *San Francisco Call-Bulletin,* Nov. 26, 1929; *San Francisco Chronicle,* May 20, July 2, 1930.

89. *Statutes of California* 49th reg. sess. (1929) ch. 763, 1489–1502.

90. The California Toll Bridge Authority was one of the very first public corporations to rely primarily on revenue bonds for its financing. Soon after its creation, the bond market collapsed, delaying construction of the Bay Bridge. However, as a self-liquidating state project, it was eligible for new sources of federal aid. The Bay Bridge was one of the first two public works projects to be financed through the Reconstruction Finance Corporation during the Hoover administration, along with the Colorado River Aqueduct, which benefited Southern California. California Legislative Auditor, *Financial History of the San Francisco-Oakland Bay Bridge* (Sacramento, 1953); Udo Sautter, "Government and Unemployment: the Use of Public Works before the New Deal," *Journal of American History* 73 (1986), 59–86.

91. *San Francisco Chronicle,* Aug. 15, 1929.

92. See Issel, "Business Power and Political Culture in San Francisco, 1900–1940"; William Issel, "'Citizens Outside the Government': Business and

Urban Policy in San Francisco and Los Angeles, 1890–1932," *Pacific Historical Review* 57 (1988), 117–45.

93. Golden Gate Bridge and Highway District, Minutes of the Regular Adjourned Meeting of Aug. 27th, 1930, box 66, Keesling Papers, M0100; Charles W. Duncan to Board of Directors, Golden Gate Bridge and Highway District, Sept. 10, 1930, box 61, Keesling Papers, M100; Keesling to A. R. O'Brien, Jan. 13, 1933, box 65, Keesling Papers, M1146; *Ukiah Republican Press*, Dec. 11, 1929; *Rafael Daily Independent*, Oct. 16, 1929; *San Francisco Chronicle*, Oct. 18, 1929.

94. Golden Gate Bridge and Highway District, *Report of the Chief Engineer with Architectural Studies*, 27–28, emphasis in original.

95. Golden Gate Bridge and Highway District, *Traffic Analysis and Report of the Traffic Engineer*, by Sydney W. Taylor (San Francisco, 1930), 28–29, A5; Golden Gate Bridge and Highway District, *Report of the Chief Engineer with Architectural Studies*, 24, 27, 37, 100; *San Francisco Chronicle*, July 2, 1930; *San Francisco Chronicle*, Oct. 27, 1930; *San Francisco News*, Oct. 27, 1930.

96. Fred R. Muhs to San Francisco Chamber of Commerce, Oct. 10, 1930, box 8, Galloway Papers; San Francisco Chamber of Commerce Bridge Committee, *Report On the Results of the Investigation of the Proposed Golden Gate Bridge* (San Francisco, 1930); Leland W. Cutler, *America Is Good to a Country Boy* (Stanford: Stanford University Press, 1954), 143–46.

97. *San Francisco Examiner*, Oct. 8, 1930; *San Francisco News*, Oct. 9, 13, 1930; *San Francisco Chronicle*, Oct. 26, 1930; Loomis, "History of the Building of the Golden Gate Bridge," 69; Fred R. Muhs to San Francisco Chamber of Commerce, Oct. 10, 1930, box 8, Galloway Papers. For Taxpayers' Committee fliers and advertisements, see box 8, Galloway Papers.

98. Advertisement, "The Truth About the Bridge!" *Sausalito News*, Oct. 31, 1930. Similar arguments were made in many other ads. E.g., *San Francisco Chronicle*, Oct. 30, 1930.

99. Advertisement, *San Francisco Examiner*, Nov. 1, 1930.

100. "The Golden Gate Bridge," *Transactions of the Commonwealth Club of California* 6 (1930), 318–19, 339.

101. Joseph B. Strauss to William Fitch Cheney, Oct. 24, 1930, box 8, Charles Derleth Papers, DERLETH, Water Resources Center Archives, University of California, Berkeley (hereafter cited as Derleth Papers).

102. Advertisement, *San Francisco Chronicle*, Oct. 22, 1930.

103. *San Francisco News*, Oct. 9, 1930.

104. *San Francisco Chronicle*, Oct. 13, 1930.

105. The bond vote totals were: San Francisco, 107,040 to 33,264; Marin, 12,704 to 1,901; Del Norte, 1,449 to 208; Mendocino, 874 to 1,020; Napa, 3,554 to 1,929; Sonoma, 11,693 to 2,235. *San Francisco Chronicle*, Nov. 5, 1930.

106. *Statutes of California* 49th reg. sess. (1931) ch. 70, 77–80.

107. *Statutes of California* 45th reg. sess. (1923) ch. 228, 452–64.

108. *Statutes of California* 49th reg. sess. (1931) ch. 169, 239–41.

109. In June 17, 1931, *Chronicle* editorial evoked the collapse of the St. Francis Dam, a major engineering disaster related to inadequate bedrock that killed more than 400 people in southern California in 1928. Other newspapers criticized the *Chronicle* for "publishing harmful propaganda." *San Francisco Chronicle*, June 13, 17, 18, 1931; *San Francisco Examiner*, June 19, 1931; *San Rafael Daily Independent*, June 19, 1931; *San Francisco Examiner*, June 11, 18, 1931; Andrew C. Lawson to Board of Directors Golden Gate Bridge and Highway District, June 9, 1931, box 8, Derleth Papers; Allan E. Sedgwick to Golden Gate Bridge and High-

way District, June 9, 1931, box 8, Derleth Papers; Joseph B. Strauss to Board of Directors, Golden Gate Bridge and Highway District, June 10, 1931, box 8, Derleth Papers.

110. Keesling to A. R. O'Brien, Jan. 13, 1933, box 65, Keesling Papers, M1146; *San Francisco Examiner,* June 18, 1931.

111. *San Francisco Chronicle,* May 16, June 19, July 9, 17, 1931; *San Francisco Examiner,* July 9, 10, Nov. 17, 1931; Francis V. Keesling to A. R. O'Brien, Jan. 13, 1933, box 65, Keesling Papers, M1146.

112. *San Francisco Examiner,* Aug. 14, Sept. 16, 1931; *San Francisco Chronicle,* Aug. 14, Sept. 16, 1931; *Golden Gate Bridge and Highway District v. Felt*; Loomis, "History of the Building of the Golden Gate Bridge," 87–89.

113. Stanley Scott and John C. Bollens, *Special Districts in California Local Government* (Berkeley, 1949); William Anderson, *The Units of Government in the United States, an Ennumeration and Analysis,* rev. ed. (Chicago: University of Chicago Press, 1949).

114. Ibid., 315–16.

115. *Golden Gate Bridge and Highway District v. Felt,* 337, 340–41.

116. Ibid., 324.

117. *San Francisco Chronicle,* Nov. 29, Dec. 10, 1931; *San Francisco Examiner,* Nov. 29, Dec. 10, 1931; *San Francisco News,* Aug. 17, Dec. 5, 9, 10, 1931; *Ukiah Republican Press,* Aug. 26, 1931.

118. *Del Norte Co. v. Filmer; Garland Co. v. Filmer* 1 F. Supp. 8 (N.D. Cal. 1932).

119. *San Francisco News,* Aug. 10, 1932.

120. Loomis, "History of the Building of the Golden Gate Bridge," 103.

121. The other major firms in the syndicate were Blythe and Co. Inc., Dean Witter & Company, and Weeden and Company. Later, the price of the bonds went up, and $3.2 million worth sold over par in 1935. Bankamerica Company, "Memorandum reviewing the history of the early financing of the golden Gate Bridge and Highway District," 1934, box 52-2, IM facility; Blythe & Co. inc., *Golden Gate Bridge and Highway District*; *San Francisco Chronicle,* Jan. 17, 1935.

122. *Ukiah Republican Press,* Oct. 23, 1929.

123. Luther Gulick, quoted in Robert G. Smith, *Public Authorities, Special Districts, and Local Government* (Washington, D.C.: National Association of Counties Research Foundatiopn, 1964), 38.

Chapter 2. A District Divided

1. *San Francisco Chronicle,* Feb. 26, 27, 1933.

2. William H. Mullins, *The Depression and the Urban West Coast, 1929–1933: Los Angeles, San Francisco, Seattle, and Portland* (Bloomington: Indiana University Press, 1991).

3. Support for large public works projects was an important part of federal economic stimulus and unemployment relief efforts during the Great Depression (though scholars disagree on their efficacy). The literature on public works in the 1930s is extensive, reflecting the spectacular scale of many of these projects, their enduring economic and physical legacies, and their centrality to the New Deal. The history of the Golden Gate Bridge and Highway District highlights how many of the strategies applied at the federal level during the Great Depression to promote economic growth were developed much earlier by city and state governments. See Udo Sautter, "Government and Unemployment:

The Use of Public Works Before the New Deal," *Journal of American History* 73 (1986), 59–86; Udo Sautter, *Three Cheers for the Unemployed: Government and Unemployment Before the New Deal* (Cambridge: Cambridge University Press, 1991). For recent discussion of the political economy of public works in the 1930s see Jason Scott Smith, *Building New Deal Liberalism: The Political Economy of Public Works* (New York: Cambridge University Press, 2006); Jordan A. Schwarz, *The New Dealers: Power Politics in the Age of Roosevelt* (New York: Knopf, 1993); Robert D. Leighninger, Jr., *Long-Range Public Investment: The Forgotten Legacy of the New Deal* (Columbia: University of South Carolina Press, 2007); Elliott A. Rosen, *Roosevelt, the Great Depression, and the Economics of Recovery* (Charlottesville: University Press of Virginia, 2005); Jeff Singleton, *The American Dole: Unemployment Relief and the Welfare State in the Great Depression* (Westport, Conn.: Greenwood, 2000).

4. The potential for waste, inefficiency, and graft associated with large public works projects has garnered concern since the nineteenth century and continues to plague them today. See Bent Flyvbjerg, Nils Bruzelius, and Werner Rothengatter, *Megaprojects and Risk: An Anatomy of Ambition* (Cambridge: Cambridge University Press, 2003).

5. *Statutes of California* 45th reg. sess. (1923) ch. 228, 452–64. In 1929, the board of directors specified that the general manager "shall approve or disapprove all demands presented against the District before the same are acted upon by the Auditing Committee." Golden Gate Bridge and Highway District, Rules Governing the Proceedings of the Directors of the Golden Gate Bridge and Highway District, [1930], box 66, Keesling Papers, M0100; *Engineering News-Record*, Jan. 5, 1933.

6. *San Francisco Chronicle*, April 11, 1929.

7. *Western Construction News* 6 (1931), 177–78.

8. "The Earth Movers I," *Fortune* 28 (Aug. 1943), 105.

9. In 1918 MacDonald helped design and build the first of very few American concrete ships, the SS *Faith*, as part of the wartime effort to conserve scarce steel. Roger Eberhardt, "Concrete Shipbuilding in San Diego, 1918–1920," *Journal of San Diego History* 41 (1995), http://www.sandiegohistory.org/journal/95spring/shipbuilding.htm (accessed July 2006); Joseph E. Stevens, *Hoover Dam: An American Adventure* (Norman, Okla., 1988), 40; Golden Gate Bridge and Highway District, *Report of the Chief Engineer with Architectural Studies* by Joseph B. Strauss, vol. 1 (San Francisco, 1930), 12.

10. Donald E. Wolf, *Big Dams and Other Dreams: The Six Companies Story* (Norman: University of Oklahoma Press, 1996), 4, 33; Christopher James Tassava, "Multiples of Six: The Six Companies and West Coast Industrialization, 1930–1945," *Enterprise & Society* 4 (March 2003), 1–27; *Western Construction News* 6 (1931) 173–79.

11. *San Francisco Chronicle*, Sept. 21, 1932; Francis V. Keesling, *Daily Calendar* (1929–1937), 42–43, 47, Keesling Papers, M1146.

12. *San Francisco News*, Sept. 21, 22, Dec. 29, 1932; *San Francisco Examiner*, Sept. 22, Dec. 15, 1932; *San Francisco Chronicle*, Sept. 21–23, 1932.

13. Keesling, *Daily Calendar*, 47–51; Stevens, *Hoover Dam*, 289, n. 19; *San Francisco Examiner*, Dec. 15, 1932.

14. *San Francisco Examiner*, Dec. 25, 27, 1932.

15. *San Francisco News*, Dec. 28, 1932.

16. *San Francisco Examiner*, Dec. 22, 1932; *San Francisco News*, Dec. 22, 1932; *San Francisco Examiner*, Dec. 23, 1932.

17. *San Francisco Chronicle*, Dec. 15, 1932.

18. After MacDonald's sudden death from a heart attack in 1935 at the age of 51, Los Angeles city attorneys filed a $2.6 million civil claim against his estate. *San Francisco News,* Dec. 28, 1932.

19. *Los Angeles Times,* May 17, June 9, 17, 1933, Nov. 30, 1935; Jared Orsi, *Hazardous Metropolis: Flooding and Urban Ecology in Los Angeles* (Berkeley: University of California Press, 2004), 70–72.

20. *San Francisco Examiner,* Dec. 19, 23, 29, 1932, Jan. 4, 1933; *San Francisco Chronicle,* Nov. 25, 1930, Dec. 29, 1932, Nov. 21, 1933.

21. Willis Leslie Winter, Jr., "The Metamorphosis of a Newspaper: The San Francisco Chronicle, 1935–1965" (Ph.D. diss., University of Illinois, 1968); Alicia C. Shepard, "Family Feud," *American Journalism Review* (1999) http://www.ajr.org/article.asp?id=541 (accessed Jan. 2006).

22. Gray Brechin, *Imperial San Francisco: Urban Power, Earthly Ruin* (Berkeley: University of California Press, 1999), 195–96, 258–60; Hoover-Young San Francisco Bay Bridge Commission, *Report* (1930).

23. *San Francisco Chronicle,* Sept. 29, 1933.

24. John van der Zee, *The Gate: The True Story of the Design and Construction of the Golden Gate Bridge* (New York: Simon and Schuster, 1986), 162–63.

25. *San Francisco Examiner,* Dec. 4, 1934; *San Francisco Chronicle,* Nov. 7, 1933, Dec. 4, 1934; *San Francisco News,* Nov. 7, 1933; Marin County Historical Society, *Marin People,* vol. 3 ([San Rafael], 1980), 317–18.

26. *San Francisco Examiner,* Dec. 29, 30, 1932.

27. "Applicants for appointment to the position of General Manager," [1933], box 63, Keesling Papers, M0100.

28. *San Francisco Examiner,* Dec. 30, 1932; *San Francisco Chronicle,* Dec. 31, 1932, Jan. 19, 1933.

29. James Reed to Frank P. Doyle, Jan. 16, 1933, box 1, James Reed Papers, JL012, Department of Special Collections, Stanford University Libraries, Stanford, Calif. (hereafter cited as Reed Papers); *San Francisco Chronicle,* Jan. 19, 1933.

30. Francis V. Keesling to A. R. O'Brien, Jan. 13, 1933, box 65, Keesling Papers, M0100.

31. *San Francisco Chronicle,* Dec. 29, 1932.

32. *San Francisco Chronicle,* Dec. 15, 1932.

33. Brechin, *Imperial San Francisco,* 195, 260.

34. Charles Derleth to James Reed, May 9, 1933, box 1, Reed Papers; James A. Keller to George H. Harlan, Sept. 11, 1933, box 62, Keesling Papers, M0100; Golden Gate Bridge and Highway District, *Facts Concerning Adoption of High Silica Cement (Pink Cement) by the Golden Gate Bridge & Highway District* (San Francisco, 1933), box 62, Keesling Papers, M0100; *San Francisco News,* Sept. 13, Oct. 2, 4, Nov. 29, 1933; *San Francisco Chronicle,* Sept. 14, 16, Nov. 5, 25, 30, 1933, Jan. 18, May 5, 1934; *San Francisco Examiner,* Sept. 18, Nov. 30, 1933, Jan. 17, 25, Feb. 1, May 5, 1934.

35. A.B. 2378, 50th reg. sess. (Ca. 1933); George J. Presley et al. to Members of the State Legislature, May 2, 1933, box 61 Keesling Papers, M0100; *San Francisco Examiner,* April 21, May 4, 1933; *San Francisco Chronicle,* April 26, May 2, 3, 1933.

36. Keesling, *Daily Calendar,* 19, 65.

37. *San Francisco Examiner,* Jan. 17, 1934.

38. *San Francisco Chronicle,* Jan. 18, 1934.

39. Russell G. Cone, "Battling Storm and Tide in Founding Golden Gate Pier,"

Engineering News-Record, Aug. 22, 1944, 245–51; *San Francisco Chronicle,* Dec. 14, 17, 1933.

40. Bailey Willis to A. D. Wilder, April 7, 1934, box 3, Derleth Papers.

41. Carl-Henry Geschwind, *California Earthquakes: Science, Risk & the Politics of Hazard Mitigation* (Baltimore: Johns Hopkins University Press, 2001), 67–96; S. S. Visher, "Bailey Willis, 1857–1949," *Annals of the Association of American Geographers* 39 (1949), 291–92; Donald C. Jackson and Norris Hundley, Jr., "Privilege and Responsibility: William Mulholland and the St. Francis Dam Disaster," *California History* (2004), 8–47, 72–78; Bailey Willis, "Report on the Geology of St. Francis Damsite, Los Angeles County, California," *Western Construction News* (June 25, 1928), 409–13; Charles F. Outland, *Man-Made Disaster: The Story of St. Francis Dam* (Glendale, Calif.: A. H. Clark, 1963).

42. Andrew Lawson to James Reed, April 10, 1934, box 3, Derleth Papers.

43. [James Reed] to Francis V. Keesling, May 21, 1934, box 61, Keesling Papers, M0100.

44. Golden Gate Bridge and Highway District, *South Pier—Investigation of Criticism of Foundation by Dr. Bailey Willis,* prepared by Harry Lutgens, Thomas Maxwell, and F. V. Keesling (San Francisco, 1934); [James Reed], Diary, Oct. 2, 1934, box 3, Derleth Papers.

45. F. L. Ransome to W. W. Felt, June 3, 1935, folder 22, Derleth Papers.

46. [Golden Gate Bridge and Highway District], "Statements made by Prof. Bailey Willis," Sept. 6, 1934, box 3, Derleth Papers; *San Francisco News,* Oct. 22, 31, 1934; *San Francisco Examiner,* Oct. 31, 1934; *San Francisco Chronicle,* Nov. 16, 1934; O. H. Ammann to James Reed, Sept. 12, 1934, box 3, Derleth Papers; James Reed to O. H. Ammann, Sept. 14, 1934, box 3, Derleth Papers; Leon S. Moisseiff to James Reed, Sept. 12, 1934, box 3, 1934; Charles Derleth to James Reed, Sept. 22, 1934, box 3, Derleth Papers; [Golden Gate Bridge and Highway District], "Memorandum on Criticisms of Golden Gate Bridge," [San Francisco, 1936], San Francisco Public Library, San Francisco History Center Vertical Files.

47. *San Francisco Chronicle,* May 9, 1935; *San Francisco News,* Sept. 12, 19, 25, Nov. 13, 1935, Jan. 14, Dec. 10, 1936; *San Francisco Examiner,* Sept. 26, 1935; *San Rafael Daily Independent,* Dec. 14, 1936.

48. On problems posed by approaches, see Golden Gate Bridge and Highway District, *Report on Conditions Affecting Traffic Which Will Use or May Be Encouraged to Use the Golden Gate Bridge,* by Sydney W. Taylor (San Francisco, 1935); *San Francisco Chronicle,* March 12, 13, 1936; *San Rafael Daily Independent,* Dec. 14, 1936.

49. *San Francisco News,* Jan. 14, 1937.

50. The Francis V. Keesling Papers are stored in the archives of Stanford University, Keesling's alma mater. They include a detailed daily calendar of Keesling's activities on behalf of the bridge district, and a wide variety of documents, newspaper clippings, and memorabilia from the construction period. Francis V. Keesling Papers, M0100 and M0258, Department of Special Collections, Stanford University Libraries, Stanford, Calif.

51. *San Rafael Daily Independent,* Dec. 4, 17, 1936; *San Francisco Chronicle,* Dec. 14, 1936; *San Francisco Examiner,* Dec. 14, 1936.

52. *San Francisco News,* Dec. 10, 1936.

53. *San Francisco Examiner,* Dec. 5, 1936.

54. *San Francisco Examiner,* Dec. 6, 1936; *San Francisco News,* Dec. 7, 1936; *San Francisco Chronicle,* Dec. 14, 15, 1936; *San Rafael Daily Independent,* Dec. 7, 1936.

55. *San Francisco Examiner,* Dec. 9, 1936.

56. For Keesling's detailed response to the charges leveled against him, see

Francis V. Keesling to Adolph Uhl, Dec. 11, 1936, box 67, Keesling Papers, M0100. Francis V. Keesling to Thomas M. Storke, Dec. 29, 1936, box 67, Keesling Papers, M0100; Francis V. Keesling to James Adam, May 3, 1937, box 66, Keesling Papers, M0100; *San Francisco Chronicle,* Dec. 24, 1936.

57. James Reed to William P. Filmer, July 26, 1937, box 1, Reed Papers. *San Rafael Daily Independent,* Nov. 7, 9, 10, Dec. 12, 14, 1936; *San Francisco Examiner,* July 28, 1937.

58. *San Francisco Examiner,* Feb. 19, 1927.

59. Peter Wiley and Robert Gottlieb, *Empires in the Sun: The Rise of the New American West* (New York: Putnam, 1982), 3–29; Stevens, *Hoover Dam,* 191–241; *San Francisco Examiner,* Feb. 21, 24, 1937; *San Francisco Chronicle,* March 15, 1937.

60. *San Francisco Chronicle,* March 16, July 20, 27, 1937, Feb. 17, 1938.

61. Rumors that Strauss's role was exaggerated persisted (see Brown, *Golden Gate,* 114–15), but his claim to be the designer of the Golden Gate Bridge was confronted directly for the first time in 1986 with the publication of *The Gate: The True Story of the Design and Construction of the Golden Gate Bridge,* by John van der Zee. Some of the details of van der Zee's evisceration of Strauss are incorrect. For example, he asserts that Strauss lied about his credentials and experience as an engineer, but records show that Strauss did indeed have a degree in civil engineering from the University of Cincinnati and did teach there briefly in the 1890s.

62. One bridge district supporter informed Keesling in 1931 that Strauss was under attack as a "promoter, a jew, and an alien." Miner Chipman to Francis V. Keesling, July 10, 1931, box 61, Keesling Papers M0100.

63. Frank J. Taylor, "A Matter of Size," *American Magazine* 119 (1935), 43–44, 86–89.

64. Moisseiff took the theoretical advances that allowed for the Golden Gate Bridge's elegant design too far with the Tacoma Narrows Bridge. See discussion in Chapter 3.

65. University of Cincinnati, *Catalogue of the Academic Department, 1891–92* (Cincinnati, 1892). Available through the University of Cincinnati Engineering Library website: http://engrlib.uc.edu/strauss (accessed July 2006).

66. A partial list of Strauss's patents is available through the University of Cincinnati Engineering Library website: http://www.engrlib.uc.edu/strauss/patents/patentslist.html (accessed July 2006); Strauss Engineering Corporation, *Bridges by Strauss* (Chicago, [1930]), http://www.engrlib.uc.edu/strauss/articles/articles.html (accessed July 2006).

67. Charles Ellis, quoted in van der Zee, *The Gate,* 103.

68. Charles Derleth, "Remarks by Prof. Derleth," transcript of speech before the Commonwealth Club, Oct. 16, 1930, box 7, Derleth Papers; van der Zee, *The Gate,* 125–26, 141–42.

69. See the following correspondence in box 2, Derleth Papers: Charles Ellis to Charles Derleth, Jr., March 23, 1932; Leon S. Moisseiff to Charles A. Ellis, Aug. 30, 1932; Charles Ellis to Charles Derleth, Jr., Sept. 7, 1932; C[harles] D[erleth] to L. S. Moisseiff, Sept. 12, 1932; Leon S. Moisseiff to Charles Derleth, Jr., Sept. 19, 1932; C. Derleth, Jr. to L. S. Moisseiff, Sept. 22, 1932; C. Derleth, Jr. to Chas. A. Ellis, Sept. 23, 1932; C. Derleth, Jr. to L. S. Moisseiff, Nov. 28, 1932; C. Derleth Jr. to L. S. Moisseiff, Dec. 5, 1932. See also John van der Zee and Russ Cone, "The Case of the Missing Engineer," *San Francisco Examiner Image,* May 31, 1992.

70. Van der Zee, *The Gate,* 115–17.

71. Cone, "Battling Storm and Tide"; Russell G. Cone, "Permanent Painting

Scaffolds for the Golden Gate Bridge," *Engineering News Record*, April 25, 1940, 52–53; *New York Times*, Jan. 22, 1961; *New York Times*, Jan. 22, 1961; Elizabeth Noble Shore, "Russell Glenn Cone," *American National Biography Online* (2000), http://www.anb.org/articles/13/13-00329.html (accessed Jan. 2006).

72. Keesling, *Daily Calendar*, 58.

73. Van der Zee, *The Gate*, 153–56, 179–80.

74. *San Rafael Daily Independent*, Dec. 15, 1934, Nov. 7, 17, 1936; *San Francisco News*, Jan. 14, 1937.

75. Van der Zee, *The Gate*, 226–28.

76. *San Francisco Chronicle*, Sept. 30, 1937; *San Francisco Examiner*, Oct. 22, 1937.

77. *San Francisco News*, May 31, 1937.

78. [*San Francisco News*], Sept. 14, 1938, San Francisco Public Library, San Francisco History Center Vertical Files.

79. *San Francisco Chronicle*, July 31, 1937.

80. O'Brien, quoted in Brown, *Golden Gate*, 143.

81. The directors rejected a resolution to hire Cone on September 16, 1937 with a vote of seven to five. It took several attempts to pass a resolution to hire Harrelson. Golden Gate Bridge and Highway District, Resolution No. 1427, Sept. 16, 1937; *San Francisco Chronicle*, Aug. 6, 19, Sept. 17, 30, 1937; *San Francisco News*, Sept. 17, 1937; Francis V. Keesling to A. R. O'Brien, Aug. 16, 1937, box 65, Keesling Papers, M0100.

82. R. G. Cone to Charles Derleth, July 15, 1941, box 2, Derleth Papers.

83. For example, the Marin County grand jury denounced the expensive statue of Strauss and accused Harrelson and the bridge directors of a "lack of concern for the best interests of the district and the taxpayers who compose it," and found evidence that already toll collectors were "chiseling," taking advantage of inadequate oversight. *San Rafael Daily Independent*, July 18, 1940, Oct. 24, 1940; *San Francisco Examiner*, Oct. 25, 1940.

84. Obviously, Finn's progressive Republican allies did not fit the dichotomy of corrupt political machines and virtuous, middle-class progressive reformers that was once a trope of urban political history. James J. Connolly, Kenneth Finegold, and others have pointed out that in reality middle-class, native whites never had a monopoly on the progressive rhetoric of reform; conversely, corruption affected both immigrant- and labor-backed politicians and patrician conservative businessmen. James J. Connolly, *The Triumph of Ethnic Progressivism: Urban Political Culture in Boston, 1900–1925* (Cambridge, Mass.: Harvard University Press, 1998); Kenneth Finegold, *Experts and Politicians: Reform Challenges to Machine Politics in New York, Cleveland, and Chicago* (Princeton, N.J.: Princeton University Press, 1995).

85. *San Rafael Daily Independent*, June 19, July 9, 1940; *Sausalito News*, July 11, 1940; *San Anselmo Herald*, July 4, 1940.

Chapter 3. The District and Its Enemies

1. In 1938, Redwood Empire Association leaders successfully fought off an attempt by the California Chamber of Commerce to usurp their position of influence in northern California, securing their organization's premier status. Gail D. Apperson to Lantz B. Smith, Dec. 29, 1936, carton 137, REA Records; [Redwood Empire Association], "Analysis of State Chamber Interference with and Duplication of Redwood Empire Association Work," ([1936]), carton 136, REA Records.

2. For discussion of New Deal work relief, including Works Progress Administration activities, see Donald S. Howard, *The WPA and Federal Relief Policy* (New York: Russell Sage Foundation, 1943); Nancy Ellen Rose, *Put to Work: Relief Programs in the Great Depression* (New York: Monthly Review Press, 1993); Edwin Amenta, *Bold Relief: Institutional Politics and the Origins of Modern American Social Policy* (Princeton, N.J.: Princeton University Press, 2000); Singleton, *The American Dole.*

3. *San Rafael Daily Independent,* March 12, 1937, May 25, 1937. Part of the expense could be attributed to the geology of the site, as state engineers observed: "This particular mountain area lacks the hard rock formation common to most mountain country of comparable topography, and the disturbance of its natural, somewhat doubtful state of equilibrium by the heavy cuts and deep fills required produced fully anticipated but unpredictable problems from slides. This situation, due to the close proximity of the bay, was aggravated by nature's deposit of soft clay over the underlying rocky formation to depths as much as forty feet." California Department of Public Works, *Chronological Statement of Work Done Upon Waldo Road in Marin County* (Sacramento, 1935), Golden Gate Bridge District File, California Director of Public Works Files—Director's Office, California State Archives, Office of the Secretary of State, Sacramento (hereafter referred to as California DPW Files).

4. Earl Lee Kelly, *Press Release* [Nov. 1935], California DPW Files.

5. [Thomas H.] MacDonald to [L. I.] Hewes, telegram, Sept. 24, 1935; James Reed to Earl Lee Kelly, telegram, Nov. 8, 1935; C. C. Carleton to C. H. Purcell, Sept. 26, 1935; H. E. Cloke to Jno. H. Skeggs, Sept. 5, 1935; Jno. H. Skeggs to C. H. Purcell, Sept. 6, 1935, all in Golden Gate Bridge District File, California DPW Files. On MacDonald's career and ideology, see Bruce E. Seely, *Building the American Highway System: Engineers as Policy Makers* (Philadelphia: Temple University Press, 1987).

6. *San Rafael Daily Independent,* Nov. 18, 1935; *San Francisco Examiner,* Nov. 16, 1935; *San Francisco Chronicle,* Nov. 15, 1935.

7. *San Francisco Examiner,* Dec. 19, 1935.

8. Earl Lee Kelly to Angelo J. Rossi, Nov. 27, 1935, Golden Gate Bridge District File, Public Works Director Files; G. T. McCoy to Earl Lee Kelly, Oct. 28, 1935, box 62, Keesling Papers, M0100.

9. Earl Lee Kelly to Directors, Golden Gate Bridge and Highway District, Nov. 20, 1935, box 61, Keesling Papers M0100.

10. *San Francisco News,* Nov. 8, 14, 15, 21, 1935; *San Rafael Daily Independent,* Nov. 8, 21, 1935; *San Francisco Chronicle,* Oct. 24, Nov. 9, 13, 14, 1935.

11. Earl Lee Kelly, Introduction to Traffic Statement, Nov. 8, 1935, Golden Gate Bridge District File, California DPW Files.

12. *San Francisco News,* Nov. 25, 1935; *San Francisco Examiner,* Dec. 4, 1935.

13. *San Francisco News,* Nov. 19, 20, 1935.

14. *San Francisco Chronicle,* Dec. 12, 1935; Mort J. Donoghue, "Earl Lee Kelly Announces Four Lane Bridge Approach," press release, Dec. 11, 1935, Golden Gate Bridge District File, California DPW Files; Richard Thomas Loomis, "The History of the Building of the Golden Gate Bridge" (Ph.D. diss., Stanford University, 1958), 148–51.

15. Clyde Edmondson, *Building the Redwood Empire . . . An Epoch of the Adventurous* West ([San Francisco, 1937]), carton 49, REA Records; Redwood Empire Association, *Supplemental Analysis—Based on Historical Fact* ([San Francisco, 1959]), carton 49, REA Records.

16. Golden Gate Bridge and Highway District, *Annual Appropriations,* [1968], box 126, IM Facility; Clyde Edmondson, memorandum, Jan. 12, 1938, box 91, IM Facility; Clyde Edmondson to Officers and Directors Golden Gate Bridge and Highway District, Dec. 21, 1938, box 91, IM Facility; Clyde Edmondson to William H. Harrelson, April 6, 1938, box 91, IM Facility; Clyde Edmondson to William Harrelson, Aug. 26, 1938, box 91, IM Facility; J. P. Kelly to William H. Harrelson, June 28, 1938, box 91, IM Facility; George P. Anderson and Clyde Edmondson to Francis V. Keesling, Dec. 2, 1936, box 61, Keesling Papers, M0100; Redwood Empire Association, press release, May 17, 1937, carton 136, REA Records.

17. *Official Souvenir Program: Golden Gate Bridge Fiesta* (San Francisco, 1937); *San Rafael Daily Independent,* Dec. 15, 1936; Keesling, *Daily Calendar,* 146.

18. While there were early plans for a scale model of the Golden Gate Bridge to be part of the Redwood Empire building at the Golden Gate International Exposition, they were never realized. Instead, the Redwood Empire was represented by huge faux stump faced with redwood bark, its interior decorated with a hunting cabin theme. However, the gate at the main entry to the fair was built to resemble the Golden Gate Bridge, as was the key that opened it. Richard Reinhardt, *Treasure Island: San Francisco's Exposition Years* (San Francisco, 1973), 67, 122; Clyde Edmondson to William H. Harrelson, April 6, 1938 and Nov. 21, 1938, box 91, IM Facility.

19. *San Francisco Examiner,* April 9, 1938, Jan. 27, 1938; *San Francisco Chronicle,* Jan. 29, 1938.

20. *San Francisco Examiner,* Sept. 29, 1938; *San Francisco Today,* Jan. 30, 1937; Frederick H. Meyer to the Board of Directors, San Francisco Chamber of Commerce, Jan. 19, 1939, box 41, Keesling Papers, M0100.

21. San Francisco Chamber of Commerce Special Committee on the Golden Gate Bridge and Highway District to Board of Directors, San Francisco Chamber of Commerce, Sept. 21, 1938, box 22, IM Facility.

22. *San Francisco Chronicle,* Sept. 27, 1938.

23. Special Committee on the Golden Gate Bridge and Highway District to Board of Directors, San Francisco Chamber of Commerce, Sept. 21, 1938, box 22, IM Facility.

24. A. R. O'Brien, Jr., A. M. Brown, and R. H. Trumbull to Board of Directors Golden Gate Bridge and Highway District, Oct. 13, 1938, box 80, DS Vault; Charles Page to President and Directors of the Golden Gate Bridge and Highway District, Jan. 30, 1939, box 22, IM Facility.

25. *San Francisco Chronicle,* Oct. 14, 1938.

26. A. R. O'Brien, A. M. Brown, and R. H. Trumbull to Board of Directors Golden Gate Bridge and Highway District, Oct. 13, 1938, box 80, DS Vault.

27. Redwood Highway Association, *Your Harvest from More Tourists Vacationists Settlers in the Redwood Highway Empire* [1925]; Leland W. Cutler to All Members of the San Francisco Chamber of Commerce, [1930], folder 50, Galloway Papers; [James Reed], Diary, Oct. 2, 1934, folder 22, Derleth Papers.

28. *San Francisco Today,* Oct. 21, 1938.

29. There was a brief resumption of limited service by Northwestern Pacific Company in 1941. Sydney W. Taylor to Board of Directors Golden Gate Bridge and Highway District, June 2, 1943, box 204, DS Vault.

30. In 1940 bridge district officials erected a sign directing motorists to the Golden Gate Bridge right next to a state sign pointing to the Carquinez Bridge,

hoping to divert San Francisco bound traffic. *San Rafael Daily Independent,* Oct. 9, 1940.

31. San Francisco Bureau of Governmental Research, "News Bulletin: A Continued Golden Gate Bridge Deficit in 1939–1940," Oct. 3, 1939; San Francisco Bureau of Governmental Research, "News Bulletin: Golden Gate Bridge Auto Traffic and Revenue," June 18, 1940; W. W. Monohan to W. H. Harrelson, Oct. 25, 1939, box 22, IM Facility.

32. *San Francisco Examiner,* Sept. 28, 1938.

33. For information on Bay Bridge tolls, see Division of Highways, California Department of Public Works, *Report on Examination of Statements Relating to Traffic, Revenues, and Revenue Funds, San Francisco-Oakland Bay Bridge* (Sacramento, 1937–1964); California Legislative Auditor, *Financial History of the San Francisco-Oakland Bay Bridge* (Sacramento, 1953). For the early Golden Gate Bridge toll structure, see Golden Gate Bridge and Highway District, *Preliminary Report on Long Range Planning,* vol. 1, *Long Range Planning Survey,* prepared by Arthur C. Jenkins (San Francisco, 1958), Table G-II.

34. For detailed objections to the comparison see A. R. O'Brien, R. A. Thompson, and James E. Rickets to Honorable Board of Directors, Golden Gate Bridge and Highway District, Jan. 8, 1941, Golden Gate Bridge and Highway District File, Randolph Collier Papers, LP 229 California State Archives, Sacramento Calif. (hereafter referred to as Collier Papers).

35. San Francisco Bureau of Governmental Research, "News Bulletin: A Continued Golden Gate Bridge Deficit in 1939–1940," Oct. 3, 1939.

36. *San Francisco Chronicle,* June 15, 1939.

37. *San Francisco Examiner,* Dec. 9, 11, 12, 1940.

38. *San Francisco Examiner,* Dec. 11, 19, 1940; *San Rafael Daily Independent,* Dec. 18, 1940.

39. *San Rafael Daily Independent,* Jan. 8, 1941, Jan. 9, 1941.

40. *San Rafael Daily Independent,* Jan. 29, 1941; *San Francisco Chronicle,* Jan. 30, 1941.

41. *Press Democrat,* Jan. 16, 1941.

42. *San Francisco Examiner,* Jan. 16, 1941.

43. *San Rafael Daily Independent,* June 18, 1941.

44. Leland M. Kaiser, *Report on the Golden Gate Bridge & Highway District* (San Francisco, [1943]), box 205, DS Vault.

45. Special Senate Interim Committee on the Administrative Affairs, Financial Status and Modus Operandi of the Golden Gate Bridge and Highway District, *Excerpts of Testimony* (Sacramento, Dec. 15–17, 1942), 195–7, 16, box 70, Keesling Papers, M0100; *San Rafael Daily Independent,* June 19, 1941.

46. John L. McNab, testimony, Special Senate Interim Committee, *[Hearing] in the Matter of Administrative Affairs, Financial Status and Modus Operandi of the Golden Gate Bridge and Highway District* (Sacramento, March 8, 1943), 76–77, box 204, IM Facility.

47. San Francisco Bureau of Governmental Research, "News Bulletin: Golden Gate Bond Refinancing Proposed," July 1, 1941.

48. Roy S. West to Board of Directors, Golden Gate Bridge and Highway District, June 20, 1941, box 204, DS Vault.

49. *San Francisco Examiner,* Feb. 14, 1942.

50. *San Francisco News,* Dec. 9, 1940, Dec. 10, 1940, Dec. 11, 1940; *San Francisco Examiner,* Dec. 10, 1940; A.B. 531, 54th reg. sess. (Ca. 1941); S.B. 1137, 54th ex. sess. (Ca. 1942); *San Rafael Daily Independent,* May 21, 24, 27, Dec. 14, 1940, Jan.

4, 7, 9, 13, 1941; *Mill Valley Record,* May 28, 1940; *Marin Journal,* June 6, 1940; *San Francisco Chronicle,* Jan. 7, 14, 1941.

51. *San Francisco Examiner,* Jan. 15, 1941; *People ex rel. Bagshaw v. Thompson,* 55 Cal. 2d 147, Oct. 27, 1942.

52. *San Francisco Chronicle,* Jan. 11, 1938; *San Rafael Daily Independent Journal,* Feb. 28, 1941; *San Francisco Examiner,* May 23, 1942.

53. Senate Interim Committee on the Golden Gate Bridge and Highway District, *Report* (Sacramento, 1943), 5.

54. Special Senate Interim Committee on the Administrative Affairs, Financial Status and Modus Operandi of the Golden Gate Bridge and Highway District, *Excerpts of Testimony* (Dec. 15–17, 1942), 4, box 70, Keesling Papers, M0100.

55. W. D. Hadeler, statement, March 4, 1943, box 204, IM Facility; Special Senate Interim Committee, *[Hearing] In the Matter of Administrative Affairs, Financial Status and Modus Operandi of the Golden Gate Bridge and Highway District* (March 8, 1943), 45.

56. *San Francisco Examiner,* Jan. 22, 1943.

57. *San Francisco Examiner,* May 27, 1943.

58. *San Francisco Examiner,* Jan. 22, 1943.

59. Senate Interim Committee on the Golden Gate Bridge and Highway District, *Report* (Sacramento, 1943); *Statutes of California* (1943) 45th reg. sess., ch. 286, 1243–60; ch. 509, 2050–51; ch. 543, 2089–90.

60. Henry Petroski, *Engineers of Dreams: Great Bridge Builders and the Spanning of America* (New York: Vintage Books, 1995), 270–71; Richard Scott, *In the Wake of Tacoma: Suspension Bridges and the Quest for Aerodynamic Stability* (Reston, Va.: ACSE Press, 2001), 31–33.

61. Washington State Department of Transportation. "Tacoma Narrows Bridge: Extreme History," http://www.wsdot.wa.gov/TNBhistory/ (accessed July 17, 2006); Scott, *Wake of Tacoma,* 40.

62. Scott, *Wake of Tacoma,* 32, 42.

63. Ibid., 49–53.

64. Private insurers and federal officials also commissioned independent panels of engineers to investigate the disaster. United States Public Roads Administration, Advisory Board on the Investigation of Suspension Bridges, *The Failure of the Tacoma Narrows Bridge: A Reprint of Original Reports* (College Station, Tex., 1944).

65. *San Francisco Examiner,* Feb. 28, 1941; *Engineering News-Record,* March 6, 1941.

66. *San Rafael Daily Independent,* March 5, 1941, March 6, 1941; *San Francisco News,* March 6, 1941.

67. *San Francisco Chronicle,* March 6, 1941.

68. *San Francisco Chronicle,* March 7, 1941.

69. R. G. Cone to Charles Derleth, July 15, 1941, folder 11, Derleth Papers; John van der Zee, *The Gate: The True Story of the Design and Construction of the Golden Gate Bridge* (New York: Simon and Schuster, 1986), 320–21.

70. [United States] Federal Works Agency, *The Failure of the Tacoma Narrows Bridge,* prepared by Othman H. Ammann, Theodore von Kármán, and Glen B. Woodruff (Washington, D.C., 1941), appendix 9; Scott, *Wake of Tacoma.*

71. *Los Angeles Times,* May 15, 1941.

72. A. R. O'Brien, "Mismanagement of the Golden Gate Bridge," June 11, 1941, box 70, Keesling Papers, M0100.

73. *San Rafael Daily Independent,* June 5, 9, 1941; *San Francisco Examiner,* June 6,

1941; Guggenheim Aeronautic Laboratory, Stanford University, *Report on Wind Tunnel Tests of Golden Gate Bridge Model,* prepared by Elliott G. Reid (Palo Alto, 1941), folder 10, Derleth Papers; C. Derleth to O. H. Ammann, July 17, 1941, folder 10, Derleth Papers; Leon S. Moisseiff to Hugo D. Newhouse, June 4, 1941, folder 11, Derleth Papers; *Engineering New-Record,* June 12, 1941.

74. O. H. Ammann to Hugo D. Newhouse, July 14, 1941, folder 11, Derleth Papers; Ammann to Arthur R. O'Brien, June 20, 1941, folder 11, Derleth Papers.

75. *San Francisco Today,* July 9, 1941.

76. *San Francisco Chronicle,* July 19, 1941; Hugo D. Newhouse to O. H. Ammann, July 12, 1941, folder 50–7, Derleth Papers; Golden Gate Bridge and Highway District, *Annual Report* (San Francisco, 1941–1947).

77. *Western Construction News,* April 1942; George S. Vincent, "Paper 1817: Golden Gate Bridge Vibration Studies," *Journal of the Structural Division, Proceedings of the American Society of Civil Engineers* (1958); Golden Gate Bridge and Highway District, *The Golden Gate Bridge: Report of the General Manager, A Symposium* (San Francisco, 1958), 34–52; Golden Gate Bridge and Highway District, *Report on Alterations of Golden Gate Bridge,* prepared by Clifford E. Paine, Othmar H. Ammann, and Charles E. Andrew (San Francisco, 1953).

78. The next decline in traffic occurred in 1973–74, when traffic volume dropped from 43.6 million vehicles to 32.8 million. Traffic figures from Golden Gate Bridge and Highway District, *Annual Report* (San Francisco, 1937–74).

79. Marinship, on the shores of Richardson Bay in southern Marin County, began production in June 1942. Initially, most of its 17,500 workers lived in San Francisco, but by the end of 1943 hastily constructed housing in Marin City reduced the number of commuters using the bridge. The committee questioned the bridge district auditor about shipyard traffic, pointing out that it was most likely temporary. Special Senate Interim Committee, *[Hearing] in the Matter of Administrative Affairs, Financial Status and Modus Operandi of the Golden Gate Bridge and Highway District* (Sacramento, March 8, 1943), 52–54; Charles Wollenberg, *Marinship at War: Shipbuilding and Social Change in Wartime Sausalito* (Berkeley, 1990), 4, 86.

80. *San Francisco Examiner,* June 13, 1950.

81. *San Rafael Daily Independent Journal,* June 20, 1950.

82. *San Francisco Examiner,* June 13, 1950.

83. *San Rafael Daily Independent Journal,* Nov. 20, 1950.

84. *San Rafael Daily Independent Journal,* June 20, Nov. 20, 21, 25, 1950; *Mill Valley Record,* Nov. 16, 23, 30, 1950.

85. Marin County Board of Supervisors, *In the Matter Of: Petition Requesting Adoption of Resolution for State Acquisition of Golden Gate Bridge and Highway District* (San Rafael, Calif., 1952), 34, box 204, DS Vault.

86. Senate Interim Committee on Problems Concerning the Inclusion of the Golden Gate Bridge into the State Highway System, *Public Hearings* (Sacramento, Feb. 26 and 27, 1951), 116.

87. Chris McCarthy, interview with author, tape recording, Petaluma, Calif., July 31, 2002; *San Rafael Daily Independent Journal,* Nov. 25, 1950.

88. *San Rafael Daily Independent Journal,* Nov. 24, 25, 1950; *San Francisco Chronicle,* Nov. 15, 1941.

89. Evelyn Morris Radford, *The Bridge and the Building: The Art of Government and the Government of Art,* rev. ed. (New York: Carleton Press, 1974).

90. Richard Walker, *The Country in the City: Urban Environmentalism in the San Francisco Bay Area* (Seattle: University of Washington Press, 2007).

91. In later campaigns, McCarthy emphasized his Irish-Catholic heritage by using a shamrock logo in his ads, e.g., *Pacific Sun*, Sept. 21, 1966.

92. The *Independent Journal* suggested that Robert McCarthy would soon be known as "the father of our legislature." *San Rafael Daily Independent Journal*, Nov. 25, 1950.

93. *Sausalito News*, Feb. 22, 1951; *San Rafael Daily Independent Journal*, Oct. 11, Nov. 2, 1950.

94. Upon hearing about the new committee, McCollister reportedly "dashed in with a series of bills," apparently undeterred in reintroducing the same legislation for a state takeover that failed in 1947 and 1949. *San Francisco Chronicle*, Feb. 5, 1951; Senate Interim Committee on Problems Concerning the Inclusion of the Golden Gate Bridge into the State Highway System, *Public Hearings* (Sacramento, Feb. 26, 27, 1951), 115.

95. State Senate Interim Committee on Problems Concerning the Inclusion of the Golden Gate Bridge into the State Highway System, *Partial Report* (Sacramento, 1951), 7.

96. Senate Interim Committee on Problems Concerning the Inclusion of the Golden Gate Bridge into the State Highway System, *Public Hearings* (Sacramento, Feb. 26, 27, 1951), 88–89.

97. California Legislative Auditor, *Materials Relating to the Operation and Financing of the Golden Gate Bridge*, prepared for the Senate Interim Committee on Golden Gate Bridge Problems (Sacramento, 1952).

98. *San Rafael Daily Independent Journal*, March 29, June 14, 19, July 24, 28, 1952; *San Francisco Chronicle*, June 14, 1952.

99. *Sausalito News*, Sept. 18, 1952.

100. Marin County Board of Supervisors, *In the Matter Of: Petition Requesting Adoption of Resolution for State Acquisition of Golden Gate Bridge and Highway District* (San Rafael, Calif., 1952), 10, box 204, DS Vault.

101. Peter A. Gasser to Honorable Board of Supervisors County of Napa, Oct. 27, 1952, box 204, DS Vault.

102. *Baywood Press*, Sept. 18, 1952.

103. *San Rafael Daily Independent Journal*, Jan. 29, 1953.

104. Marin County Board of Supervisors, *In the Matter Of: Petition Requesting Adoption of Resolution for State Acquisition of Golden Gate Bridge and Highway District* (San Rafael, Calif., 1952), 42, box 204, DS Vault.

105. *Sausalito News*, Oct. 25, 1951.

106. McCarthy protested to Marin supervisors, and they confronted the bridge directors with a demand that their Sacramento agent "cease and desist" from obstructing the construction of the long-sought span. The directors protested that Adam was not acting upon their direction, but the move was not uncharacteristic for Adam, who was given free rein in Sacramento and an ample expense account. *San Rafael Daily Independent Journal*, Feb. 26, 1952.

107. Statement of James E. Rickets before the Senate Interim Committee on Golden Gate Bridge Operations, San Francisco, Nov. 18, 1952, box 204, DS Vault.

108. *San Rafael Daily Independent Journal*, Nov. 19, 1952.

109. B. J. Talvacchia to Howard C. Wood, Nov. 20, 1952, Golden Gate Bridge District File, California DPW Files.

110. *San Rafael Daily Independent Journal*, Nov. 19, 1952.

111. *San Rafael Daily Independent Journal*, Nov. 11, 1952.

112. *Sausalito News*, Dec. 15, 1952; *San Francisco Examiner*, Nov. 21, 1952.

113. S.B. 558, 1941 leg., ex. sess., (Ca. 1942).

114. *San Francisco Chronicle,* March 19, April 18, 1953.

115. The board resolved to "withhold further reductions until such a time as the total of outstanding insurance covering the destruction or damage of the bridge, plus reserves on hand equals the outstanding bonded indebtedness of the Bridge District." *San Francisco Chronicle,* March 21, May 9, 1953; *San Francisco Examiner,* May 14, 1953.

116. *San Francisco Chronicle,* May 23, 29, June 7, July 10, 1953.

117. *San Rafael Daily Independent Journal,* March 28, 1953; *San Francisco Examiner,* Jan. 18, 1953.

118. *San Francisco Chronicle,* Dec. 31, 1954, April 26, 1955; *San Rafael Daily Independent Journal,* April 26, 30, June 11, 1955.

119. *San Rafael Daily Independent Journal,* March 14, 1953; *San Francisco Chronicle,* March 16, 1953; *San Francisco Chronicle,* April 11, 1953.

120. *San Rafael Daily Independent Journal,* July 10, 1953.

121. *San Rafael Daily Independent Journal,* July 21, 23, 1954, May 10, Aug. 27, Sept. 2, Oct. 15, 1955, Nov. 14, 1960; *San Francisco Chronicle,* May 7, 1953, July 25, 1954, Aug. 2, 1954.

122. James Adam to William J. Varley, April 24, 1950, box 204, DS Vault.

123. Radio broadcast, "California Commentaries" ([San Francisco], KNBC, Sept. 19, 1952), box 204, DS Vault.

124. Golden Gate Bridge and Highway District, *The Golden Gate Bridge,* prepared by Charles W. Reinking (San Francisco, 1950).

Chapter 4. The Defeat of the Golden Gate Authority

An earlier version of this chapter appeared in the *Journal of Urban History* 34 (2008), 287–308.

1. In addition to the Golden Gate Bridge and Highway District, the Bay Area had the East Bay Municipal Utility District (1934), the San Francisco Bay Regional Water Pollution Control Board (1949), the Bay Area Air Pollution Control District (1955), the Alameda–Contra Costa Transit District (1956), and the Bay Area Rapid Transit District (1957). For an overview of their creation, see Mel Scott, *The San Francisco Bay Area: Metropolis in Perspective,* 2nd ed. (Berkeley: University of California Press, 1985).

2. Senate Interim Committee on Bay Area Problems, *Final Report Recommending the Creation of a Golden Gate Authority in the San Francisco Bay Area* (Sacramento, 1959); John F. McCarthy to Edgar F. Kaiser, July 15, 1958, carton 48, Edgar F. Kaiser Papers, The Bancroft Library, University of California, Berkeley (hereafter cited as E. F. Kaiser Papers).

3. Senate Fact-Finding Committee on San Francisco Bay Ports, *Ports of the San Francisco Bay Area: Their Commerce, Facilities, Problems and Progress; Final Report* (Sacramento, 1951); Walter P. Hollmann, "The Metropolitan Picture in California to 1980," paper presented at the Conference of the Governor's Metropolitan Commission, [Sacramento], 1959; Terry Hoy et al., *The Use of the Port Authority in the United States: With Special Reference to the San Francisco Bay Area* (Berkeley: Bureau of Public Administration, 1959); California Interim Committee on Transportation and Commerce, *Transcript of Proceedings: Hearing on Mass Transportation Problems of the San Francisco Bay Area* ([Sacramento], 1959); Richard M. Zettel, *Urban Transportation in the San Francisco Bay Area* (Berkeley: Institute of Govern-

mental Studies, University of California, 1963); Bay Area Transportation Study Commission, *Bay Area Transportation Report* (Berkeley, 1969); Seymour Mark Adler, "The Political Economy of Transit in the San Francisco Bay Area, 1945–1957," Ph.D. diss., University of California, Berkeley, 1980.

4. Planning Subcommittee on Bay Area Regional Problems of the Assembly Committee on Conservation, and Public Works, *First Progress Report* (Sacramento, 1952), 102–3.

5. John C. Bollens, *Problems of Government in the San Francisco Bay Area* (Berkeley: University of California Bureau of Public Administration, 1948), 120–21; Hoy et al., *The Use of the Port Authority in the United States*, 3.

6. The Reber Plan, decisively rejected by a joint Army-Navy board in 1946, inspired several more proposals for Bay infills and barriers. For an interesting overview of these proposals, see California Department of Transportation, Division of Bay Toll Crossings, *A Progress Report to Department of Public Works on a San Francisco-Marin Crossing of San Francisco Bay* (Sacramento, 1962). Also see David R. Long, "Mistaken Identity: Putting the John Reber Plan for the San Francisco Bay Area into Historical Context," in *American Cities and Towns: Historical Perspectives*, ed. Joseph F. Rishel (Pittsburgh: Duquesne University Press, 1992).

7. Bollens, *The Problems of Government*, 112–13; T. J. Kent, Jr., "Regional Planning and Metropolitan Government Proposals for the San Francisco Bay Area," paper presented at the National Convention of the American Institute of Planners, Seattle, July 1959.

8. Keesling was the first chairman of the BAC executive committee. In many urban areas, new business-oriented civic associations sponsored efforts to coordinate metropolitan area policy and to plan on a large scale in the post–World War II period, including the Allegheny Conference on Community Development in Pittsburgh, Civic Progress in St. Louis, the Citizens' League in Minneapolis-St. Paul, and the Greater Boston Economic Study Committee. The business-initiated Regional Plan Association of New York, created in 1923 and funded by the Russell Sage Foundation, was an important model for these and other civic groups advocating regional planning and government. Thomas Adams developed the controversial *Regional Plan of New York and Its Environs* on behalf of this association, which became a defining document for "metropolitan regionalism" in the post–World War II era. See Chapter 7, n. 1. Sy Adler, "Infrastructure Politics, The Dynamics of Crossing San Francisco Bay," *The Public Historian* 10 (1988), 19–41; Mel Scott, *American City Planning Since 1890* (Berkeley: University of California Press, 1979), 430–52; Richard A. Walker and Michael K. Heiman, "Quiet Revolution for Whom?" *Annals of the Association of American Geographers* 71 (1981), 67–83; Jon C. Teaford, *The Rough Road to Renaissance: Urban Revitalization in America, 1940–1985* (Baltimore, Md.: Johns Hopkins University Press, 1990), 44–81; Roy Lubove, *Twentieth Century Pittsburgh: Government, Business and Environmental Change* (Pittsburgh: University of Pittsburgh Press, 1995), 106–41; Joseph Heathcott and Máire Agnes Murphy, "Corridors of Flight, Zones of Renewal: Industry, Planning, and Policy in the Making of Metropolitan St. Louis, 1940–1980," *Journal of Urban History* 31 (2005), 151–89; Peter Hall, *Cities of Tomorrow*, 3rd ed. (Malden, Mass.: Blackwell Publications, 2002), 164–69; G. Ross Stephens and Nelson Wikstrom, *Metropolitan Government and Governance: Theoretical Perspectives, Empirical Analysis, and the Future* (New York: Oxford University Press, 2000), 29–50.

9. *Trends* 16 (March 1961), carton 47, E. F. Kaiser Papers; William Issel, "The New Deal and the Wartime Origins of San Francisco's Political Culture: The

Case of Growth Politics and Policy," in *The Way We Really Were: The Golden State in the Second Great War*, ed. Roger Lotchin (Urbana: University of Illinois Press, 2000), 68–92.

10. Frank E. March, quoted in Bollens, *The Problems of Government*, 115.

11. Richard Allen Sundeen, "The Bay Area Council, Analysis of a Non-Governmental Metropolitan Organization," M.A. thesis, Stanford University, 1963.

12. San Francisco Bay Area Council, *Regional Planning Needs of the San Francisco Bay Area*, prepared by V. B. Stanbery (San Francisco, 1954).

13. *Oakland Tribune*, April 1, 1969; *San Francisco Examiner*, Oct. 25, 1964; *Fortune Magazine*, July 1951; *Business Week*, June 12, 1954; Cartons 3 and 4, E. F. Kaiser Papers. On Henry J. Kaiser's career and legacy, see Mark S. Foster, *Henry J. Kaiser: Builder in the Modern American West* (Austin: University of Texas Press, 1989); Albert Heiner, *Henry J. Kaiser: Western Colossus* (San Francisco: Halo Books, 1991); Stephen B. Adams, *Mr. Kaiser Goes to Washington: The Rise of a Government Entrepreneur* (Chapel Hill: University of North Carolina Press, 1997).

14. Jackson K. Putnam, "The Progressive Legacy in California: Fifty Years of Politics," in *California Progressivism Revisited*, ed. William Deverell and Tom Sitton (Berkeley: University of California Press, 1994); William Issel, "Business Power and Political Culture in San Francisco, 1900–1940," *Journal of Urban History* 16 (1989), 52–77.

15. In three decisions between 1962 and 1964, the U.S. Supreme Court ruled that representation in state legislatures had to be based on population. County-based representation in the California senate made it the most egregiously mal-apportioned body in the United States, with vastly greater power for northern than southern California, particularly as population growth in and around Los Angeles had far outpaced that of any other area for decades. For various reasons, several voter initiatives to balance representation failed, and as in many other states, reapportionment had to be forced with lawsuits and court intervention. Don Allen, *Legislative Sourcebook: California Legislature and Reapportionment, 1849–1965* (Sacramento, [1965]), 5–68; Leroy C. Hardy and Charles P. Sohner, "Constitutional Challenge and Political Response: California Reapportionment, 1965," *The Western Political Quarterly* 23 (1970), 733–51; Bruce W. Robeck, "Legislative Partisanship, Constituency and Malapportionment: The Case of California," *American Political Science Review* 66 (1972), 1246–55; John R. Owens, Edmond Constantini, and Louis F. Weschler, *California Politics and Parties* ([New York]: Macmillan, 1970), 284–91.

16. Consulting Engineers Coverdale & Colpitts to Edgar F. Kaiser, July 16, 1958; John F. McCarthy to Edgar F. Kaiser, July 15, 1958, both in carton 48, E. F. Kaiser Papers.

17. San Francisco Bay Area Council, *Report on a Proposed Public Authority for the Bay Area*, prepared by Coverdale & Colpitts (San Francisco, 1958), 1–2, 132.

18. Ibid., 135.

19. Edgar F. Kaiser to Robert Bradford, Jan. 10, 1961, carton 48, E. F. Kaiser Papers.

20. Ibid., 4.

21. Ibid.

22. San Francisco Bay Area Council, *Report on a Proposed Public Authority*, 135.

23. Ibid., 7.

24. Edgar F. Kaiser, Address to the San Francisco Downtown Association, Feb. 16, 1959, carton 50, E. F. Kaiser Papers.

25. San Francisco Bay Area Council, *Report on a Proposed Public Authority*, 40, 43, 127–29.

26. San Francisco Bay Area Council, press release, Dec. 10, 1958, carton 48, E. F. Kaiser Papers.

27. Norm Nicholson to Edgar F. Kaiser, Dec. 1, 1958, carton 47, E. F. Kaiser Papers.

28. [William S. Downing], "Mr. Kaiser's Activity on Behalf of Golden Gate Authority," Dec. 17, 1959, carton 48, E. F. Kaiser Papers.

29. San Francisco Bay Area Council, press release, Dec. 10, 1958, carton 48, E. F. Kaiser Papers.

30. Edgar F. Kaiser, Address to the San Francisco Downtown Association, Feb. 16, 1959, carton 50, E. F. Kaiser Papers.

31. Kaiser described efforts of this early campaign: "We did not take the creation of the Golden Gate Authority lightly. To the contrary, having had the cooperation of experts in every possible field in determining (1) would an authority work to the advantage of California and the Bay Area and (2) could an act be drafted to make its creation physically possible, we launched the most intensive drive possible to take this vital question to the people, the organizations and the local government bodies of the nine-county Bay Area. . . . We have been in contact with over 8,000 individuals and organizations in a period of three months to tell the Golden Gate Authority story. As the authority is explained and detailed, support has been almost universal. In this short period of time, nearly 300 community leaders have joined the Citizens Committee for the Golden Gate Authority. These people come from throughout the Bay Area. There are labor men, business men, governmental officials, housewives, farmers, Democrats, Republicans and men and women from every other walk of life who have joined us in this effort." Edgar F. Kaiser, quoted in Senate Interim Committee on Bay Area Problems, *Final Report*, 140–41. Also see Nicholson to Chad F. Calhoun, Jan. 31, 1959, carton 47, E. F. Kaiser Papers; Frank E. Marsh, "Statement of Frank E. Marsh, Executive Vice President, San Francisco Bay Area Council, Before the Legislative Committee of the Golden Gate Bridge and Highway District," [San Francisco, 1959], box 94, DS Vault.

32. Senate Interim Committee on Bay Area Problems, *Final Report*, 64.

33. Hutchison served as dean at UC Berkeley from 1930 through 1952, and then spent two years in the same position at the University of Nevada. After retiring from academia, he was elected mayor of Berkeley in 1955 and served until 1963. Claude B. Hutchinson, "Presentation to Sub-committee on Planning of the Assembly Interim Committee on Conservation, Planning and Public Works" (Berkeley, 1958); John D. Phillips, "A Report to the Berkeley City Council on Metropolitan Government" (Berkeley, 1958); Minutes of the Alameda County Mayors' Conference, April 10, 1959, Oakland, Calif., and July 10, 1959, San Leandro, Calif.; Revan Tranter, *ABAG: A Concise History* (Berkeley: Institute of Government Studies, University of California, Berkeley, 2001).

34. For Kent's argument in favor of ABAG (just before it was named) and regional planning through a federation rather than a new governmental agency, see T. J. Kent Jr., "Regional Planning and Metropolitan Government Proposals for the San Francisco Bay Area," paper presented at the National Convention of the American Institute of Planners, Seattle, July 1959. Hutchison also worked closely with the Berkeley city manager John D. Phillips in developing the case against the authority. Claude B. Hutchison, "Presentation to Sub-committee on Planning of the Assembly Interim Committee on Conservation, Planning and

Public Works," Berkeley, Dec. 16, 1958; John D. Phillips, "A Report to the Berkeley City Council on Metropolitan Government," Berkeley, Nov. 1958.

35. Dale Radach Bartley, "A Micro View of Intergovernmental Relations and Councils of Governments: The Case of the Association of Bay Area Governments," Ph.D. diss., University of Colorado, 1979, 29.

36. League of California Cities, *A Statement of Principles on Metropolitan Problems* (n.p., 1959), vol. 4, [Collected ABAG Materials], Institute of Governmental Studies Library, University of California, Berkeley.

37. *Oakland Tribune,* March 21, 1959; Kaiser, "Draft—Statement for Edgar Kaiser, Mayors' Meeting," March 20, [1959], carton 47, E. F. Kaiser Papers.

38. Wes McClure, "The Development of a Metropolitan Government Structure in the San Francisco Bay Area," paper presented at the Meeting of Mayors of Cities of the Nine Bay Area Counties, Berkeley, Calif., March [20], 1959, box 94, DS Vault.

39. *Marin Independent Journal,* Feb. 29, March 6, 10, 1959; *San Francisco Examiner,* March 12, 1959; Golden Gate Bridge and Highway District, Resolution No. 5078, March 9, 1959; James Adam, General Manager's Report, March 13, 1959, and April 10, 1959, Golden Gate Bridge and Highway District, [San Francisco], box 94, DS Vault.

40. Matt A. Graham, Radio KTIM, San Rafael, March 12, 1959, box 94, DS Vault. Emphasis is his.

41. Resolutions for the measure were passed by the Marin Board of Supervisors, the San Rafael City Council, the San Rafael, Novato, and San Anselmo Chambers of Commerce, the Marin Development Foundation, and the Marin County Labor Council. "List of Organizations Which Have Endorsed the Authority," March 30, 1959, carton 48, E. F. Kaiser Papers.

42. Dan London to San Francisco Board of Supervisors, March 12, 1959, box 94, DS Vault.

43. Dion R. Holm, "Digest of Senate Bill No. 853 Creating a Golden Gate Transportation Commission," San Francisco, March 29, 1961.

44. Edgar F. Kaiser, "Statement of Edgar F. Kaiser President, San Francisco Bay Area Council," San Francisco, March 26, 1959, carton 48, E. F. Kaiser Papers.

45. *Marin Independent Journal,* Nov. 28, 30, 1960; *San Francisco Chronicle,* Nov. 29, 30, 1960.

46. *San Francisco Chronicle,* Feb. 7, 1961, Feb. 22, 1963; *San Francisco Examiner,* Feb. 7, 1961.

47. Senate Interim Committee on Bay Area Problems, *Final Report,* 10; *Marin Independent Journal,* April 24, 1959.

48. San Francisco Board of Supervisors, Resolution Endorsing Senate Bill No. 576 Provided Amendments Proposed by City and County are Adopted, April 20, 1959.

49. Brown announced the creation of the Governor's Commission on Metropolitan Area Problems on March 26, 1959: "California's growth, occurring mainly in urban regions, has crowded our streets, over-burdened our transit lines, threatened a dangerous pollution of our air, created water shortages, and led to new cost and complexity in local government. These tensions and troubles, properly called metropolitan area problems, require our earnest and immediate study." Edmund G. Brown, quoted in Assembly Interim Committee on Municipal and County Government, *Multipurpose Districts* (Sacramento, 1962).

50. Governor [Edmond G.] Brown, Statement Re: Golden Gate Authority, April 24, 1959, carton 48, E. F. Kaiser Papers.

51. *San Francisco Chronicle,* May 27, 1959.

52. The new Golden Gate Authority Commission included Kaiser; Bradford; Thomas Carlson, Contra Costa attorney; Joseph L. Eichler, a Palo Alto developer; William M. Malone, San Francisco attorney; Sam Eubanks of the San Francisco-Oakland Newspaper Guild; and Leo Strauss, a Marin resident and outspoken critic of the bridge district. A fourteen-member advisory council was headed by Oakland developer Robert Nahas and Joseph Martin, Jr., attorney and member of the San Francisco Public Utilities Commission, the founders of the Committee for Trade and Transportation, and included one Golden Gate Bridge director, Leland S. Murphy. Golden Gate Authority Commission and Advisory Council, *Directory of Members* ([Sacramento, 1959]), Golden Gate Authority Commission Papers, California State Archives, Sacramento (hereafter referred to as GGAC Papers); *Marin Independent Journal,* June 30, 1960; "Marin Sounding Board Program: Golden Gate Authority Commission," San Rafael, Sept. 1, 1960, box 104, DS Vault; "Golden Gate Authority Commission—the Background Story," [San Francisco], 1960, GGAC Papers.

53. Golden Gate Authority Commission, [*Summary of All Public Hearings Held by the Commission* (Sacramento, 1960)], 3, Golden Gate Authority Commission Papers.

54. Ibid.

55. Golden Gate Authority Commission, *Report,* prepared by Ernst & Ernst (San Francisco: Golden Gate Authority Commission, 1960), 131–39.

56. Ibid.

57. Ibid.; Golden Gate Authority Commission, *Transcript of Public Hearing: Golden Gate Bridge and Highway District* (San Rafael, May 12, 1960), GGAC Papers; *Marin Independent Journal,* May 13, 1960.

58. Golden Gate Authority Commission, *Transcript of Public Hearing: Golden Gate Bridge and Highway District* (San Francisco, Aug. 10, 1960), 25, GGAC Papers.

59. For Adam's written response see Golden Gate Authority Commission, Minutes of Meeting, Oct. 4, 1960, GGAC Papers.

60. *San Francisco Examiner,* Aug. 14, 15, 16, 1960.

61. Ed Salzman, Radio KFAX, San Francisco, Aug. 18, 1960, box 85, IM Facility.

62. Golden Gate Authority Commission, *Transcript of Public Hearing: Governmental Aspects of a Regional Bay Area Authority* (Berkeley, June 8, 1960), 5, GGAC Papers.

63. Ibid., 3.

64. Lantos later became a U.S. Congressman representing San Francisco and San Mateo Counties. Ibid., 40.

65. Ibid., 7

66. Golden Gate Authority Commission, *Report,* prepared by Ernst & Ernst (San Francisco, 1960), 131–39.

67. Golden Gate Authority Commission, *Preliminary Report on the Feasibility of a Regional Transportation Agency for the San Francisco Bay Area* (San Francisco, 1961).

68. Golden Gate Authority Commission, *Preliminary Report,* 9.

69. Ibid., 16. Many of the commission members feared that this would reduce the "quality" of the governing board, but decided to compromise on this issue. William S. Downing to Edgar F. Kaiser, Dec. 16, 1960, carton 48, E. F. Kaiser Papers; William S. Downing, memorandum, "GGA Situation and Miscellany" [1960], carton 48, E. F. Kaiser Papers.

70. Golden Gate Authority Commission, *Preliminary Report on the Feasibility of a Regional Transportation Agency for the San Francisco Bay Area* (San Francisco, 1961).

71. *Oakland Tribune,* Feb. 4, 1961.

72. Arthur C. Jenkins to James Adam, Sept. 16, 1960, box 85, IM Facility.

73. Golden Gate Bridge and Highway District, "Senate Bill 853—Opposition," press release, May 10, 1961, box 94, DS Vault; S.B. 853, 1941 leg., reg. sess., (Ca. 1961).

74. Broadcast, Radio KQBY, San Francisco, March 8, 1961, box 94, DS Vault.

75. *Independent Journal,* April 18, 1961. Marin County's remarkable shift, from unanimous support for the district to unanimous opposition, reflected the polarization of the supervisors in an escalating power struggle in the county over land use, growth, and transportation, as well as the success of bridge district propaganda. Two of the supervisors who voted to condemn the bill would soon face a recall election. See Louise Nelson Dyble, "Revolt Against Sprawl: Transportation and the Origins of the Marin County Growth-Control Regime," *Journal of Urban History* 34 (2007), 38–66.

76. M. A. Graham, Remarks before the San Francisco Board of Supervisors, San Francisco, April 3, 1961, box 94, DS Vault. All of the resolutions, letters, and press releases issued by the Golden Gate Bridge and Highway District during this period can be found in box 94, DS Vault.

77. Collier had a strong record of supporting state highway construction and was a proponent of rural interests generally. The Collier-Burns Act, passed in 1947, launched a massive construction boom in California, funded with gas tax revenue. For biographical information see folder 88, Senator Randolph Collier Papers, California State Archives, Sacramento (hereafter cited as Collier Papers). Randolph Collier, *"The Legislature Takes a Look at California Highway Needs" and Other Addresses by Senator Randolph Collier* (Sacramento, 1947); Werner Z. Hirsch and Daniel J. B. Mitchell, "Warren's Way Back from the Budget Cliff: 'Action, Action, Action,'" paper 909, UCLA School of Public Affairs, California Policy Options, Jan. 1, 2005, http://repositories.cdlib.org/uclaspa/cpo/909 (accessed June 2008).

78. *San Francisco Chronicle,* Oct. 28, 1968.

79. Senate Transportation Committee Hearing, April 25, 1961, box 104, DS Vault.

80. *San Francisco Chronicle,* May 27, 1962.

81. Stephan C. Leonoudakis, "Stephan Leonoudakis: Oral History," interviewed by Trubee Schock ([San Francisco], 2000), 11.

82. Senate Transportation Committee, *Transportation Committee Hearing on Senate Bill 853* (Sacramento, May 11, 1961), 4.

83. *San Francisco Chronicle,* June 9, 11, 1961; *San Francisco Examiner,* May 15, June 12, 1961.

84. *San Francisco Examiner,* June 12, 1961.

85. *San Francisco Examiner,* May 15, 1961.

86. Edgar F. Kaiser, *Report on GGTC Bill to All Bay Area Council Trustees* ([June 15, 1961]), carton 47, E. F. Kaiser Papers.

87. "Marin Sounding Board Program," Radio KTIM, San Rafael, June 25, 1966, box 94, DS Vault.

88. *San Francisco Chronicle,* Nov. 28, 1962.

89. Dan E. London to Randolph Collier, May 13, 1959, folder 632, Collier Papers; Golden Gate Bridge and Highway District, Publicity and Advertising Committee, "Reply to Allegations of State Senator John F. McCarthy Relating to

Administrative, Financial and Managerial Affairs of the Golden Gate Bridge and Highway District," Dec. 6, 1962, box 204, DS Vault.

90. San Francisco Bay Area Council, "Report of the Year's Activities for 1961," [San Francisco], 1961; *Trends* 16 (May 1961), 1, carton 47, E. F. Kaiser Papers.

91. Bechtel headed one of the largest construction and engineering firms in the country, and was one of the founding members of the BAC. San Francisco Bay Area Council, "Report of the Year's Activities for 1961," [San Francisco], 1961; *Trends* 16 (May 1961), 1, carton 47, E. F. Kaiser Papers. On Bechtel's career and legacy see Laton McCartney, *Friends in High Places: the Bechtel Story: The Most Secret Corporation and How It Engineered the World* (New York: Simon and Schuster, 1988).

92. Privately, BAC partisans were worried about ABAG's implications and agenda. After the antagonistic statement of the Berkeley City Council to the proposed authority on Jan. 24, 1961, Downing wrote, "This is a rough draft [response] to Berkeley's statement. And while it has been very difficult, I have tried to use a conciliatory tone because I am afraid they could hurt us in this new ABAG organization." Downing to Thomas Carlson, Feb. 2, 1961, carton 47, E. F. Kaiser Papers; *Trends* 16 (May 1961), 1, carton 47, E. F. Kaiser Papers; San Francisco Bay Area Council, "Report of the Year's Activities for 1961," [San Francisco], 1961.

93. Sonoma County citizens voted to withdraw from ABAG in 1970 after the publication of its first (noncompulsory) regional plan. The City of Oakland and the City and County of San Francisco did not join until 1964, and Solano County did not become a member until 1977.

94. Accounts of ABAG's history include Victor Jones, "Bay Area Regionalism: Institutions, Processes, and Programs," in Advisory Commission on Intergovernmental Relations, *Regional Governance: Promise and Performance*, vol. 2 (Washington, D.C., 1973), 75–110; Douglas D. Detling and Ann-Louise Bacon, *Areawide Environmental Management: Six Decades of Regional Approaches in the Bay Area* (Berkeley: n.p., 1977); Diedre A. Heitman, "The Association of Bay Area Governments: A Critical Look at the Bay Area's Regional Planning Agency," M.A. thesis, University of California, Berkeley, 1982; Tranter, *ABAG: A Concise History*.

95. On federal planning requirements and their implications for metropolitan areas and councils of governments, see Melvin Mogulof, *Governing Metropolitan Areas: A Critical Review of Councils of Governments and the Federal Role* (Washington, D.C., 1971); Nelson Wikstrom, *Councils of Governments: A Study of Political Incrementalism* (Chicago, 1977); David K. Hamilton, *Governing Metropolitan Areas: Response to Growth and Change* (New York: Garland, 1999), 217–52; Kenneth Fox, *Metropolitan America: Urban Life and Urban Policy in the United States, 1940–1980* (Jackson: University Press of Mississippi, 1986); John J. Harrigan, *Political Change in the Metropolis*, 4th ed. (Glenview, Ill.: Scott Foresman, 1989), 343–47. Contemporary analysis of ABAG's regional planning aspirations include Ora Huth, "Regional Organization in the San Francisco Bay Area—1970," paper presented at the Regional Conference—1970, Berkeley, 1970; Victor Jones, "Bay Area Regionalism: The Politics of Intergovernmental Relations," in *The Regionalist Papers*, ed. Kent Mathewson (Detroit: Metropolitan Fund, 1973); Victor Jones, *Government of the San Francisco Bay Area* (Berkeley: Institute of Governmental Studies, University of California, 1964), 64–80; Robert G. Miller and the Association of Bay Area Governments, *Regional Home Rule and Government of the San Francisco Bay Area, Statement to the Assembly Committee on Municipal and County Government* (Berkeley, 1967); Stanley Scott and John C. Bollens, *Governing a Metro-*

politan Region: The San Francisco Bay Area (Berkeley: Institute of Governmental Studies, University of California, 1968).

96. Joseph F. Zimmerman, quoted in Harrigan, *Political Change in the Metropolis,* 346.

97. Golden Gate Bridge and Highway District, *Traffic Analysis, Capacity Factors, and Volume Projections,* vol. 2, *Long Range Planning Survey on Traffic, Facilities, Finance, Toll Rates, Operation and Maintenance of the Golden Gate Bridge,* prepared by Arthur C. Jenkins (San Francisco, 1959), A1–A2.

Chapter 5. Rapid Transit Versus the Golden Gate Bridge

1. Golden Gate Bridge and Highway District, *Supplementary Report on Rapid Transit,* prepared by Charles Derleth, Jr. (San Francisco, 1935), box 204, DS Vault.

2. Charles Derleth to O. H. Ammann, Oct. 20, 1934, box 1, Reed Papers.

3. Ibid.; Golden Gate Bridge and Highway District, Minutes of Meeting of the Board of Engineers, Dec. 11, 1934, box 63, Keesling Papers M0100; Golden Gate Bridge and Highway District, *Special Report on Rapid Transit—Golden Gate Bridge,* prepared by Joseph B. Strauss (Chicago, 1935), box 204, DS Vault.

4. By the late 1960s *San Francisco Bay Guardian* reporters were condemning BART backers as elite businessmen conspiring to establish San Francisco as headquarters for a global empire and to pay for it with regressive taxes on Bay Area residents. Voters, they argued, were duped by promises of congestion and air pollution relief even though the intensive downtown development that proponents anticipated would predictably generate more traffic in San Francisco despite BART. *San Francisco Bay Guardian,* June 18, Aug. 30, 1968, Feb. 14, 1972, Feb. 4, 1973, Nov. 15–28, 1973. Also see J. Allen Whitt, *Urban Elites and Mass Transportation: The Dialectics of Power* (Princeton, N.J.: Princeton University Press, 1982), 40–80. Less overtly critical accounts of the origins of BART include: Stephen Zwerling, *Mass Transit and the Politics of Technology: A Study of BART and the San Francisco Bay Area* (New York: Praeger, 1974); United States Department of Transportation and Department of Housing and Urban Development, *A History of the Key Decisions in the Development of Bay Area Rapid Transit,* prepared by McDonald & Smart, Inc. (Washington, D.C., 1975); United States Congress Office of Technology Assessment, *An Assessment of Community Planning for Mass Transit: Volume 8—San Francisco Case Study* (Washington, D.C., 1976); Seymour Mark Adler, "Political Economy of Transit in the San Francisco Bay Area, 1945–1963," Ph.D. diss., University of California, Berkeley, 1980; Adler, "Infrastructure Politics: The Dynamics of Crossing San Francisco Bay," *The Public Historian* 10 (1988), 19–41; Peter Geoffrey Hall, *Great Planning Disasters* (Berkeley: University of California Press, 1980), 109–37; Frederick M. Wirt, *Power in the City: Decision Making in San Francisco* (Berkeley: University of California Press, 1974), 187–93.

5. San Francisco Bay Area Rapid Transit Commission, *Preliminary Report* (San Francisco, 1953), 15.

6. Ibid., 35; Adler, "The Political Economy of Transit," 99.

7. Senate Interim Committee on San Francisco Bay Area Metropolitan Rapid Transit Problems, *Final Report* (Sacramento, 1957).

8. Ibid.

9. *Independent Journal,* May 12, 1955.

10. San Francisco Bay Area Rapid Transit Commission, *Technical Report on the*

Golden Gate Bridge, prepared by Parsons, Brinckerhoff, Hall and MacDonald (San Francisco, 1955), quoted in Golden Gate Bridge and Highway District, *A Preliminary Report on Long Range Planning,* vol. 1, *Long Range Planning Survey on Traffic, Facilities, Finance, Toll Rates, Operation and Maintenance of the Golden Gate Bridge,* prepared by Arthur C. Jenkins (San Francisco, 1958), H7–H11.

11. San Francisco Bay Area Rapid Transit Commission, *Regional Rapid Transit,* prepared by Parsons, Brinckerhoff, Hall and MacDonald (Sacramento, 1956).

12. Ibid., 89.

13. San Francisco Bay Area Rapid Transit Commission, *Report on Organizational and Financial Aspect of a Proposed Rapid Transit System for the San Francisco Bay Area,* prepared by J. Knight Allen and Morgan Sibbett (Sacramento, 1956), 21.

14. M. N. Quade to San Francisco Bay Area Rapid Transit District, Oct. 9, 1959, box 204, DS Vault; San Francisco Bay Area Rapid Transit Commission, *Report on Organizational and Financial Aspect,* 47–48.

15. *Independent Journal,* Jan. 6, 1956.

16. Senate Interim Committee on San Francisco Bay Area Metropolitan Rapid Transit Problems, *Final Report* (Sacramento, 1957).

17. San Francisco Bay Area Rapid Transit Commission, *Regional Rapid Transit,* 18.

18. [Arthur C. Jenkins] to Charles [W. Reinking], June 15, 1960, box 87, IM facility.

19. Adler, "Political Economy of Transit."

20. Arthur C. Jenkins, "Future of Urban and Interurban Transportation," paper presented at the 11th annual session of the Institute of Government, University of Southern California, June 15, 1939, 10.

21. Arthur C. Jenkins, *Report on Preliminary Considerations to Improving the Net Earning Position of Key System Transit Lines* (San Francisco, 1948); Arthur C. Jenkins, "Outline of Education and Experience" [1949], box 6, Arthur C. Jenkins Papers, Harmer E. Davis Transportation Library, Institute of Transportation Studies, University of California, Berkeley (hereafter referred to as Jenkins Papers); Arthur C. Jenkins, "Professional Biography of Arthur C. Jenkins," 1963, box 85, IM facility.

22. Adler, "Political Economy of Transit," 29–30.

23. A widespread misconception exists that well-functioning streetcar systems were intentionally put out of business by a conspiratorial alliance of tire and auto manufacturers in the 1940s and 1950s. This theory started with a 1974 government report by Bradford Snell and was propagated by several popular histories and the 1996 documentary film, *Taken for a Ride.* Bradford C. Snell, "American Ground Transport," report presented to the Subcommittee on Antitrust and Monopoly, Committee of the Judiciary, United States Senate, Feb. 26, 1974; Stanley I. Fischler, *Moving Millions: An Inside Look at Mass Transit* (New York: Harper and Row, 1979); *Taken for a Ride* (dir. Jim Klein and Martha Olson, 1996). In reality, many streetcar companies were never reliably profitable, and they suffered from overcapitalization, inadequate maintenance, and poor service. They were unpopular with riders who often viewed their operators as monopolistic opportunists, and they were regulated by public officials who responded to public pressure to keep fares low regardless of the financial circumstances. An extensive literature on the decline of mass transit in the United States stresses the political and financial difficulties faced by private transportation companies and the popularity of automobiles and publicly subsidized roadbuilding. See, for example, Robert M. Fogelson, *The Fragmented Metropolis: Los Angeles, 1850–1930*

(Cambridge, Mass.: Harvard University Press, 1967), 164–85; Stanley Mallach, "The Origins of the Decline of Urban Mass Transportation in the United States, 1890–1930," *Urbanism Past and Present* 8 (1979), 1–17; Brian J. Cudahy, *Cash, Tokens, and Transfers: A History of Urban Mass Transit in North America* (New York: Fordham University Press, 1990); Paul Barrett, *The Automobile and Urban Transit: The Formation of Public Policy in Chicago, 1900–1930* (Philadelphia: Temple University Press, 1983); David W. Jones, *Urban Transit Policy: An Economic and Political History* (Englewood Cliffs, N.J.: Prentice Hall, 1985); and Jones, *Mass Motorization + Mass Transit: An American History and Policy Analysis* (Bloomington: Indiana University Press, 2008); Scott Bottles, *Los Angeles and the Automobile: The Making of the Modern City* (Berkeley: University of California Press, 1987); Sy Adler, "The Transformation of the Pacific Electric Railway: Bradford Snell, Roger Rabbit, and the Politics of Transportation in Los Angeles," *Urban Affairs Quarterly* 27 (1991), 51–86; George M. Smerk, *The Federal Role in Urban Mass Transportation* (Bloomington: Indiana University Press, 1991); Martha J. Bianco, "Technological Innovation and the Rise and Fall of Urban Mass Transit," *Journal of Urban History* 25 (1999), 348–78; Zachary M. Schrag, "'The Bus Is Young and Honest': Transportation Politics, Technical Choice, and the Motorization of Manhattan Surface Transit, 1919–1936," *Technology and Culture* 41 (2000), 51–79. For a scholarly perspective that is more sympathetic to Snell's fundamental contentions, see Glenn Yago, *The Decline of Transit: Urban Transportation in German and U.S. Cities, 1900–1970* (New York: Cambridge University Press, 1994).

24. Arthur C. Jenkins and Pacific Electric Railway Company, *Before the Public Utilities Commission of the State of California: A Report on Statistical Data and Trends Applying to the Transit Industry of the United States* (Los Angeles, 1948), box 5, Jenkins Papers; Jenkins, "Professional Biography." The Harmer E. Davis Transportation Library at the Institute of Transportation Studies Library at the University of California, Berkeley, includes dozens of reports and studies prepared by Jenkins for public and private transit operators throughout California, both in the general collection and in the Arthur C. Jenkins Papers. It also includes the minutes of all early BART meetings.

25. Historian Sy Adler describes Jenkins's position on the Pacific Electric Railway: "the era of rail transit, indeed, of transit generally, was drawing to a close and PE ought to grow old as gracefully as possible while it bowed to the realities of technological progress represented by the automobile." Adler, "Transformation of the Pacific Electric Railway," 60–63.

26. Pacific Electric Railway Company, *Report on Operations, Facilities, Organization, Financial Status and Modernization Program of Pacific Electric Railway Company, Los Angeles, California,* prepared by Arthur C. Jenkins (San Francisco, 1949), 7.

27. Pacific Electric Railway Company, *A Report on Statistical Data and Trends Applying to the Transit Industry in the United States,* prepared by Arthur C. Jenkins ([Sacramento], 1948), 6.

28. Arthur C. Jenkins, "Before the Interstate Commerce Commission: Report on A Modernization Program Passenger Transportation Operations of Pacific Electric Railway Company Replacing Nonprofitable Passenger Rail Service with Modern Coach Service and Abandoning of Certain Portions of Rail Lines," Los Angeles, April 3, 1950; Arthur C. Jenkins, "In the Matter of the Application of Pacific Electric Railway Company, Los Angeles, California for the Authority to Make Certain Changes in Passenger Rail and Motor Coach Service, Operations, and Facilities Pursuant to Franchise Ordinance No. 90344," Los Angeles, Jan. 5, 1950.

29. Golden Gate Bridge and Highway District, *Summary Review of Technical Report on Rapid Transit Facilities as Recommended for Installation on the Golden Gate Bridge by Parsons, Brinckerhoff, Hall & MacDonald, Engineers in a Report to The San Francisco Bay Area Rapid Transit Commission*, prepared by Arthur C. Jenkins (San Francisco, 1956).

30. Ibid.

31. The three-volume *Long Range Plan* was completed in October 1959 and announced at a press conference, but bridge district officials never actually released it publicly. The *Independent Journal* ran in a front-page headline, "Gate Span Improvement Plan Ignores Transit," which further antagonized BART officials. *Independent Journal*, Nov. 13, Oct. 30, 1959.

32. Golden Gate Bridge and Highway District, *Preliminary Report on Long Range Planning*, H1.

33. Ibid., A5.

34. Ibid., H11.

35. [Arthur C. Jenkins] to Charles [W. Reinking], June 15, 1960, box 87, IM facility.

36. Ibid.

37. Bay Area Rapid Transit District, Minutes of the Meeting of the Board of Directors, Aug. 13, 1959.

38. Ibid.

39. Bay Area Rapid Transit District, *Route Selection and Development Status Report* (Oakland, 1959).

40. Thorpe J. DeLasaux, "Redwood Empire Association [Report]," Oct. 23, 1959.

41. *Independent Journal*, Oct. 24, 1959.

42. *Independent Journal*, Aug. 19, 1959.

43. Jenkins was appointed part-time in 1962 as the first bridge district engineer officially on staff since Richard G. Little's dismissal in 1953. *San Francisco Chronicle*, Feb. 15, 1964.

44. Arthur C. Jenkins to James Adam, Oct. 16, 1959, box 83, IM facility.

45. Ibid.

46. Arthur C. Jenkins, memorandum, Subject: Conference on Rail Rapid Transit on Golden Gate Bridge, Nov. 5, 1959, box 85, IM facility.

47. Ibid.

48. Bay Area Rapid Transit District, Minutes of Meeting of the Board of Directors, Dec. 10, 1959.

49. Golden Gate Bridge and Highway District, *Brief Analysis of Issues Relating to Installation of Rail Rapid Transit Facilities on the Golden Gate Bridge as Proposed by the San Francisco Bay Area Rapid Transit District With Suggestions as to Engineering Procedure*, prepared by Arthur C. Jenkins (San Francisco, 1959), 8, box 33-1, IM facility.

50. Ibid., 5.

51. John C. Beckett, Report to the Board of Directors, Dec. 10, 1959, box 85, IM facility.

52. Ibid.

53. San Francisco Bay Area Rapid Transit District, *Golden Gate Bridge Rapid Transit Investigation: Semi-Final Report*, prepared by D. B. Steinman (Oakland, 1960), 3.

54. *Independent Journal*, June 16, 1960.

55. *Independent Journal*, June 23, 1960.

56. San Francisco Bay Area Rapid Transit District, *Golden Gate Bridge: Final Report on Engineering Feasibility of Proposed Rapid Transit Facilities,* prepared by C. H. Gronquist (Oakland, 1961).

57. *Independent Journal,* April 20, July 15, 1961.

58. Arthur C. Jenkins to Peter [A. Gasser], [Sept.] 1961, box 87, IM facility.

59. John van der Zee, *The Gate: The True Story of the Design and Construction of the Golden Gate Bridge* (New York, 1986), 156.

60. R. G. Cone to Charles Derleth, July 15, 1941, box 2, Derleth Papers.

61. Clifford E. Paine, "Comments [on] Supplementary Report by Carl H. Gronquist August 1961 on Engineering Feasibility of Rapid Transit Facilities on Golden Gate Bridge," San Francisco, Aug. 29, 1961, box 204, DS Vault.

62. Golden Gate Bridge and Highway District, *Report on Proposed Operation of Rapid Transit Trains over Golden Gate Bridge,* prepared by Clifford E. Paine (San Francisco, 1961), 19.

63. Ibid., 10.

64. Ibid., 16.

65. While Paine's concern about this may have been sincere at the time, in 1953 he coauthored a report that recommended replacing the existing sidewalk "partially or entirely" with open grating. Golden Gate Bridge and Highway District, *Report on Alterations of Golden Gate Bridge,* prepared by Clifford F. Paine, Othmar H. Ammann, and Charles E. Andrew (San Francisco, 1953), 16, 28.

66. Ibid., 14.

67. Ibid., 20.

68. Golden Gate Bridge and Highway District, "Meeting of the Rapid Transit Committee With the Committee of the Whole of the Board of Directors of the Golden Gate Bridge and Highway District," San Francisco, Sept. 5, 1961, 4, box 87, IM facility.

69. Arthur C. Jenkins to Peter [A. Gasser], [Sept.] 1961, box 87, IM facility.

70. The resolution identified Paine as the "chief designer of the Golden Gate Bridge." Golden Gate Bridge and Highway District, Resolution No. 5484 Opposing Rail Rapid Transit Facilities on the Golden Gate Bridge, Sept. 5, 1961.

71. Adrien J. Falk, Report of President Relating to Golden Gate Bridge, Minutes of the 80th Meeting of the San Francisco Bay Area Rapid Transit District, Sept. 7, 1961.

72. *San Francisco Chronicle,* Sept. 8, 1961.

73. The bridge district received letters from the Marin County Board of Supervisors, the San Francisco Board of Supervisors, the Marin Industrial Development Foundation, the Marin County Real Estate Board, the San Rafael Chamber of Commerce, the Downtown Association of San Francisco, the Mill Valley Commuters Club, the Novato Chamber of Commerce and City Council, the City Council of the Town of Ross (in Marin), the San Francisco Junior Chamber of Commerce, the Bay Area Council and the newly formed Association of Bay Area Governments. Golden Gate Bridge and Highway District, Rapid Transit Communications, 1961, box 204, DS Vault.

74. *San Francisco Examiner,* Sept. 10, 1961.

75. Jenkins also reviewed a draft of Gasser's speech before it was presented to the board. Arthur C. Jenkins to [Peter A. Gasser, 1961], box 87, IM facility.

76. Gasser, *Golden Gate Bridge and Rapid Transit.* Gasser distributed copies of his statement at the meeting, along with the only supportive editorial published on the decision, from his hometown. *Napa Register,* Sept. 27, 1961.

77. *Statutes of California* 1959 reg. sess., ch. 1755; Bay Area Rapid Transit

District, *Composite Report: Bay Area Rapid Transit, San Francisco,* prepared by Parsons Brinkerhoff-Tudor-Bechtel (San Francisco, 1962); Adler, "Infrastructure Politics."

78. San Francisco Bay Area Rapid Transit District, Minutes of the 81st Meeting of the San Francisco Bay Area Rapid Transit District, Sept. 14, 1961; San Francisco Bay Area Rapid Transit District, Minutes of the Regular Meeting of the Board of Directors, Oct. 13, 1962.

79. Golden Gate Bridge and Highway District, Excerpts from Board of Directors Meeting Re: Rapid Transit, Oct. 13, 1961, box 204, DS Vault.

80. Ibid.

81. Othmar H. Ammann was an ambitious, politically savvy, and celebrated engineer, and was either the principal designer or a consultant on most of the major suspension bridges that were built in the mid-twentieth century, including the Golden Gate Bridge. He also had a longstanding and bitter rivalry with David Steinman that made him all the more likely to contradict his findings. Darl Rastorfer, *Six Bridges: The Legacy of Othmar H. Ammann* (New Haven: Yale University Press, 2000); Henry Petroski, *Engineers of Dreams: Great Bridge Builders and the Spanning of America* (New York: Knopf, 1995), ch. 5: Jameson W. Doig and David P. Billington, "Ammann's First Bridge: A Study in Engineering, Politics, and Entrepreneurial Behavior," *Technology and Culture* 35 (1994), 537–70; David P. Billington, *The Tower and the Bridge: The New Art of Structural Engineering* (Princeton, N.J.: Princeton Unversity Press, 1985), ch. 8.

82. O. H. Ammann, Frank M. Masters, and N. M. Newmark to James Adam, Feb. 5, 1962, box 87, DS Vault. San Francisco Chronicles, Dec. 7, 1962.

83. O. H. Ammann, Frank M. Masters, and N. M. Newmark, "Golden Gate Bridge Rapid Transit Study by Engineering Board of Review: Proposed Scope of Investigations," [San Francisco], Feb. 5, 1962.

84. *Independent Journal,* Dec. 15, 1962.

85. Studies of BART over the Golden Gate Bridge were again initiated in the late 1980s but dropped because of vehement opposition from Marin County environmentalists, who by then dominated the politics of the county. Bay Area Rapid Transit District, *San Francisco-North Bay BART Connection: A Conceptual Study,* prepared by Bechtel Engineering ([San Francisco], 1989); *San Francisco Chronicle,* March 11, July 7, 1989; *Independent Journal,* April 7, July 7, 1989; Louise Nelson Dyble, "Revolt Against Sprawl: Transportation and the Origins of the Marin County Growth-Control Regime," *Journal of Urban History* 34 (2007), 38–66.

86. *Independent Journal,* April 13, 1962.

87. *Independent Journal,* April 27, 1962.

88. *Independent Journal,* May 5, 10, 11, 15, 1962.

89. *Independent Journal,* April 16, May 18, 1962.

90. Zwerling, *Mass Transit and the Politics of Technology;* Adler, "Political Economy of Transit."

91. United States Congress Office of Technology Assessment, *An Assessment of Community Planning for Mass Transit,* 16.

92. Ibid., 20.

93. Robert O. Self, *American Babylon: Race and the Struggle for Postwar Oakland* (Princeton, N.J.: Princeton University Press, 2003), 191–98.

Chapter 6. James Adam, Boss of the Golden Gate Bridge

1. *San Francisco Examiner,* June 11, July 5, 13, Aug. 2, 1932, Dec. 14, 1936, Sept. 18, 1939, Nov. 30, 1943, Jan. 13, 1944; *Call-Bulletin,* Nov. 8, 1944; *San Rafael Independent,* Feb. 28, 1941; Golden Gate Bridge and Highway District, *Annual Report* (1948).

2. *San Francisco Examiner,* Dec. 2, 1950.

3. *San Francisco Examiner,* June 14, 1952.

4. For an incisive portrait of the scene in Sacramento, the legislature, and its lobbyists in this period, see William Buchanan, *Legislative Partisanship: The Deviant Case of California* (Westport, Conn.: Greenwood Press, 1978). See also Carey McWilliams, *California: The Great Exception* (New York: Current Books, 1949), 192–213; Winston W. Crouch, John C. Bollens, and Stanley Scott, *California Government and Politics,* 2nd ed. (Englewood Cliffs, N.J.: Prentice Hall, 1960), 53–75; Dewey Anderson, *California State Government* (Stanford, Calif.: Stanford University Press, 1942), 131–80; Lester Velie, "The Secret Boss of California," *Collier's Magazine,* Aug. 13, 1949, Aug. 20, 1949; Arthur H. Samish and Bob Thomas, *The Secret Boss of California: The Life and High Times of Art Samish* (New York: Crown, 1971); Ivan Hinderaker, "Regulation of Lobbying in California," in David Farrelly and Ivan Hinderaker, eds., *The Politics of California: A Book of Readings* (New York: Ronald Press, 1951), 197–205.

5. *Independent Journal,* Jan. 29, June 27, Oct. 19, 21, 31, 1953; *San Francisco Examiner,* July 30, 1953; *San Francisco Chronicle,* Aug. 1, 1953.

6. *San Francisco Examiner,* April 10, 1954.

7. *Independent Journal,* July 28, 1953, April 10, 1954.

8. *San Francisco Chronicle,* Feb. 12, 1955; *Independent Journal,* Feb. 12, 1955.

9. *San Francisco Examiner,* May 15, 1953.

10. Garland, a Democrat from Tulare County, managed to win election as speaker in 1940, despite the opposition of Governor Culbert Olson, who was also a Democrat. He became an important ally of Governor Earl Warren and many other prominent Republicans. Buchanan, *Legislative Partisanship,* 16–19.

11. James Adam, "Administration of Highway Toll Facilities," paper presented at the annual meeting of the American Bridge, Tunnel and Turnpike Association, 1955, box 19, IM facility.

12. *Independent Journal,* Aug. 6, 1954.

13. *San Francisco Examiner,* April 14, 1956.

14. *San Francisco Examiner,* April 28, 1956.

15. *San Francisco Examiner,* Oct. 8, 1956.

16. *San Francisco Examiner,* Aug. 15, 16, 1960.

17. *Independent Journal,* Nov. 28, 30, 1960; *San Francisco Chronicle,* Nov. 29, 30, 1960.

18. *San Francisco Chronicle,* May 24–27, 1962.

19. *San Francisco Chronicle,* May 29, 1962.

20. *San Francisco Chronicle,* May 30, 1962.

21. *San Francisco Chronicle,* Nov. 28, 1962.

22. *Independent Journal,* Nov. 27, 1962.

23. *San Francisco Chronicle,* Nov. 28, 1962.

24. The next day, to show that he had not been fired, Hendricks produced an acknowledgment of his resignation that had been signed by Adam. *San Francisco Chronicle,* Dec. 11, 1962.

25. Golden Gate Bridge and Highway District, Publicity and Advertising Com-

mittee, *Reply to Allegations of State Senator John F. McCarthy Relating to Administrative, Financial and Managerial Affairs of the Golden Gate Bridge and Highway District,* by Dan E. London (San Francisco, 1962), box 127, IM facility.

26. Dan E. London to Honorable Board of Directors, Golden Gate Bridge and Highway District, Dec. 14, 1962, box 204, DS Vault.

27. *San Francisco Chronicle,* June 28, Oct. 12, Nov. 9, 1962; *Independent Journal,* Nov. 9, 1962.

28. *San Francisco Chronicle,* Dec. 2, 14, 15, 19, 1962.

29. Marin County Grand Jury, *Special Report on the Golden Gate Bridge and Highway District* (San Rafael, 1963), 29.

30. Ibid., 30.

31. Ibid., 32.

32. Ibid., 31.

33. Ibid.

34. *San Francisco Chronicle,* Jan. 12, 1963.

35. *San Francisco Chronicle,* Jan. 26, 1963.

36. *San Francisco Chronicle,* April 13, 1963.

37. *San Francisco Chronicle,* July 18, 1963.

38. *San Francisco Chronicle,* May 11, 1963; *Independent Journal,* March 1, May 7, 1963; S.B. 183, 184, 610, and 611 1963 leg., reg. sess. (Ca.).

39. *Independent Journal,* April 3, 1963.

40. *San Francisco Chronicle,* July 1, 1964

41. *Santa Rosa Press Democrat,* Dec. 3, 1962.

42. "This partnership really paid off," declared a headline in one Mendocino paper: "we hail this profitable partnership. . . . Long may it endure, to the profit of us all." *Ukiah Daily Journal* June 27, 1967.

43. Carney J. Campion to E. W. Fraser, June 21, 1965, box 126, IM facility.

44. Ibid.; Edwin A. Frediani to Redwood Empire Supervisors, Golden Gate Bridge Directors, Legislators, County Officials, Executive Board, News Media, May 17, 1968, Collier Papers.

45. *San Francisco Chronicle,* Nov. 10, 1966.

46. *San Francisco Chronicle,* March 8, 1966.

47. California Fair Employment Practice Commission, *In the Matter of the Accusation of Golden Gate Bridge and Highway District, Board of Directors of the Golden Gate Bridge and Highway District, and James Adam, General Manager of the Golden Gate Bridge and Highway District: Reporter's Transcript* (San Francisco, Sept. 11–15, Nov. 13–17, 1967), 134–40, private collection of James Haugabook. There are FEPC case files in the California State Archives from this period, but they are not accessible to researchers as of 2008.

48. *San Francisco Chronicle,* Dec. 21, 1965.

49. *San Francisco Chronicle,* March 8, 9, 1966.

50. *San Francisco Chronicle,* March 22, 1966.

51. California Fair Employment Practice Commission, *In the Matter of . . . Golden Gate Bridge and Highway District,* 90–92.

52. Ibid., 87.

53. Ibid., 30, 97, 160, 215.

54. *San Francisco Chronicle,* March 22, 1966.

55. *San Francisco Chronicle,* May 27, June 3, 8, 1967.

56. *San Francisco Examiner,* May 30, Nov. 15, 1967; *San Francisco Chronicle,* Oct. 27, 1967.

57. James Haugabook to author, email, March 7, 2003.

58. California Fair Employment Practice Commission, *In the Matter of . . . Golden Gate Bridge and Highway District,* 346–47, 536, 546.

59. Ibid., 80.

60. Ibid., 57, 197–209.

61. Ibid., 33.

62. Ibid., 36–37.

63. *San Francisco Chronicle,* April 1, 1967.

64. *San Francisco Examiner* [May 1967], private clipping file of James Hauga-book.

65. *San Francisco Chronicle,* April 1, 1967.

66. *San Francisco Chronicle,* May 19, 1967. Later, union officials claimed that "one of the main charges used against Paul Powell is that he picked the wrong place to sit on the rail" in practicing the longstanding painters' method of reliev-ing themselves on the job. The only toilet facilities at the time were at the toll plaza. *San Francisco Chronicle,* June 3, 1967.

67. *San Francisco Chronicle,* April 28, 29, 1967.

68. *San Francisco Chronicle,* April 29, 1967. Dearman was the friend and law partner of Willie Brown, a state assemblyman and later, mayor of San Francisco. When Dearman was dropped from the bridge district delegation after only two years to make room for a supervisor to serve (to fulfill the requirements of a 1968 reform bill, see Chapter 7), Brown vowed revenge. Dearman was assigned to the Metropolitan Transportation Commission instead, an organization that Brown described as "less than powerless." *San Francisco Chronicle,* Dec. 20, 1968, Dec. 16, 1970.

69. *San Francisco Examiner,* May 25, 1967; *San Francisco Chronicle,* May 23–25, 1967.

70. *San Francisco Chronicle,* July 20, 1967. Dellums was one of the founders of the Brotherhood of Sleeping Car Porters and became West Coast regional direc-tor of the NAACP in 1948. Dellums also supported the creation of the FEPC in 1959, and served as its first chairman. On Dellums's career, see Robert O. Self, *American Babylon: Race and the Struggle for Postwar Oakland* (Princeton, N.J.: Princeton University Press, 2003).

71. *San Francisco Chronicle,* July 22, 1967.

72. California Fair Employment Practice Commission, *In the Matter of . . . Golden Gate Bridge and Highway District,* 12, 638–39; California Streets and High-ways Code, sections 27150–27151 (as of 1968): "The General Manager shall be the Executive Officer of the District. He shall employ and discharge all subordi-nate officers, employees, and assistants, prescribe their duties . . . and fix their compensation. He shall have full charge and control of the construction, main-tenance, and operation of all works of the District."

73. *San Francisco Chronicle,* July 20, 22, 1967.

74. California Fair Employment Practice Commission, *In the Matter of . . . Golden Gate Bridge and Highway District,* 21–23, 116–17.

75. Ibid., 24.

76. Ibid., 220.

77. Ibid., 156–93, 228–30, 325–27, 384–85.

78. Ibid., 39, 51–54, 76–78, 413, 398, 527.

79. Ibid., 257.

80. *San Francisco Chronicle,* Nov. 14–16, 1967.

81. The panel was comprised of three of the seven commissioners. Pier Gherini, a Republican from Santa Barbara County, chaired the panel. He and

Stella Sandoval, a Republican appointed by Governor Ronald Reagan, voted to dismiss Haugabook's complaint. John Anson Ford, a Democrat appointed by Governor Pat Brown, dissented. California Fair Employment Practice Commission, *Report* (Sacramento, 1967–68); *San Francisco Chronicle,* Dec. 6, 9, 1967.

82. *San Francisco Examiner,* Dec. 5, 1967.

83. *San Francisco Chronicle,* Dec. 19, 1967.

84. On the California FEPC, its powers, and its politics, see Richard B. Couser, "The California FEPC: Stepchild of the State Agencies," *Stanford Law Review* 18 (Nov. 1965), 187–212; Self, *American Babylon,* 85–86, 187–91.

85. Paul Peterzell, a young reporter for the *Independent Journal,* charged that the closed meeting was a violation of the Ralph M. Brown Act, which required public access to government meetings. He forced his way into the board room in a rather dramatic confrontation. *Independent Journal,* Dec. 8, 1967.

86. *San Francisco Chronicle,* Dec. 9, 1967.

87. The union business representative said that they had already spent thousands on Haugabook's case and could not afford the $10,000 that a court appeal would cost. *San Francisco Chronicle,* Dec. 19, 1967. Powell sued the district for reinstatement and $500,000 in damages, and settled for $25,000. *San Francisco Examiner,* May 21, 1968; *San Francisco Chronicle,* May 30, 1968.

88. This demonstration was attended by Willie Brown. *San Francisco Chronicle,* Aug. 24, 26, 1967.

89. *San Francisco Chronicle,* June 8, 1968; *San Francisco Examiner,* June 8, 1968.

90. *San Francisco Chronicle,* June 15, 1968.

91. *San Francisco Chronicle,* Sept. 14, 1967.

92. California Fair Employment Practice Commission, *In the Matter of . . . Golden Gate Bridge and Highway District,* 483, 515.

93. Ibid., 933–92; *San Francisco Chronicle,* Sept. 16, 1967.

94. California Fair Employment Practice Commission, *In the Matter of . . . Golden Gate Bridge and Highway District,* 518.

95. A. R. O'Brien, A. M. Brown, and R. H. Trumbull to the Board of Directors, Golden Gate Bridge and Highway District, Oct. 13, 1938, box 63, Keesling Papers, M0100; Russell G. Cone, "Permanent Painting Scaffolds For the Golden Gate Bridge," *Engineering News-Record,* April 25, 1940.

96. Golden Gate Bridge and Highway District, *Golden Gate Bridge, Report on Inspection of Condition and Major Structural Units,* prepared by Ammann & Whitney (San Francisco, 1969).

97. *San Francisco Chronicle,* Oct. 26–28, Nov. 22, 1967.

98. *San Francisco Chronicle,* Oct. 28, 1967.

99. Redwood Empire Association, press release, Oct. 27, 1967, box 126, IM facility; *San Francisco Chronicle,* Nov. 22, 1967.

100. *San Francisco Chronicle,* Sept. 9, 1967; *San Francisco Examiner,* April 4, 1968.

101. *San Francisco Chronicle,* June 1, 1968.

102. *Independent Journal,* Sept. 15, 1967.

103. Marin County Grand Jury, *Report* (San Rafael, 1967); *San Francisco Chronicle,* June 1, 1968; *San Francisco Chronicle,* June 1, 1968.

104. *Independent Journal,* May 31, 1968.

105. *Independent Journal,* May 30, 31, 1968.

106. *San Francisco Examiner,* March 22, 1968.

107. *San Francisco Chronicle,* Aug. 13, 1968.

108. Jules Dundes, editorial, Radio KCBS, San Francisco, Dec. 7, 10, 1962, box 127, IM Facility.

109. *Independent Journal,* June 14, 1968.
110. *San Francisco Examiner,* March 4, 1968.
111. *San Francisco Examiner,* April 4, 1968.

Chapter 7. Regionalism, Transportation, and Perpetual Tolls

1. Regionalism as it was understood in the 1950s and 1960s referred to the structural, technocratic reform movement that was popular with civic and business leaders, including members of the Bay Area Council (see Chapter 4). Its roots can be traced to structural reformers in the field of public administration, including Herbert Croly and Woodrow Wilson. Members of the Chicago school of sociology, particularly Roderick D. McKenzie, were also influential in its development. I call this movement "pro-growth regionalism" in the Bay Area context, and others have used the term "metropolitan regionalism." Metropolitan regionalism was predicated on the belief that the metropolis had become the fundamental unit of the economy and society by the early twentieth century, and that effective and efficient government must correspond to that scale. Its proponents insisted that the decentralized, fragmented governments of metropolitan areas had to be consolidated for the sake of efficient public administration, optimal distribution of resources and services, and the effective management of social and environmental problems. Among the chief concerns of metropolitan regionalists was the ongoing proliferation of narrow, single-purpose special districts contributing to governmental fragmentation. Leading advocates in the 1960s included Luther Halsey Gulick, John C. Bollens, and Robert Wood. The federal Advisory Commission on Intergovernmental Relations (ACIR), created in 1959, published a series of reports based on the principals of metropolitan regionalism, and the elite, industry-led national Council for Economic Development was another major proponent. Important contributions to metropolitan regionalism, all of which expressed concern about special districts, include Paul Studenski, *The Government of Metropolitan Areas in the United States* (New York: National Municipal League, 1930); Roderick D. McKenzie, *The Metropolitan Community* (New York, 1933); Charles Edward Merriam, Spencer Delbert Parratt, and Albert Lepawsky, *The Government of the Metropolitan Region of Chicago* (Chicago, 1933); Victor Jones, *Metropolitan Government* (Chicago: University of Chicago Press, 1942); Council of State Governments, *The States and the Metropolitan Problem,* prepared by John C. Bollens (Chicago: Council of State Governments, 1956); John C. Bollens, *Special District Governments in the United States* (Berkeley: University of California Press, 1957); Robert C. Wood, *1400 Governments: The Political Economy of the New York Metropolitan Region* (Cambridge, Mass.: Harvard University Press, 1961); Luther Halsey Gulick, *The Metropolitan Problem and American Ideas* (New York: Alfred A. Knopf, 1962). See also "A Symposium on Metropolitan Regionalism: Development Governmental Concepts," *University of Pennsylvania Law Review* 105 (1957), 439–616. For discussion, see G. Ross Stephens and Nelson Wikstrom, *Metropolitan Government and Governance: Theoretical Perspectives, Empirical Analysis, and the Future* (New York: Oxford University Press, 2000); Peter Hall, *Cities of Tomorrow: An Intellectual History of Urban Planning and Design in the Twentieth Century,* 3rd ed. (London: Blackwell, 2002), 143–87; Richard A. Walker and Michael K. Heiman, "Quiet Revolution for Whom?" *Annals of the Association of American Geographers* 71 (1981), 67–83; Margaret Weir, "Coalition Building for Regionalism," in *Reflections on Regionalism,* ed. Bruce Katz (Washington, D.C.:

Brookings Institution Press, 2000), 127–53; Allan D. Wallis, "Inventing Regionalism: The First Two Waves," *National Civic Review* 83 (1994), 159–76.

2. Mel Scott, *San Francisco Bay Area: Metropolis in Perspective*, 2nd ed. (Berkeley: University of California Press, 1986), 297, 314–17; *Statutes of California* 1965 reg. sess, ch. 1351.

3. Melvin B. Lane to T. Louis Chess, Adrien Falk, Nils Eklund, and Grant Burton, April 13, 1966, vol. 4, [Collected ABAG Materials], Institute of Governmental Studies Library, University of California, Berkeley.

4. Walter P. Hollmann, "The Metropolitan Picture in California to 1980," paper presented at the Conference of the Governor's Metropolitan Commission ([Sacramento], 1959); Richard M. Zettel, *Urban Transportation in the San Francisco Bay Area* (Berkeley: Institute of Governmental Studies, University of California, 1963); Bay Area Transportation Study Commission, *Bay Area Transportation Report* (Berkeley, 1969); Golden Gate Bridge and Highway District, *Report of the Chief Engineer with Architectural Studies*, vol. 3, *The Golden Gate Bridge at San Francisco California* (San Francisco, 1930); Golden Gate Bridge and Highway District, *Statistical Report on Traffic on the Golden Gate Bridge and Approaches*, prepared by Arthur C. Jenkins and Robert L. Davidson (San Francisco, 1965).

5. San Francisco Bay Area Rapid Transit Commission, *Regional Rapid Transit*, prepared by Brinckerhoff, Parsons, Hall, and MacDonald (San Francisco, 1956), 18.

6. U.S. Department of Commerce, *Future Development of the San Francisco Bay Area 1960–2020* (San Francisco, 1959), 25, D-2, Plate 1.

7. David W. Jones, *California's Freeway Era in Historical Perspective* (Berkeley: Institute of Transportation Studies, University of California, 1989); California Department of Public Works Division of Highways, *The California Freeway System: A Report to the Joint Interim Committee on Highway Problems of the California Legislature* (Sacramento, 1958). For discussions of the federal road and highway programs, see Mark H. Rose, *Interstate: Express Highway Politics, 1939–1989*, rev. ed. (Knoxville: University of Tennessee Press, 1990); Bruce E. Seely, *Building the American Highway System: Engineers as Policy Makers* (Philadelphia: Temple University Press, 1987); Tom Lewis, *Divided Highways: Building the Interstate Highways, Transforming American Life* (New York: Viking, 1997).

8. California Department of Public Works Division of Bay Toll Crossings, *A Preliminary Report to Department of Public Works on a San Francisco—Tiburon Crossing of San Francisco Bay* (Sacramento, 1957).

9. William Issel, "'Land Values, Human Values, and the Preservation of the City's Treasured Appearance': Environmentalism, Politics, and the San Francisco Freeway Revolt," *Pacific Historical Review* 68 (1999), 611–46; Stephanie Sabine Pincetl, *Transforming California: A Political History of Land Use and Development* (Baltimore: Johns Hopkins University Press, 1999); Katherine M. Johnson, "Captain Blake Versus the Highwaymen, or How San Francisco Won the Freeway Revolt," paper presented at the Conference of the American Association of Geographers, San Francisco, 2007; Jones, *California's Freeway Era*; Zettel, *Urban Transportation in the San Francisco Bay Area*.

10. Richard Walker, *The Country in the City: Urban Environmentalism in the San Francisco Bay Area* (Seattle: University of Washington Press, 2007); Charles Wollenberg, *Golden Gate Metropolis: Perspective on Bay Area History* (Berkeley: Institute of Governmental Studies, University of California, 1985); L. Martin Griffin, *Saving the Marin-Sonoma Coast: The Battles for Audubon Canyon Ranch, Point Reyes & California's Russian River* (Healdsburg, Calif.: Sweetwater Springs Press, 1998); Louise Nelson Dyble,

"Revolt Against Sprawl: Transportation and the Origins of the Marin County Growth Control Regime," *Journal of Urban History* 34 (2007), 38–66.

11. Scott, *The San Francisco Bay Area*, 315–17; San Francisco Bay-Delta Water Quality Control Program, *Final Report to the State of California: San Francisco Bay-Delta Water Quality Control Program*, prepared by Kaiser Engineers ([San Francisco], 1969), ch. 22.

12. T. J. Kent Jr., "Statewide and Regional Land-Use Planning in California, 1950–1980," an interview conducted by Malca Chall, Regional Oral History Office, The Bancroft Library (Berkeley, 1983); Walker, *Country in the City*, 132–42; Fukuo Akimoto, "T. J. Kent, Jr.: A City and Regional Planner in the Bay Area," paper presented at the Tenth National Conference on Planning History, St. Louis, Mo., 2003.

13. Kent's view of regional planning was very different from that of the mainstream metropolitan reformers of the time, influenced by his conservationist sympathies and also ideas associated with Mumford and the short-lived Regional Planning Association of America. The differences between these two regionalist schools were thrown into striking contrast in 1932 when Mumford attacked the *Regional Plan of New York and Its Environs* and its primary author, Thomas Adams, in the pages of the *New Republic*. Mumford's brand of regionalism, with socialist overtones, more sensitivity to the value of the natural environment, and more attention to areas outside of the urban core, was rooted in a cultural and intellectual critique of industrialization and development that appealed to a new generation of environmentally sensitive, left-leaning planners emerging in the 1960s and 1970s. Kent, in his position in the Department of City and Regional Planning at the University of California, Berkeley, helped train this new generation. Robert Fishman, "The Metropolitan Tradition in American Planning," in *The American Planning Tradition: Culture and Policy*, ed. Robert Fishman (Washington, D.C.: Woodrow Wilson International Center, 2000), 65–85; John L. Thomas, "Holding the Middle Ground," in *The American Planning Tradition*, 33–63; Hall, *Cities of Tomorrow*, 143–87, 357–58; Matthew Dalbey, *Regional Visionaries and Metropolitan Boosters* (Boston: Kluwer Academic Publishers, 2002).

14. T. J. Kent, Jr., *City and Regional Planning for the Metropolitan San Francisco Bay Area* (Berkeley: Institute of Governmental Studies, University of California, 1963), 1–2.

15. Scott contributed to the campaign for a Golden Gate Authority as well as the BATS Commission. Jones and Bollens were veteran critics of fragmented government and special district proliferation. The monthly *Public Affairs Report* published by the Institute of Governmental Studies at UC Berkeley included extensive discussion of efforts for regional government in the 1960s. The major conferences on the subject held in the Bay Area included: "Future of the Bay Area Conference," sponsored by the Bay Area Council, San Francisco Planning and Urban Renewal Association, and the Association of Bay Area Governments Oakland, 1963; "Bay Area Regional Organization: Scope and Shape," sponsored by the University Extension and the Institute of Governmental Studies on behalf of the Joint Legislative Committee on Bay Area Regional Organization University of California, Berkeley, Sept. 14, 1968; "Regional Conference—1970," sponsored by the Institute of Governmental Studies, University of California, Berkeley, April 18, 1970. See also Victor Jones, *Government of the San Francisco Bay Area* (Berkeley: Institute of Governmental Studies, University of California, 1964); San Francisco Bay Area Council, *Review of Background Developments and Present Status of Consideration of Governing Regional Problems in the San Francisco Bay*

Area, prepared by Stan McCaffrey (San Francisco, 1967); Stanley Scott and John C. Bollens, *Governing a Metropolitan Region: The San Francisco Bay Area* (Berkeley: Institute of Governmental Studies, University of California, 1968); Scott and Willis D. Hawley, "Organizing to Solve Regional Problems in the San Francisco Bay Area," *Public Affairs Report* 9 (1968).

16. Pincetl, *Transforming California,* 140–42; Bay Area Federation of Planning Councils, *Regional Planning for the Bay Area: Proposed Regional Planning District Legislation* (San Francisco, 1960); T. J. Kent, "Regional Planning and Metropolitan Government Proposals for the San Francisco Bay Area," paper presented at the National Convention of the American Institute of Planners, Seattle, July, 1959, 6–13; League of Women Voters of San Francisco, *Resource Material on Bay Area Problems* (San Francisco, 1960); Governor's Commission on Metropolitan Area Problems, *Meeting Metropolitan Problems* (Sacramento, 1960).

17. Association of Bay Area Governments, *Preliminary Regional Plan* (Berkeley, 1966); Ora Huth, "Regional Organization in the San Francisco Bay Area—1970," paper presented at the Regional Conference—1970, Berkeley.

18. Bay Area Transportation Study Commission, *Prospectus for a San Francisco Bay Area Transportation Study* (Sacramento, 1962).

19. Harbor Carriers, Inc. operated a ferry from Tiburon to San Francisco in the 1960s. California Department of Public Works Division of Bay Toll Crossings, *San Francisco-Marin Crossing* (Sacramento, 1967), 21.

20. Arthur C. Jenkins, "Engineering Proposals for Second Deck on the Golden Gate Bridge," Sept. 23, 1966, box 205, DS Vault.

21. Golden Gate Bridge and Highway District, *Financial Analysis and Projection,* vol. 3, *Long Range Planning Survey on Traffic, Facilities, Finance, Toll Rates, Operation and Maintenance of the Golden Gate Bridge,* prepared by Arthur C. Jenkins (San Francisco, 1959), 4–6.

22. Arthur C. Jenkins, "Outline of Elements Recommended for Inclusion in a Long-Range Planning Program," Jan. 16, 1956, box 33-1, IM facility.

23. Jenkins, "Outline of Elements," 5; California Department of Public Works Division of Bay Toll Crossings, *Preliminary Report to Department of Public Works on a San Francisco—Tiburon Crossing of San Francisco Bay* (Sacramento, 1957).

24. In 1961 state engineers revised plans for the Angel Island span with landings that avoided residential areas in Marin, but opposition was just as bitter and vehement, and once again the project was abandoned. California Division of Bay Toll Crossings, *San Francisco-Marin Crossing*; California Department of Public Works Division of Bay Toll Crossings, *A Progress Report to Department of Public Works on a San Francisco—Marin Crossing of San Francisco Bay* (Sacramento, 1962); *Independent Journal,* March 11, 12, 21, 1955, Jan. 14, Feb. 9, 1956, Jan. 7, March 7, 1957, Oct. 8, 1966, Jan. 5, 1968; *San Francisco Examiner,* April 30, May 8, July 18, 1957; *San Francisco News,* June 4, 1957; *San Francisco Chronicle,* May 9, 1957, March 22, 29, 1966. See also Walker, *Country in the City,* ch. 4; Dyble, "Revolt Against Sprawl."

25. S.B. 905 1965 leg., reg. sess. (Ca.)

26. *San Francisco Examiner,* June 14, 1965.

27. *San Francisco Chronicle,* March 22, 29, 1966; Division of Bay Toll Crossings, *San Francisco-Marin Crossing,* 107–10.

28. *Independent Journal,* April 27, 1962; Aug. 24, Sept. 28, Oct. 19, 1962; Jerome B. White to Board of Directors Golden Gate Bridge and Highway District, Dec. 21, 1965, box 127, IM facility; Jerome B. White to James Adam, May 19, 1964, Collier Papers.

29. *Independent Journal,* May 1, 1962.

30. *Independent Journal,* Oct. 11, 1962.

31. Golden Gate Bridge and Highway District, *Report on Feasibility of Installation of a Lower Deck for Automobile Traffic on Golden Gate Bridge,* prepared by Ammann & Whitney ([San Francisco], 1964); *Independent Journal,* Aug. 6, 1964; Redwood Empire Association, press release, "Second Deck Looms for Golden Gate Bridge," Jan. 10, 1966, box 126, IM facility.

32. *San Francisco Chronicle,* Aug. 15, 1964.

33. E.g., *San Francisco Chronicle,* May 20, 1966.

34. *San Francisco Chronicle,* June 11, Aug. 27, 1966; Arthur C. Jenkins to James Adam, Sept. 6, 1964, box 83, IM facility; Golden Gate Bridge and Highway District, *Status of Current Planning for Design and Construction of a Second Deck of the Golden Gate Bridge* ([San Francisco], 1966) box 82, IM facility.

35. In 1970, Marin journalist Paul Peterzell described the "Ammann & Whitney syndrome" as the "circular reasoning that assures consultants a steady income. Ammann & Whitney . . . traditionally captures contracts with the district on the ground that since it got the last job it naturally knows best how to do the next one. Naturally." *Independent Journal,* Oct. 19, 1970.

36. *Independent Journal,* Feb. 15, April 29, 1965.

37. The Tudor Engineering Company had been a major contractor on the San Francisco-Oakland Bay Bridge and was working in partnership with the Bechtel Corporation on the BART system at the time. United States Congress Office of Technology Assessment, *An Assessment of Community Planning for Mass Transit: Volume 8—San Francisco Case Study* (Washington, D.C., 1976).

38. Golden Gate Bridge and Highway District, *A Report on a Study of: the Ammann & Whitney report, August 1964; the Tudor Engineering Company Report, March 1966; Relating to the Installation of a Lower Deck for Vehicular Traffic on the Golden Gate Bridge,* prepared by Clifford E. Paine (San Francisco, 1966).

39. *Independent Journal,* Oct. 19, 1965, Oct. 22, 1966; *San Francisco Chronicle,* Oct. 30, 1965, May 27, July 8, 1966; Golden Gate Bridge and Highway District, *Preliminary Feasibility Report: Double-Decking Golden Gate Bridge, San Francisco, California,* prepared by Tudor Engineering Company (San Francisco, 1966); Golden Gate Bridge and Highway District, *Supplementary Report: Double-Decking Golden Gate Bridge, San Francisco, California,* prepared by Tudor Engineering Company (San Francisco, 1966); Milton Brumer to James Adam, April 1, 1966, box 205, DS Vault.

40. *San Francisco Chronicle,* Sept. 12, 1967.

41. *San Francisco Chronicle,* April 8, 1966.

42. *San Francisco Chronicle,* Aug. 26, 1966.

43. Redwood Empire Association, press release, "Gate Span Tolls Could Pay for 2nd Deck, Auditor Says," Oct. 12, 1967, box 126, IM facility; *San Francisco Chronicle,* June 2, 15, 1966.

44. *Independent Journal,* Nov. 21, 1962, April 3, 1963, Dec. 2, 1964; *San Francisco Chronicle,* Nov. 21, 28, Dec. 8, 25, 1962, Dec. 20, 1966.

45. *San Francisco Chronicle,* July 29, 1966; [Arthur C. Jenkins] to Dan E. London, Oct. 7, 1966, box 82, IM facility; Redwood Empire Association, press release, "No Bridge Deck Without S. F. Supervisors' OKEH," July 28, 1966, box 126, IM facility; *San Francisco Chronicle,* July 29, 1966.

46. *San Francisco Chronicle,* Aug. 2, 1967.

47. *San Francisco Chronicle,* Aug. 8, 1967.

48. Redwood Empire Association, press release, "Bridge Board Upholds Deck Survey, 7-5," Oct. 13, 1967, box 126, IM facility; Redwood Empire Association,

press release, "Second Deck Looms for Golden Gate Bridge," Jan. 10, 1966, box 126, IM facility; *San Francisco Chronicle,* June 26, 28, July 4, 1963. Clearly, there was an affinity; bridge district officials had been working alongside state engineers to convince San Francisco to approve plans to widen approaches for the bridge for years, and Jenkins was deeply frustrated about the recalcitrance of San Francisco freeway opponents. Responding to an ad by a neighborhood group against the Golden Gate Freeway, Jenkins composed this letter: "Here you have it! The means by which the small—very small—segment of the public gains or attempts to gain its advantage over the far greater representation by use of the . . . 'money be damned' process of buying spin in the local press to give you a 'forced enema' on the issues of a program of traffic control that will without valid challenge benefit the greater majority of the people including those residents the article helped to influence to take the path of opposition. . . . San Francisco is not self sufficient as to its economy and its tax roll! This city is dependent upon its reputation as one of the important and controlling financial centers of the world! . . . These narrow minded, financially indifferent individuals who make up less than one percent of the population, in their effort to preserve their self-styled sanctity as residents of Telegraph Hill, Nob Hill, and other such areas who have nothing to do but sit [and] look at the scenery, searching for freeways that may mar their view, try to inculcate the masses through costly advertisements. [T]hey do not know what they are talking about and . . . they are deliberately spending their unlimited funds to influence you to join their ranks as opportunists. . . . Use your own judgment on this issue—don't let the hill dwellers tell your story for you." Arthur C. Jenkins to [editors of the *San Francisco Chronicle*], May 26, [1965], box 84, IM facility.

49. *San Francisco Chronicle and Examiner,* Aug. 6, 1967.

50. *San Francisco Chronicle,* Oct. 25, 1967.

51. Speakers represented the San Francisco Planning and Urban Renewal Association, the Telegraph Hill Dwellers Association, the Marin Property Owners' Association, the League of Women Voters, San Francisco Beautiful, Marin Transportation Action Committee, San Francisco Women's Chamber of Commerce, the San Francisco chapter of the Sierra Club, the San Francisco Council of Women's Clubs, the Marin Civic Improvement Property Owners' Association, the California Roadside Council, and several San Francisco unions. *San Francisco Chronicle,* Nov. 18, 1967.

52. Golden Gate Bridge and Highway District, Resolution 6526, Nov. 24, 1967; Redwood Empire Association, press release, "Alioto Speaks, Gate Span Deck Halt Confirmed," Nov. 24, 1967, box 126, IM facility; Redwood Empire Association, press release, "S.F. Freeway Lack May Block Gate Span Deck," Oct. 27, 1966, box 126, IM facility; *San Francisco Chronicle,* Oct. 3, Nov. 8, 1967.

53. *San Francisco Chronicle,* Nov. 25, 1967; Redwood Empire Association, press release, "Alioto Speaks, Gate Span Deck Halt Confirmed," Nov. 24, 1967, box 126, IM facility.

54. The resolution, which was introduced by Dearman, was adopted at the next meeting of the board of directors on December 15. Redwood Empire Association, press release, "Ferry Studies Sought by Gate Span Board," Dec. 15, 1967, box 126, IM facility.

55. A.B. 2628, 1963 leg., reg. sess. (Ca.); *Independent Journal,* April 9, July 29, 1963.

56. A.B. 75, 1963 leg., ex. sess. (Ca.). The measure was endorsed by the BART

board of directors. San Francisco Bay Area Rapid Transit District, Resolution No. 340, Feb. 27, 1964.

57. Greyhound also faced labor relations problems, including a crippling strike in 1966. For analysis of Greyhound operations, see Marin County Transportation District, *Report on Public Transportation in County of Marin,* prepared by Coverdale and Colpitts (San Rafael, Calif., 1966). Studies of the problem commissioned by the MCTD include *Report on Public Transportation in County of Marin*; Marin County Transportation District, *Public Transportation Survey for Marin County,* prepared by De Leuw and Cather Company (San Rafael, Calif., 1964); Paul J. Fanning, "Report to the Board of Directors, Marin County Transit District: Presenting a Plan of Transit Operation for Marin County," San Rafael, Calif., June 1965; Marin County Transportation District, *Basic Considerations of Transit Planning Marin County Transit District,* prepared by Arthur C. Jenkins (San Rafael, Calif., 1967).

58. *Independent Journal,* July 21, 1965, Jan. 6, 1966.

59. *San Francisco Chronicle,* May 11, 1963; Golden Gate Bridge and Highway District, Resolution No. 6003, Aug. 28, 1994; Arthur C. Jenkins to James Adam, Dec. 28, 1965, box 83, IM facility; [Jerome B. White] to Board of Directors Golden Gate Bridge and Highway District, Sept. 3, 1965.

60. Thomas T. Storer to Marin County Transit District Board of Directors, March 14, 1968, carton 5, Bagley Papers.

61. Technical Sub-Committee of the Tri-Partite Transportation Committee, *Current Status of Rapid Transit on the Golden Gate Bridge* (San Francisco, 1968), carton 5, Bagley Papers.

62. Redwood Empire Association, press release, "Bridge Member Quits Tripartite Group," June 12, 1968, box 126, IM facility; Redwood Empire Association, press release, "Demand Gate Bridge Quit 3-Agency Transit Study," June 14, 1968, box 127, IM facility.

63. California Legislative Analyst, *The San Francisco-Marin County Transportation Corridor Problem* (Sacramento, 1967).

64. John F. Foran, "Oral History Interview with John F. Foran," interviewed by Laura McCreery, State Government Oral History Program, California State Archives (Sacramento, 2003).

65. *Pacific Sun,* Oct. 29, 1966; Foran, "Oral History," 23.

66. *San Francisco Examiner,* March 5, 1968; A.B. 855, 1968 leg., reg. sess. (Ca.); A.B. 2057, 1968 leg. reg. sess. (Ca.); Bagley, press release, March 5, 1968, carton 5, William T. Bagley Legislative Papers, BANC MSS 77/109 c, The Bancroft Library, University of California, Berkeley (hereafter cited as Bagley Papers).

67. William T. Bagley to Eugene C. Lee. March 12, 1968, carton 5, Bagley Papers.

68. *People ex. rel. Bagshaw v. Thompson,* 55 Cal. 2d 147 (1942).

69. *San Francisco Chronicle,* July 6, 9, 23, 31, 1968; *Independent Journal,* July 27, 30, Aug. 21, 30, 1968; Bagley, press release, March 5, 1968, carton 5, Bagley Papers.

70. Redwood Empire Association, press release, "Engineer Leaves Golden Gate Bridge," March 31, 1967, box 126, IM facility; *San Francisco Chronicle,* June 16, 29, July 13, Aug. 1, 9, Oct. 20, 22, 1968, Jan. 11, 1969.

71. One-way tolls were recommended by the state as early as 1960, but Adam predicted that "toll-free northbound traffic would cause traffic to merge at high speed beyond the toll plaza, and would endanger the movement of rescue vehicles . . . very little time, if any would be saved in passing cars through toll gates."

Adam also worried that they would encourage joy riders circling the bay without paying tolls. Jenkins dismissed them as not worth the effort. *Independent Journal,* July 10, 1962; Redwood Empire Association, press release, "Bridge Board Upholds Deck Survey, 7-5," Oct. 13, 1967, box 126, DS Vault; *San Francisco Chronicle,* Oct. 18, 1968.

72. *San Francisco Chronicle,* Dec. 15, 1967.

73. Ibid, 3.

74. *Independent Journal,* Jan. 16, 1969.

75. Former Marin bridge director Thomas Hardcastle remarked that he was "just amazed at the unanimity here." *Independent Journal,* Feb. 6, 1969.

76. T. J. Kent, Jr., "Home Rule and Regional Government for the San Francisco Bay Area: A Statement Presented to the Committee on the Future of the League of California Cities," Berkeley, June 1971, 3; San Jose Planning Department, *Metropolitan Open Space and Regional Government: Next Steps in Shaping the Metropolitan Future of the San Francisco Bay Area—1970–2020,* prepared by T. J. Kent (San Jose, 1968).

77. Kent, "Home Rule and Regional Government," 3. Kent emphasized the importance of local sovereignty in his influential 1964 textbook, *The Urban General Plan,* asserting that local elected officials should control the planning process and that planners should defer to their wishes. T. J. Kent, *The Urban General Plan* (San Francisco: Chandler Publishing Company, 1964); Patrick S. McGovern, "San Francisco Bay Area Edge Cities: New Roles for Planners and the General Plan," *Journal of Planning Education and Research* 17 (1998), 246–58; Mel Scott, *American City Planning Since 1890* (Berkeley: University of California Press, 1969), 616–17.

78. Association of Bay Area Governments, *Preliminary Regional Plan* (Berkeley, 1966); Association of Bay Area Governments, *Regional Plan 1970–1990, San Francisco Bay Region* (Berkeley, 1970); Kent, "Statewide and Regional Land-Use Planning," 57.

79. San Francisco Bay-Delta Water Quality Control Program, *Final Report,* ch. 2, pp. 21–27, ch. 22; San Francisco Bay Conservation and Development Commission, *The San Francisco Bay Plan* ([San Francisco], 1969), 35; Bay Area Transportation Study Commission, *Bay Area Transportation Report* (Berkeley, 1969), 82.

80. Association of Bay Area Governments, *The Emergence of a Regional Concept (1910–1973)* ([Berkeley], 1973); *San Francisco Examiner & Chronicle,* April 6, 1969.

81. ABAG formed a goals and organization committee in 1965 to study the issue of regional government. Its members concluded that ABAG should be transformed into an "umbrella agency" to oversee and advise existing regional agencies. In 1967, a bill to allow ABAG to take over the functions of the BCDC failed. Its 1969 version, Assembly Bill 1846, would have made ABAG an advisory agency for existing regional special districts and would have given it the power to "function in . . . problem areas in order to meet regional needs," including planning, pollution control, conservation, and regional parks and open space. Association of Bay Area Governments Goals and Organization Committee, *Regional Home Rule and the Government of the Bay Area: Report to the General Assembly* (Berkeley, 1966).

82. Victor Jones, "Bay Area Regionalism: Institutions, Processes, and Programs," in *Regional Governance—Promise and Performance,* ed. Advisory Commission on Intergovernmental Relations (Washington, D.C., 1973), 79; Revan

Tranter, *ABAG: A Concise History—Celebrating 40 Years of Service* ([Berkeley], 2001).

83. McCarthy's politics went out of favor in Marin, and he resigned as it became clear that his chances for re-election were remote. McCarthy was contending with a bitter divorce and the effects of years of heavy drinking as well, according to those who knew him. McCarthy died of a heart attack in 1981 at the age of fifty-seven. *Independent Journal,* Dec. 26, 1969, Jan. 24, 1968, Jan. 7, 13, 1970, Jan. 25, 1981.

84. Stanley Scott, "The Regional Jobs to Be Done and Ways of Getting Them Accomplished," paper presented at the Regional Conference—1970, Berkeley; Jones, "Bay Area Regionalism: Institutions"; Tranter, *ABAG: A Concise History;* Huth, "Regional Organization in the San Francisco Bay Area—1970"; Scott, *The San Francisco Bay Area,* 315–17; *San Francisco Chronicle,* Aug. 19, Sept. 16, 1970; John T. Knox, "Statewide and Regional Land-Use Planning in California, 1950–1980," interview conducted by Malca Chall, Regional Oral History Office, The Bancroft Library (Berkeley, 1982).

85. The *San Francisco Chronicle and Examiner* described its plan as the "Orwellian Future by BATS." July 13, 1969.

86. Stanley Scott described an "umbrella agency" as an alternative to a multipurpose regional government shortly after the defeats of 1969. Stanley Scott, "Choosing Representatives for a Bay Area Umbrella Agency: Another Possibility," in *Adapting Government to Regional Needs: Report of the Conference on Bay Area Regional Organization, April 18, 1970,* ed. Stanley Scott and Harriet Nathan (Berkeley, 1971).

87. Foran, "Oral History," 87.

88. David W. Jones Jr., Robert Taggart, and Edith Dorosin, *The Metropolitan Transportation Commission: An Innovative Experiment in Incremental Planning; A Cautious Experiment in Regionalism* ([Palo Alto, Calif.]: Stanford Transportation Research Program, 1974), 38.

89. Mel Scott concludes that the lack of MTC authority ultimately had a progrowth effect on the Bay Area: "the agency does not guide local and regional growth through its decisions; it tends to authorize transit services after growth has taken place." Scott, *The San Francisco Bay Area,* 322. See also James Houston Banks, "Political Influence in Transportation Planning: The San Francisco Bay Area Metropolitan Transportation Commission's Regional Transportation Plan," Ph.D. diss., University of California, Berkeley, 1977; Jones, Taggart, and Dorosin, *The Metropolitan Transportation Commission;* Metropolitan Transportation Commission, *The Metropolitan Transportation Commission: A New Regional Agency* ([Oakland, Calif.], 1971).

90. Donald N. Rothblatt and Victor Jones, "Governance of the San Francisco Bay Area Revisited," in *Metropolitan Governance Revisited: American/Canadian Intergovernmental Perspectives,* ed. Donald N. Rothblatt and Andrew Sancton (Berkeley: Institute of Governmental Studies Press, University of California, 1998).

91. *Statutes of California* 1969 reg. sess, ch. 805, pp. 1625–27.

92. The San Francisco chapter of the Sierra Club, People for a Golden Gate National Recreation Area, and San Francisco Beautiful all endorsed bridge district ferry plans. Golden Gate Bridge, Highway and Transportation District, *Draft Environmental Impact Statement on the Proposed Expansion of Ferry Services Between San Francisco and Marin County* (San Francisco, 1971); Redwood Empire Association, press release, "Ferry Studies Sought by Gate Span Board," Dec. 15, 1967, box 126, IM facility; Thomas T. Storer, press release, Oct. 26, 1965, box 127, IM

facility; Golden Gate Bridge and Highway District, *Golden Gate Commuter Ferryboat System: San Francisco-Marin Crossing*, prepared by Philip F. Spaulding and Associates (Seattle, 1970); California Legislative Analyst, *Analysis of the Golden Gate Bridge, Highway and Transportation District: Final Report* (Sacramento, 1975), 8–9; *San Francisco Chronicle*, Dec. 30, 1969, June 12, 16, July 11, Aug. 15, 18, 19, 24, April 4, 25, Nov. 14, 1970; *San Francisco Business*, April 1, 1981.

93. *Independent Journal*, Oct. 20, 1969, Jan. 27, 1970.

94. *Independent Journal*, Sept. 16, Oct. 17, 1969; *San Francisco Chronicle*, Sept. 16, 17, 19, Nov. 6, 15, 1969; Dale W. Luehring to the Board of Directors, Golden Gate Bridge and Highway District, Feb. 14, 1969.

95. Marin County Transit District, *Optimum Bus System and Summary of Water Transportation Study: Staff Report*, prepared by R. L. Banks and Associates (San Rafael, Calif., 1969).

96. The directors even considered offering coffee and cocktail service on the buses. Golden Gate Bridge and Highway District, *Report on Prospective Participation in a Public Transit System*, 27; *San Francisco Chronicle*, March 20, 1970.

97. *San Francisco Chronicle*, Oct. 10, 1970, Jan. 1, Feb. 25, 1972.

98. *San Francisco Chronicle*, Feb. 12, 1969.

99. *San Francisco Examiner and Chronicle*, Dec. 20, 1970.

100. *Independent Journal*, Aug. 30, 1968, Jan. 7, 1970.

101. *Independent Journal*, March 23, 1970.

102. *Independent Journal*, Oct. 20, 1969, Jan. 30, Feb. 6, Aug. 8, 17, Oct. 14, 1970, Jan. 18, Feb. 22, June 30, 1971, July 18, Aug. 18, 1975, March 22, 1976.

103. Donald M. Van Dyke to Lowell Edington, July 20, 1971, box 156, IM facility.

104. *Pacific Sun*, Feb. 11, 1970.

105. *San Francisco Chronicle*, April 10, 1971.

106. Golden Gate Bridge, Highway and Transportation District, *Golden Gate Bridge, Report on Inspection of Condition and Major Structural Units*, prepared by Ammann & Whitney (San Francisco, 1969); *San Francisco Chronicle*, Jan. 31, 1970, Aug. 14, 1971; Golden Gate Bridge, Highway and Transportation District, *Toll Plaza Modernization, Preliminary Engineering Report*, prepared by PBQ&D, Inc., Engineers (San Francisco, 1970); Golden Gate Bridge, Highway and Transportation District, *Golden Gate Corridor: Long Range Transportation Alternatives: Engineering Report*, prepared by Kaiser Engineers (San Francisco, 1970).

107. *San Francisco Chronicle*, July 1, 1971.

108. *San Francisco Chronicle*, Jan. 30, July 20, 1972.

109. *San Francisco Examiner*, May 3, 1970.

110. The Federal-Aid Highway Act of 1962, the Urban Mass Transportation Act of 1964, and the Demonstration Cities and Metropolitan Development Act of 1966 all included requirements for regional transportation planning. The Intergovernmental Cooperation Act of 1968, which required greater governmental coordination at the regional level, was followed by the Office of Management and Budget Circular A-95, which provided funding. David K. Hamilton, *Governing Metropolitan Areas: Response to Growth and Change* (New York: Garland Publishing, 1999), 153–61; Mark H. Rose and Bruce E. Seely, "Getting the Interstate Built: Road Engineers and the Implementation of Public Policy, 1955–1985," *Journal of Policy History* 2 (1990), 23–55.

111. Willis D. Hawley, "On Understanding Metropolitan Political Integration," in *Theoretical Perspectives on Urban Politics*, ed. Hawley et al. (Englewood Cliffs, N.J.: Prentice Hall, 1976), 100. See also Robert Fishman, "The Death and Life of

American Regional Planning," in *Reflections on Regionalism*, ed. Bruce J. Katz (Washington, D.C.: Brookings Institution Press, 2000), 107–23; Advisory Commission on Intergovernmental Relations, *Substate Regionalism and the Federal System* (Washington, D.C., 1973).

112. The founding statement of public choice theory was Charles Tiebout, "A Pure Theory of Local Expenditures," *Journal of Political Economy* 64 (1956), 416–54. Tiebout introduced the oft-cited concept of urban residents "voting with their feet," and therefore forcing localities to compete for population and for investment. In the 1960s and 1970s, scholars including Werner Z. Hirsch, Robert Warren, Robert L. Bish, Vincent Ostrom, and Elinor Ostrom elaborated and refined public choice theory. A landmark publication that broadened the influence of these ideas was Paul E. Peterson's 1981 book, *City Limits*, which interpreted the policy implications of public choice theory, emphasizing the imperative of economic development for city officials and the positive effects of the competitive market forces motivating their decision-making. Paul E. Peterson, *City Limits* (Chicago: University of Chicago Press, 1981). For an overview of public choice theory, see Stephens and Wikstrom, *Metropolitan Government and Governance*, 105–21.

113. On the "new federalism" as it developed during the Nixon and Reagan administrations, which complemented public choice or home rule ideology, see Timothy J. Conlan, *From New Federalism to Devolution: Twenty-Five Years of Intergovernmental Reform* (Washington, D.C.: Brookings Institution Press, 1998).

114. Urban historians have long recognized that a decentralized state is not necessarily weak, but for an important recent refutation of the idea that American government is exceptionally powerless see William J. Novak, "The Myth of the 'Weak' American State," *American History Review* 113 (2008), 752–72.

115. Henry Cisneros, *Interwoven Destinies: Cities and the Nation* (New York: W. W. Norton, 1993); Anthony Downs, *New Visions for Metropolitan America* (Washington, D.C.: Brookings Institution Press, 1994); Myron Orfield, *Metropolitics: A Regional Agenda for Community and Stability* (Washington, D.C.: Brookings Institution Press, 1997); David Rusk, *Cities Without Suburbs* (Washington, D.C.: Woodrow Wilson Center Press, 1993); Peter Calthorpe and William Fulton, *The Regional City: Planning for the End of Sprawl* (Washington, D.C.: Island Press, 2001). For analysis of the "new regionalism," see contributions to a special issue of the *Journal of Urban Affairs,* including Frances Frisken and Donald F. Norris, "Regionalism Reconsidered," *Journal of Urban Affairs* 23 (2001), 467–78; Todd Swanstrom, "What We Argue About When We Argue About Regionalism," *Journal of Urban Affairs* 23 (2001), 479–96; Juliet F. Gainsborough, "Bridging the City-Suburb Divide: States and the Politics of Regional Cooperation," *Journal of Urban Affairs* 23 (2001), 497–512; Andrew Sancton, "Canadian Cities and the New Regionalism," *Journal of Urban Affairs* 23 (2001), 543–55; Donald F. Norris, "Prospects for Regional Governance Under the New Regionalism: Economic Imperatives Versus Political Impediments," *Journal of Urban Affairs* 23 (2001), 557–71. See also Todd Swanstrom, "Philosopher in the City: The New Regionalism Debate," *Journal of Urban Affairs* 17 (1995), 309–14; H. V. Savitch and Ronald K. Vogel, "Paths to New Regionalism," *State and Local Government Review* 32 (2000), 158–68; Clyde Mitchell-Weaver, David Miller, and Ronald Deal, Jr., "Multilevel Governance and Metropolitan Regionalism in the USA," *Urban Studies* 37 (2000), 851–76.

116. Norris, "Prospects for Regional Governance Under the New Regionalism," 560.

Conclusion. Subsidies, Suicides, and Sensitivity

1. Annmarie Hauck Walsh, *The Public's Business: The Politics and Practices of Government Corporations* (Cambridge, Mass.: MIT Press, 1978), 231–32.

2. John C. Bollens, *Special District Governments in the United States* (Berkeley, 1957), 30.

3. U.S. Census Bureau, *2002 Census of Governments*, vol. 1, no. 1 *Government Organization* (Washington, D.C., 2002); U.S. Census Bureau, *2002 Census of Governments, vol. 4, no. 5 Government Finances* (Washington, D.C., 2005).

4. E.g., Donald Axelrod, *Shadow Government: The Hidden World of Public Authorities—and How They Control $1 Trillion of Your Money* (New York, 1992).

5. California Legislative Analyst, *Analysis of the Golden Gate Bridge, Highway and Transportation District: Preliminary Report* (Sacramento, 1975), 6; *Analysis of the Golden Gate Bridge, Highway and Transportation District: Final Report* (Sacramento, 1975), 76–81.

6. Golden Gate Bridge, Highway and Transportation District, *Golden Gate Commuter Ferryboat System: San Francisco-Marin Crossing,* prepared by Philip F. Spaulding and Associates (San Francisco, 1970); *San Francisco Chronicle,* Aug. 6, 1970; *San Francisco Chronicle,* Dec. 12, 1970, Jan. 29, May 29, 1971, March 31, 1972.

7. San Francisco-Marin Water Transportation Study Committee, *Feasibility Study of San Francisco–Marin Ferry System,* prepared by Arthur D. Little Inc. (San Francisco, 1969); Golden Gate Bridge, Highway and Transportation District, *Report on Proposed Operational Plan for Integrated Bus-Ferry Service,* prepared by Kaiser Engineers (San Francisco, 1971); Golden Gate Bridge and Highway District, *Golden Gate Commuter Ferryboat System*; Golden Gate Bridge, Highway and Transportation District, *Golden Gate Corridor: Long Range Transportation Alternatives,* prepared by Okamoto-Liskamm (San Francisco, 1970).

8. U.S. General Accounting Office, *Increased Cost of Implementing Commuter Ferry System on San Francisco Bay* (Washington, D.C., 1975), 4–27.

9. California Legislative Analyst, *Analysis of the Golden Gate Bridge, Highway and Transportation District: Preliminary Report,* 54.

10. Marin County Grand Jury, *Final Report, 1974–1975* (San Rafael, Calif., 1975).

11. California Legislative Analyst, *Analysis of the Golden Gate Bridge, Highway and Transportation District: Preliminary Report,* 6, 50.

12. *San Francisco Examiner,* March 5, 1975.

13. California Legislative Analyst, *Analysis of the Golden Gate Bridge, Highway and Transportation District: Preliminary Report,* 56–57.

14. *San Francisco Chronicle,* April 1, 2, 1975, April 9, 10, May 29, June 15, 1976, July 7, July 25, Oct. 15, 1979, Oct. 21, 1979, Dec. 15, 1984, March 6, 1988; *San Francisco Examiner,* May 24, 1975; *San Francisco Examiner and Chronicle,* Feb. 8, 1981.

15. Golden Gate Bridge and Highway District, *1987–1988 Annual Report* (San Francisco, 1988), 2.

16. *San Francisco Chronicle,* July 6, 1994; *San Francisco Examiner,* April 22, 29, June 25, 1981, Dec. 24, 1987; *San Francisco Chronicle,* April 25, May 26, 1981, June 10, 1988.

17. *San Francisco Examiner,* Aug. 8, 1937, Nov. 27, 28, 1940; *San Francisco Call-Bulletin,* Nov. 23, 1940.

18. Golden Gate Bridge, Highway and Transportation District, *Suicide Prevention Study: Report on the Concept, Phase I,* prepared by Anshen & Allen (San Fran-

cisco, 1971); *San Francisco Examiner*, Jan. 31, 1948, Jan. 31, Feb. 14, 1951; *San Francisco Chronicle*, Feb. 6, 1954, Aug. 17, 1970; *Independent Journal*, Sept. 12, 1964.

19. Subsequently, bridge district officials have abandoned efforts to win federal historic landmark designation because it would restrict their ability to modify the bridge in other ways. Mervin C. Giacomini to Building and Operating Committee, "Golden Gate Bridge, Suicide Deterrent—Report on Previous Studies, Actions, and Future Actions (Information)," San Francisco, Dec. 30, 1994.

20. The agency's legal immunity was established in a published state court decision in 2004. The case confirmed that bridge district officials had no responsibility for the death of fourteen-year-old Marissa Imrie because she failed to use "due care" when she climbed the railing and jumped. *Milligan v. Golden Gate Bridge Highway and Transportation District, et al.*, 120 Cal. App. 4th 1 (2004). Maria Martinez also sued after her son, Leonard Branzuela, died in 1993, but her case was dismissed. *San Francisco Chronicle*, Aug. 18, 1994.

21. *San Francisco Chronicle*, March 13, 31, 1977.

22. Richard H. Seiden, "Can a Physical Barrier Prevent Suicides on the Golden Gate Bridge?" School of Public Health, University of California, Berkeley, 1973; Richard H. Seiden, "Where Are They Now? A Follow-Up Study of Suicide Attempters from the Golden Gate Bridge," *Suicide and Life Threatening Behavior* 8 (1978), 203–16.

23. *San Francisco Chronicle*, Aug. 18, Oct. 5, 1994; July 11, 12, 28, 1995, Dec. 22, 2002.

24. For the entire *Chronicle* series as well as supplementary material, see http://www.sfgate.com/lethalbeauty/ (accessed Nov. 2006). *San Francisco Chronicle*, Jan. 19, 2005, Feb. 25, March 11, May 24, 2006; Tad Friend, "Jumpers: The Fatal Grandeur of the Golden Gate Bridge," *New Yorker*, Oct. 13, 2003; Eric Steel, director, *The Bridge* (2006), documentary film.

25. Ken Holmes, "Marin County Coroner's Office Releases Ten-Year Study on Golden Gate Bridge Suicides," press release, July 30, 2007; Holmes, "Gate Bridge Suicide Death Toll: At Least 35 in 2007," press release, Jan. 9, 2008.

26. *San Francisco Chronicle*, Oct. 18, 2007.

27. In July 1945, five-year-old Marilyn De Mont jumped from the bridge at the command of her father—climbing over the railing without assistance, according to witnesses. Nearly fifty years later, the father of three-year-old Kellie Page ended her life in a murder-suicide from the bridge in January 1993, and a Thanksgiving murder-suicide took a two-year-old boy the same year. Teenagers jump frequently; at least seven people age nineteen or younger jumped from the bridge between 1997 and 2007. Brown, *Golden Gate*, 201; *San Francisco Examiner*, July 24, 1945; *San Francisco Chronicle*, Jan. 30, Nov. 25, 27, 1993, Dec. 23, 24, 31, 1997; *San Francisco Examiner*, Dec. 23, 24, 1997; Marin County Deputy Coroner Jeff Sherman to the author, Jan. 22, 2008.

28. *San Francisco Chronicle*, April 21, 1988.

29. *San Francisco Examiner and Chronicle*, Jan. 30, 1977.

30. Doyle Drive was financed and built by the bridge district but transferred to the California Department of Transportation in 1945. A state plan to widen and improve the approach was rejected by the San Francisco supervisors in 1963, a casualty of the city's freeway revolt. More recent plans for the outdated roadway that maintained its scenic parkway characteristics and did not expand its traffic capacity garnered opposition from North Bay residents and bridge district officials. San Francisco planners proposed a toll and congestion pricing on Doyle

Drive traffic in 2007 pay for its retrofit and reconstruction and to enhance mass transportation, in part to take advantage of federal money available to support congestion pricing schemes. When the bridge district was asked to collect the fee, San Francisco directors favored cooperating but northern California representatives, a majority of the board, overruled them. They argued that any new toll put an unjust and unduly heavy burden on North Bay commuters. *San Francisco Chronicle,* Oct. 7, Nov. 3, 1972, Aug. 16, 1981, Dec. 11, 1982, March 22, Dec. 23, 1983, Dec. 25, 1983, March 10, 1984, June 13, 1988, June 26, 1996, July 18, Sept. 5, 1996, July 2, 2001, Feb. 19, March 14, 2008; *San Francisco Examiner,* Oct. 14, 1972, Oct. 14, March 23, 1972, Nov. 10, 1981, Feb. 19, 1985, June 27, June 28, 1996. For an overview of the Doyle Drive controversy, see Laura Stonehill, "Congestion Pricing on Doyle Drive," M.A. thesis, University of California, Berkeley, 2007.

31. Several bridge directors formed a group called "Friends of the Bridge" to promote its "historical glorification and edification." Members sought to establish a museum, though they made little progress toward that goal. California Office of the Auditor General, *A Review of the Golden Gate Bridge, Highway and Transportation District and the 50th Anniversary Celebration of the Golden Gate Bridge: Report* (Sacramento, 1987); *San Francisco Chronicle,* June 26, 1987; *Examiner and Chronicle,* June 21, 1987.

32. *San Francisco Chronicle,* Feb. 6, March 23, April 3, 25, 2002.

33. *San Francisco Chronicle,* June 4, 2002.

34. *New York Times,* Nov. 29, 2002.

35. *San Francisco Chronicle,* May 31, 2002, April 7, 25, July 12, Sept. 26, 2003; *Marin Independent Journal,* May 31, 2002, March 1, April 2, 26, May 21, 2003.

36. Bridge officials released the executive summary of the report (the rest was withheld from the public to protect "trade secrets" of the consultants) on August 24, 2007, which was greeted with denunciations and mockery by the Bay Area press. Bridge director and San Francisco supervisor Jake McGoldrick complained that he had "never seen something that so lacked transparency. . . . I think it's a terrible abuse of the public process. The public doesn't know what's going on." *San Francisco Chronicle,* Nov. 18, 2006, Aug. 25, 2007; Golden Gate Bridge, Highway and Transportation District, *Corporate Partnership Program to Preserve the Golden Gate Bridge: Phase I Findings* (San Francisco, 2007).

37. *San Francisco Examiner,* Sept. 10, 2007; *San Francisco Chronicle,* March 15, 2008.

Index

Gulick, Esther, 175
Gulick, Luther Halsey, 44, 263n1

Haas, Walter A., 87
Hadeler, William, D., 61, 84, 188
Hardcastle, Thomas D., 185
Harlan, George H., 5, 36, 38; proposal for
  special district to build Golden Gate
  Bridge, 12, 21–24, 227n35; effort to en-
  roll of counties in bridge district, 24,
  28, 229n60; appointed bridge district
  attorney, 32; and revised terms of con-
  struction bonds, 38–39; conflict with
  Strauss, 68–69
Harrelson, William, 69–70, 238n81,
  238n83
Harris, Maurice, 166
Haugabook, James, 161–66, 262n87
Havenner, Franck P., 30–31
Hearst, William Randolph, 18, 56
Hendricks, William, 155–57, 259n24
Henry, C. A., 31
Hetch Hetchy Dam, 17–18, 25, 39,
  225n20, 229n54
Hibbard, I. N., 21
Hickey, James, 192
high-density development, 135
Highway 101 (U.S.), 127, 179
Hirschberg, Abraham "Murphy," 31, 51,
  52, 54, 59–61, 70, 230n76
historical institutionalism, 218n9
Holland Tunnel (New York): financing of,
  82
Holm, Dion R., 111
Holmes, Ken, 211
home rule, 9, 95, 101, 108–9, 120, 123,
  172, 176, 192, 193, 273n113
Hoover, Herbert, 231n90
Hoover, Kenneth, 129, 137
Hoover Dam, 50–51, 62, 103
Hoover-Young Commission, 53
Hotchkiss, W. J., 21, 24, 30
Humboldt County: membership in North
  Bay Counties Association, 13; environ-
  ment, landscape, economy, 14; refusal
  to join bridge district, 27, 229n60; and
  Golden Gate Authority proposal, 110
Hutchinson, Claude B., 101, 108–9,
  116–17, 248n33, 248n34

Imrie, Marissa, 275n20
Ingalls, R. R., 31

Independent Journal: coverage of 1952 hearings on bridge district administration,
  96; praise for McCarthy, 97; on rapid
  transit, 129, 136, 139, 145–46; criticism
  of bridge district administration, 16,
  152–53, 169, 199. See also *Marin Independent Journal*; *San Rafael Independent*
infrastructure, 86, 91, 98, 101, 102, 104,
  106, 138, 194. See also public works
Intergovernmental Coordination Act
  (1968), 122, 272n110
Interstate and Defense Highway System,
  173

Jack, Helen, 185–86
Jenkins, Arthur C., 7, 96, 115, 118, 122–23,
  205, *131*; opinions about mass transit,
  125, 130–32; opposition to BART on
  the Golden Gate Bridge, 133–38,
  140–42, 147–48, 255n25; appointed as
  part-time bridge district engineer,
  256n43; recommendations for bridge
  district planning and policy, 179–80; on
  San Francisco freeway opposition,
  267n48; plan for bridge district mass
  transportation operations, 190–91, 198
jobs, 36, 39, 46. See also unemployment
  relief
Johnson, Hiram, 17, 31, 59
Johnson, Katherine M., 224n12
Jones, Victor, 7–8, 177, 265n15
Jordan, Frank C., 28
Josephine County, Oregon: membership
  in North Bay Counties Association, 13

Kahn, Felix, 50, 52
Kaiser, Edgar F., 176, 205: support for
  Golden Gate Authority proposal, 100,
  103–4, 106, 108–9, 112–14, 120–21,
  248n31, 250n52; support for BART,
  126
Kaiser, Henry J., 51, 91, 103
Kaiser, Leland M., 82–83
Kaiser Industries Corporation, 103
Keesling, Francis V., *60*, 70, 103, 204,
  230n76, 236n56, 31; member of bridge
  district committee on information and
  publicity, 36; as bridge district leader,
  50, 52–54, 56, 58; ouster from bridge
  directorship, 59–61; conflict with
  Strauss, 67, 68; as first chairman of the
  BAC, 103, 246n8

Acknowledgments

This book is the product of many years of research in archives and libraries throughout the San Francisco Bay Area. It would be impossible to thank all of the people who helped with this research and with its interpretation. However, the staff of the Golden Gate Bridge, Highway and Transportation District deserves credit for the assistance they gave me, especially Trubee Schock, who was appointed as the bridge district archives coordinator during the time I spent inspecting their records. I am grateful to Carney J. Campion, John F. Foran, James Haugabook, John T. Knox, Quentin L. Kopp, Stephan C. Leonoudakis, Dale W. Luehring, and Paul Peterzell for the time they devoted to discussing their relationship with the bridge district. All of them made important suggestions for interpreting its history. Chris McCarthy was very generous in allowing me to examine family papers, and in sharing his recollections of time spent as a youth in his father's Sacramento office. Wende Mintz, the niece of Arthur C. Jenkins, provided valuable details about his life and career as well as a rare portrait. I would especially like to thank William T. Bagley, not only for discussing his role in Golden Gate Bridge history, but also for sponsoring the California Public Records Act. David Greene at the First Amendment Project in Oakland offered very helpful legal advice on gaining access to bridge district records and deserves special thanks.

Many librarians and archivists assisted me in innumerable and important ways, but a few of them were especially helpful. I would like to thank Jocelyn Moss of the Marin History Museum and the staff and volunteers of the Anne T. Kent Room of the Marin County Public Library. I am grateful for the assistance of the knowledgeable staff of the Bancroft Library at the University of California, Berkeley, and the librarians and archivists of the California Department of Transportation Library, the San Francisco History Room of the San Francisco Public Library, and the Institute of Governmental Studies at the University of California, Berkeley. I would also like to thank the staff of the Harmer E. Davis

Transportation Library of the Institute of Transportation Studies, and library director Rita Evans in particular.

Funding for this project came from many sources, most significantly the Weisman Fellowship of the California Institute of Technology, the Ahmanson Fellowship of the Huntington Library, and the Kevin Starr Fellowship of the Humanities Research Institute at University of California, Irvine. This research was also supported with funding from the Henry J. Vaux Chair in Forest Policy, held by Sally K. Fairfax of the Department of Environmental Science, Policy and Management at the University of California, Berkeley. The University of California Transportation Center, directed by Elizabeth Deakin, supported a crucial year of research with a fellowship. Numerous scholarships, grants, and teaching fellowships from the History Department of the University of California, Berkeley made it possible as well. Thank you to Michael Keston and Richard G. Little of the Keston Institute for Public Finance and Infrastructure Policy at the University of Southern California for support in the final stages of its completion.

I am also grateful for the high standards and thought-provoking commentary of my mentor, Robin L. Einhorn, who is not only a brilliant historian, but also a truly gifted and dedicated teacher. Sally K. Fairfax deserves special thanks, not only for helping me to expand the breadth of my research and encouraging me to delve into theory, but also for her patience. Richard A. Walker has made many important contributions to this book as well, and his work on the Bay Area has been inspirational. Among the many other people who challenged and helped improve the book are Mansel G. Blackford, Kathleen A. Brosnan, Nora Heaphy, William Issel, Richard R. John, Karen McNeil, Wendell E. Pritchett, Peter Richardson, Matthew Roth, Zachary M. Schrag, and Sarah L. Thomas. Thanks to the editors of this series, Pamela Walker Laird, Richard R. John, and Mark H. Rose, who were all very helpful in refining the manuscript. Rose in particular devoted an enormous amount of time to helping me shape the book, offering detailed and thoughtful criticism at many stages in its development. Thanks to Robert Lockhart and the many other conscientious people at Penn Press who helped produce this volume.

Finally, thank you to my family. Because of the hospitality of my uncle and aunt, Russell and Marguerite Burbank, I wrote and rewrote many chapters surrounded by lovely redwoods in Mill Valley. My grandmother Louise Burbank, my parents, Ann and Ken Nelson, and my sister, Elizabeth Cady, read the manuscript as it progressed and offered invaluable encouragement. I would never have made it this far without their love and support.